NARRATING REALITY

Also by Harry E. Shaw

The Forms of Historical Fiction:
Sir Walter Scott and His Successors

Critical Essays on Sir Walter Scott:
The Waverley Novels (editor)

Narrating Reality

Austen, Scott, Eliot

Harry E. Shaw

CORNELL UNIVERSITY PRESS

ITHACA AND LONDON

THIS BOOK HAS BEEN PUBLISHED WITH THE AID OF A GRANT FROM
THE HULL MEMORIAL PUBLICATION FUND OF CORNELL UNIVERSITY

First published 1999 by Cornell University Press

Printed in the United States of America

Material from "Loose Narrators: Display, Engagement, and the Search for a
Place in History in Realist Fiction" by Harry E. Shaw reprinted by permission
from *Narrative*, Vol. 3, No. 2 (May 1995). Copyright 1995 by
Ohio State University Press. All rights reserved.

Library of Congress Cataloging-in-Publication Data

Shaw, Harry E., 1946–
    Narrating reality : Austen, Scott, Eliot / Harry E. Shaw.
        p.   cm.
    Includes index.
    ISBN 0-8014-3672-9 (alk. paper)
    1. English fiction—19th century—History and criticism.
2. Realism in literature.   3. Scott, Walter, Sir, 1771–1832—
Fictional works.   4. Scott, Walter, Sir, 1771–1832—Technique.
5. Eliot, George, 1819–1880—Technique.   6. Austen, Jane, 1775–1817—
Technique.   7. Reality in literature.   8. Narration (Rhetoric)
9.   Fiction—Technique.   I. Title
PR868.R4S53   1999
823'.70912—dc21   99-24817

Cornell University Press strives to use environmentally responsible suppliers
and materials to the fullest extent possible in the publishing of its books. Such
materials include vegetable-based, low-VOC inks and acid-free papers that are
recycled, totally chlorine-free, or partly composed of nonwood fibers. Books
that bear the logo of the FSC (Forest Stewardship Council) use paper taken
from forests that have been inspected and certified as meeting the highest
standards for environmental and social responsibility. For further information,
visit our website at www.cornellpress.cornell.edu.

Cloth printing   10 9 8 7 6 5 4 3 2 1

FOR JUDY, CHRISTOPHER, AND KATY

Contents

Preface   ix

1. Realism and Its Problems   1

2. Realism and Things   38

3. An Approach to Realist Narratives   90

4. Austen: Narrative, Plots, Distinctions, and Life in the Grain   126

5. Scott: Realism and the Other   168

6. Eliot: Narrating in History   218

Afterword   265

Appendix: On Tropes and Master Tropes   269

Index   277

Preface

Prefaces are written at the end of projects. Issues that linger in my mind as I leave this one may help to introduce the reader to it. My book begins with three chapters on realist representation, in which novelists, philosophers, and literary theorists and critics mingle. Though such a state of affairs has become too common to require justification, some comment on the twist I give this familiar structure may prove helpful. When I turn to philosophy or theory, my intent is not to solve the problems of realist representation from outside or beneath, or to find a justification for realism. My purpose tends instead to be either to clear the ground of obscuring theoretical underbrush or to seek out examples to help define a realist habit of mind. Working through the grain of the realist novel, I don't expect to find in philosophy a justification for realist practice. In a real world, the claims of practice may come first. I draw on philosophy to clarify and put in perspective some of the ways we have come to talk about realism, and especially about whether realism is "possible." I look to certain kinds of philosophical practice as examples of a mode of engaging reality in which such terms as "realism," "realist," and even "reality" itself regain their vitality and credibility.

One way of making sense of the claims to realism of the range of novels I'll be concerned with is just to say that they are doing work with respect to the real world that more abstract modes of thought can't do. If this is so, it would be odd if those more abstract modes of thought could provide definitive grounds for judging how well they are doing the work. If my net can catch things that yours can't, because my net has a finer weave, are you really justified in proving to me, on the basis of how your net is constructed, that the catches I've made are impossible? Nineteenth-century realism responds to a historical and ideological situation of which, it believes, philosophy can no longer give an adequate account.

I spend time, especially in my opening chapter, with authors and positions that today are most alive (though not always vibrant) in the unspoken assumptions of books, articles, and student papers. In the course of the general development of literary theory in the past fifty years, a multifaceted discourse about realism has made its presence felt, increasingly as a silent, uninspected partner in critical discussions in which realism is cast in the role of the defining and bad opposite of more acceptable modes. This discourse has in my view stabilized since its enrichment by Foucauldian modes of thought; many of its components reached effective stability much earlier. It seems part of the world's furniture by now, which is all the more reason to polish it up so that we'll be prompted to ask if it's either ornamental or useful. The most interesting formulations are often the early ones, produced when it still seemed necessary to define and contest the issues.

You can simply turn your back on this discourse; the chances are, though, that it will turn its back on you with greater general effect. But you can't get anywhere by addressing it on its own peremptory terms, and at a certain point you do need to turn away. Before I do so, I will try to put it in its place. This doesn't mean ignoring or denigrating the critical achievements of what we've come to call theory or of ideological critique. It does mean recognizing that much recent criticism has been relatively ineffective in dealing with realism as more than a negative contrast to other ways of doing or thinking about literature. This book is not, however, intended to be a defense of realism. I admire the novels and novelists with which I am here concerned. I am inclined to approach them with a ceremonious respect, as one would an honored guest. I have not considered it my main task to point out their shortcomings. But they neither ask for nor require an uncritical acceptance. The idea of defending them would seem presumptuous—and odd. If pressed, I suppose I'd settle for defending the potentialities of realism. Mainly, I'd like us to listen to the realist narrator.

Over the period during which the discourse about realism has taken hold, significant work has been done that enlarges or escapes its confines, in modes that range from the neorealist epistemology and ethics of S. P. Mohanty to the Hegelian formalism of Marshall Brown. Some of these modes have left their mark on my own work, and my agreements and disagreements with them will I hope sufficiently emerge as my discussion proceeds. My choice to focus for a positive example less on such contemporaries than on Erich Auerbach, who would appear to have been left well behind in current discussions of realism, may seem perverse. The logic of concentrating on a figure who can function as both an example and an object of hermeneutical inquiry, and whose work is not entangled with our present discussions, will, I trust, become clear. Readers who grasp it will have followed much of what I mean to say in this book.

I turn next to an issue that has occupied me throughout my work on this project, the issue of formal procedures versus substantive discussions. The modern bias in favor of formal solutions to philosophical and cultural problems is deep-rooted. One feels it in the movement from ontology to epistemology. When you ask not what is true or what is real, but how we can reliably know about truth and reality, you are moving into the realm of the procedural. But the question arises of whether procedures will in the end suffice. Will they indeed reach any end? Or will it turn out that a quest for the right procedure involves an infinite postponement of addressing matters of substance? Such questions have lately made things warm for certain ethical and political thinkers, including one I draw on here, Jürgen Habermas. Habermas relies heavily on the notion of the ideal speech situation, in which participants discuss and decide upon means and ends in a situation where power relations and personal interests have been erased, and the only force that is respected is the force of the better argument. In framing such a conception, Habermas is not naively assuming that it exists or could readily be made to exist: he presents it as a counterfactual, regulative ideal. He is, however, assuming that the way to imagine just solutions to social problems is to envisage a procedure that can act as a conceptual yardstick. But, critics have asked, can you really use an "ideal speech situation" to discuss justice, when the participants in that situation are described at a level of abstraction that erases differences of gender and class? Shouldn't these considerations form a substantive component of the discussion from the ground up? Don't supposedly general standards of rationality have powerful, unacknowledged biases built into them? Couldn't one say that in his proceduralism Habermas is edging toward giving primacy to the very supremacy of "instrumental reason" that his thought as a whole so vigorously contests? Is the best way to bring the question of substantive goals back into our intellectual, social, and political lives really to imagine abstract procedures? Then again, it may turn out that this proceduralism itself has real and potentially productive ties to the substance of history.

Nineteenth-century realist fiction can be seen as an attempt to balance procedure and substance, in the concrete modes by which it invites the reader to come to terms with realities, imagined and real. In my own definition of realism I attempt a similar balancing act, by arguing that realism insists that certain mental procedures are needed to make sense of those substantial aspects of the world it selects as significant. A dialectic between substance and procedure is also implicit in my claim that historicist realism involves a movement between positions in and above a given historical moment. On a theoretical plane, this all seems to me justifiable (and for that matter accurate). In practice, however, I remain uneasy that my account may postpone the claims of the substantial too long. Isn't there something suspect about a mode of viewing realism that keeps insisting on what realism "might" accomplish, instead of drawing up a bill of indictment based on what, so far as we can determine, it actually helped to accomplish in the nineteenth century and beyond, by way of cultural domination? The answer remains to be seen. I am somewhat heartened, however, by coming to realize that nineteenth-century realism itself was aware of just this problem. I'll be arguing that Scott provides a telling critique of the potential murderousness of abstract understanding, and that Eliot bends her narrative forms in order to engage her readers in the moral substance of life in history. This is not the only instance in which, in working on this book, I have discovered that realism has a good deal to tell us about the questions we find ourselves bringing to it in the light of subsequent developments. I believe that this happens because the reality it brings into focus remains, for good and ill and despite strenuous attempts to leave it behind, very much our reality, in form if not always in substance.

Here, in the form of a brief synopsis, is what lies ahead for the reader. The first part of this book considers the discourse that has grown up about novelistic realism in the last half century, and proposes an alternative. Chapter 1 centers on the question of whether the representation typical of the nineteenth-century realist novel is totalistic. As is well known, an affirmative answer to this question would not be good news for realism in most critical camps these days, for totalistic visions tend to be equated with coerciveness, hegemony, and a general attempt to pass off as natural and inevitable what is actually the ideology of a dominant social group. Looking back in time, however, I show that the equation of realism with totalization is itself neither natural nor inevitable. Some critics have found realist novels dispersed, not totalistically centered, in their representation; realism here is identified as an avatar of freedom, not a ruse of coercive power, because of its supposed aversion to viewing the world as a closed and totalized system. Other critics have agreed that realism creates a dispersed mode of representation, but consider this dispersal itself subtly and effectively coercive. Still others have found realism totalistic, but admirable because of the completeness of its vision. I follow the major twists and turns of this issue for two reasons. On the negative side, the variety of considered opinions here ought to make us question the assumption that realist representation is simply totalistic. On the positive side, the variety of views about this issue, I contend, are in fact responding to various facets of realism's own divided response to the problem of modernity.

In the second chapter, I take an extended look at another prevalent piety about realism, the notion that it trades in something called "transparent" representation. Here again my intentions are both positive and negative. I discuss the philosophical problem of how words refer to things to show that prevalent notions of transparent representation are irrelevant to the aims and workings of nineteenth-century realism. In the course of my discussion, however, I offer a view of reference as productive—a view that better describes the part reference plays in realist novels, as well as in the realist narration employed by J. L. Austin. My third chapter extends the analyses of the first two, drawing upon the critical insights and narrative practice of Erich Auerbach to mount a general theory of how the realism of nineteenth-century novels operates. I argue that the central claim of these novels to be realistic is procedural. By versing and involving us in the workings of a historicist metonymy, they promise to involve us in a way of taking in reality which, when we turn from their pages to the world itself, will bring our own distinctively historical mode of being into focus. As part of this argument, I distinguish between the kind of narrative Auerbach creates as he writes literary history and the end-driven, "providential" narrative mode sometimes attributed to him, and to the plotting of realist novels.

In the second part of this book, the focus rests on narration, as I explore the nature and implications of realist metonymy in Austen, Scott, and Eliot. Realist plotting and the plotting of history form the subject of the chapter on Austen, which interrogates Walter Benjamin's notion of brushing history against the grain. I propose an alternative both to an explosive reading against the grain and to its straw opposite, a slavish reading with the grain. I refer to this alternative as reading *through* the grain, and I suggest that it is called for by the density and cunning of Austen's representation of life in society. A chapter on Walter Scott follows. Here, I trace the assessment Scott's fiction projects of the possibility of knowing the culturally Other in a mode of mutuality and respect. I suggest that Scott's realism demonstrates a lively, sober awareness of the difficulties involved in working through the grain of one's own cultural position to understand the situation of another culture, and to act on that understanding. The final chapter takes a close look at the narrative poetics of George Eliot's realism. My consideration of Eliot emphasizes two dominant motifs of this book as a whole: my belief that nineteenth-century realism is historicist in conception and execution, and my insistence that grasping what realism is about depends upon responding to the full rhetorical powers of the realist narrator.

It is a pleasure to acknowledge the help I have received down what has turned out to be a long road. I am grateful to the Society for the Study of Narrative Literature for giving my ideas on a number of subjects treated here an initial hearing in its annual conferences. James Phelan facilitated much of this; I join the queue of those beholden to him. The published work of another member of the society, Robyn Warhol, on the "engaging narrator" encouraged my own thoughts along similar lines. Richard Moran put his philosophical expertise at my disposal during the early stages of this project, Audrey Jaffe and John Kucich provided valuable critiques at its conclusion, and Biodun Jeyifo and Arthur Groos furnished discerning advice. Bernhard Kendler and Kay Scheuer were model editors. To the President and Fellows of Clare Hall in Cambridge, I extend thanks for their hospitality during my year as a visiting fellow. Amanda Anderson and Alison Case have responded to my work generously, with care and remarkable insight; at times, they understood better than I what I was about. Their support and friendship have meant a great deal to me. Finally, I owe an abiding debt to colleagues who read and commented on parts of this work when it and I needed help: Laura Brown, Walter Cohen, Paul Sawyer, and Mark Seltzer. For this relief much thanks.

Earlier versions of parts of this book have appeared in various venues. Portions of "With Reference to Austin," *diacritics*, 20 (1990), 75–92, appear in Chapter 2. "Scott's 'Daemon' and the Voices of Historical Narration," *JEGP*, 88 (1989), 21–33 (published by the University of Illinois Press), is the basis for my discussion of Jeanie Deans at the end of Chapter 4. My commentary on narration in Eliot in Chapter 6 draws on "Loose Narrators: Display, Engagement, and the Search for a Place in History in Realist Fiction," *Narrative*, 3 (1995), 95–116. Finally, Chapter 5 and the Appendix contain brief excerpts from "Realism and Metonymy," in *Narrative Poetics*, ed. James Phelan, vol. 5 of Papers in Comparative Studies (Center for Comparative Studies in the Humanities: Ohio State University, 1987), 127–35. I am grateful for permission to use this material.

HARRY E. SHAW

Ithaca, New York

NARRATING REALITY

1

Realism and Its Problems

"Is this real?" said Redgauntlet. "Can you mean this?—Am I—are all, are any of these gentlemen at liberty, without interruption, to embark in yonder brig, which, I see, is now again approaching the shore?"

"You, sir—all—any of the gentlemen present," said the General, —"all whom the vessel can contain, are at liberty to embark uninterrupted by me; but I advise none to go off who have not powerful reasons, unconnected with the present meeting, for this will be remembered against no one."

"Then, gentlemen," said Redgauntlet, clasping his hands together as the words burst from him, "the cause is lost for ever!"

—Scott, *Redgauntlet*

At the climax of the novel that bears his name, Hugh Redgauntlet exclaims in incredulous despair, "Is this real?" He and a score of other Jacobite conspirators, including the Stuart pretender to the throne of England, have just become aware that their plot to overthrow George III has been discovered and that they are surrounded by Government troops. In their midst stands the King's representative, who delivers the unexpected message that all of them can depart without fear of punishment. Their attempt to foment a rebellion will be ignored, because the King is persuaded that, in the 1760s, it is hopelessly behind the times. This news delights the rest of the conspirators, whose participation in the abortive rebellion has been an expression of nostalgia, not of a desire to fight. It may even relieve the Pretender. But it thoroughly dismays Redgauntlet, who questions its "reality" because he grasps its implications. One might have thought that the King's clemency would grant the Jacobite cause, or what was left of it, a reprieve and a new lease on life. In fact, as Redgauntlet realizes, the Jacobite cause is doomed because what Colin Campbell has said is, in several senses, "real." All along, Redgauntlet has wished, hoped, pretended that he and his cause might make a difference in history, might threaten and overturn its course. The King's sangfroid demonstrates the emptiness of such aspirations. He can afford to be generous, but Redgauntlet cannot afford to be taken so lightly.

When Redgauntlet asks "Is this real?", his locution seems odd. His next words, "Can you mean this?", seem more to the point: they suggest that when he blurts out "Is this real?", he does so in a flustered attempt to produce the sentence, "Can you really mean this?" Or we may take "Is this real?" to be an elliptical version of "Is this [a] real [offer]?" Such parsing carries us over a rough spot in Scott's dialogue, but Redgauntlet's ringing phrase remains poignant. Particularly in its closing chapters, *Redgauntlet* depicts characters in situations that prevent them from grasping the reality in front of them. The hero mistakes a sister he's never met for an inexplicably "forward" girl who keeps throwing herself at him; his best friend believes himself to be in the presence of a Jesuit priest when actually he's in the presence of Bonnie Prince Charlie. Both less and more deluded, Redgauntlet throughout the novel seems able to force reality to bend to the demands of his political imagination. By sheer strength of will and devotion, he momentarily succeeds in leading a group of half-hearted, sentimental Jacobites to the brink of actual rebellion. When such a character is brought to utter the question, "Is this real?", the moment has a resonance exceeding any attempt to get the facts straight or sort out the King's offer. Redgauntlet suddenly finds himself confronted by a reality whose power he had tried to ignore, the reality of the world-situation that makes the King's offer possible. He must face the fact that history has made the idea of a successful Jacobite rising ludicrous and thereby rendered his own efforts futile, an attempt to stay a rising tide.

Redgauntlet's exclamation captures something crucial about the nineteenth-century realist novel. As he speaks, we see before us a character coming to recognize the power of a reality external to him; or, to put it another way, we see a character forced to become a "realist." Redgauntlet is not the only realist here. Walter Scott himself, if not in person then as the creator of the novel's implied author, presents himself as a realist of a more encompassing sort, one who is able to render with fidelity and truth the objective reality, not merely of certain kinds of human behavior, or even of the contours of a certain social order, but of the course of history itself. Scott claims the ability to tell us what really happened to the Jacobites and why it matters. That he does so by depicting a series of events that never occurred in history does not lessen his novel's realism, it simply reveals that Scott is dealing with underlying realities—and makes (or should make) it difficult to imagine that his realism depends on what is sometimes called "direct" or "photographic" representation.

There was a time in the not-too-distant past when the various kinds of realism embodied in the scene would have evoked critical delight. When Lionel Trilling suggested that the novel has functioned as the conscience for modern society, he was thinking of its depiction of such moments of illumination and the part they play in enriching the esthetic possibilities of fictional characters, and in illuminating our social and historical situations.[1] The depiction of fictional characters struggling against illusion was thought to be salutary for real readers, who doubtless had their own illusions to contend with. The demonstration of the power of objective reality was, to be sure, sobering, but it told us where we stood—unless, of course, it went to extremes and left us with a sense that the individual will is entirely determined by external forces. The objective depiction of the ways of society and history provided the ultimate justification for the novel, a form lacking the grace of lyric poetry and the intensity of Shakespearean drama.

More recently, the delight has all but vanished and the applause ceased. Realism has become not a form that can tell us about life in the modern world, but a form that can tell us nothing useful, and doesn't even know it. In commentary after commentary, the realist novel proves most useful as a foil, throwing into relief other, better forms and genres. Naive where it should be subtle, confident because unreflective, realism has become the form which, far from showing the way past illusion, itself perpetuates the illusions on which our blind, ideology-ridden life in society depends.

That realism has come under increased attack should not be surprising. In part, realism is now paying the price of success, and of its association with what has come to seem doubtful company. The attack on realism is part of what is by now a familiar story, the story of what happens when, for various historical reasons, liberal ideology comes to be considered another god who has failed us. Realism, formerly seen as the finest fruit of the Liberal Imagination, now becomes the target of attacks that assume that liberalism has become entirely bankrupt. If we ask not so much about the intellectual origins of certain rhetorics of suspicion, but rather about the causes of their swift and nearly complete acceptance by large segments of the American critical establishment, at least part of the an-

---

[1] Lionel Trilling, "Manners, Morals, and the Novel," in *The Liberal Imagination* (New York: Viking, 1950).

swer must involve the damage done to a certain horizon of beliefs by the spectacle of Vietnam. Viewed in a wider context, the attack on realism may be seen as part of a revolt against the heritage of the Enlightenment itself. But now that, with the help of such thinkers as Habermas, we are seeing a resurgence of interest in defending enlightenment, it may be time to take another look at the question of realism.

This is a book about the realist novel, but it is not a history of the realist novel. Instead, it deals, first with a set of general theoretical issues, and then with the work of three British novelists. In the first part, my aim is both negative and positive: I wish to suggest that certain objections to the project of realism are misguided, and to offer a more useful conception of realism. In the second part, as I confront works by three major novelists, the focus is more specific and the criticism more practical. I shall be much concerned with realism as a narrative phenomenon, exploring issues that include general questions about the intersections of history, ideology, knowledge, and narrative form, but also more specific narratological concerns, such as the use and significance of free indirect discourse. Throughout, I attempt to define and assess the claims of realism. Much unuseful commentary has arisen from those who choose to impute to realism a set of claims no reasonable person would advance. Yet realism does make certain claims that ought to give us pause. Despite the imagery such realist novelists as Zola sometimes employ to describe their aspirations, no realist novel with which I am familiar claims, for example, to offer us unmediated and "transparent" access to reality. Realist novels do, however, claim that certain ways of capturing reality are better (for their purposes) than others, and this latter claim deserves our scrutiny and our skepticism. Since my ultimate quarry is something like a realist "habit of mind" as it confronts what I take to be a set of central and defining problems, I shall sometimes turn to the works of philosophers and critics as well as novelists. Though my main concern is the nineteenth-century realist novel, I shall speak of "realism" in more general terms when it seems appropriate to do so—for instance, when I'm critiquing positions that use the term "realism" in a broad sense.

As it develops, my discussion will mention critics whose work was published some time ago, and the work of Erich Auerbach will assume pivotal importance. I'm tempted to explain this predilection for the dead by invoking a story like the one Habermas tells of how in the works of the early Hegel, philosophy took a wrong turn and has been suffering the consequences ever since. In fact, my claims are less dramatic. Critics like Auerbach have come to be seriously misread, when they're not simply ignored. They deserve better. I am not advocating a "return to Auerbach." The attempt to meet such a figure on his own ground can be rewarding, but my interest is in what his work, viewed without blinking what must now seem historically inevitable errors and omissions, might offer to help us past our current confusions and impasses.

Problems of definition prove notoriously difficult when it comes to realism and realist fiction. The greatest study of realism we possess, Auerbach's *Mimesis*, chooses to avoid a "front-loading" of definitional and theoretical material. Auerbach plunges directly into a narrative in which the nature of the problem is concretely exemplified and theoretical and definitional matters are brought up as opportune moments arise. Such a procedure, beautiful to contemplate and to read, seems nearly inconceivable for a critic today; it is certainly out of the reach of a book that does not claim to be a history of realist fiction. But though I do not intend to follow Auerbach's asceticism with regard to preliminary discussions of relevant issues on a theoretical plane, I will (nearly) follow it with regard to the definition of realism itself. What I mean by realism and particularly by the "realist novel," and why I mean it, will emerge centrally only as my discussion proceeds, especially in my third chapter, where I indicate what a useful theory of realist fiction might look like. Here, I shall pause only to indicate in the broadest and most elliptical of fashions the working concept of the realist novel that lies behind my project. The fiction with which I'm concerned arises in the eighteenth century and becomes widespread in the nineteenth. In my view, its richest examples are substantially informed by what I shall be calling historicism. (That another opaque and heavily contested term arises so quickly in even a brief attempt to define the opaque and heavily contested term "realism" may suggest why it's wiser to allow a substantial definition to emerge in the telling of one's tale.)[2] Such an assertion recalls Georg Lukács's view of realism, which suggests that modern realism comes into being when Walter Scott discovers for fiction the workings of history, and subsequent authors such as Balzac take advantage of this advance to achieve representations of "the present of history."[3] Now to some extent I am indeed echo-

---

[2]   Like realism, historicism has taken a beating, from both the left (Althusser) and the right (Popper). Perhaps the publication in the "New Critical Idiom" series of Paul Hamilton's wide-ranging study *Historicism* (London: Routledge, 1996) may mark a revaluation—and one that is not limited to dividing the conceptual world between the New Historicism and its bad other. I should add that I take the New Historicism to involve a set of complexly interrelated critical practices: to employ that tired but serviceable Wittgensteinian concept, "the New Historicism" designates a family group. Relating those practices to underlying theoretical positions is beyond the scope of this book. For a stimulating placement of some New Historical practices in the perspective of the development of radical American critique, see Catherine Gallagher, "Marxism and the New Historicism," in *The New Historicism*, ed. H. Aram Veeser (London: Routledge, 1989), 37–48.
[3]   Georg Lukács, *The Historical Novel* (1937), trans. Hannah Mitchell and Stanley Mitchell (London: Merlin, 1962), 83; Erich Auerbach also uses the term "the present as history"

ing Lukács, and I certainly mean to give Scott a central place in the story I am telling. But I wish to find a place for Jane Austen as well, and this requires an underlying model rather different from Lukács's vision of Scott's fiction as a stream that branches off from the mainstream of fiction to discover history and, rejoining the mainstream, to make history available to his successors. I think we need to suggest instead that fiction's discovery of history itself is a prime expression of a set of cultural and intellectual practices that gathered strength in the eighteenth century. These practices found expression in Scott's fiction, but they also affected fiction significantly different from Scott's.[4] Jane Austen's fiction, for instance, shares a sense of specific social density that is allied to the historicist insight, but is not quite identical with it. The defining mark of the realism with which I am concerned is that it can be placed in a determinate, positive relationship with historicism, not that it expresses a historicist essence. It responds to similar problems with similar tactics. Though the representation of historical forces may not provide the overt subject matter for all the novels I'd define as "realist," nearly everything important about realism stems from its attempt to come to grips with the fact that we live in a historical world. By the same token, nearly every challenge to realist fiction involves a wish to rewrite its notions of what history involves.

The term "realism" resists the status of the purely descriptive: it always tends to attract epistemological and moral claims.[5] Lukács's work on realism exemplifies both the strengths and the weaknesses that can result. The problem with Lukács's analysis of modernism in general, and of his angry dismissal of the works of Kafka and Joyce in particular, is well known and hardly requires exemplification.[6] His judgments of such novelists can be offensive and obtuse—though they do remind us forcefully

---

(which derives from Hegel) to describe Balzac: see *Mimesis* (1946), trans. Willard R. Trask (Princeton: Princeton University Press, 1953), 480.

[4] In suggesting that the rise of historicism involved "practices" and not simply "insights," I mean something quite specific. The historicist vision was made possible by the accretion not only of techniques for dealing with old documents, but also of documentary sources of information about the past. Only when there was a critical mass of information about past periods could historicism really take hold; without this critical mass, all the theorizing in the world could never have produced a substantial historicism. Realist fiction bears the marks of this origin, as we shall see. So does the best criticism of realism, as we see in Auerbach and his belief that the history of realism can be apprehended only in concrete historical instances, not by means of free abstractions.

[5] For a good discussion of this point, see J. P. Stern, *On Realism* (London: Routledge and Kegan Paul, 1973), 33–43; hereafter cited in the text.

[6] Georg Lukács, *Realism in Our Time* (1957), trans. John Mander and Necke Mander (New York: Harper, 1971).

of areas of human experience these authors avoid. Such obtuseness in a major critic cries for explanation. One might conclude that Lukács's problem stems from a myopic fixation on nineteenth-century models, which provide him with a set of assumptions that simply can't prove fruitful for later fiction; one might add that a theory of realism that cannot come to grips with modernism cannot come to grips with its own preferred subject either. But this doesn't necessarily follow, either for Lukács or for other critics who find the pivot of realism in the nineteenth century. In the case of Lukács, it's more likely that a set of prior philosophical and political assumptions led him to aggrandize certain aspects of nineteenth-century fiction. Yet that Lukács holds a flawed view of modernism doesn't mean that his view of realism is simply wrong. He might simply be *misapplying* a fertile view of realism when he castigates much of the art of the twentieth century. Some admirers of realism have attempted a simpler refutation of avant-garde denigration by reminding us that realism is alive and well right now, no matter what its detractors may say about it. Just look at the novels most people read: they're hardly postmodernist works! Perhaps. But nothing is more common in the history of artistic production than the dwindling of genres from more than a documentary cultural significance.

Brecht refuted Lukács by mimicking the advice he seemed to be giving the modern writer: "Be like Balzac—only up-to-date!"[7] Isn't it just as pointless to advise the nineteenth-century novel to "be like Joyce—only a century earlier!"? Whatever our allegiances, it seems unpromising to link our view of nineteenth-century realism directly to our view of what's fruitful, or alarming, about the literary scene today (or yesterday). If, for example, we try to account for realism and modernism in the same breath, we run the risk either of doing injustice to one or to the other, or of being forced to a level of considerable abstraction before we can make the two terrains merge.[8] If we believe that something it's sensible to call realist fiction reached maturity during the nineteenth century, in close association with the rise of historicist thinking, this needn't commit us to using nineteenth-century realism as a universal yardstick. It might, however, make sense to enter into a dialogue with nineteenth-century realism, and to consider the answers it could offer to our own concerns. I attempt this in the second part of this book.

---

[7] Bertolt Brecht, "On the Formalistic Character of the Theory of Realism" (written in 1938), in Ernst Bloch et al., *Aesthetics and Politics* (London: Verso, 1977), 76.
[8] This is not to say that the quite different enterprise of assessing continuities between realism and modernism cannot provide useful results—as it does in the work of George Levine and Elizabeth Deeds Ermarth.

Is Realism "Centered" or "Dispersed"?

In the last twenty years or so, anything approaching dialogue has been largely absent in discussions of realism. Despite some promising recent developments, the realist novel has taken a beating. David Lodge captures the central impetus of this attack on realism when he suggests that "Post-structuralist criticism, especially that which derives from the work of Roland Barthes, has identified the 'classic realist text' as an instrument of ideology, a genre founded on bad faith, on the pretense that bourgeois culture is 'natural,' using the dominance of the authorial voice over all the other discourses in the text to limit meaning in the interests of control, repression and privilege." Lodge himself takes a more generous view. Yet he inadvertently reveals how deeply what has become the standard critique of realism has taken root when, a few sentences later, he suggests that "part of the problem is that realism is a literary effect that works by disguising its own conventionality."[9] I shall have more to say about the issue Lodge raises here, the issue of "transparency," in the next chapter; for now, I invite the reader to consider how a novel might go about *disguising* its own conventionality. Should we assume that, unless a novel gives primary attention to metafictional maneuvering, it is disguising something?

That a dominant genre should come in for criticism and even repudiation is unsurprising, particularly if the attackers are trying to make way for artistic experimentation. Early in this century, modernist writers and their supporters felt the need to attack the sprawling social novels of the century that preceded and dwarfed them. (Even today, writers of distinguished prose fiction rooted in everyday reality can get huffy if the term "realism" is used to describe their works, fearing that their creativity is being called into question and their writing reduced to "mere photographic representation" or "simple reportage.") Writing in the twenties, Roman Jakobson sought to undermine the prestige of realism by demonstrating that critics had used the term "realism" to describe so many different things that it had come to mean everything and nothing; in his analysis, the most plausible of the many uses of "realism" turned out to involve historically variable effects of estrangement that make a reader say, "this is real!" when faced with a novel. Jakobson's stated purpose was to clean up a particularly messy part of the critical terrain, to help sort out the critical vocabulary, and no doubt such a desire was indeed part of his motivation. Yet the conclusions he drew are so hospitable to the "estranging" avant-garde art he and the other Russian Formalists

[9]   David Lodge, *After Bakhtin* (London: Routledge, 1990), 121–22.

championed that it's difficult to believe that his ultimate object was not to make room for such work.[10]

Avant-garde art would appear to have long since carved out a secure place for itself. Why, then, should the outmoded and outmaneuvered realist novel remain the focus of such sustained critical polemics in our own recent past? Answers may be sought in two directions. First, avant-garde art has indeed won a battle—for status and perhaps even hegemony in the sphere of high culture. It has not, however, quite so evidently won the war with respect to our cultural production as a whole. Second—and perhaps this will turn out to be the same point, arrived at from another direction—when realism is attacked, it may simply be serving as a convenient stand-in for attitudes seen as pervasive in our culture as a whole, for "ideology" or "commodified culture." Thus even a critic quite well disposed to realism can claim that the high-theoretical attack on realism is justified because "it prevents—or would prevent if it were more accessible—the total dominance of our literary culture by expressive realism."[11]

What has become the standard case against realism rests on objections that may be grouped under two heads. Realist representation is said to be naively *transparent* and malignantly *totalistic*. On the one hand, realism supposedly promises its reader a "direct" mirroring of reality, one that provides "literal transcriptions of reality, forms in which, as it were, reality writes itself."[12] On the other hand, realism supposedly attempts to make the world of the bourgeoisie seem "natural" and "full," thereby giving its vision of reality a peremptory power over our imaginations. According to this logic of naturalization, the realist attempt to represent the complexities of a given historical moment turns out to be simply an attempt to "naturalize" that moment, to make its workings seem part of nature, not culture, to deny that it is a product of contingent historical forces.[13] Are these two issues really a single issue? From certain points of view, they certainly begin to merge. It's easy enough to make the issues of transparency and totalization slide into each other. We can, for instance,

[10] Roman Jakobson, "On Realism in Art" (1921), in *Readings in Russian Poetics*, ed. Ladislav Matejka and Krystyna Pomorska (Cambridge: MIT Press, 1971), 38–46.
[11] Lodge, *After Bakhtin*, 17.
[12] Tony Bennett, *Formalism and Marxism* (London: Methuen, 1979), 24.
[13] The poet of "naturalization" is Roland Barthes; perhaps the most influential transmission of this concept to English-speaking audiences was made by Jonathan Culler in *Structuralist Poetics* (Ithaca: Cornell University Press, 1975). On "naturalization" as adding to the Russian Formalist concept of "motivation" the idea that content is selected not simply to reinforce form, but to reinforce form that has arisen to meet specific ideological requirements, see Terry Eagleton, *Criticism and Ideology* (London: Verso, 1976), 76.

observe that the means by which realism renders its view of the world co-ercively and totalistically "present" is by suppressing our sense of its own workings, so that, as the quotation above suggests, reality seems to write itself. Where more opaque and self-referential artistic forms would lead us to realize that they are offering one *version* of reality, transparent rep-resentation allows a single view to impose itself on us in a total, in-escapable fashion. Transparency leads to totalization; totalizing views present themselves as transparently self-evident.

In practice, however, discussions of transparency on the one hand, and of totalization on the other, tend to occur at different levels of abstraction and generalization. Arguments about "transparency" tend to be cleaner, brisker, more self-assured, more abstract and global, and more hermeti-cally sealed; arguments about totalization tend to involve appeals to ac-tual states of affairs in the world—to history, gender relations, and poli-tics. As a result, assertions of the transparency of realism tend to seem either irrefutably ("transparently"?) correct or simply wrong, depending on one's prior philosophical commitments. Assertions that realism is to-talizing lead into murkier waters: we may reject their stated grounds and the conclusions drawn from them, but still feel that they raise significant issues. In the next chapter, I shall try to show that, in its purer forms, the notion that realism as a genre attempts to provide a transparent view of the world has little merit, because the view of realist language on which it is based has little reference to realist practice—and is in any case incoher-ent. Given my confidence on this score, it would be convenient to take at their word those critics who ground their belief in realism's tendency to-ward totalization on its alleged attempt to hoodwink us into thinking that it provides a transparent view of the world. One could readily agree that the entire attack on realism as totalistic rests on the notion of trans-parency, but then happily add that, since the idea of realism's trans-parency is implausible, the notion of realism's totalizing tendencies falls with it. But a root-and-branch response really won't do. Among other things, the attack on realism as totalizing raises issues that realist novels themselves find interesting and important.

My discussions of particular novels in the second part of this book will recur repeatedly to the problem of totalization, in various guises that seem particularly relevant today. For the moment, I'll deal on a more the-oretical level with the question of whether there's something inherently and malignantly "totalistic" about realism. As I do so, a curious fact will emerge. If we move beyond the powerfully influential circle of those who warn us against realism's totalizing ambitions, we will find critics who consider realism's signal virtue to be its power to give something ap-proaching a total picture of society. Such disagreement about values, based on an agreement about the pretensions of realism, is only to be expected. What is surprising is that if we expand our scope further, we'll find champions of realism who consider its prime virtue its *refusal* to totalize, and we'll also discover critics who find realism reprehensible because of this very refusal. In the remainder of this chapter, I shall describe and assess representative examples of these antithetical views, and then address a problem perhaps even more interesting than that of weighing their relative merits. How could such multiple disagreements about the same body of works arise in the first place?

I begin with the preeminent Marxist critic of realism, Georg Lukács. Lukács, as is well known, played a fundamental role in making "totality" a central concept for twentieth-century thought as a whole. The larger story of his contribution to the discourse of totality is far beyond the scope of this discussion.[14] What I will offer here is a brief discussion of Lukács's views on the importance of totality for the realist novel, as he formulated them during the period when realist literature had become his primary intellectual concern—the thirties.

One important function the notion of totality served for Lukács throughout his career was to counter the power of the random object. In his earlier writings, imagining a time in the past when life, art, and vision formed a totality gave Lukács a norm which he could use to measure the anomie of the modern condition. By the thirties, the use of the notion of totality had become more aggressive. When Lukács proclaimed that all worthy art was realist, and that all realist art strove to capture the totality of life, he did so to defend the possibility that historical process can be understood and artistically represented. Those who discuss realism often use it as a scapegoat genre that helps them affirm values they find antithetical to the values they impute to it. With Lukács, the role of scapegoat falls not to realism, but to a mode he calls "naturalism"—a mode of writing which, instead of mastering the totality of modern life in history, allows itself to be overwhelmed by its individual aspects, either by simply describing them directly, or by falling uncritically in with the mere subjectivity of individual characters. For Lukács, it's not that modern writers aren't faced with enormous complexities around them. Indeed, the complexities have grown, because of the development of history itself, to the point where the solution of an earlier age will no longer suffice: we need to strive for totality of vision precisely *because* of the complexities we face. There was a time when the genre of tragedy could do justice to life in history by representing the essence of historical conflicts, more or less shorn

---

[14]   Martin Jay, in *Marxism and Totality* (Berkeley: University of California Press, 1984), provides a superb discussion of the concept of totality in twentieth-century thought; my discussion of totality in Lukács is much indebted to him.

of the details of a particular historical milieu; in the modern world, it is necessary to present not simply the essence of a conflict, but a representation of the "totality of objects" that places that conflict in its particular moment in history (*The Historical Novel*, 89–95). Lukács's insistence on the importance of creating a totalistic representation, then, results from a fear of becoming enmeshed in a trivial immediacy of meaningless details; for him, *naturalism* succumbs to the immediate and therefore chaotic, while realism grasps the underlying patterns and dynamics that in fact inform and render intelligible the movement of history. The stress on totality goes hand in hand with a stress on piercing beneath the epiphenomena of history: both imply the existence of an objective, interrelated set of structures that inform reality and by so informing it make it potentially comprehensible. Just because life in history is complex, we must demand that realism make visible its essentials, pierce beneath a confusing surface to a comprehensible core. For Lukács, "the essential aim of the novel is the representation of the way society moves" (*The Historical Novel*, 144). In this formulation, the concepts both of "movement" and of "society" bear crucial meanings. The "movement" is a vector, the product of historical forces; once we grasp its direction, we possess an instrument that allows us to discriminate between those aspects of a historical milieu that are "typical" and those that are merely epiphenomenal. The "society" in question is modern society, which can be adequately represented only if seen with a certain density of concrete specification, one which the attention to milieu of a Balzac is better suited to produce than are the sublime generalizations of tragedy.

Lukács's insistence that realism captures "the way society moves" finds a counterpart in his notion of the way it represents individuals. As is well known, the key category in Lukács's realist aesthetics is the category of the "typical." Its most famous incarnation in his work on realism in the thirties involves the notion that realism above all else creates "typical" characters—characters who concentrate within themselves the prime historical determinants of an age, the indicators of the forces that allow us to grasp the movement of history itself. Insisting that the movement of society through history can be known and represented by using "typical characters under typical circumstances"[15] does several things for Lukács. It allows him to insist that novels mirror the social and historical aspect of life in history, instead of concentrating solely on individual psychology or feelings of alienation and *angst*. A coherent and powerful sub-

---

[15]   The phrase comes from Engels: it occurs in his celebrated letter to Margaret Harkness (April 1888), in which he also refers to Balzac's novels as constituting, through their historically accurate depiction of French society and despite Balzac's own political allegiances, "one of the greatest triumphs of Realism."

jectivity and agency are implied here, for characters and for readers, at least on the level of contemplation. Historical knowledge centers on typical characters and realist readers.[16]

It would be possible to write the history of recent critiques of realism in schematic fashion as a series of rebuttals to Lukács's championing of the category of totality. Insofar as it suggested that all critics of realism have directly responded to Lukács, such a history would be a fiction: though many influential critics answered him, others did not. Yet fictions have their uses, and the category of totality is important enough both to realism and to the history of our own recent critical preoccupations to merit a central place. So does the split we've already noted between positive and negative attitudes toward realism. Combining these two issues leaves us with four ways of assessing realism. Realism can be viewed positively either because it is totalistic or because it is not, or negatively either because it is totalistic or because it is not. In the last half-century, *powerful critical minds have advanced every one of these four positions*. The following grid defines these critical positions according to whether they take a positive or negative view of the realist enterprise, and whether they believe realism to be totalistic and "centered" or nontotalistic and "dispersed." It also names (in brackets) exemplary critical schools:

	Centered	*Dispersed*
Positive	1 [Lukácsian]	2 [Liberal; Symptomatic]
Negative	3 ["Guerrilla Theater"]	4 [Foucauldian]

In schematizing positions toward realism, it's well to remember all the various issues "realism" has focused for critics: it has involved, among other things, modes of reading, modes of perceiving the world in general, different personal and social uses of literature, the place and efficacy of the intellectual, and the state and functioning of ideology in the modern world. The critical schools included in brackets are not meant to be exhaustive; they do point to what I take to be the most typical and significant critiques. Nor do the positions this schema organizes include all recent attempts to theorize the realist text. (I shall address other views as

---

[16] Lukács's "reflection theory" has been charged with involving a belief in "transparent" representation. In fact, Lukács always insists that artistic representation involves a *selection* of reality, not its mere "transparent" replication. Yet, as part of his inheritance from German romantic aesthetics, he sometimes makes it seem as if he's offering an aesthetics of transparency, in suggesting that though works of art are really necessarily selective, they must *seem* to readers to leave no gaps. This characterization of realism is in my view flawed: in any case, it might be better described as an aesthetics of illusionist *intensity* or *wholeness* than by using a rhetoric of transparency.

the book progresses.) What I'm interested in defining here are the positions that seem to me to have organized everyday critical discourse about the realist novel. This discourse makes itself felt most unanswerably not in extended discussions of realism, but in passing comments by those who are busy with other issues. Discussions of any complexity can hardly avoid relying on penumbral assumptions. From time to time, though, they require scrutiny, not least because they can allow positions no longer of vital interest to have an unfortunate afterlife.

Lukács dominates the first block of my critical grid. A significant body of criticism, less influential now than it was in the fifties and sixties, identifies realism with the second block, viewing realism as a genre that is both benign and what I'm calling "dispersed"—indeed, benign precisely because it is dispersed. For reasons that will become apparent, we may call this the liberal view of realism. It's a view that J. P. Stern's book, titled simply *On Realism*, represents admirably. For Stern, the realist novel is faithful to the individual and the concrete, as opposed to the abstract and ideological. Because of its interest in human and historical particularity, realism can save us from our own cultural solipsism, providing a route to the historically and culturally other. Realism is a mode of criticism as well as a form of literature: Stern's commentary on the realist novel provides the occasion for a defense of determinant readings of literature and indeed of life itself, as against the indeterminacy and special pleading of "interested" reading (179–83).

Stern views realism as, in crucial respects, "naive." Realism doesn't worry about epistemological issues, it simply posits a real world. It also doesn't worry that the cultural relativism it seems to imply might undercut its own claims. Though realism is acutely aware of cultural differences over time, it simply supposes that, at any one time, there exists only one reality: "Realism (unlike a discussion of what it is) is philosophically incurious and epistemologically naive" (54). It's doubtless worth pointing out that novels are not philosophical tracts. Something odd, however, seems to be going on—or rather, something sadly familiar—when we are told that realism gives us access to the other and the alien, providing an escape from solipsism, but that at the same time realism is and must be "naive." How can a "naive" genre solve our most sophisticated problems? Why should critics be allowed to raise questions that works and authors are categorically denied? Why, indeed, should Stern, in talking of realism and the realist author deny what seems self-evident to a reader of realist novels, that at least some realist authors are obsessed with such problems? The role realism is asked to play here is uncomfortably reminiscent of the role women and children are often asked to play, in literature and culture: by their own simplicity, purity, and above all inability to comprehend or ask certain questions, they guarantee stability for those of us who are more knowing. Stern finds himself in this position for political reasons. His bluff, no-nonsense, practical rhetoric is designed to promote compromise and a sense of the immediate, and thereby to stave off "ideology," which for him means thought that is totalistic and abstract.

A fear of systems, a belief that totalizing thought inevitably leads to totalitarian practice, is strong in Stern. His book itself embodies dispersal at every level. Realism, a perennial and partial mode, is defined as appearing in works dispersed widely over time and space. The claims of realism are dispersed (following a hint from Ian Watt) into realism of presentation and realism of assessment. What critique there is of other critical positions is dispersed throughout the book: a running attack on Lukács is overtly directed at substitute figures and shoehorned into irate parentheses and footnotes. The very form of Stern's book is a model of elegant dispersal, with its mixture of modes of exposition (a dialogue intervenes at one point); its elegant skipping from one topic to another and back again; and its numerous cross-references, retrospective and proleptic.

The political motivations underlying Stern's account become apparent in his discussion of the politics of realism itself. Early in his book, Stern suggests that realism is simply apolitical, that it can be either subversive or reactionary or liberal or anything else. But further on—in a passing comment that remarkably enough refers to this very early passage as its justification—we find a reference to "realism's skeptical attitude to all utopian and revolutionary ideologies which propose to sacrifice the concrete particular to the abstract general" (83). It appears that for Stern, liberal politics aren't really politics at all, but instead merely a sensible recognition of the claims of the concrete and the immediate. This is the sort of slipping and sliding that has helped to give both liberalism and realism a bad name, the sort of analysis that has helped to make plausible the notion that realism attempts to make a certain bourgeois view of the world seem as "transparently" natural and inevitable as tables, chairs, and banks.

Before we move to those critics who view realism in a negative light, it will be useful to pause to take stock of the remarkably disparate approving pictures of realism Lukács and Stern paint. How can we explain their differences? It would be possible to conclude that, given the pressure of their critical and ideological commitments, both Stern and Lukács have lost sight of realism as an actual literary practice. Instead, they simply use it as a surrogate and project onto it the normative aesthetic and political visions that appeal to them. Such a conclusion embodies a partial truth, and one that applies not simply to these two figures alone. Critics of realism have regularly used it as a surrogate, to embody either what they value or what they hate. It is a measure of the success realist modes of art have enjoyed that they should choose to do this. (Lukács is, as usual, only being more overt than others when he proclaims that all good art is in fact realist art.)[17] Yet there is something in the nature of the realist enterprise, something more specific and inherent than its prestige or lack of prestige in a given critical climate, that attracts the concerns about the aesthetic and political issues that lie hidden in debates about its alleged "transparency" or "totalism." As I shall try to show more fully in the next two chapters, historicism reveals a world that needs to be known in terms of concrete details of a seemingly infinite variety and complexity. Realism embodies a set of attempts to discover in such a world a knowable order, without losing its salient particularities. Lukács and Stern, then, can find evidence for their diametrically opposed notions of whether realism is or is not "totalistic," simply by emphasizing the different poles of realism's response to the problematic that defines it. Neither has captured the essence of historicist realism; both are responding to its central and defining problematic. By the same token, Stern is echoing something important about realism when he creates a book that itself embodies the mindset he finds characteristic of realism. For the central claim of realist fiction is that the set of mental operations it elicits in us can adequately apprehend the reality of society as it moves through history.

The critiques of realism grouped in the third position on our grid identify this claim as the result of a totalizing impulse that is inherently totalistic and covertly (here radical politics joins hands with Stern's liberalism) totalitarian.[18] Many of the theorists I have in mind here were influenced by Althusserian Marxism, or by the use the journal *Screen* made of Lacan in the service of film theory. Probably most influential in the 1970s, they include, among many others, the early Roland Barthes, Pierre Macherey, Stephen Heath, Colin MacCabe, and Terry Eagleton (in

---

[17]   Lukács, *Realism in Our Time*, 48: "realism is not one style among others, it is the basis of literature; all styles (even those seemingly most opposed to realism) originate in it or are significantly related to it."

[18]   Jay (*Marxism and Totality*, 536–37) offers a thoughtful corrective to the fashionable assumption that the concept of "totality" is inherently oppressive, reminding us that global problems may require global solutions: "The search for a viable concept of totality, which we have seen animating Western Marxism, should not therefore be written off as no more than a benighted exercise in nostalgia for a past plenitude or the ideology of intellectuals bent on legitimating their domination of the rest of mankind. For if the human race is to avoid the negative totality of nuclear catastrophe, we may well need to find some positive alternative. As [Nietzsche,] the philosopher who has so often been used against the concept of totality once observed, decadence means 'that life no longer dwells in the whole.' " The threat of nuclear catastrophe may have diminished in the period since Jay wrote these words, but global thinking on other fronts (especially the ecological front) continues to be a pressing need.

some of his early critical incarnations). The list of names will itself suggest that they are by no means identical in their outlooks, either with one another or (in some cases) across their own careers. But the motivations behind their attacks on realism, and especially their antitotalistic bent, provide a reasonable amount of continuity.

Some of these critics react to realism in a simple and straightforward fashion: they deplore its totalizing tendencies, usually as a prelude to an attempt to imagine an art form that would be different and better—perhaps, with the *Screen* critics, a new form of film; perhaps, with the early Eagleton and others, "guerrilla theater" finding its inspiration in the works of Brecht. By insisting on the totalistic bent of "the classic realist text" or "the classic realist film," they make realism serve as the antitype of a truly liberating artistic practice. Lukács had asked the question "Franz Kafka or Thomas Mann?" and hardly paused before giving the answer "Thomas Mann." These critics ask "Georg Lukács or Bertolt Brecht?" and immediately opt for the latter. Where for Stern, realism serves not only as a genre that embodies democratic values, but also as a habit of mind that supports the notion of stable texts and determinate readings, "guerrilla theater" opponents of realism find themselves suggesting that texts exist, if at all, only as pretexts for performances. The cultural pressures that helped to evoke, and to render plausible to readers, such critical opinions as Colin MacCabe's assertion that the narrative voice in George Eliot is completely without what we have more recently come to call "dialogic" possibilities now seem clear enough, and indeed their influence on much recent criticism has become a commonplace.[19] Realism here serves as a surrogate and indeed a scapegoat for political, social, and technological forces that seemed to possess a limitless capacity to co-opt and neutralize anything that might serve as a negation of the dominant ideology. Critics who like to think that their work might have an impact on such a social formation could only view this power with alarm, anxiety, and a good deal of aggressiveness. (Thus, in an exuberant display of bad-boy role-playing, Eagleton tells us regretfully that though we cannot completely ignore the literary text in favor of our own revolutionary desires, we can and should "at least round on it, torture and interrogate it with a critical rigour.")[20] Such critics had a way of announcing that one or another of their analytic discoveries bore on "nothing less" than a grand cultural or political theme. Do such grandiloquent phrases mask a legitimate anxiety that literary criticism is politically ineffectual, a

[19] For a restrained but decisive refutation of the notion that the narrator of *Middlemarch* is an entirely controlling presence, see Lodge, *After Bakhtin*, 45–56. I shall have more to say about Eliot's narrators in my final chapter.

[20] Eagleton, *Criticism and Ideology*, 68.

fear that "nothing" could be "less" important than the role of the literary critic?[21]

It is easy to sympathize with frustration in the face of the power of modern society to co-opt and deflect oppositional energy. Yet identifying realism as an agent in this process necessitates doing a certain amount of violence to the realist text and its reader—and more than that, neglects what might be useful resources in dealing with the modern realities one finds so stultifying. Colin MacCabe provides a striking example in an analysis of the film *American Graffiti*. As many readers will know, this film lovingly and amusingly enacts life in a California town at the moment just before Vietnam changed reality in America. At the very end of the film, cameo pictures of its four main (male) characters appear on the screen, with a phrase describing the fate of each. The protagonist has moved to Canada; another character ("Toad") was killed at An Loc on a certain date. Now MacCabe wishes to use *American Graffiti* as an example of the ways in which what he calls "classical realism" prevents the emergence of "contradiction" by installing a master discourse that overrules to the point of obliteration any other discourses that happen to find their way into the text. The cameo pictures and their captions might seem to raise problems for such an interpretation, but MacCabe finds that they actually reinforce it:

> What is politically important about [the film's] textual organisation is that it removes the spectator from the realm of contradiction. But it is not just contradiction in general that is avoided but a specific set of contradictions—those raised by the impact of the Vietnam war on American society. Portrait of a pre-Vietnam America, the film presents to us the children of the Kennedy generation in the age of innocence—an innocence that we can regard from our position of knowledge. But this knowledge presupposes us outside politics now, outside contradiction. Indeed, Curt Henderson is a writer living in Canada, reflecting on an earlier reality of America that could not be sustained. (The fact that the writer is living in Canada is a further index of the repression of Vietnam—he has presumably dodged the draft, but this remains unspoken: to interrogate that de-

[21]   Raymond Tallis in *In Defense of Realism* (London: Edward Arnold, 1988), 159–70, embroiders on this possibility with enormous glee, discussing with considerable schadenfreude a phenomenon he describes as *Kritikerschuld*. That ad hominem attacks like the one he makes on Said in this section will raise the level of the discourse about realism by promoting dialogue seems doubtful; that they lead to an oversimplification of significant issues is certain. A valuable aspect of Tallis's discussion is his recognition that for realism, capturing the real is a challenge that can be approached only asymptotically.

cision would introduce contradiction.) The passing of innocence is reduced in the film to the process of growing up—there is no way in which external forces could be introduced into the homogeneous society of small-town California. Toad grows up and goes off to die at An Loc but this is simply part of a human cycle. The position of the viewer after the Vietnam war is simply held to be the same but different—the position of the imaginary [in Lacanian parlance]. The Vietnam war is repressed and smoothed over.[22]

I cannot believe that any of the "children of the Kennedy generation" (i.e., Americans who were adolescents during the Kennedy years) could possibly experience the ending of *American Graffiti* in the way MacCabe suggests the film's form makes inevitable. On some level MacCabe must himself realize this, else why would he seek to insinuate that there's any doubt why Curt Henderson went to Canada, and how could he make the extraordinary suggestion that the viewer will take the death of "Toad" at An Loc as a "natural," nonpolitical part of a life cycle? An Loc, California? You simply cannot mention the death of a late-adolescent American at An Loc to someone of my generation and expect to evoke the response that it was "part of the life cycle"—particularly after you've just raised in our minds a vividly absorbing picture of what life was like before Vietnam (or of what, after Vietnam, we wish to think it was like). This bizarre reading of the film's ending points to problems at a number of levels. To begin with, it graphically demonstrates how the attempt to define realism as the thoughtless genre demotes the powers of the reader or viewer as well. How ignorant or insensitive would you have to be to view the film that way? But of course this raises the further question of just who "the reader" is, and how helpful it is to suppose that global structures of a psychological or epistemological nature can control the responses of readers.

Beyond that, MacCabe's reading of the ending of *American Graffiti* may serve as an inadvertent endorsement for one of the prime agendas of realism: its attempt to provide a palpable, textured, complex picture of the culturally "other." How was MacCabe, from his side of the Atlantic, sup-

---

[22]   Colin MacCabe, "Theory and Film: Principles of Realism and Pleasure" (1976), in *Tracking the Signifier* (Minneapolis: University of Minnesota Press, 1985), 73–74. A footnote informs us that the films MacCabe uses as examples were pre-set by the exigencies of the conference where he first delivered it. This may help to explain why the *American Graffiti* analysis seems weak; the question remains of what would have been required to make its analysis stronger, especially since the general line about realism taken in his analysis of that film appears in other essays in this volume. Terry Lovell in *Pictures of Reality* (London: British Film Institute, 1980), 79–87, provides a useful critique of MacCabe's views on realism and of straw-man pictures of realism that oversimplify the ways language refers to the world. I pursue the issue of reference in the following chapter.

posed to know what the cameos would mean to its American audience of a certain age, one might ask? Well, one answer would be that he might have taken more seriously other realist representations of American society. By the same token, he might have tried reading the film "with the grain"—asking himself what you'd have to assume the audience is expected to know for the ending to have some interest and integrity, instead of asking himself how it could be proved to be politically nefarious. Had he done so, he might nevertheless have come up with the justified complaint that the film's ending can work only for a limited audience. Realism at its most successful provides a model of how we might go about processing social and historical realities, of the sorts of things we'd need to take into account and the sorts of connections we might usefully draw. This *American Graffiti* does not do. The ending of *American Graffiti* tends to presuppose, by contrast, that we have such a model already in place. The closest thing it provides to a model centers in the sensibility of the protagonist, the one who has presumably written the movie in his exile in Canada—a sensibility that is formed during the film (*pace* MacCabe) not by the protagonist's quest for a father, but by his attempt to exist without a father, through experimenting with a series of different cultural roles in search of a mixture of detachment and inclusion in multiple cultural possibilities. Henderson would know what to make of the cameos that end the film: indeed, he'd know how to make them.

MacCabe has little interest in half-detached, half-engaged observers like Curt Henderson. Instead, he wants to produce "engaged" readers, who have been jolted out of their normal pattern of response by his criticism. Here we again come upon the remarkably ambivalent view of the reader that arises from the way such criticism seeks to take the edge off realism's own critical potential. The reader has two choices, either to be completely and simplemindedly enslaved by the realist work, or to be jolted by the enlightened critic to a new plane of consciousness that will leave realism behind.

Some of those who see in realism the attempt to create a malignant totality have, however, taken a less single-minded view. They begin by suggesting that realism attempts to present a totalized and "naturalized" vision of the world, and they view this as a bad thing. (Thus realism either occupies, or attempts to occupy, position three on my chart.) But they continue their analysis to suggest that, usually despite itself, realism cannot make good on this attempt. To the properly equipped critic, realism in fact reveals the incoherencies of the ideology it embodies, and of the historical situation from which it arises, and this is at least potentially a good thing. (Thus realism finds itself, against its own deepest wishes, occupying position two on my chart: realism is good because it fails to achieve totalization.) The version of position two these critics embrace is, to be sure, significantly different from Stern's. We might say that they give this position a theoretically self-conscious turn in opposition to Stern's bluff empiricism; or we might borrow Schiller's terminology to suggest that they substitute a "sentimental" version of the notion that realism is good because noncentered for Stern's "naive" version. Realism becomes "good" despite its own wishes and its own defining project: the critic's reading of its symptoms *makes* it good.

A confrontation between Barthes and Macherey on the subject of Jules Verne is exemplary here. In *Mythologies*, Barthes had suggested that, despite their exoticism, Verne's works really have little to do with a genuine quest for adventure and the extraordinary. Instead of valuing the image of the ship as an image of "genuine exploration," Verne in fact prized it as a fully enclosed, pleasingly compact and full habitat, a microcosm perfectly attuned to the bourgeois love of appropriation and withdrawal to the hearth. The ship provides a space full of a plenitude of objects, the gathering together of which Barthes elsewhere consistently identifies with the project of realism itself. This fantasy of fullness and enclosure, like the other social forms and products Barthes examines in *Mythologies*, is objectionable in that it presents ideological phenomena as if they were "natural." On Captain Nemo's *Nautilus*, "the enjoyment of being enclosed reaches its paroxysm when, from the bosom of this unbroken inwardness, it is possible to watch, through a large window-pane, the outside vagueness of the waters, and thus define, in a single act, the inside by means of its opposite"—no bad image (though Barthes doesn't say so explicitly) of the bourgeois desire for a world secure from what has come to seem to the member of a historically dominant class the "chaos" of life in history.[23] Thus Verne's representation would find itself firmly placed in position three on our chart: it presents itself, on every level, as "full" and "centered," and it is self-mystified in doing so.

In *A Theory of Literary Production*, Macherey sees Verne quite differently. Macherey finds in Verne's work a set of determinate gaps, incongruities, and absences that triangulate upon or gesture toward the nature of the real, instead of embodying it in a direct and centered fashion. He thus puts Verne's work in our category two: it is dispersed, not centered, and for that very reason it has value. At the deepest level, I believe, what Macherey is objecting to in Barthes's account is the "centering" involved in the very practice of demythologizing cultural artifacts. He doesn't like the way in which Verne can be made to seem a "transparent," centered

[23] Roland Barthes, *Mythologies* (1957), trans. Annette Lavers (New York: Hill and Wang, 1972), 66–67.

exemplum of a crucial contradiction in bourgeois ideology, since the apparent ease with which the result is produced ignores the real difficulties ideology presents because of its protean adaptability and its blunting of overt contradictions. Macherey objects to Barthes's *brio*, the powerful and at the same time eminently personal intelligence Barthes's writing projects, an intelligence fully able to defy the ideological mystifications of his society and show them for what they are. Macherey implicitly puts Barthes as critic himself in our category three: he is centered and therefore defective. That Macherey is able in the end to avoid a similar centering in his own treatment of Verne is something I would deny, but one cannot deny the lengths to which he goes in his attempt to avoid this. Macherey takes pains to prevent us from assuming that he is imputing to Verne a heroic intelligence or struggle that wrests the truth from a recalcitrant reality, even though one of Verne's central symbols turns out to suggest the incoherence of bourgeois ideology.[24]

Barthes's subsequent distinction in *S/Z* between the "readerly" (position three) and "writerly" (position two) potentiality of the classic realist text represents a subtle response to the point of view expressed in Macherey's work. The distinction preserves the indictment of realism's allegedly nefarious tendency to "totalize," as well as an Althusserian vision of the nature of ideology and a Barthesian endorsement of taking pleasure in the text. In creating this distinction, Barthes allows the "classic realist text" to occupy both positions two and three on our chart simultaneously——or perhaps better, to oscillate between them at the will of the reader.

Macherey's criticism follows clearly and overtly from his belief in Althusser's anti-Lukácsian version of Marxism. What we observe in *A Theory of Literary Production*, however, becomes at times an inverted Lukácsianism. Like Lukács, Macherey is interested in literature's "mirroring" of reality (though he takes pains to give a very different definition of how the mirror works). The notion of "realism" and the notion of "literature that has a determinate relationship to social and historical process" tend to coalesce for him, as they do for Lukács. Thus Macherey talks of Verne's art and indeed literary art in general as constituting "a form of final *perception* of reality" (239), suggesting that it draws upon elements from earlier fiction in such a way as to create "an instance of the real" (235). Indeed, with Macherey, an emphasis on realism as a means of approaching and processing reality becomes so strong that he finds himself denying the standard opposition between the "classic realist text" and Brechtian

[24]   Pierre Macherey, *A Theory of Literary Production* (1966), trans. Geoffrey Wall (London: Routledge and Kegan Paul, 1978), 235; hereafter cited in the text.

aesthetics. For critics who find classic realism malignantly totalizing, it would be more than an understatement to suggest, as Macherey does, that "it has hardly been noticed that Balzac's compositional principles are those adopted in another domain by Brecht." Not only have they not "noticed" it; they would loudly deny it. He continues in a way they might find acceptable (if they could believe its description to be true of Balzac): "Balzac puts the world into his work as Brecht puts the dialectic on the stage: both culminate in a ·broken plot" (271). This certainly distances his view of realism from that of Lukács, moving it definitively to our "dispersed" or "fractured" position two.

Those in the fourth position on our grid would agree that there's something "broken" about realist representation, but they would find this dispersal hardly cause for enjoyment. The fourth position considers realism at least as politically suspect as does the third, but (like "liberal" criticism), it makes room for an appreciation of the complexities with which realism tries to come to terms. When D. A. Miller suggests that Dickens's "Chancery . . . names an organization of power that is total but not totalizable, total *because* it is not totalizable," he echoes a central Foucauldian thesis about power: power hardly requires visible monoliths, thriving better through invisible micropractices.[25] From such a point of view, when a liberal critic like Stern finds a guarantee for freedom in the recalcitrant details of everyday life, he merely hands himself over to that which polices life better than the police; when a critic like Eagleton pins his hopes on guerrilla theater tactics which promise freedom by exploding totalizing practices, he deludes himself. The struggle against totalization, like its acceptance, simply acts as a useful diversion, reinforcing the main event. The major contribution of realism to domination is to serve as a kind of training ground whereby readers learn to perform, and to accept as natural, practices that promote the continuation and extension of power.[26]

[25]   D. A. Miller, "Discipline in Different Voices: Bureaucracy, Police, Family, and *Bleak House*" (1983), in *The Novel and the Police* (Berkeley: University of California Press, 1988), 61–62. My talk of Miller's view of "realism" (and, for that matter, of "the Foucauldian view of realism") is a convenient and potentially misleading shorthand. Miller's subject in *The Novel and the Police* is imbricated with but not identical to realism: "Few of course would dispute that, with Dickens, the English novel for the first time features a massive thematization of social discipline, or that, in direct and undisguised response to Dickens, Trollope and Collins develop the two most important inflections of this thematization in the 'realist' and 'sensation' traditions respectively" (ix).
[26]   Miller's criticism can in this respect be seen as an extension of the side of MacCabe ("Theory and Film," 70–72) that allows realism to include moments that contest its dominant ideological force, but only so that those moments can be finally suppressed.

The Foucauldian position on realism balances realism's quest for order and its admission of disorder with an elegance denied the other positions on our chart: while the others tilt one way or another or oscillate between the two poles of the realist problematic, the Foucauldian view holds the two in perfect suspension.[27] Lukács, by contrast, admits the diversity of historical reality, but only in the guise of samples, already organized into "totalities." Radical diversity and disjunction cannot have a place within Lukács's view of realism; instead, it is projected onto realism's "bad other," naturalism. Foucault conveys a vision of reality at least as tightly organized as Lukács's, but he does not need to pit its logic against naturalistic dispersal. For Foucault, reality is made up of disjunct, local particulars knit together by dispersed relays of power.

Foucauldian criticism has an unsettling ability to accept whatever aspect of a literary representation one might assume would create either knowledge or freedom, but then to show that in fact it only perpetuates dominant relations of power. Thus if we wish to argue, with George Levine and against critics who find realism "naive," that realism in fact is full of self-consciousness, the Foucauldian critic is happy to agree. He simply adds that the self-consciousness in question enmeshes one all the more effectively in a conceptual grid that furthers the designs of power: it provides schooling and recreation for the prisoner.[28] If we say that realism is totalistic, it turns out that the lure of totality is a mere diversion from the actually dispersed workings of power on the microlevel. If, by contrast, we say that realism is tentative and uncertain about problems involving the constitution of personality or the power of society, we discover that such doubts act only to help us toward a feeling of wise mastery over imponderables, again giving us a libidinal investment in creating and then failing to solve problems that divert us from the true workings of power. Should such lines of argument turn out to be valid, nearly everything I shall have to say on behalf of the realist novel would be radically undercut. There is much that's salutary in the relentless single-mindedness of Foucauldian criticism. The guerrilla theater notion

[27]   In suggesting this, I am offering a tribute to the aesthetic appeal of Foucault's work, not its truth. To the extent that Foucault's analysis depends for its ultimate plausibility on the notion that reality is really an incoherent mass of impressions that rush in on the observer (and can therefore be organized without internal constraint into "discourses" and "disciplines"), it joins the mass of modern positions that forget that such an epistemology is itself a product of abstraction. As we'll see in the next chapter, a critic who has been taken to be the prophet of realism, Ian Watt, holds this view, which is very widespread. For a discussion that points out that narrative is more "primitive" than the notion that life in history is really random, see David Carr, *Time, Narrative, and History* (Bloomington: Indiana University Press, 1986).

[28]   George Levine, *The Realistic Imagination* (Chicago: University of Chicago Press, 1981).

that self-reflexivity is in and of itself revolutionary becomes hard to sustain against this withering attack, as does the liberal notion that simply buried oneself in the particulars of one's society will guarantee freedom and political probity. Particularly remarkable has been the revaluation of the aesthetic branch of this theory, the novel criticism that has marched under the banner of Henry James. Mark Seltzer has shown that a disappearing narrator may disappear so as to be the more controlling, and that certain kinds of artistic and social "care" can betoken not a liberal compassion that would allow room for the claims of the other and of "life," but an extraordinary level of coercion.[29]

To suggest that our normal distinctions between, say, "care" and "coercion" can mask deeper identities is one thing; to follow a critical method which effectively depends upon such masking's *always* being the case—indeed, which insists that the very making of distinctions is itself simply an extension of the ruses of power—is quite another. D. A. Miller finds in the theory of "limited schism" voiced by Arabin, a clergyman in *Barchester Towers*, a telling description of how Trollope's realism works, and indeed of how power in general works. Arabin considers the existence of a certain amount of disagreement regarding the Church of England no bad thing, for it focuses people's attention on religion as something worth considering and fighting over. Miller extends this insight as follows:

> To contend over introducing Sabbath-day schools, or intoning the Sunday service, is not just to advertise the supreme importance of the Church of England in the national life. Even better, it is to make this importance vital in the contending subjects themselves, whose conflicts (amounting to so many cathexes) attach them not only to "religion" but also to the general social condition of bondedness that not inaptly passes here under that name. The entelechy of a war game, therefore, is not, as with a war, to be over, but, as with a game, to secure a maximum of play. What matters most in this game is not whether you win or lose, or even how well you play it, but that you play it at all. (115)

The insight Miller so deftly unfolds here applies to many parts of our lives. Indeed, it is profoundly true of realism, but not necessarily with the implications Miller gives it—if one can imagine the "game" as involving more than self-amused indoctrination. One wonders, however, if it doesn't apply best of all to the kind of criticism that Miller himself is writ-

---

[29] Mark Seltzer, *Henry James and the Art of Power* (Ithaca: Cornell University Press, 1984).

ing. The language game he makes us enjoy playing involves, among many other things, the repeated use of such words as "police" and "discipline," until a darkly irresistible insinuation builds that these are everywhere—that, for instance, any attempt at knowledge is a covert extension of power, and that any self-scrutiny is self-policing.

This brilliantly elaborated line of argument leads to some implausible accounts of the reading experience. The passage from our private reading of novels to our more public everyday life and back again, we are told, simply and univocally trains us to accept the privatizing rhythms of bourgeois life. That novels are too long to read at one sitting also has unfortunate consequences: "No doubt, both as a system of distribution and as a text, the Victorian novel establishes a little bureaucracy of its own, generating an immense amount of paper work and sending its readers here, there, backward and forward, like the circumlocutory agencies that Dickens satirizes. On this basis, it could be argued that, despite or by means of its superficially hostile attitude toward bureaucracy, a novel like *Bleak House* is profoundly concerned to train us—as, at least since the eighteenth century, play usually trains us for work—in the sensibility for inhabiting the new bureaucratic, administrative structures" (88–89). The phrase, "despite or by means of" says it all here, is itself an example of the language game that insinuates a remarkably persuasive rhetoric of suspicion throughout Miller's works. But what, indeed, of Miller's work itself? Is this training too—and that despite a "superficial" critique of power? The essays *are* pretty long, do contain a lot of paper, and they require us to negotiate the interstices of a rather complex, highly self-contained and self-supporting intellectual system. Or should we suspect only novelists and readers of novels? At one point in his essay on Trollope, Miller makes evident the political stakes of his critique, reminding us that "much as, in late twentieth-century America, unseemly political activity against imperialist wars or for various civil rights is opportunistically converted into the very evidence of the 'free society' that this activity is in fact trying to bring about, or a scandal like Watergate comes to vindicate a system that, even so severely tried, stll triumphantly 'works,' so the bickering in Trollope's Church and the fallibility of its ministers are all to the good" (118). However much one may share the sense of outrage here, it sits oddly with a discussion that suggests that co-optation is not an abuse, but simply an inevitable extension of power. What prevents us from concluding that the civil rights activists were themselves merely serving power, by engaging in what in the end will always turn out to be a superficial hostility toward a state that always already has the last word? Is there any way that the protesters' actions could have been more than superficial, and if so, is there any way in which they could have gauged this? If we try to make such distinctions, aren't we simply indulging in activities that will further the designs of power?

Another version of position four brings us back to our starting point, Lukács. Lennard Davis, working with presuppositions very different from those of Miller and other Foucauldians, suggests that one of the many ill consequences of reading realist novels is that they train one to perceive the objects in the world as cut off from oneself. Here, as with Foucauldian criticism, realism is suspect because its representation is essentially dispersed, but whereas Foucauldian criticism sees this dispersal as an extension of the workings of power in the (rest of the) world, Davis sees it as a simple falsification, which substitutes a mystified, reified relationship to objects for the organic connections that would emerge in a more just society, the sort of society imagined by Marx and Engels as the product of the Revolution. Like Lukács (from whom he derives his notion of "reification"), Davis sees the world as at least potentially "centered" and indeed "organic" in its connections; unlike Lukács, Davis finds in realism not a revelation of the logic of reality, but a training in alienation from it.[30]

The work of two other critics importantly engaged with realism relates to my schema in ways that are complex enough to require special notice. Both may seem initially to fit into one of the boxes in my diagram; neither can be contained there. Fredric Jameson presents a complicated case. [31] There are indications that Jameson would fit into the same category to which I have assigned Lukács, as one who views realism as good because totalistic. This would be relatively unsurprising, given Jameson's (unfashionable) regard for Lukács as "the greatest Marxist philosopher of modern times."[32] But such an assignment won't quite do. The "ethical" categories "good" and "bad" are foreign to Jameson; they are insufficiently historicized. (This is perhaps more a judgment on the material they *do* accommodate than on the categories themselves.) For a critic of Jameson's synthesizing ambitions, either supporting or opposing realism (or any other literary genre or type) would be jejune. The point is not to understand literary genres, but to mediate them and thereby determine

[30] Lennard J. Davis, *Resisting Novels: Ideology and Fiction* (New York: Methuen, 1987).
[31] In the brief comments that follow, I'll be drawing indifferently from older and newer writings by Jameson. On the issues relevant here, he appears to me to have maintained a consistent line throughout his career.
[32] Fredric Jameson, *The Political Unconscious* (Ithaca: Cornell University Press, 1981), 13. Jameson's sophisticated, wary approval of the "totalizing concept" also appears in more recent work: "in my opinion, it is diagnostically more productive to have a totalizing concept than to try to make one's way without one" (Jameson, *Postmodernism, or, The Cultural Logic of Late Capitalism* [Durham: Duke University Press, 1991], 212).

what they can contribute to the "one grand narrative" of Marxism. As a result of this orientation, Jameson feels no need to scapegoat realism (or any other genre) in the service of another genre he prefers. Instead, he himself analyzes that scapegoating.[33] In reacting to the Brecht/Lukács debate, for instance, he suggests that at our own particular moment in history and with suitable reworking, invoking the concept of realism could have the merit of reminding us of the importance of the concept of "totality" and thus of denaturalizing a now wholly co-opted modernism.[34]

Jameson thus consciously avoids the kind of partisanship that would place him in one or another of our categories. The synthesis he creates between impulses to praise or to castigate realism as totalizing is particularly noteworthy. Jameson believes in the importance of a movement toward totality; at the same time, he believes that that which is objectively total, history itself, cannot be grasped "directly" because it is inherently nontextual and cannot be rendered in a text.[35] What we have, then, is a movement toward totality balanced by the notion that the ultimate reality is, for us, an absent cause—and thus cannot produce what the enemies of totality would identify as a totalistic, closed ideology.

With Jameson as with George Eliot, one feels preempted at every turn: both authors always seem to have arrived there first, anticipating and incorporating into their own projects all objections and all shades of meaning and distinction. Nevertheless, Jameson's stress on history as that which eludes language may not provide an ideal climate for understanding the workings of realism. I shall be exploring realism as a mode that claims, not implausibly, to engage us in ways of thought and feeling that open onto reality as a presence, and as something we can represent and apprehend in our language. Given Jameson's view of history as beyond representation, it seems unsurprising that he focuses on ways in which past and present modes of apprehending can be mediated and moved through; given my interest in positive historical representation, it follows that my own analysis will want to press the possibility of engaging realist texts more on their own terms and in their own moments. This in turn means that my focus will be more formal and aesthetic: how realism makes its claims will become a more central concern than how its ideology might enter our present dialectical situation. When I turn to realist texts in the second part of this book, my interest will be focused on narrative and narrators in the works, and not on the sort of "one grand narra-

[33]   See, for instance, Fredric Jameson, "The Ideology of the Text," in *Situations of Theory*, vol. 1 of *The Ideologies of Theory* (Minneapolis: University of Minnesota Press, 1988), 57–59.
[34]   Fredric Jameson, "Reflections on the Brecht-Lukács Debate," Afterword to Bloch et al., *Aesthetics and Politics*, 211–12.
[35]   Jameson, *The Political Unconscious*, 102.

tive" Jameson insists is required for us to make ultimate sense of society, history, and literature.

Jameson's position with regard to history as necessarily "absent" from representation seems to me an excellent example of a principle Mark Sacks finds operative in Kant: by granting that there exists a realm of the unknowable and demarcating it strictly from the knowable, you support the claim that phenomena on the near side of the line are indeed knowable.[36] You cordon off a category of the unknowable, so that it will not contaminate the knowable. Hence Jameson's assuredness that the phenomena on the near side of the line (in part because of their very ideological distortions) can ultimately be made to cohere, positively or negatively, with the one grand story he wishes to unfold. At the same time, this procedure removes "real" history itself from the possibility of being tainted by the ideologies everywhere operative on the knowable side of the epistemological line.[37] In my view (and of course this doesn't necessarily contradict Jameson, since it operates at a different level of generality from his), nineteenth-century realist fiction makes most sense when it is viewed as an attempt to deal with situations which involve partial knowledge and continual approximation, and in which history, existing on a continuum with our other forms of experience and being, can be known and represented with varying degrees of accuracy. Realism therefore feels no need to place "real" history in a category like the noumenal.

As with Jameson, Mikhail Bakhtin cannot be contained within any of the four categories I've outlined above. To be sure, when Bakhtin contrasts the closed, "monologic" representation of Tolstoy with the open, "dialogic" representation of Dostoevsky, we seem to be in the universe of my second category, the one in which realism is seen as "bad because totalistic."[38] Yet elsewhere Bakhtin indicates that dialogic possibilities needn't be enacted solely within a work itself. Dialogue can occur with other works and with the audience (whether by rhetorical instigation or address); beyond that, dialogue is always present in the variously sedimented meanings of words themselves. Working on the level of the word in "Discourse in the Novel," Bakhtin discovers the monologic "other" of dialogism not in a group of novelists set in opposition to Dostoevsky, but in poetry. On this level of analysis, Tolstoy becomes the exemplar of a bipartite novelistic dialogism, in which his discourse "harmonizes and

[36] Mark Sacks, *The World We Found* (London: Duckworth, 1989), 27; I return to this issue in the following chapter.

[37] My own view of realism is touched by Kant, but in a different way; it emphasizes the importance of mental categories and operations, concerning itself with a realist frame of mind.

[38] Mikhail Bakhtin, *Problems of Dostoevsky's Poetics* (1929, revised 1963), trans. Caryl Emerson (Minneapolis: University of Minnesota Press, 1984), 69–75.

disharmonizes (more often disharmonizes) with various aspects of the heteroglot socio-verbal consciousness ensnaring the object, while at the same time polemically invading the reader's belief and evaluative system, striving to stun and destroy the apperceptive background of the reader's active understanding."[39] Tolstoy activates the multi-sedimented potentialities of the word to create modes of dialogism that reveal the complexities hidden in the world he describes, and challenge the ways in which the reader understands and values. Not only does this allow Tolstoy back into the fold of dialogic writers, it suggests ways of imagining the workings of realism that do not rely on the passive images of mirror or window pane. When novelistic language itself becomes inherently dialogic, however, any special claims for realism seem ready to evaporate. Reality is already immanent in all language and all language uses; monologic intentions can, it seems, always be defeated by dialogic reading and indeed are defeated in advance by the historical sedimentation of dialogic layers of reference and meaning immanent in the word itself. For all of that, Bakhtin's emphasis on dialogue is important; at the very least, it can act as an antidote to a characteristic shared by much work on realism, an implicit denigration of the reader. I shall follow Bakhtin's emphasis on dialogue and communication in conceiving of realist fiction as entirely dependent upon maintaining a strongly rhetorical circuit of communication between narrator and reader.[40]

Critiquing the Critiques

My categorization of these critiques of realism suggests a fundamental question: How could any mode of representation attract such utterly divergent views, not simply about its merits, but about its fundamental character? One answer involves the company it keeps. As we've seen repeatedly, realism has tended to be invoked either as the type of all good literature, or as the "bad" opposite that allows us by contrast to define more progressive literary possibilities.[41] Lukács is unusually brash in sug-

---

[39]   Mikhail Bakhtin, "Discourse in the Novel" (1934–35), in *The Dialogic Imagination*, trans. Caryl Emerson and Michael Holquist (Austin: University of Texas Press, 1981), 283.

[40]   Lilian R. Furst, in *All is True* (Durham: Duke University Press, 1995), also invokes Bakhtin in emphasizing the importance of the complex acts of cognition realism elicits in its readers.

[41]   Bruce Robbins, "Modernism and Literary Realism: Response," in *Realism and Representation*, ed. George Levine (Madison: University of Wisconsin Press, 1993), 227, adds a further dimension to our understanding of this phenomenon, viewing the recourse to strawman notions of realism as a fundamental way in which the discipline of literary criticism seeks to legitimate itself: "realism is not any old subject for criticism; it's what we have told ourselves we exist by not being."

gesting that good literature is and always has been realist, but he is hardly alone in creating a discourse in which the question of the value of realism bleeds into the question of the value of literature in general. The issues with which realism becomes entwined are sufficiently broad to activate contrary opinions and assessments. (We discover here the explanation for the "positive" and "negative" poles on our chart.)

Yet the characterizations of realism we've encountered are not infinite in their variety, and as I've already suggested, the attacks on realism have a certain appropriateness. Realist fiction offers itself up as a scapegoat, because of the claims it makes and the problems it attempts to solve. There is for instance a recognizable center of gravity in the attitude realist fiction takes to the predicament of the individual (more recently, and with clear gains, the "subject") in history. Because of its complex awareness of the power and intricacy of the forces at work in shaping any historical milieu or moment, realist fiction tends to depict human beings as relatively weak in the face of circumstance. (This assumption is never more obvious than when a realist novel enters the mode of wish-fulfillment, by having history and society arrange themselves so that characters in whose welfare we have an investment survive or even thrive in the face of destructive historical change.) Realist fiction's fascination with the particular conditions of social and historical existence tends to translate into an assumption that all we are given is, precisely, our place and our moment, that the resources of our situation here and now will have to suffice. The responses that realist novels have enacted to the weakness of the individual in the face of history are quite various, though there is a recognizable shift of focus as the nineteenth century progresses. One of the more interesting historical stories one might tell about realist fiction would trace the way in which Scott's delight in depicting how individuals are embedded in the rich cultures of the past becomes transformed, in the works of naturalist writers at the end of Scott's century, into a fear that we are cogs in the social machine. But the linked recognition of the complexity of societies as they move through history, and the fragility of the individuals who face them, remains constant. One purpose of the attack on realism has been to refresh the terms in which we think about this problem, either by dissolving the notion of the individual into a set of codes, or by trying to imagine and promote powerful forms of avant-garde literary practice that would provide a substitute agency for the individual (or for certain groups of individuals). I have mentioned that the critiques of realism lead to a certain enslavement of the reader, and I'll return to this problem in a moment. I'd like to mention here, however, that a hemming-in of the reader may inadvertently reflect respect for the forces of history on the part of those who favor realism, and fear of their power on the part of those who attack it. The "naive" reader of realism tends to be cast in the role critics suppose the fiction's characters are in, a role the critics themselves may fear they're not immune to.

Another, perhaps more fundamental explanation for the contradictory ways realism has been described stems from the nature of the realist project itself. The critiques of realism build, in selective ways, on the problematic situation to which realist fiction responds. Faced with a world of diverse historicist particularity, realism attempts to give that world some degree of order while remaining true to its concrete specificity. (Here we discover an explanation for the "centered" and "dispersed" poles on our chart.) Lukácsian and Foucauldian criticism take both aspects of this situation into account, with Lukácsian criticism giving a heavier weight to an organizing and totalizing moment in the historical dialectic, and Foucauldian criticism achieving a remarkable balance between the two, by imagining a coercive mode of dispersal. The critiques that lie on the other diagonal of my diagram tend to ignore either realism's drive toward order or its attempt to honor historicist particularity. For Stern, realism is all diversity (and therefore good); for the guerrilla theater critics, realism is all totalization (and therefore bad). Yet an irony arises here, for these attempts to ignore one of realism's constitutive moments are inherently unstable. Critics like Macherey and Barthes find themselves oscillating between positions, so that even as they deny its dual nature, their own work *with* realism engages with both poles of its problematic. Indeed, absolutely pure forms of position two and (especially) position three on our chart are rather hard to come by. Stern's very fixation on the dangers of totalization, for instance, seems to result from a kind of return of the repressed, in which the full spectrum of the project of realism reasserts itself, in demonized form, against his insistence on the essentially dispersed nature of realism. Here another irony arises. The critical positions on the Lukács/Foucault axis of our diagram seem much more intellectually powerful than those on the other axis. Yet the tendency toward oscillation we find on the other axis (where, for instance, an inert realist "readerly" text finds itself supplemented by an active "writerly" text) seems more in keeping with the genius of realism, which involves dialogue and a reaching for totality, not the simple presentation of a powerfully achieved totality. Again, however, we might counter this appearance by suggesting that the very intellectual power of the Lukácsian and Foucauldian analyses itself seems destined to lead to a rich dialogue, though not an internal one—a dialogue with the reader, the sort of dialogue that's fundamental to the claims of the realist project.

If we set aside these potentialities for a dialogue that replicates realism's own constitutive dialogue, the various positions about realism we have been canvassing (with a few exceptions) assume a somewhat depressing flatness. For, whether they are approving or disapproving, they can be reduced to a two-step operation. First, you form a picture of realism by emphasizing one moment of its reaction to its constitutive problematic, its wish to put in order a reality in which the particulars are viewed as inherently resistant to abstract generalization. By emphasizing the attempt realism makes to see things whole, you can produce the picture of a "centered" realism; by emphasizing the recalcitrance of the materials it seeks to come to terms with, you can produce a "dispersed" realism. Second, you either praise or disparage the vision of realism you've constructed, depending on the values you bring to it. Such a procedure goes against the grain of realism. Realism supposes that, in our encounters with reality, we can produce new and more adequate knowledge. The two-step critical procedure I've outlined, by contrast, suggests that the general, global, abstract schemes we bring to reality have a total power to construct reality for us in advance of our encounters with it.[42]

Much is lost when this is assumed. Problems arise with respect not only to the realist text, but to its reader as well. The accounts of realism we have been considering seem strangely inattentive to the task of imagining what might be involved in a willing reader's encounter with the narrative and rhetorical particularities of realist texts. It is difficult to cast realism as either a stupid or a manipulative genre without making its readers seem chumps. We learn, for instance, that "it is clear that the classic realist text, as defined above, guarantees the position of the subject exactly outside any articulation—the whole text works on the concealing of the dominant discourse as articulation—instead the dominant discourse presents itself exactly as the presentation of objects to the reading subject."[43] This is a subject-position no reasonable person would wish to inhabit. If this is really all realism has to offer, it would indeed be better for its readers to turn to other literary forms.

Things are better for readers with the symptomatic readings of Macherey and the Foucauldian readings of Miller. Here their power is en-

---

[42]   If we grant such overwhelming power to preexisting epistemological and ideological investments, it becomes difficult to see how anyone could reliably unmask realism—or anything else! The by now familiar confessions that the critic is "complicit" with the designs of the text attempt to deal with this problem by acknowledging it so loudly as to preempt further discussion; in fact, they do precisely nothing, either for society at large or for solving the theoretical problem at hand.

[43]   Colin MacCabe, "Realism and the Cinema" (1974), in *Tracking the Signifier*, 47. Precisely what "guarantee" means here, and how far the guarantee extends, are thorny problems. If the guarantee were complete, the possibility of seeing the film in any way but the one it expects would be zero; if the guarantee isn't complete, why call it a guarantee in the first place? To ask this is to ask just how coercive the supposed deep psychological structures are that such criticism invokes.

hanced by demoting the power of the text, though the text does retain substantial interest. Verne's novel turns out to know more than Verne does, but not more than we as readers can discover. Dickens may be reinforcing the workings of power, but we can see this dynamic at work. It's necessary to add, however, that this enhancement depends upon the creation of two classes of readers: we promote some to the status of knowing (tenured?) readers by envisioning a group of very differently endowed "normal" readers, to whom the ruses we are able to decode are in the first instance directed. This is a common enough tactic in many kinds of criticism; in this context at least, it brings with it certain liabilities. Expert reading becomes synonymous with unmasking, and (here is the fundamental problem) any other experience of the realist text sinks to the level of mass hypnosis. To those who value the possibility of a dialogue with that which they read, these alternatives are likely to seem impoverishing. One must add that realism's friends have been only slightly kinder to the reader of realism than have its enemies.[44] Even the genial Stern finds himself creating a slightly obtuse (though quite likable) realist reader, when he gives realism the image of being "philosophically incurious" and assigns philosophical curiosity to the critic instead. But it may be that realist fiction has something valuable to tell us on several levels, if we are willing to listen.

I conclude with Lukács and the reader. For all its flaws, Lukács's work on realism provides fundamental insights. His reflection theory is more complex and valuable than his detractors would allow. It directs our attention to what matters centrally in realist fiction, its attempt to deal with a historical world. His insistent rationalism, his lack of embarrassment in claiming that it's necessary to make sense of the world if we are to change it, aligns him with an important aspect of the project of realist fiction. Yet his picture of how realism achieves its ends seems incomplete. When I read his description of how the typical characters concentrate within themselves the essential determinants of a historical collision, I am of two minds. I believe he has identified a crucial aim of the novels he describes; I believe he has only partially described how this aim is accomplished. The notion of passive spectatorship that always lurks in the image of "mirroring" asserts itself at this point, to Lukács's disadvantage. If typical characters really accomplished what Lukács says they do, there would be

---

[44]   A recent exception is Darío Villanueva, *Theories of Literary Realism*, trans. Mihai I. Spariosu and Santiago García-Castañón (Albany: State University of New York Press, 1997). Villanueva's book provides a wide-ranging discussion of theorists of realism as a step toward a phenomenologically inflected discussion of the role of the reader in realist fiction. Tallis, *In Defense of Realism*, 55, 152–59, also notes and deplores the demotion of the realist reader.

little more left for the reader than to sit back and contemplate them. Lukács himself seems uneasy with this aspect of his analysis, as it begins to seem that typical characters directly represent objective knowledge about history. He tells us that typical characters do in fact bring such knowledge into focus, but adds that the author must disguise this knowledge so that the work will maintain its aesthetic nature.[45] (This double movement anticipates the Althusserian distinction between ideology and science, and it is just as unsatisfactory.[46]) Lukács's account leaves out the way narrative fiction sets the mind in motion, instead of freezing knowledge into static, concentrated images. That Lukács's immediate goal is to discredit the use of literature as simple propaganda should not be allowed to obscure this fundamental problem. In fact, there is for realist fiction no question of the achievement of a crystalline embodiment of the essential structure of an age, which then must be occluded to produce aesthetic pleasure and to avoid making claims that only philosophy (or Marxist "science") could make good. The narrative apparatus of realism involves us in emotional and cognitive activities that allow us to experience what it would be like to come to grips with the way history moves. Contemplation of the already achieved typicality of figures is not the primary mode in which we experience realist representation. An evolving participation in a set of mental processes that promises to help us grasp the typical determinants of a historical situation is.

Early in the nineteenth century, Jürgen Habermas has suggested, philosophy in the person of the young Hegel took a decisive turn in the wrong direction. Hegel faced the difficulties that arise from recognizing that one's own society is historical, and as a result finding it no longer possible to ground one's values in an unquestioning acceptance of traditional values, which are themselves revealed to be products of history, and hence to lack religious or metaphysical inevitability. With the advent of historical consciousness comes the discovery that we are not only historical, but "modern" as well, modern by virtue of our now disjunct relationship to the past. But how, in such a situation and bereft of an appeal to traditional values, can modernity make peace with itself, justify its existence? Hegel's early work seemed to be leading toward a recognition of the primacy of interpersonal discourse situations for the solution of such a prob-

---

[45]   This is a pervasive theme in Lukács's writings of the thirties. See, for instance, *The Historical Novel*, 91–92.

[46]   For a sympathetic account of Althusser's significance which nonetheless insists on the fundamentally destructive consequences of his antithesis between science and ideology, see Joseph McCarney, "For and Against Althusser," *New Left Review* 176 (July/August 1989), 115–28.

lem. According to the young Hegel, we can no longer justify the punishment of criminals as obedience to God's will; we can, however, justly attempt to bring criminals to the consciousness that crimes have rent the
fabric of our common life. God's will is not our own, but our common life
is: we create its values together as we seek to be free. At a certain point,
however, Hegel abandoned this insight and produced instead a contribution to the "philosophy of the subject," in which he justifies modernity as
a phase in the evolution of Mind, and in which "Mind" as a category
elides the interpersonal, gaining its identity instead from the classical
epistemology of the single subject/observer, facing a world of objects.
Modernity in the later Hegel attempts to justify its own existence in the
guise of an individual mind becoming Mind itself.[47]

The realist novel, which was establishing itself at roughly the same
time as Hegel was wrestling with modernity, has a similar bifurcation at
its heart. In Scott's works, as I've argued at length elsewhere, the individual is seen, so to speak, from the skin out, not from the skin in: the focus
rests almost entirely on the social and historical aspects of human life,
with the inner life being relegated to the realm of the ineffable.[48] In the realist novels that succeed Scott, the inner life gains a voice. This creates opportunities and enrichments, but also problems. The attacks on realism
we have canvassed were indeed prepared for and to some extent anticipated by a dominant tradition of twentieth-century novel criticism that
preceded them. That criticism responded to the realist novel by concentrating largely on its discovery of the inner life. This emphasis led either
to the misrepresentation or to the devaluation of what I take to be the central claim of nineteenth-century realism, the claim to place us in history. I
would argue, however, that the realist novel always retains the potentiality for registering the interpersonal realm. This potentiality is present
above all in the ways realist novels employ their narrators to engage
readers in different modes of imaginative dialogue. The increasing
prominence of the inner life in realist novels tends to lead toward the
"philosophy of the subject," for it can install a lone observer at the center
of things. Yet the reading situation these novels create leads, or can be
made to lead, in other directions as well.

To determine exactly how it is that realist novels have actually been
read would require a study quite different from this one—and from the
critiques I have discussed in this chapter. I believe that realist novels *ask*
to be read in quite complex and interactive ways—an obvious enough as-

---

[47] Jürgen Habermas, *The Philosophical Discourse of Modernity* (1985), trans. Frederick
Lawrence (Cambridge: MIT Press, 1987), 23–44.
[48] For a discussion of the significance of Scott's avoidance of the "inner life," see Harry E.
Shaw, *The Forms of Historical Fiction* (Ithaca: Cornell University Press, 1983), 128–49.

sertion, were it not so often negated in theory and practice. They require us neither to participate in the passive acceptance of a "naturalized" reality, nor to engage in an endless process of self-reflexive unmasking. My critique of the critiques of realism suggests that we need to respond to the realist problematic as a whole, and not simply to one of its poles. It also suggests that political judgments will always be part of a reading of the claims of realism: for that very reason, we should make them as overt as we can. One way of doing this is to attempt to engage realist novels in a dialogue concerning the issues that most concern us. I believe that realist novels ask to be read in such ways. To wish to engage in such reading, however, we will need to believe that the realist project is neither impossible in conception nor impossibly flawed in execution. The purpose of this chapter and the two that follow it is to define the realist project and to suggest that its claims might possibly be made good.

2

Realism and Things

> "I wonder whether one oftener learns to love real objects
> through their representations, or the representations through
> the real objects," he said, after pointing out a lovely capital
> made by the curled leaves of greens, showing their reticulated
> under-side with the firm gradual swell of its central rib.
> "When I was a little fellow these capitals taught me to ob-
> serve, and delight in, the structure of leaves."
> —Eliot, *Daniel Deronda*

During the production of one of his films, Erich von Stroheim is said to have made an extreme demand upon the wardrobe department. He required that the soldiers who appeared to swell his scenes be equipped not simply with authentic Prussian uniforms, but with authentic Prussian underwear. (This was not because at a climactic moment in the film the uniforms, or the underwear itself, would be removed.) Antirealist criticism of the novel could give a ready explanation for Stroheim's obsessiveness. Stroheim was a naive realist. He forgot that the uniforms his soldiers wore weren't transparent, in his hopes of achieving a representation of reality that would be transparent. He was trying to dress his actors in (pieces of) the referent.

This chapter will explore attitudes toward representation and language that have helped to make the attack on the realist novel convincing. In the previous chapter, I discussed "totalization," one of the issues that have organized (and confused) the critical discourse on realism. Now I turn to a second—the issue of whether realism seeks to engage in something called "transparent" representation. It has become commonplace to suggest that realism promises to give us "direct" and unproblematic access to the world, pretending that what is really a *version* of the world is in fact natural, inevitable, objective, and immediately available for our inspection. This chapter will cast doubt on all aspects of this analysis. Though I freely admit that the language of realist fiction isn't transparent, the conclusions I draw from this undoubted fact are quite different from those typically produced by critics who introduce the issue of transparency in the first place. My denial of realist transparency is radical: I find the very raising of the issue as it is normally raised inadmissible. Talk of transparency typically produces the following pattern. You divide the possibilities of linguistic representation into two camps, transparent representation and its opposite (which is generally taken to be some sort of linguistic self-referentiality). In the process (and this is the key maneuver) you create the impression that realism could gain a purchase on the real world only through linguistic transparency. Then, when you quite properly show that the notion of linguistic transparency is a fallacy, you have thereby preempted other possible ways in which realist representation might make contact with the world. Your own definition of the nontransparent then rushes in to fill the vacuum thus created.

I hope to show that realism doesn't trade in "transparent" representation, because it doesn't need to and doesn't want to. Realism doesn't need to, because nothing about the nature of language requires that an attempt to make contact with the real world must involve "transparent reference" to a putative "world prior to language." Realism doesn't want to, because it's often interested in the issue of how we can best come to grips with the world, and because it's always interested in engaging the reader, not in some sort of illusion of "direct" contact with the world, but in a dialogue in which the stakes are more rhetorical than epistemological and have more to do with the will than with a certain (inadequate) model of knowing.

As in my discussion of realism's allegedly "totalistic" pretensions in the previous chapter, however, my aim is not simply to demonstrate to realism's detractors the palpable error of their ways. I believe that those who ascribe to realism an interest in "transparent" reference are discussing something real about realism, though they are misdescribing it. I shall be particularly interested in why this misdescription quickly achieved broad acceptance in Anglo-American critical circles; by the same token, I shall try to assess what these arguments seemed to offer in a positive way. I'll suggest that at their best, they offered or seemed to offer a way to focus our attention on the ideological components of literary practice—an offer all but impossible to refuse in the last twenty years. In this chapter as in the last, I will be much concerned with the unexamined discourse about realism. One of my purposes will be to show that much of this discourse comes from sources that are anything but up-to-date.

A convenient way to open a discussion of transparent representation and its alleged connection with realism is provided by considering the role that objects play in realist novels. And a good place to begin such a consideration is with Ian Watt's discussion of objects and novels in *The Rise of the Novel*. Watt's account does not condemn the realist novel for being "transparent": transparency is indeed a concept Watt (to his credit) doesn't employ. But the terms of his discussion set the stage for such an accusation, and for others. Beyond that, a path Watt later regretted he had not taken in writing *The Rise of the Novel* helps to suggest a better set of answers than the theorists of "transparency" provide in understanding the objects of realist representation.[1]

Beginning with objects will involve us with problems of reference and "the referent." The classic objections to "transparent realism" often suggest that it is based upon a naively direct notion of reference. Novels think that they are simply and directly referring to things in the world, when in fact they've never passed beyond their own language. The model such accounts provide for reference tends to involve an individual's affixing a label to a physical entity—which brings us back to the question of the status of objects in realist novels.

Haven't realist novelists themselves stated their belief in a theory of "transparent language"? A famous case is Zola's wish to create "a clear language, something like a house of glass that allows the ideas inside it to be observed."[2] Darío Villanueva suggests that Zola's pronouncements (he

[1] Doubts about whether "transparency" is useful in analyzing realism needn't involve doubts about the usefulness of the concept to describe other aspects of nineteenth-century culture, particularly the attitude that women should be morally and epistemologically transparent. Also useful, for work in ethical and political philosophy, is the concept of a transparency of social institutions, which Bernard Williams, in *Ethics and the Limits of Philosophy* (Cambridge: Harvard University Press, 1985), 101, defines as involving "the sense that the working of its ethical institutions should not depend on members of the community misunderstanding how they work." (One notes that the negative definition here avoids implying that the community's understanding must be simple and immediate.) Analytical philosophers employ the dyad opacity/transparency in discussions of reference. Antony Flew gives the following example of a failure of this kind of transparency: "The sentence 'The police are looking for Jones's murderer' will not necessarily remain true if 'Jones's murderer' is substituted by 'the man in a black hat,' even if both terms are, in fact, applicable to the same individual." Here, because the two terms "Jones's murderer" and "the man in the black hat" cannot be substituted for each other, even though they may both refer to the same person, the context is said to be referentially opaque, not referentially transparent. (See *A Dictionary of Philosophy*, 2d ed. [New York: St. Martin's, 1984], under "opacity and transparency.") I suppose we could imagine someone who keeps mistaking contexts of opaque reference for contexts of transparent reference, but this is not what those who refer to realism's naive belief in the transparency of language have in mind. Behind the portentousness that can accompany mentions of linguistic and epistemological transparency may stand the specter of the self-transparency Mind will attain at the end of history, according to Hegel.
[2] Quoted (in French) in Darió Villanueva, *Theories of Literary Realism*, trans. Mihai I. Spariosu and Santiago García-Castañon (Albany: State University of New York Press, 1997), 22; hereafter cited in the text. Villanueva provides a wealth of similar citations from Zola and other authors; Zola's reference to the "pane of glass" is also quoted on 22.

calls them "arguments") along these lines—and there are a good number of them—"possess a high theoretical value, summing up most accurately the various ways of understanding mimesis and realism that had immediately preceded him" (16). This is not the place to undertake a critique of the accuracy of the historical aspect of such a claim. I will however say that Zola's pronouncements, and many others like them, do not appear to me to have theoretical status. Zola is speaking in terms of total effects, structures (like that of a house, though elsewhere he does to be sure compare the realist "screen" to "a pane of glass"), and crucially, aspirations. But to say that you *want* to create a house of glass suggests that, at best, it might be possible to *make* language (usually, an artistic form as a whole) behave *as if* it were transparent, which in turn implies that in its normal state, language is anything but transparent. (Compare Auerbach on how Flaubert's belief in the *mot juste* involves not a simple assumption, but a "mystical-realistic insight.") In brief, the evidence usually adduced doesn't seem to me to imply that realists and naturalists such as Zola "believed in" a "theory" that language is normally transparent, and I'm certain that they didn't simply *assume* the transparency of language (whether one means by this phrase that language is normally transparent—or that it can under special circumstances be made transparent, or indeed with regard to whatever meaning you give the phrase). In the Zola passage cited above, I'd say that the image of a "house of glass" is in fact a metaphor for a phenomenon better described as linguistic adequacy, with a strong guarantee that the author isn't being rhetorical *in the sense of manipulative* thrown in.[3] It is at any rate important not to lose sight of the fact that statements like Zola's do not themselves *entail* any one theory of how language operates, but are compatible (or can be made compatible) with many. Even if realists of the nineteenth century all subscribed in an utterly naive fashion to a theory of transparent language, the question of how language actually behaves in their novels would remain open.

---

[3]   It is instructive to see how easily a realist such as Trollope can move from talk of what could easily be described as "transparent representation" to talk of rhetoric. After citing with approval Hawthorne's comment that Trollope's own novels seem "just as real as if some giant had hewn a great lump out of the earth and put it under a glass case," Trollope adds, "I have always desired to 'hew out some lump of the earth,' and to make men and women walk upon it just as they do walk here among us,—with not more of excellence, nor with exaggerated baseness,—so that my readers might recognize human beings like to themselves, and not feel themselves to be carried away among gods or demons. If I could do this, then, I thought, I might succeed in impregnating the mind of the novel reader with a feeling that honesty is the best policy, that truth prevails while falsehood fails" and so on. See Anthony Trollope, *An Autobiography*, ed. David Skilton (Harmondsworth: Penguin, 1996), 96.

Watt, Lukács, and the Realist Object

Why are there so many objects in realist novels? Ian Watt sought an answer to this question in epistemology and the philosophy of language. Watt notes the rise in the eighteenth century of a fuller depiction of "interiors": we learn much about Mr. B's mansions, about Grandison Hall, about the dwellings of Robinson Crusoe and Moll Flanders and the objects that fill those dwellings. This is information with which earlier and other genres do not provide us. According to Watt, the realist novel provides it as part of an aim it "shares with the [realist/Descartian] philosopher—the production of what purports to be an authentic account of the actual experiences of individuals." Achieving such an aim requires the use of suitable linguistic means. Whereas earlier literature had employed language that tended toward "linguistic ornateness" and the self-referential, the realist novel's language is more self-effacing. Realism, as part of a general cultural movement toward an empiricist philosophical orientation, tends to employ language not as "a source of interest in its own right," but as "a purely referential medium."[4]

The defining opposite of "referential" language thus becomes for Watt "self-referential" language, language that does provide "a source of interest in its own right." The extreme cases of the choice Watt offers are euphuism on the one hand and the police blotter on the other. But in the process, something crucial has entered the picture, and some very significant possibilities have left it. The criterion for "truth to reality" has become whether or not we feel that we're in a position of "eavesdropping"(29) on the situations the novel presents. In "eavesdropping," linguistic mediation appears to drop away: there we are at the keyhole, listening and watching as reality unfolds. To achieve the effect of eavesdropping, the novel must short-circuit our self-consciousness, duping either us or itself or both: we must somehow *think we're there*, but not think about how we got there. "Formal realism" appears to involve the production of a certain intensity of experience, but little else.

[4]   The quotations here come from Ian Watt, *The Rise of the Novel* (1957; Berkeley: University of California Press, 1965), 27–29; hereafter cited in the text. Watt suggests that the "closeness" to "what is being described" Richardson wishes to convey is "mainly emotional" (29). In a valuable assessment, John Richetti, "The Legacy of Ian Watt's *The Rise of the Novel*," in *The Profession of Eighteenth-Century Literature*, ed. Leo Damrosch (Madison: University of Wisconsin Press, 1992), 97, points out that "the eighteenth-century novel's realistic transparency is from the first identified by Watt as a response to cultural circumstances and not as a move, as some of his critics think, toward an improved access to some sort of transhistorical realm of actuality." On Watt's achievement and influence, see also Daniel R. Schwarz, *The Humanistic Heritage* (Philadelphia: University of Pennsylvania Press, 1986), 99–117. Let me make clear from the outset that I do not intend to call into question Watt's remarkable achievement in *The Rise of the Novel*, taken as a whole.

Watt answers the question of why there are so many objects in novels, then, by suggesting that, like the philosophers who decided that truth and reality must be reached through individual experience, the realist novelist tries to replicate this experience.[5] A convincing "report" on the world must present large groups of objects with a maximum of immediacy, and with something of the randomness that allegedly characterizes our experiences of objects in real life. Watt suggests that "the function of language is much more largely referential in the novel than in other literary forms; that the genre itself works by exhaustive presentation rather than by elegant concentration" (30). In reaching this conclusion, he helped to create one of his book's more remarkable achievements, its seminal effect in promoting Richardson and demoting Fielding as the central eighteenth-century novelist. The drift of his subsequent statements about his book suggests that this is an effect he may not have intended to create in so dramatic a way. An earlier form of the book, he tells us, more equally balanced "realism of presentation" with "realism of assessment"; a greater stress on "realism of assessment" would have given Fielding more of his due.[6] Yet in the book Watt published, the realism that calls the tune is "realism of presentation," and nowhere more so than in the matter of the relationship of words to things, as expressed by the notion of the language of realism as being basically a "referential" language.

Watt's discussion of "realism of presentation," however, contains an interesting ambiguity. In describing the new, referential style favored by Locke and his progeny, Watt suggests such a style valued "the closeness with which" an author "made his words correspond to their objects" (28–29). "Object" can mean "thing"; it can also mean "purpose." Richardson's novels may contain descriptions of a relatively large number of physical objects, for instance the "round-eared caps" to which Pamela repeatedly refers, to the amusement of Henry Fielding. They also, as Watt points out, strive to bring us "close" to less tangible entities, especially the emotional states of his characters. But anyone who turns over the pages of Richardson's novels will find a good deal of writing that can only be described as "rhetorical" in several senses of the word. One thinks, for instance, of the long speeches Clarissa and Lovelace deliver. Rhetoric is more concerned with purposes existing in an intersubjective field than with objects extended in space. When Richardson provides a detailed de-

---

[5] Watt, to be sure, does have an interest in the modalities by which we process experience, but this is a practical interest. He uses such categories as time and space to describe the *content* of an empiricist view of reality; he doesn't use them to speculate on the possibilities and limitations of our ways of knowing.
[6] See Ian Watt, "Serious Reflections on *The Rise of the Novel*" (1968), in *Towards a Poetics of Fiction*, ed. Mark Spilka (Bloomington: Indiana University Press, 1977), 98–100. I'll have more to say about "realism of assessment" below.

scription of Clarissa's coffin, his purpose transcends an interest in the coffin as an object. He wants to tell us something about her, her society, and ourselves. He wants to impinge on and mold our sensibilities and our wills. Such examples suggest that Richardson's interest in "objects" hardly ends with the creation of a sense of "direct" contact with the world. What Richardson discovers as he reinvents the novel is not exhausted by the possibility of creating a "more largely referential" mode of representation. His novels may require that his language bring us "close" to objects and sensations, but a language limited to "direct" and "transparent" representation could never have achieved this.

Why do realist novels contain so many objects? For Georg Lukács, the answer to this question involves the answer to the question of why novels are the preferred genre for representing history after the advent of historicism. Drawing heavily on Hegel, Lukács (as we've seen in the previous chapter) invokes different kinds of totalities in an attempt to give an answer. Though no artistic form can hope to capture the entire manifold of human existence, some can capture more than others. Where drama depends on an extreme concentration of human factors into the actions of a few characters, the novel casts a wider net. The many-layered nature of historicist reality requires this greater capaciousness. The components of a truly historical representation must be various and disparate. They will include, among other things, physical objects, individual characters, entire social systems, and lines of historical development. Realist representation cannot find its organizing principle at the level of the epiphenomena, of concrete objects or even individual destinies. Realism must always be concerned with the deeper structures that give the epiphenomena form and significance. But to imagine those structures with anything like an appropriate complexity requires that we imagine them in dynamic relation to the epiphenomena. As soon as particularities are subsumed into generalities, the nature of the generalities shifts and we've lost their historically characteristic flavor. History is, to be sure, a process so complex as to elude summary statement, dramatic concentration, or synecdochic symbolization. Yet it is not, as some would have it, that which is always other than representation or language. Instead, it is that which can never be fully indicated, but can be best indicated by representation. The materials in the historical milieu are so disparate, exist on so many levels, and are woven together by such multifarious and complexly overdetermined mediations, that an extensive reduplication is impossible and anyway would be pointless. The best one can do is to provide a model, but the model must emulate the mode of concreteness which characterizes historical existence. Such a model shows us how to make connections; without a sufficient range of appropriately disparate objects to connect, it cannot do its work.

For Lukács, then, realist novels contain so many objects because history does. In both realist novels and the world, there obtains a level and quality of socio-historical complexity that require (among other things) the inclusion of concrete objects if it is to be represented at all. (You can't play a sonata in C minor on a piano with no black keys, any more than from music that lacks clefs.) The stakes of realism are higher for Lukács than for Watt. Watt is happy enough to describe how it is that formal realism correlated with the epistemology characteristic of modernity, but he has no intention of making any claims about the nature of the real itself: he introduces a note of relativism into his analysis by reminding us that "realism" in the Middle Ages involved a belief in the reality of universals, not of particulars; and he's quick to assure us that formal realism is "only a convention" (32). Lukács's claim, by contrast, has an ontological force: he's suggesting that realism's interest in things (and, more centrally, in their relationships) attempts to accommodate the actual nature of the historical reality that surrounds us. Watt's more modest claims allow him to stop short of Lukács's demand that realism's interest in details be accompanied by an interest in the historical structures that accompany them and provide the motor for history. As a result, Watt's "formal realism" can easily become a "material realism," in which the mere presence of discrete objects will serve to indicate a certain set of epistemological priorities. It's a short step from "formal realism" to "transparent representation"—and, as we'll see, to Barthes's "reality effect."

Lukács's ontological claim for realism is likely to make us feel uneasy, especially when it leads him to declare that all true art is "realistic," a claim that can easily slide into the claim that all art must mirror the nineteenth-century realist novels Lukács so admires. (I myself would be inclined to parse it to mean that all true art puts itself into some sort of relationship to the social and historical realities that Lukács believes to be at the heart of life in our world: this would authorize a large number of different artistic forms.) Watt's wish to confine the question of realism to matters of epistemology seems more judicious. I shall nonetheless be suggesting in the next chapter that realism must bring with it ontological as well as epistemological commitments. For the present, I'd like to consider the results these two positions produce, at least in Watt and Lukács. Whose account of the status and function of objects in realist fiction seems truer to the workings of at least one nineteenth-century realist novel?

One of the purposes of *Waverley* is to explain why the Jacobite Rebellion of 1745 failed. Scott assumes that he can convey the truth about this tract of history. He believes that certain individuals and social groups existed with ascertainable economic and ideological characteristics, and that they interacted in ways his readers can understand to produce results with which they are still living. Must such a set of beliefs entail a belief in, or use of, "transparent" reference to the world? Scott's representational mode fills his novel with objects that catch our attention, in part because they come from a culture foreign to ours. Does representing such objects involve using language as a "more largely referential medium"?

One important truth about the Jacobite Rebellion of 1745 that Scott wanted to convey is that the conditions of its early success and the causes of its inevitable failure were one and the same, on any number of levels. The Pretender's army penetrated far into England because it was small and mobile, and unencumbered by the English recruits it had hoped to gain on its march. The English army was, by contrast, large and unwieldy and therefore difficult to set in motion. But of course once the English army got itself moving, it was bound to prevail, the more so because the Pretender's army had failed to raise English supporters (again, because English society itself had become in several senses more "unwieldy" than the society of the Highlands). On the level of ideology a similar contradiction obtained. To raise his troops, the Pretender had only to appeal to a small number of clan leaders, because of the fanatical adherence of the members of a clan to its head. Thus the Pretender could provide himself quickly with fiercely loyal adherents, the more loyal because their country was economically backward and their very way of life threatened by the incursions of the more modern English society. Yet this power base was inherently unstable. The fierce loyalty of the clansmen was inextricably bound up with a hatred of rival clans. It had a certain anarchic and anachronistic side as well, with war serving as a way of testing and demonstrating martial prowess, and also as a way of gaining booty, but not as an organized, long-term paid profession in which soldiers fight for wages, for the benefit of people to whom they are not related and whom they may not even know. Under the strain of a long campaign that took them farther and farther from their ancestral lands, the Highland army was bound to disintegrate. Thus the Pretender's decision to retreat at Derby was the inevitable consequence of the historical forces and milieu that allowed him to reach Derby in the first place.[7]

To represent this historical inevitability concretely and to measure its human consequences requires much of the narrative of *Waverley*. For our

---

[7]   Scott's view of the truth about the Forty-Five has of course not gone unchallenged. A recent attempt to redefine the status of the Highlanders within the Jacobite rising is Murray G. H. Pittock, *The Myth of the Jacobite Clans* (Edinburgh: Edinburgh University Press, 1995).

present purposes, we may concentrate on a single sequence that makes a characteristic contribution. During the march to Derby, the Pretender becomes aware of a disturbance in the ranks. What has caused the disturbance is that Edward Waverley, the hero of the novel and an Englishman with Jacobite connections who is participating in the rebellion, has quarreled with Fergus MacIvor, the Highland Chief with whom he had chosen to serve. The quarrel occurs because Waverley, for good reason, refuses to consider himself engaged to MacIvor's sister, and MacIvor feels himself personally affronted and politically weakened by this refusal. Word of the quarrel penetrates the ranks, and one of MacIvor's followers takes a potshot at Waverley when Waverley, in a huff, joins the ranks of a company under the command of a Lowlander. The two groups are at the point of fighting a pitched battle, but the Pretender arrives in the nick of time and with marvelous adroitness blunts the situation, soothing the pride of the various contenders and getting them to consider their mutual grievances in a more measured fashion. As a result, MacIvor assembles his clan, asks who it was that took the shot at Waverley, is told, ascertains that the pistol of the clansman in question has been recently fired, and proceeds to club him with it. The offender, who survives, makes no attempt to avoid the blow and feels no resentment at having received it; the fanatical attachment that had initially motivated the shot at Waverley remains intact. At the close of the scene, the Pretender gets the line of march moving again, remarking to his aide-de-camp (speaking in French) that this sort of thing may be boring, but is also the stuff of which grand enterprises are made.

In all of this, it is hard to detect the use of a "referential" language that seeks to give a "direct" report of reality, for which the model is reference to a single, palpable physical object taken in by a lone observer. Scott clearly believes that he's telling the truth about an objectively real historical situation, but the means to that truth are simply not "referential" in the sense required. They are instead heavily mediated through and through. To demonstrate how full this mediation is would require many pages of complex analysis. We would notice, to give only one example, that nearly all the characters involved have been presented as parts of a self-consciously simplified network of types: the mendacious, thieving, violent Highlander who shoots at Waverley from behind a bush, for instance, is balanced from his first appearance by a much more noble Highlander. If we say, then, that Scott has captured the reality of the historical situation, what we must mean is that he has presented us with a representation that contains its essential determinants (in this case partly through a set of palpably oversimplified stereotypes) and shows how they produced the outcome we know has occurred.

Similarly, if we feel that Scott has painted a picture of what the Pretender must really have been like, it's improbable that we suppose we've been given the equivalent of a videotape recording of what the Pretender actually did and said on the way to Derby. Instead, our feelings might be verbalized along the following lines: "This is the sort of adroitness the Pretender must have possessed to get his troops as far as he did." Or better: "The scene as a whole shows what the Pretender was up against, and how a certain kind of intelligence would cope with the problem." Or even better: "In composing the scene in this way, Scott reveals the variety of historical determinants and human qualities we would need to take into account if we were to understand a phenomenon like the march to Derby. He shows us, in short, what would be involved in registering the historically real." The ultimate object of realist representation is to involve us in the movements of a mind that would be capable of grasping the reality of human life in history—no doubt a superhuman achievement, if realism ever imagined success in its task possible.

The simply "referential" language Watt characterizes wouldn't serve Scott's purposes. What is real for Scott is not exhausted by concrete physical objects, much as he prized (and collected) them. He cares much less about the gun in the scene than about who falls under its sights and why it was fired. He's interested in objectives, not just objects. What Scott finds most real are the connections between things, and these connections cannot be presented simply by "direct reference" to individual objects as such. Though embodied in practices, the connections are invisible.

It is worth adding that, just as the gun isn't seen as "transparent," so it is not presented as "natural" (that is, marked by a pregiven and preaccepted significance). *As* an object, it has no significance whatever, natural or otherwise. It acquires significance in the uses that can be made of it in a given social context. This becomes particularly clear in historical fiction like Scott's: hence the importance of writing him back into a central place in the history and theory of realism. Waverley couldn't have made the same use of the gun as Calum Beg did, or even as MacIvor did. (In case we miss the latter point, Scott has Waverley ask MacIvor why he hit Calum Beg so hard. The answer: if he didn't hit hard, his men would forget themselves.) It's very unlikely that Waverley would have performed the same physical action with the gun; even if he had, it would have borne a radically different significance, because of his cultural differences from the Highlanders.

I hope I have said enough to cast doubt on the notion that the realist novelist uses a "more largely referential" language, the "exclusive aim" of which is, as Watt would have it, to "make the words bring his object home to us in all its concrete particularity" (29). Yet the reader may feel that I have explained too much. For surely the world of a realist novel does have an immediacy that shifts attention from the workings of language as such. Such an objection has enough merit to deserve further exploration. Two kinds of issues seem important here: the possibility that the objects in realism will seem not just concrete and particular, but *in the aggregate* "natural" and inevitable, and the question of whether realism does indeed tend toward effacing the presence and workings of language as such (whereas poetry foregrounds language).

Realism seeks to create an imagined world that functions using the same referential materials and acting according to the same laws as our own.[8] Historicist realism is also fascinated by the complex systematicity of social milieus. These considerations themselves suggest that, though one does find a fascination with individual objects as such in Defoe (as Watt clearly demonstrates), such a fascination is unlikely to characterize realist fiction as a whole. What realism likes to make vivid are systems in which objects play a part. Of course, realism might still imagine those systems, so to speak, behind the backs of its readers, in a way calculated to make them seem "natural" and inevitable to us, thereby removing them from the category of things we feel called upon to conceptualize and contest. This would be possible. But is it true? As often with realism, the crucial question is how we define the typical instance of our object of inquiry. What kinds of realist novels are we discussing? If we define the typical as the average or mediocre, gesturing mentally toward a mass of popular fiction depicting everyday life, it might be possible to make a case for the notion that realism "inherently" naturalizes, though distinguished work on popular fiction strongly suggests that consumers of such fiction are in fact acutely aware of its fantasy elements—and, for that matter, of its general constructedness.[9] If, however, we follow Lukács in taking the typical to be that which most fully represents the tendency or potentiality of an entity, then our view will be different. In the major British realist novelists—in Eliot or Gaskell, for instance—we indeed recall scenes in which a given milieu is depicted as natural and unmediated, but it is so for those who inhabit it, not for us. For us, the Poysers' farm in *Adam Bede* is framed: it is an object of nostalgia, and the affect of nostalgia marks a gap.

What of the notion that realism habitually turns its attention away

---

[8]   For interesting uses of "possible worlds" philosophy to describe the orientation toward reality of realism and other genres, see Thomas G. Pavel, *Fictional Worlds* (Cambridge: Harvard University Press, 1986), 43–72, and Marie-Laure Ryan, *Possible Worlds, Artificial Intelligence, and Narrative Theory* (Bloomington: Indiana University Press, 1991).

[9]   The seminal study is Janice A. Radway, *Reading the Romance* (Chapel Hill : University of North Carolina Press, 1984).

from the medium of language as such? Here, it all depends on what we mean by "language." It would be idle to quarrel with Watt's contention that the language of realist fiction eschews the intense self-referentiality we find in euphuism, to use Watt's own example. But if we shift our attention to the issue of artistic mediation, the general activity that makes itself specifically felt on the level of individual words in euphuism, our conclusions will alter. (This is only one area in which coming to grips with realism means moving beyond the individual word, to larger structures of meaning.) For, as Wayne Booth has taught us, the larger narrative apparatus is something that doesn't disappear even in fiction written under the aegis of Percy Lubbock. It rarely makes even an attempt to do so in the great realist novels of the nineteenth century.

This is not to say that realist novels, even those with the most intrusive of narrators, do not generate from time to time intense moments that seem immediate and that may blend into our perceptions of everyday life. These are moments when our awareness of the linguistic medium that creates them does indeed slip away. But the creation of a certain *illusionism* (which is the common achievement of a very wide range of literary forms) and its rhetorical manipulation need to be distinguished from an attempt to create a language which, because of its supposedly "referential" nature, attempts to put us into a "direct" contact with reality. The aims of illusionism in realist fiction are many, not the single aim of escaping or seeming to escape mediation. Often, what is at issue is an attempt to make us focus on what it would be like for a human being to be in a certain situation: what is imitated in moments of seemingly transparent representation can be a certain concentration of attention that accompanies tension and excitement. Such moments do indeed seek to keep certain kinds of self-referentiality at bay, at least for the moment. You can't think of everything at once—or perhaps better, you can't *feel* everything at once—and there are times when an author wishes to make rather strenuous demands on a limited range of attention and emotion.

Thackeray is a master of this: at certain high points in his narratives, such as the moment in *Vanity Fair* when Rawdon Crawley discovers Lord Steyne with Becky, the sentences grow tense and short, and we receive what appears to be a simple and direct report of events occurring before us:

> But Rawdon Crawley springing out, seized him by the neckcloth, until Steyne, almost strangled, writhed, and bent under his arm. "You lie, you dog!" said Rawdon. "You lie, you coward and villain!" And he struck the Peer twice over the face with his open

hand, and flung him bleeding to the ground. It was all done before Rebecca could interpose. She stood there trembling before him. She admired her husband, strong, brave, and victorious.

"Come here," he said.—She came up at once.

"Take off those things."—She began, trembling, pulling the jewels from her arms, and the rings from her shaking fingers, and held them all in a heap, quivering and looking up at him. "Throw them down," he said, and she dropped them. He tore the diamond ornament out of her breast, and flung it at Lord Steyne. It cut him on his bald forehead. Steyne wore the scar to his dying day.[10]

Such moments include the depiction of telling objects, presented with an overwhelming immediacy. We see the jewelry lying there, scattered on the floor. We see Steyne's scar. But such moments are also deeply rhetorical, and on some level we perceive them as such, if only because their very "immediacy" stands in contrast to the normal narrative texture. We make them immediate, and we know it. Indeed, at the deepest level, the power of the tense, dramatic spareness of Thackeray's style here stems from its vivid consummation of our desire for fully self-contained, self-explanatory scenes that would give life a simple meaning and deal justice where it is due, for a mastery of life figured in Rawdon's perfect mastery of the situation and of Becky. We long for an *ethical* transparency. It is, however, part of the nature of realist narrative that such effects never last very long. In *Vanity Fair*, the seemingly immediate and self-evident meaning of the scene between Rawdon and Becky blurs as soon as it ends, as the narrator begins to ask, "Was she guilty?" And the notion of Rawdon's mastering Becky is absurd, as a moment's reflection reveals. When we realize that it's also distasteful, we have entered into the critique of the desire for transparency and finality in which this instance of "transparent realism" has momentarily involved us.

Often, a sense of immediacy is something realism urges us to acquire. George Eliot demands that we look carefully at the everyday and the commonplace. Dickens, with characteristic excess, urges us to take the rooftops off the buildings and peer inside, and in *Bleak House* cranks himself up to rub our noses in the commonplace death of Jo. A truly transparent reality would require no such efforts, on our part or on the part of the narrator. What is being insisted on instead is that certain aspects of external reality matter, or can be made to matter as part of a larger web of relations, if only we'll pierce beyond the veil of the familiar—not that

---

[10]   Thackeray, *Vanity Fair*, ed. J. I. M. Stewart (Harmondsworth: Penguin, 1968), 620–21.

they are self-evidently and unproblematically present for our inspection. Eliot knows the necessary limitations of even the most penetrating human vision. We must be well wadded in stupidity to escape being overwhelmed by the realities that confront us; we must nonetheless respond to the irony in her description of our condition with an attempt to overcome our inevitable blindness. Such pronouncements raise the issue of what we might call the "narrator's privilege." It's frequently suggested that however it may be for the characters in a novel, reality is indeed made to seem transparent for the narrator. The fully rhetorical nature of realist invocations of reality tells against such a view.[11] When Eliot tells us that *we* are all well wadded in stupidity, she means it; the language of her novels betrays time and again the narrator's own subjection to desire and the myopia that attends it.[12]

I shall have more to say about realist narrators in the second part of this book. The claims of realism grow complicated indeed in the matter of the narrator's privilege. There is a sense in which authorial omniscience acts as a teleological, regulative principle, miming the wholeness of vision we need to strive for if we are to make any sense of the world at all, but can in fact never entirely achieve in our own world. Teleology has a bad name these days, especially in circles that distrust totality. The teleology in question here, however, which takes the point of view of finite beings in a historical world, involves process, not achieving static closure at the end of the line. Regulative principles set in motion an open-ended process, the nature of which they help to define; they do not provide definitive blueprints that predict in advance everything that will be discovered along the way. The narrator's privilege is most likely to look like a closed, coercive blueprint, I suspect, from a vantage point that does not

[11]   In the process of differentiating his own kind of rhetorical reading from Wayne Booth's, James Phelan, in *Narrative as Rhetoric* (Columbus: Ohio State University Press, 1996), 19, outlines an approach to narrative texts that, mutatis mutandis, can help with the problem of the "narrator's privilege": "The approach I am advocating shifts emphasis from author as controller to the recursive relationships among authorial agency, textual phenomena, and reader response, to the way in which our attention to each of these elements both influences and can be influenced by the other two."

[12]   In *The Subject of Modernism* (Ann Arbor: University of Michigan Press, 1994), Tony E. Jackson suggests that the coexistence of narrative desire with the pretensions of the realist narrator to produce "unproblematic right reading acts" (46) creates a simple contradiction unnoticed by classical realism, at least until *Daniel Deronda*. Jackson's study, admirable in pursuit of its modernist concerns, provides a recent example of the persistence of the assumptions about realism we've been considering, sounding the notes of realist naiveté, transparency, and totalization (though these terms themselves aren't central to his discussion). The realist narrator is said to be coercive, and in realism, plot determines meaning. Realism here functions primarily as a negative, defining other on behalf of modernism: we're told that George Eliot "never seems aware that her own claims about realism imply the need for a new form of fiction" (47).

allow for the emergence of knowledge through a dialectical interplay between language and the world, subject and object.

Realism, Reference, and the Sign

Two major attacks on realism flow from the conception of realist language Watt defined in *The Rise of the Novel*. These attacks did not develop solely or even primarily in response to Watt. Tracing the continuities between Watt and later critics of realism doesn't involve discovering a direct line of descent or influence. Some critics mention him; many do not. Many of the views in question are imports with their own genealogy. Yet even for these, Watt's work provides a useful context. Careful attention to Watt's view of realism may help to answer the question of why Anglo-American criticism accepted these critiques of realism so readily. Watt's position, I shall argue, drew upon and solidified a set of literary and philosophical beliefs that were relatively easy to turn against the realist project.

Watt's characterization of realist language as pursuing pure referentiality sets the stage, first, for a direct attack on realism, in which realism becomes the genre that seeks to give us the illusion that we're in simple and unproblematic contact with a nondiscursive "real world," in an attempt to obscure the role our linguistic practices play in creating the objects we perceive. For those who invoke a well-known version of Saussurean linguistics Vincent Descombes has called the "semiological hypothesis," that role is total.[13] Realism thereby becomes totally suspect in its alleged attempt to move directly from signifier to referent, ignoring the workings of the signified. As Roland Barthes puts it in a celebrated moment from his seminal essay "L'effet de réel," realism depends upon "the *direct* collusion between a referent and a signifier: the signified is ejected from the sign."[14]

Those who subscribe to the semiological hypothesis know that any at-

[13] Vincent Descombes, "The Quandaries of the Referent," in *The Limits of Theory*, ed. Thomas M. Kavanagh (Stanford: Stanford University Press, 1989), 51–75; hereafter cited in my text.

[14] Roland Barthes, "L'effet de réel," *Communications* 11 (1968), 88, my translation. For Barthes, the essence of the "reality effect" comes from "unnecessary details," details that cannot be fitted into any pattern of significance and therefore must exist in the text simply to cry to us "We are real!" Barthes suggests that in fact "realism" as he defines it can exist only in the detail, never in narration, for narration must introduce rhetorical elements that could hardly be accounted for on the model of the "unnecessary detail" (88). The question then arises of what is gained, and what lost, by identifying realism's essence with one aspect of its means of representation, and in the process ignoring the use to which that aspect is put—especially since those who refer to Barthes's notion of the "unnecessary de-

tempt to employ a "more largely referential" language will be doomed from the start. There are no real degrees of pure referentiality, only seeming degrees. According to the hypothesis, the connection between the language in a novel and the world that reference promises to supply is illusory; we actually connect one ideological construct with another. A compact illustration of this view is provided by Catherine Belsey's discussion of how Saussure's insights imply the bankruptcy of the immediate reference supposedly assumed by realism and its simple reflection theory :

> The claim that a literary form reflects the world is simply tautological. If by "the world" we understand the world we experience, the world differentiated by language, then the claim that realism reflects the world means that realism reflects the world constructed in language. This is a tautology. If discourses articulate concepts through a system of signs which signify by means of their relationship to each other rather than to entities in the world, and if literature is a signifying practice, all it can reflect is the order inscribed in particular discourses, not the nature of the world.[15]

Belsey's statement bears out Thomas Pavel's summary of what a semiotic approach concludes about the possibility of moving from literature to the world: "Seen as governed by semiotic conventions, literary texts do not describe real or fictional worlds, but merely manipulate an amorphous purport on which they impose their arbitrary rule. Mythic and realist discourse are equally conventional and unmotivated; Balzac's novels do not resemble reality any more than do chivalry novels; they just make use of a different semiotics, as conventional and artificial as any."[16] In her general discussion, Belsey takes pains to emphasize that language can create new and more adequate meanings, and that speakers of a language can gain an awareness of its ideological freighting. Yet how this can occur remains unclear.

Pavel suggests that the semiotic hypothesis arose from Saussure's novel combination of two ideas: the idea that linguistic signs are unmotivated (they have no necessary connection with that which they signify), and the idea that, as romantic theorists of language and culture held, language expresses the worldview of the community that uses it. Those who

---

tail" rarely add his proviso that the sort of realism to which it supposedly gives rise cannot inform a larger narrative.

[15]   Catherine Belsey, *Critical Practice* (London: Methuen, 1980), 46.

[16]   The quotations from Pavel, *Fictional Worlds*, in this paragraph and the next are drawn from 114–16.

rely on Saussure tend to emphasis the unmotivated nature of the sign, but the idea that language is culturally expressive is at least as important. Once we accept an extreme romantic expressivism, supposing that language reflects in a pure, seamless, and untranscendable fashion the ideology of the culture that produces it (or, in a variant reading, that it produces), the other claims of the semiotic hypothesis become impossible to resist. We are then bound to accept, as Pavel puts it, "an implicit notion of semiotic convention that includes the traits of arbitrariness, obligatoriness, and unconscious character." Arbitrariness is, as we've seen, perhaps the most stressed aspect of the Saussurean linguistic theory: the systems of difference which constitute both the signified and signifier are said to be arbitrary both in the way they divide up the phonetic and conceptual continuum, and also in their application to the external world. As I read Pavel, the traits of obligatoriness and unconsciousness involve the way we are implicated in this arbitrary structure, which is obligatory and unconscious in the sense that we simply cannot "mean" in any other way: the semiotic hypothesis specifies globally (obligatoriness) and inescapably (unconsciousness) our relationship both to words and to the world. It seems useful to specify a further trait that sometimes informs the semiotic vision, a belief that semiotic systems are self-adjusting totalities. It's often said that "at least in principle" a change in any part of a diacritical system implies a change in all the others, and this belief is often attached to ideological frameworks viewed as wholes.

Despite its extraordinary influence on our intellectual life since the rediscovery of Saussure in the middle of this century, the semiotic hypothesis is open to fundamental criticism on several counts.[17] Pavel's identification of the role that an extreme romantic expressivism plays in it suggests a remarkable irony in the use of the semiotic hypothesis as a stick with which to beat realism. An acceptance of romantic cultural expressivism paves the way for a view of language that undermines the claims of realist representation, in particular by suggesting the notion that our place in our untranscendable cultures is "unconscious." But a central precondition for nineteenth-century realism was the rise of . . . romantic cultural expressivism. As we'll discover in discussing the works of Scott and Eliot, realist novels provide excellent fields for considering the problem of whether we can transcend the limits of our own cultures, and indeed, they meditate on these problems themselves. Can we really believe that realism could provide, at one and the same time, both the

---

[17]   See, for instance, Robert Scholes, *Textual Power* (New Haven: Yale University Press, 1985), 86–110. It has become standard to suggest that the semiotic hypothesis has no way of explaining how its own insights could be known to be true.

prime example of an inability to transcend one's own culture because we cannot think beyond it, and the literary form in which this concern was for the first time painstakingly represented and explored?

Other objections to the semiotic hypothesis arise. To begin with, its use of Saussure has begun to seem increasingly un-Saussurean. There's no reason, for instance, to assume that any realist theory of language must deny the existence of linguistic "arbitrariness" we associate with the work of Saussure. Indeed, there are the best possible grounds for believing that if language didn't possess an element of arbitrariness, it would be useless for the realist enterprise, or any other.[18] Because realism is centrally interested in social relations and the ways societies move through time, it couldn't possibly make do with a language that limited itself to the task of sticking labels on things, working on the model, one supposes, of onomatopoeia. The same goes for an influential idea that amounts to the suggestion that realist narrative is a form of labeling with a temporal dimension—the notion that realist narratives are "providential narratives," narratives pointed toward and controlled by a foreordained end. The idea that realism is dominated by "providential history" is to the idea that realism naively pastes words to things in a "direct" manner, as running movies are to still frames: instead of naively pasting labels on the things lying around us, we now naively roll down providential tracks, pasting labels on the parts of the landscape which the positioning of the train's windows and tracks allows us to see as we travel toward the end of the line.[19]

One aspect of the semiotic hypothesis that makes the hedge of the signifieds seem impenetrable is the notion that *all* the signifieds interact in a systematic and self-regulating fashion—the belief that they constitute what I've called a self-adjusting totality. But is this really what Saussure claimed, and is it plausible? A global claim from someone as interested in phonetic differences as Saussure would be surprising. In the realm of phonetics—which, after all, provides the model for the notion of a system constituted purely by differences—we have spectacularly clear evidence that diacritical relationships are *not* universal, but obtain only between members of subsets. When the Great Vowel Shift took place, *it did not affect the consonants*. That systems as large as language itself, or as the total-

---

[18]   See Linda R. Waugh, "Against Arbitrariness: Imitation and Motivation Revised, with Consequences for Textual Meaning," *diacritics*, 23 (Summer 1993), 71–87. Waugh argues that it is necessary for any linguistic system to combine elements of arbitrariness with elements of "iconicity" (that is, linguistic imitation and motivation). A large diacritical system without *any* elements of imitation and motivation would be impossibly clumsy to operate, and probably unlearnable.

[19]   The relationship between realism and "providential history" is explored in the following chapter.

ity of the signifieds, could be systematically linked and self-adjusting seems overwhelmingly unlikely.[20] That such a claim should have been seriously maintained and uncritically accepted suggests that a strong interest must be served by erecting a system that denies in advance all reliable forms of access to the world.

A more likely claim would be that, within *related* subsets of phonemes or of signifieds, systematic and self-adjusting diacritical relationships obtain. A claim on this order would, however, begin to suggest breaks in the hedge of the signifieds. We do not see them regrouping themselves in a unified fashion whenever a new member joins their ranks—an image that suggests that the new concept/signified is overpowered and co-opted by the system it joins (and for that matter that it joins the system in a seamless fashion). It might also undercut perhaps the most insidious force of the semiotic hypothesis: the feeling that its global, uni-dimensional account of reference to the world must be countered by another global account. The image of a globally self-adjusting system of language generates the counterimage of a homogenous set of users of language. Belsey tells us that the only world available to us is "the world we experience, the world differentiated by language." But just who is the "we" we're talking about here? Is my experience of "the world" allowed to include the experience of reading texts by people from other ages, genders, races, and of different ideological persuasions? Does the "I" who experiences persist over time? Does it grow up and grow old? If so, are all its various experiences identically mediated through the diacritical apparatus? When we begin to consider such questions, it becomes increasingly clear that the "we" being posited here must really be a Cartesian "I." But if we go beyond this "I," if we imagine ourselves as employing linguistic and conceptual systems that are in fact partial, local, evolving, and potentially contradictory, both internally and with respect to one another, the emergence of new knowledge and the modification and mutual illumination of different subsets of our linguistic competence would be anything but surprising.[21] The semiotic hypothesis seems most plausible if we grant two things: first, that the best model for how we might come in contact with the world is the model of a single observer and his impressions; sec-

[20]   Compare Jonathan Culler, *Structuralist Poetics* (Ithaca: Cornell University Press, 1975), 13–14: "When structuralists like Lévi-Strauss, attracted by the rigour of Saussure's principle, propose as an elementary methodological requirement that a structural analysis reveal a system of 'elements such that modification of any one entails modification of all the others,' they are setting their sights on a goal seldom achieved in linguistics itself."

[21]   My argument here converges, to be sure in an informal mode, with arguments for the existence and potentially salutary effects of multiple "subject-positions" for the individual. For an early statement, see Ernesto Laclau and Chantal Mouffe, *Hegemony and Socialist Strategy*, trans. Winston Moore and Paul Cammack (London: Verso, 1985). Explorations of multiple subject-positions are now legion.

ond, that diacritical systems are in principle globally self-adjusting, obligatory, and unconscious. Why should we grant either of these premises?

One of the prime attractions of the semiotic hypothesis is that it alerts
us to the workings of ideology in language.[22] Presumably it does this for a
purpose; presumably we are more likely to learn something about ideology if we come to realize that its operations are subtle and pervasive. But
how is it that our language can refer to ideology, which constitutes such a
large component of what we might call the "social referent," but not to
the referent itself? At this point, the referent begins to look like Kant's
realm of the "noumenal," a realm that functions chiefly, as Mark Sacks
has suggested, not to describe what we can't know, but to delineate and
guarantee what we can know: "in effect what [Kant] does is to protect
empirical knowledge by pushing the philosophical problems beyond our
philosophical boundaries—confining them to transcendent reality, and
our knowledge, on the other hand, to empirical reality."[23] The semiotic
hypothesis can serve the same function: it precludes knowledge of the
referent, but in return it places us in epistemological control of the workings of ideology in language.

At this point, I realize that in trying to follow up the implications of the
semiotic hypothesis, I have followed its lead by misrepresenting the significance and power of reference itself. In discussions like Belsey's (or
mine up to this point), the status of reference is radically inflated: it's
made to seem that all kinds of important issues have been settled *in advance* if we decide that reliable reference is or is not possible. In fact, reference refers, and then the interesting work begins. Reference is always
associated with other linguistic means in its dealings with the world; it
acts as one component of many packages. As Vincent Descombes puts it,
to arrive at a single answer to the question of whether books refer to
themselves or to the world would be "quite surprising." He adjures us to
think of such questions with respect to the capacities of grammar as a
whole, and not simply of the noun-object relationship.[24] By the same
token, the notion that there could be a "referential language," or even that

---

[22]   To be sure, the attempt to make us attend to ideology by attacking a naive and transparent realism was not invented by semiological criticism. As part of his effort to remind
us that "manners and morals" (in current parlance, "ideological practices") are central to
the novel, Lionel Trilling, in an essay first published in 1940, attacked V. L. Parrington for
failing to realize "there is any other relation possible between the artist and reality than
this passage of reality through the transparent artist" (*The Liberal Imagination* [New York:
Viking, 1950], 5).

[23]   Mark Sacks, *The World We Found* (London: Duckworth, 1989), 27.

[24]   "Does language turn outward toward something else, or inward toward itself? Does a
book refer to the world, or only to *a* world constructed in the book? To find any single answer to these questions would be quite surprising" (Descombes, "The Quandaries of the
Referent," 51).

language could approach a state of more or less pure referentiality, is misleading. When we refer to something, the important work remains to be done. Reference is the beginning, not the end, of a process that may or may not eventuate in knowledge of the various worlds in which we live.[25] When Bertrand Russell wrote his classic article on reference, he made the stakes of referring appear to be very large—as indeed they were for him, given his priorities. He wanted to preclude uncertainty about the truth claims of propositions; he didn't want his calculus complicated or vitiated by admitting that what appeared to be veridical statements could have for their subject matter nonexistent objects. And he was certainly right to suppose that statements about the attributes of "the present King of France" (in the twentieth century) would seem to elude the watertight distinctions he wished to create, in which all propositions could be definitely said to be either true or false, period. But the usefulness of such a logical calculus to the work of the literary or cultural critic would appear to be rather limited.[26] Especially if our aim is to account for the claims and workings of realism, we will escape a good deal of confusion and stultification if we conceive of reference as open-ended and more than that, potentially *productive*.

An account of reference as productive quickly finds itself enmeshed in linguistic, ideological, social, and historical complexities. It does not seek to render such matters "transparent"; in fact, because it doesn't settle questions in advance, it may provide an excellent way of focusing on them. A passage from Scott, in which a schoolmaster named Jedediah Cleishbotham defends the memory of the landlord of his village inn, provides an example. Various dignitaries have accused the landlord mentioned in the passage of having served illicit food and drink:

> His honour, the Laird, accused our Landlord, deceased, of having encouraged, in various times and places, the destruction of hares, rabbits, fowls black and grey, partridges, moor-pouts, roe-deer, and other birds and quadrupeds, at unlawful seasons, and contrary to the laws of this realm, which have secured, in their wisdom, the slaughter of such animals for the great of the earth, whom I have remarked to take an uncommon (though to me, an unintelligible)

[25] For Lydgate, an imperfect act of reference opens up a new vision of the world when he looks into an old book: "The page he opened on was under the heading of Anatomy, and the first passage that drew his eyes was on the valves of the heart. He was not much acquainted with valves of any sort, but he knew that *valvae* were folding doors, and through this crevice came a sudden light startling him with his first vivid notion of finely adjusted mechanism in the human frame" (*Middlemarch*, ed. Rosemary Ashton [Harmondsworth: Penguin, 1994], 144).
[26] For a useful commentary on views of reference, beginning with Russell, see Pavel, *Fictional Worlds*, 11–42.

pleasure therein. Now, in humble deference to his honour, and in justifiable defence of my friend deceased, I reply to this charge, that howsoever the form of such animals might appear to be similar to those so protected by the law, yet it was a mere *deceptio visus*; for what resembled hares were, in fact, *hill-kids*, and those partaking of the appearance of moor-fowl, were truly *wood-pigeons*, and consumed and eaten *eo nomine*, and not otherwise.

Again, the Exciseman pretended, that my deceased Landlord did encourage that species of manufacture called distillation, without having an especial permission from the Great, technically called a license, for doing so. Now, I stand up to confront this falsehood; and in defiance of him, his gauging-stick, and pen and inkhorn, I tell him, that I never saw, or tasted, a glass of unlawful aqua vitae in the house of my Landlord; nay, that, on the contrary, we needed not such devices, in respect of a pleasing and somewhat seductive liquor, which was vended and consumed at the Wallace Inn, under the name of *mountain dew*. If there is a penalty against manufacturing such a liquor, let him show me the statute; and when he does, I'll tell him if I will obey it or no.[27]

What's in a name? The laird is incensed at the landlord's evident collusion in poaching, the obvious source of what he and the statute book refer to as "hares." Jedediah defends his old friend by refusing the laird's act of naming. He suggests that, because the animals were in fact not "hares" but "hill-kids," no poaching took place, since the law does not concern itself with "hill-kids." (Students of reference will recognize here a novelistic analogue to Frege's example of the morning and evening stars.) The passage occurs in one of Scott's many fictionalized Introductions, which commonly serve the purpose of preparing us for the mode of the fiction that follows them. Does this passage prepare us to experience a world in which reference is transparent and natural? Hardly. We might wish to refer to it as a critique of transparency: the laird claims to make a direct, transparent, "natural" reference to the world, and Jedediah catches him up on this. What seems most live in the passage, though, isn't the nature or propriety of the references it contains, but what those references allow their speakers to accomplish. Jedediah's quibble seeks to remove his old friend from being answerable to the legal force of the laird's accusation, but its force for us as readers exceeds this aim as surely as it would fall short of it in a court of law presided over by the laird. By referring to the

---

[27] Jedediah is here providing an Introduction to "Tales of My Landlord," which in its first installment included *The Black Dwarf* and *Old Mortality*; I quote from Scott, *Old Mortality*, ed. Angus Calder (Harmondsworth: Penguin, 1975), 53–54; hereafter cited in the text.

animals the laird has accused Jedediah's crony of killing as "hill-kids," Jedediah seeks to activate a set of associations that will defeat the underlying tenor of the laird's accusation—that the innkeeper and his guests are disreputable. The laird's real quarry isn't hill-kids, it's the life of a class of men who frequent the landlord's inn. Jedediah uses vernacular terms to revivify the communal bonds that strengthen themselves round the landlord's fire, fed by hill-kids and mountain dew. This is the setting that makes intelligible the *real* landlord, whatever men of the laird's class may think about him. Jedediah's way of referring to the food, drink, and company he has enjoyed is a rhetorical attempt to *do* something.

There is, then, little that's "transparent" to us as readers about either the laird's reference or Jedediah's. Both use language to refer to things in the world in a way that activates contexts to create meaning and rhetorical effect. Jedediah's use of folk language, combined with his schoolmaster's Latin (which parodies the Latin of the law courts), contests and demystifies the laird's nominations, evading the concrete, punitive realities associated with the abstract, "universal" legal system that refers to "hares," and defending the honor of his tavern associates while pretending that the only issue at hand is a confusion about names. In the same breath, Jedediah hints that the "universal" legal system in fact serves the quite specific interests of his "betters": *he* can't make heads or tails of their addiction to the chase. It is moments like this for which nineteenth-century realist fiction, thick with cultural particularity and uniquely hospitable to the vernacular, was born. This is why this vignette deserves its place in the material that prepares us to experience the series of novels it prefaces. Jedediah's parting shot in the Introduction—"So, gentle reader, I bid you farewell, recommending you to such fare as the mountains of your own country produce" (56)—offers an incitement to an ever-broader enjoyment of cultural specificity and subversive reference-making.

Reference always occurs as part of a larger rhetorical situation, in which readers are implicated with a complexity that talk of abstract referential relationships can hardly begin to capture. We forget this at our peril. Flaubert's Emma Bovary has been seen as a reader who puts to use the naively realistic viewpoint that the realist novel itself is so often supposed to embody:

> Don Quijote and Emma Bovary are literary examples of what happens when the referent of fiction is presumed to be real and operative. Emma is the most serious of realists, for she truly believes that art, even the romantic literature she reads, is a vehicle for experiences which really exist or can be made to exist in her own world. Her belief raises the question of how both ordinary and literary lan-

guage can ever correspond to the precise nature of non-verbal realities.[28]

Is this really Emma Bovary's malady? Can we rise above her simple mistake simply by eschewing "naive realism"? Whatever may be the case with Don Quixote, I doubt her predicament stems from an epistemological delusion. There is, after all, a difference between believing that something exists and believing that something *must* exist. Reading helps to awaken certain desires in her, and thereby to make her unbearably aware of the insufficiency for their fulfillment of the world in which she lives. The question is not one of naive or stupid realism, but of passionate, egotistical desire, desire so strong that it must bend the world to fit its needs. Emma Bovary finds herself in one variant of the realist situation, faced with a reality that is both more powerful than she, and also radically unpalatable. One problem with an analysis that finds in her a naive realism is that it remains at a purely formal level. For such an analysis, Emma's "mistake" occurs at the level of large categories: she's a bad or naive reader. But in fact, there's nothing wrong with using literature to make oneself more aware of the potentialities of life and to bring into focus one's inchoate emotions. The problem is not that Emma betrays literature by being stupid about its ontology, the problem is that a certain kind of literature betrays Emma by giving her only an impoverished language by which to understand her own desires—a language which does nothing to help her enter into a dialogue with the possibilities of her environment or her self. Emma's gesture is not to be despised, for it is a version of one of the most important possibilities literature opens to us, the possibility of a utopian revolt against the insufficiencies of the present. What can be ultimately thin and depressing about Flaubert's world is, however, that it withholds from the novel's characters access to a language in which a utopian revolt might gain vibrancy and substantiality. In Flaubert's world, access to linguistic possibilities that would transcend the banality of the world Emma finds herself in is entirely reserved for the author and reader, in a way that recalls the unexplained semiotic privilege of offering a true analysis of how it is impossible to offer a true analysis. Yet Flaubert remains in the realist camp. If we pass beyond the circuit of the characters and their world to include the reader in our analysis, Flaubert's pitiless exposure of the insufficiency both of Emma Bovary's world and of her revolt against it might raise in us as readers a desire to do better, fueled by the discomfort and fear the spectacle of her fate evokes. We might at-

---

[28]   Linda Hutcheon, "Metafictional Implications for Novelistic Reference," in *On Referring in Literature*, ed. Anna Whiteside and Michael Issacharoff (Bloomington: Indiana University Press, 1987), 4.

tempt to channel the intelligence of the authorial voice in more fruitful directions, though what those directions might be remains unclear. At any rate, we should be wary of dealing with the frustrations raised by Flaubert's mode of representation by making Emma Bovary a scapegoat, from whose mistake about referentiality we can distance ourselves. If Emma Bovary has a lesson to teach us about reference, it is that assumptions about simple, transparent reference play no great role in our dealings with reality, whether in life or through fiction.

Reference and Self-Reference

When Watt suggested that realism is based on a "more purely referential" use of language, and employs "self-referential" language as the defining opposite of that use of language, he set the stage not only for the denial of the possibility of reference, but for a range of more complex critiques that would see realism not so much as mystified or misleading, but as banal. If realism employs language in a more purely referential way than do other genres, then those who are interested in the workings of a densely self-referential literary language, or an inherently self-deconstructing language, may well find realism thin. Watt himself appears sympathetic to this feeling. At the end of *The Rise of the Novel*, he fleshes out his earlier hints about a self-referential language that stands over and against the more purely referential language of formal realism, adding the category of "realism of assessment" to his characterization of the realist novel.[29] Realism of assessment is a very broad category: it involves the whole realm of traditional value and human wisdom with which novels deal, and from it arises the wisdom we identify with the narrative voice in Fielding or in Austen. Its ties with traditional values and its function as a "counterpoise" to formal realism make it a distinctly literary phenomenon. Formal realism involves "a narrative surface that is more or less identical with its meaning," whereas realism of assessment tends to create an "obtrusive [narrative] patterning" that has "an autonomous aesthetic appeal."[30]

---

[29] In "Serious Reflections," Watt reveals that realism of assessment was more prominent in the thirteen-chapter book he originally planned: "the emphasis on 'realism of presentation' in chapters 2–8 was counterpoised by that on 'realism of assessment' in the last five chapters" (92).

[30] Watt, "Serious Reflections," 100. This view filiates with the notion that, say, Eliot (at least in her early works) wishes simply to transcribe reality, but keeps running into a contradiction created by her simultaneous wish to make ethical judgments, which necessitates an antirealist authorial patterning of her fiction. The view I am offering of realism takes this to be a false dichotomy. It has to be sure had its virtues, facilitating explorations of Eliot's values and her artistry, in such hands as Ulrich C. Knoepflmacher, *George Eliot's*

Watt's description of formal realism suggests that realism interests it-self in putting us in contact with a world external to itself. But the cate-gory of formal realism impoverishes the mode of that contact to such an extent that it becomes hard for anyone, including Watt himself, to take it as in itself the basis for a serious literary project. If we care about the full powers of a distinctively literary language, why should we settle for a genre that, in its characteristic linguistic bias, relegates them to the status of a "counterpoise"?

In this vein, one critic suggests that although in reading metafictions, "we move beyond the purely mimetic in reading, we never manage to eradicate it completely." What matters about literature, it appears, is pre-cisely the power of its language to move beyond the "merely" mimetic: "the essence of literary language lies not in its conforming to the kind of statement found in factual studies, but in its ability to create something new, a coherent, motivated 'heterocosm.' " Because literature operates at a series of removes from the real world and from normal referentiality, it can effect something valuable, "the liberation of the reader from the world he knows only through the senses." Reference to the world be-comes an unavoidable precondition not for discovering meaning in the world, but for passing on to more interesting matters, which have to do not with the world but with a play of language and imagination.[31]

It is possible to insist that reference is more important and complex than this, while still maintaining an ultimate allegiance to the workings of language as such. In one of the more stimulating recent treatments of lit-erary reference, for instance, Ora Avni asks us to recognize simultaneous movements in language toward reference to the world and toward self-reference. Insisting on this dual aspect of language, Avni echoes a recog-nizable poststructuralist paradigm; but she employs the paradigm with a difference. For Avni, recognizing the dual nature of language should lead to a redefinition of the role of theory in literary studies, away from the hegemony it has tended to assume in structuralist and poststructuralist criticism. It may be a sign both of the past successes of structuralist and poststructuralist theory and of the more recent turn to historicist thinking that, in Avni's work, there's a significant shift in what she assumes we will take for granted about reference, and what we need to be urged to add to our normal model. Much previous theorizing had tended to sup-pose that we naively assume that language exhausts its capacities by

Early Novels: The Limits of Realism (Berkeley: University of California Press, 1968) and John P. McGowan, *Representation and Revelation: Victorian Realism from Carlyle to Yeats* (Colum-bia: University of Missouri Press, 1986), 132–57.

[31]   Hutcheon, "Metafictional Implications for Novelistic Reference," 6–9.

sticking labels on objects in the world; it insisted that we complicate this naive view by adding to it a recognition of language's materiality and self-reference. Avni, by contrast, supposes that we'll assume that language is a self-enclosed system: she seeks to complicate our view by reminding us that language also gestures toward the world. Thus she makes a convincing case that recent readers of Saussure have falsified his thought by depicting the linguistic sign as being too neatly and completely severed from "the referent." For Avni, Saussure is an interesting figure just because his system requires both that the sign be self-enclosed, yet that it also be open to the referent—and he recognized and worried about this very problem.[32]

Yet even for such a critic as Avni, who consciously offers a corrective to much poststructuralist thought, it's not quite the case that the implication of language in an external or "real" world gains an importance equal to its self-referential powers. For in the end, Avni joins those poststructuralist thinkers who admit the existence of "reference-plus-something-that-works-to-oppose-it" for the ultimate purpose of focusing on the very hesitation between reference and its opposing force. This hesitation itself is what makes language interesting, and makes literature literary. Even for Avni, reference to the world comes close to serving as a necessary but in itself rather uninteresting precondition that helps to bring into being something more important. The objection one might want to raise against this set of priorities would not be that language as such isn't interesting; nor would it, as we'll see more fully in a moment, involve the false accusation that such an account "denies reference" altogether. We'd object on more pragmatic grounds. The question would become where a given kind of criticism leads us to focus our time and energy, and in doing what. To insist that language always refers is not necessarily to explore what such reference can help us to see in the world.

A pervasive characteristic of philosophical speculation, since the first stirrings of "modernity," has been a movement from considering how things occur to assessing the conditions of possibility for their occurrence, a movement from ontology to epistemology. We ask not what truth is, but how the mind could come to true conclusions; not what happened in history, but how we could reliably know what happened. This movement seems to possess an endless internal momentum. As Descombes has amusingly and tellingly shown, it's always possible to turn one's scrutiny onto the very mechanism that, in a previous moment of self-reflexivity, had promised to take us beyond "simple reflection theories":

---

[32] Ora Avni, *The Resistance of Reference* (Baltimore: Johns Hopkins University Press, 1990), 59; 76–77.

Today, we say *referent* rather than *object*. "Referent" means: an object to which reference is made by means of an expression belonging to language and used in discourse. Implicit in this definition is the assumption that our access to things is mediated through language. It is this language that must be analyzed if we are to determine anything whatsoever about the relation between a person and the world.

Such is the argument we might make to convey the essence of the linguistic turn. Curiously, this argument bears a strong resemblance to that used by the old philosophy—the "philosophy of representation"—against an adversary that was, at the time, called "common sense" or "naïve realism." The "turn," then, was an "idealistic turn in philosophy." Prior to this idealistic turn, naïve realists believed that they apprehended things directly, oblivious to the fact that things are given to us only in the representation we have of them. But the representation we have is that which we *can* have, given the constitution of our capacity to represent.

Language has replaced *representation*, but the "philosophy of representation" is perhaps not faring so badly. (53–54)

We might escape such a constant regress by providing a more complex account of reference, which explains how its partial but crucial contribution joins forces with other linguistic resources to produce knowledge about the world. The student of realism should be wary about accepting an account of language that has the practical effect of making realist representation seem "naive" in comparison to speculations about countervailing forces obtaining within language itself.

Recently, significant efforts have been made to bridge the gap between language and the world (and especially the world's political and historical aspects) by those who seemed to some intent on keeping us within the veil of language and its aporias. Deconstruction has often been accused of imprisoning us in a windowless chamber, cut off from the possibility of political action and social relevance, because it "denies reference." This accusation is and always has been spectacularly misinformed.[33] Deconstruction—and nowhere more so than in the work of Paul de Man—actually posits and depends upon a linguistic movement of reference to the world. To be sure, it simultaneously insists on the existence of opposing forces that complicate this referential moment. In an account of reference

[33]   As have certain political and ethical conclusions drawn from this account. Critical stances have no predictive relationship to political stances (more on this in a moment); to say that the deconstructive account of reference *entails* rightist politics, leftist politics, or any other politics seems to me a simple (and by now tiresome) mistake.

as productive, by contrast, we would concern ourselves with what occurs after referential contact with the world is made, and we would thereby avoid setting self-referential and outwardly referential properties of language against one another.

In defense of those who sense a denial of referentiality in deconstructive accounts of reference, we may add that the net result of their double movement is indeed to limit the power of referentiality in a radical way: anti-poststructuralist critics might truly say that *their* notion of referentiality has been effectively "denied" in the process, in that the meaning of all the relevant terms has undergone a radical change. Recent deconstructive work, however, goes significantly further than engaging in what some might consider a grand hijacking of terms and their meanings.[34] To be sure, in recent deconstructive explorations of reference we hear echoes of concerns and attitudes that I've tried to demonstrate characterize many of the familiar attacks on realism. There remains a strong focus on the dangers of "totalizable meaning" and "totalizing narratives," a positing of the fiction that other approaches naively assume that the individual is unified and that meaning is given in advance, and an indication that other critics believe in the possibility of direct reference to the world. All of this seems redolent of the attacks on realism that construct it as their stupid and naive antitype. Yet simply using naive realism as a bad other isn't at the heart of the deconstructive analyses I have in mind. They emphasize referential problems and uncertainties in order to explore significant ground—ground, I'd like to add, that an account of reference as productive itself approaches in a different way and finds no less significant. The deconstructive interrogation of reference is meant to counter the identification of the real with the immediately intelligible, working against a state of affairs in which, as Cathy Caruth puts it, "anything that is not accessible as a semantic content that can be 'seen' or understood cannot be recognized as real." It wishes to "recognize [reference] where it does not occur *as knowledge*."[35] As we have already seen with respect to Jedediah Cleishbotham's hill-kids, an account of reference as productive

[34]   Some brilliant appropriation of terms has of course occurred. From the point of view of realism, the most damaging has been the turn of the concept "rhetorical" away from acts of persuasion in an intersubjective field.

[35]   My quotations in this paragraph are drawn from Caruth's Introduction to the anthology *Critical Encounters: Reference and Responsibility in Deconstructive Writing*, ed. Cathy Caruth and Deborah Esch (New Brunswick: Rutgers University Press, 1995), 1–8. Caruth provides a brilliant commentary on de Man and reference in the chapter "The Claims of Reference" (92–105). For another stimulating deconstructive treatment of reference, see Werner Hamacher, "LECTIO: de Man's Imperative," trans. Susan Bernstein, in *Reading de Man Reading*, ed. Lindsay Waters and Wlad Godzich (Minneapolis: University of Minnesota Press, 1989), 171–201.

is not exhausted by knowing what is being referred to. To be sure, such an account does not go on to create "a surprising realignment of reference with what is *not fully masterable by cognition*": here the parallels end. Another similarity, again accompanied by a series of profound differences, is that "deconstruction does not deny reference, but denies that reference can be modeled on the laws of perception or of understanding": so too with an account of reference as productive, so far as laws of *perception* are concerned. Finally and crucially, the deconstructive account of reference seeks to provide ways of registering and coping with a world in which we must act with only partial knowledge of ourselves, our situations, and the implications of our choices. But this is precisely the world of the realist novel.

Whatever convergences there might be, an account of reference as productive opens itself up to accusations of ignoring the overriding importance of fundamental philosophical issues and therefore behaving in a way that is antitheoretical and lacking in philosophical rigor. For underlying my emphasis on reference as an open-ended beginning is the tendentious belief that problems concerning the adequacy (or indeed the possibility) of language's connection with reality arise only in concrete application, only in the use of language. In this matter, you can't specify impossibilities in advance, as a matter of philosophical necessity or philosophical logic. One of the main contentions of this book is that the presuppositions built into certain conceptions of philosophical rigor are likely to prejudge the case of realism (and other cases) in advance. What such abstract demands mask is a choice between views of reality, not a situation in which one view can simply invalidate the other on shared ground. When faced with such philosophical demands, I am therefore inclined to adopt Jedediah Cleishbotham's discreet response to the attempts of laird and exciseman to override his assumptions with theirs in the matter of *mountain dew*: "If there is a penalty against manufacturing such a liquor, let him show me the statute; and when he does, I'll tell him if I will obey it or no."

Reference and Knowledge

The notion that access to the referent could only mean "transparent" reference is radically misconceived. As a result, accounts of realism that depend, positively or negatively, on such a notion are likely to be skewed. The notion that the inevitable failure or inadequacy of reference can serve to reveal not only philosophical complexities but also complexities attendant upon action in the world is subtler and more attractive, but it too fails to do justice to what reference can help to accomplish in and with the world. A more plausible connection between philosophical problems concerning reference and the claims of realist fiction would involve the possibility of producing knowledge about the world through linguistic mediation, which begins with reference but hardly ends there. To be sure, questions of power, action, and disposition are closer to the heart of realist fiction than questions of knowledge: Jedediah Cleishbotham is, above all else, doing something with his words. If we nevertheless choose to focus on epistemology as such, Frege, with his interest in how different instances of referring to the same referent can produce nontautological knowledge, seems relevant. When, to cite Frege's best-known example, in history (instead of in the fiction of a diachronic present) and through a developing science, human beings less pragmatically involved than Jedediah learn that "the morning star" and "the evening star" both refer to a single planet, they've produced new knowledge about the world. Frege's analysis has a modern ring to it: we can read him as questioning and then rejecting the view that our words determine in advance everything we can know. More generally, as Michael Dummett has argued, Frege's conceptualization of how different "senses" indicate different paths to the referent suggests a framework that can help us to understand the process by which we constantly adjust our ideas to cope with the exigencies of life and action in the world.[36]

More recent work on reference along these lines has sought to transcend the simple "either/or" thinking (reference is either completely transparent or completely opaque) that finds in the hedge of the signifieds such a congenial concept. The discussion of reference moved to a new level with the work of Hilary Putnam (and, in a somewhat different and more uncompromising form, that of Saul Kripke) on reference to "natural kinds." It had generally been assumed that the range of objects or situations to which a word refers (a rough formula for what philosophers call a word's "extension") is fixed by a word's meaning ("intension"). We know what objects "water" refers to because we know the meaning of "water." Putnam, by contrast, has shown that on the one hand, we needn't have any particular "concept" of water to succeed in referring to water, and on the other hand that the things in the world that we refer to as water can help to enrich our understanding of water. We knew that water was water before we discovered that water is H_2O. But

---

[36] Michael Dummett, *Frege: Philosophy of Language*, 2d ed. (London: Duckworth, 1981), 105–7. In another context, Dummett suggests that "it seems that we ought to interpose between the platonist and the constructivist picture an intermediate picture, say of objects springing into being in response to our probing"—see *Truth and Other Enigmas* (London: Duckworth, 1978), 185. This is close (but *not* identical: see Sacks, *The World We Found*, 84, n. 22) to Putnam's notion that "the mind and the world jointly make up the mind and the world."

when we discover that the substance out there that we call "water" *is* H_2O, we might as a result decide that a seemingly similar substance we had previously called water is in fact something else. Though reference may be tied to individual words (not concepts), our understanding of the world is not. There is a dialectical interplay between our understanding of the world and the extension of words, in which the production of knowledge figures as both cause and effect. Our knowledge of natural-kind substances shifts and grows as the dialectic progresses, but not either because of, or in a way that could be predicted by, synchronic shifts in a diacritical "signified."[37]

Putnam has complicated his theory in ways that make it impossible to suppose that the world somehow frames its own categories, extensions, and paths of reference without respect to the frames of reference we bring to it. In the Mind of God, an understanding of and a fixed extension for natural-kind terms may be "always already" there; they are not always already there for us. They are waiting there to be at once discovered and constructed, in conjunction with our minds and ideologies. "The mind and the world," as Putnam puts it, "jointly make up the mind and the world."[38] Even as modified, however, Putnam's views on reference do not begin to assume the idealistic rigidity and the antihistorical temporality of the "semiological hypothesis." And they reinforce what may be the most interesting implication of his work: his theory of reference to natural kinds makes implausible the notion that any single mechanism of reference (or nonreference) could possibly cover the whole field. Talk of *the* referent appears misguided from the start, as do attempts to guarantee a theory of literary meaning or cultural significance by showing that literature must always refer to the same mega-entity in the same way. Putnam thus reminds us that there is a "division of linguistic labor" in determining meanings and fixing extensions.[39] Particularly with regard to scientific knowledge, we defer to the judgment of experts. This deference is merely a special case of the general phenomenon that, as Putnam puts it, meaning just isn't "in the head" of the individual.[40] Our ascriptions of meaning and reference take a variety of forms, supported by interpersonal discussion, learning, and their sedimentation in language and culture.

[37]   For Putnam's earlier work on reference, see the essays in Hilary Putnam, *Philosophical Papers*, vol. 2 (Cambridge: Cambridge University Press, 1975), especially "The Meaning of 'Meaning.' "

[38]   Hilary Putnam, *Reason, Truth, and History* (Cambridge: Cambridge University Press, 1981), xi. For Putnam's more recent views on reference, see also his *Philosophical Papers*, vol. 3 (Cambridge: Cambridge University Press, 1983) and *The Many Faces of Realism* (LaSalle, Ill.: Open Court, 1987).

[39]   Putnam, "The Meaning of 'Meaning,' " 227.

[40]   Putnam, *Reason, Truth, and History*, 19; see also "The Meaning of 'Meaning,' " 227.

Considerations such as these begin to erode the notion that we can make a hard and fast distinction between language (or the signifieds) on one hand, and a "world beyond language" (or the referent) on the other. Or to put it another way: they remind us that such a distinction convincingly arises only when we subscribe to the fiction of synchronicity, only when we bracket the inherently historical nature of our existence. I believe that once we allow such a distinction, the semiotic hypothesis becomes a foregone conclusion: we will indeed find ourselves, as one critic has put it, "pitilessly barred" from the referent.[41] It is on these grounds that George Levine's important book on the realist novel needs to be challenged. No one has done more laudable work than Levine in revealing how self-conscious realism is with respect to problems of which it is so often supposed to be oblivious. But by making that self-consciousness stem from a realist quest for a "reality beyond language," he risks covertly reinstating a single-observer epistemology that may be aware of itself and its problems, but still lacks a route out of the individual head. In such circumstances, is it surprising that, for Levine, the reality beyond language which realism seeks always turns out to be "monstrous" in the sense of passing human understanding?[42] Further, if one accepts a framework that centers on a boundary between that which is language and that which is beyond language, even the subtlest sophistications of realism are bound in the end to seem not sophisticated enough. The project of trying to find a way "past" language will seem at best quixotic; the serious project will then become the attempt to make sense of our linguistic imprisonment. The way beyond this impasse is to recognize that language is already past any one incarnation of itself, and already past single-observer epistemology. The possibility of producing knowledge about the referent, obscured by the semiological hypothesis, follows from the potentialities of language most fully realized not in single words striving to attach themselves to single things, but in sentences and in narratives. As Paul Ricoeur reminds us, "if (following Benveniste rather than de Saussure) we take the sentence as the unit of discourse, then the *intended* of discourse ceases to be confused with the signified correlative to each signifier within the immanence of a system of signs. With the sentence, language is oriented beyond itself."[43]

[41]   Sandy Petrey, *Realism and Revolution* (Ithaca: Cornell University Press, 1988), 13. For a study that focuses on the thematization of problems of reference in nineteenth-century realism, see H. Meili Steele, *Realism and the Drama of Reference* (University Park: Pennsylvania State University Press, 1988).

[42]   George Levine, *The Realist Imagination* (Chicago: University of Chicago Press, 1981).

[43]   Paul Ricoeur, *Time and Narrative*, vol. 1 (1983), trans. Kathleen McLaughlin and David Pellauer (Chicago: University of Chicago Press, 1984), 77–78. The entire section in which this quotation appears, "Narrativity and Reference," is of interest.

I hope that my discussion thus far has thrown enough doubt on the notion that we are barred from the referent to make questions concerning the nature and validity of realist representation seem open. Were we barred from the referent, the realist enterprise would from the start be futile, and my wish to ascertain the extent to which and the ways in which realist fiction might involve us in useful thinking about an external world would be doomed from the start. A hallmark of antirealist thinking along these lines involves the matter of "guarantees." Realist representation supposedly thinks it has an unproblematic, guaranteed in advance referential capacity vis-à-vis the world; but in fact, the semiotic hypothesis proves (that is, guarantees in advance) that any such relationship is impossible. (At this point, we begin to observe mirror images.) A primary thesis of my study is that *it is impossible in advance and as a matter of analytic necessity to determine the degree of ideological infiltration present in any given act of representation.* If this supposition is true, the realist novel might turn out to be particularly useful because of its concrete rendering of particular cases, and not simply as an object for symptomatic analysis.

Given the multitude of problems we have uncovered in the account of reference provided by the semiotic hypothesis, one might ask why it was so readily accepted by such a wide spectrum of critics. I have invoked Watt to suggest that the native philosophical and critical traditions his work synthesizes could offer little resistance to the semiotic hypothesis; indeed, their own accounts of reference and also their own conception of and value for "the literary" had already prepared the way for an impoverished notion of what realist reference to the world might entail. Beyond that, I suspect that the semiotic hypothesis has been attractive mainly on political grounds. The semiotic hypothesis has helped to place squarely in view the possibility that ideology infiltrates even seemingly value-free areas. In a somewhat contradictory vein, the idea that we are cut off from the real world can also promise a liberation from the constraints of the real world. Those who are interested in metafiction can liberate an area of imaginative freedom when they downplay the importance of "direct" referentiality. Those who invoke the semiotic hypothesis can, following the Barthes of *S/Z*, slide along the chain of signifiers, instead of being subjected to the control of a spuriously objective external reality.

In the end, critiques that impute to realism a belief in "direct" referentiality do so to solidify views of the world, and worldviews are in general successfully opposed not by arguments against their self-consistency, but by other worldviews. I hope that this book as a whole will suggest that such critiques, by constructing an entirely inadequate picture of realism to act as their negative identities, have prevented their adherents from recognizing that realism might provide significant responses to the very political problems that most concern them.

Reference as Performative

Though I believe its influence is waning, it would be premature to write the obituary of the view of realism based upon the notion that we are barred from the referent. An exceptionally interesting study of realism, Sandy Petrey's *Realism and Revolution*, has remodeled this view in a way designed to extend its usefulness. Petrey employs the semiotic hypothesis not to demonstrate the bankruptcy of realism's supposedly "transparent" representation, but to focus our attention on a knowable and representable social praxis. Petrey grants the case that language cannot give us knowledge of an external world, but he adds that linguistic practices themselves, rightly understood, can tell us all we need to know about how it is that societies create and sustain themselves politically. It may be that language cannot reach the referent, but the language that societies employ for political purposes doesn't need to reach beyond itself. "Realist specificity" involves not "an impossible fidelity to a sociohistorical referent but successful activation of the process by which sociohistorical collectivities make language appear referential."[44] (Just as the phrase "simple reflection theory" is rarely used to suggest that there might be complex reflection theories, so the notion here is that *any* fidelity to a sociohistorical referent is "impossible.")

For Petrey, "language's absolute separation from objective reality goes hand in hand with its absolute dependence on social reality" (73). Accordingly, "the referent, pitilessly barred from a world prior to language, keeps all its force as a component and consequence of language" (13). If we wish to understand the French Revolution, what we actually need to grasp is how the linguistic protocols of the day defined a coercive reality and imposed that reality on society as a whole. Petrey's analysis is fascinating in its demonstration of how certain uses of language can make a politically contrived situation appear to be "natural" and inevitable, and in showing how much power depends upon making one set of political definitions (say, of the status of the National Assembly during the Revolution) stick, rather than another. His work is also valuable in insisting that the question of the ultimate "grounds" of political action or of politi-

---

[44] Petrey, *Realism and Revolution*, 49; hereafter cited in the text.

cal language may be entirely irrelevant.[45] You can show that language is groundless or indeterminate to your own satisfaction and perhaps to the satisfaction of others; this won't prevent people from using language to create results that *become* objective, that create not an illusion but historical reality itself.

With this truly radical focus on the ways in which societies perform themselves, Petrey turns the tables on the two main objections to realism we have been considering in this chapter. Holders of the semiotic hypothesis may find realism's being "barred" from the referent a scandal. Petrey doesn't. Indeed, he finds the bar enabling: it's precisely that which ensures that the language of realism will involve the true, performative basis of society. The bar, in short, functions for Petrey *within* realism in precisely the way I've argued it functions for those who invoke the semiotic hypothesis against realism: it guarantees that, on the right side of the bar, knowledge will be possible. What's "mystified," according to Petrey, isn't realism's attempt to achieve "pure referentiality" or "transparent reference," it's the notion that realism wants or needs to achieve such reference if it is to further its project. Petrey also has an answer to critics who, because of their interest in the inner contradictions and incommensurabilities of language itself, would find realism neither more nor less mystified than other forms of writing, but almost certainly less interesting. I've suggested above that the operative problem such a point of view poses for realism tends to occur on a pragmatic level. Given the assumption that certain contradictions in language are fundamental, it's natural that critics should spend their time exploring their workings. This very focus, however, is likely to divert attention from the workings of language on other levels—and particularly on the level at which realism does most of its work. Petrey's theory of realism leads to much the same conclusion as mine. Thus he counters de Man's use of J. L. Austin by suggesting that although de Man focuses on an undecidability between the performative and the constative functions of language, in realist representation the performative has become so dominant that we are authorized to attend instead to the uses of performative speech to create and maintain society: "Whereas de Man . . . strategically foregrounds the opposition between performative and constative in the early sections of *How to Do Things with Words*, that opposition becomes irrelevant when Austin makes verbal statement a subcategory of verbal performance, when what words say becomes one of the many things they do" (71).

---

[45]   A similar point, on a more general level, was made with economy some years ago by Charles Altieri, in a Wittgensteinian analysis: "for the agents involved in particular practices, metaphysical standards of arbitrariness are irrelevant." See "Culture and Skepticism: A Response to Michael Fischer," *Critical Inquiry*, 6 (1979), 351.

The power of Petrey's vision of realism becomes apparent in his treatment of the issue with which this chapter began—the question of the place of objects in realist novels. His reading of a scene in which the striking miners in *Germinal* confront their manager demonstrates how physical objects can assume meanings that differ in accordance with the set of linguistic and social conventions one brings to them. The very furniture in the manager Hennebeau's house embodies and enforces bourgeois dominance, a dominance interrupted when, for a brief moment, the miner Maheu takes control of the field of language. At least for this part of the novel, Petrey demonstrates, Lukács's characterization of Zola's "naturalist" world as full of unconnected, meaningless things is remarkably unhelpful. Objects have been a source of embarrassment for many critics of the realist novel, who seem to want to assure themselves and others that *they* don't have a taste for Victorian gewgaws. To cite a single, distinguished example, it's dismaying to find Paul Ricoeur announcing that what's truly historical about realist fiction has *nothing whatever to do* with the depiction of historical milieu, but arises instead from experiments with temporality.[46] One imagines the disappointment Balzac and Thomas Mann would have felt at discovering the vanity of so many of their words. There is, to be sure, a critical tradition of valorizing in novels the depiction of objects so long as they are interpretable as "spiritual symbols" illuminating the interiority of individuals. The horizon of Petrey's analysis is much wider: questions of epistemology, symbolism, class, and ideology are raised by Hennebeau's rug, becoming inseparable from the way the cut of his furniture is perceived from moment to moment. It's refreshing that Petrey, because of his focus on social process and convention, finds in his analysis an honored place for the physical object. In Petrey's analysis, reference to objects could never be "pure," in the sense of involving a relationship not mediated through social uses of language. Petrey's analysis would indeed lead naturally to a vision of man-made objects as constituting a kind of congealed humanity, a sedimentation of the social. Such a vision might in turn help us to imagine the possibility of an ongoing conversation with aspects of the world that had looked to be inanimate.

There is, however, an important sense in which Petrey's analysis appears incomplete. When the miner Maheu suspends the power of Hennebeau's furniture by speaking of the actual conditions of his social existence, the authority of his speech can stem only from his direct experience of the referent of which he speaks. He knows his life and his suffering, but little else. His mode of knowing the world suggests a (truncated) phi-

---

[46] Paul Ricoeur, *Time and Narrative*, vol. 3 (1985), trans. Kathleen Blamey and David Pellauer (Chicago: University of Chicago Press, 1988), 191.

losophy of praxis, recalling Barthes's contention that only the woodcut-
ter, who alone escapes through labor in the world the impasses of representation, can name the tree truly.[47] No practice crossing the referential
bar can exist in Petrey's account. For all his analysis can tell us, Maheu's
speech occurs by magic. And in that analysis, the only lasting authority
Maheu's words could possibly have would result from the success of the
miners' strike, for only such a success would make their nominations prevail.

Yet Zola's scene suggests the ultimate insufficiency of mere experience,
even when it is voiced. There is no question of the miners' understanding
how the furniture oppresses them; they only feel *that* it oppresses them.
By speaking, they can (briefly) assert an alternative reality that eclipses
the reality of Hennebeau's furniture; but this assertion is a simple act of
will. It is therefore unsurprising that when Maheu's words cease, the furniture reasserts itself as an agent of bourgeois domination. Petrey's account of the workings of realist language tends to remind us *that* language can help to make social reality occur; it *shows* us the workings of
language. In consonance with this emphasis, Petrey asserts that "the
point of moment is not *what* Maheu says about the miners' poverty but
that he says it" (172). At the end of the scene, Hennebeau adroitly alludes
to mysterious economic realities centered in "Paris," territory truly alien
to the miners, and they find themselves confronting a force that leaves
them feeling helpless and dejected, though still defiant. They are pitilessly barred from the referent. They cannot know it; it chooses not to recognize them. Their strike will fail.

For all its usefulness, Petrey's analysis of realist language would leave
us as readers in the situation of Zola's miners. His continued adherence
to the semiological hypothesis, with its notion that we are barred from a
unitary entity called "the referent," takes an ultimate toll. One of the
promises of the realist novel is to provide us with a model for how we
might place ourselves in a productively knowing relationship with the

---

[47]   Roland Barthes, *Mythologies* (1957), trans. Annette Lavers (New York: Hill and Wang,
1972), 145–46. I believe that Colin MacCabe's attempt to find a mode of reference that can
produce knowledge, but at the same time to keep faith with the semiological hypothesis,
leads him into similar difficulties: see "Realism: Balzac and Barthes," in *Tracking the Signifier* (Minneapolis: University of Minnesota Press, 1985), 131–50. For MacCabe, knowledge
can arise because what Frege calls "sense" involves a *nonlinguistic* route to the referent; by
opening up new routes, reference positions us in new places, and hence we can produce
(not see) a new reality. A number of familiar themes arise here—the passive observer who
must be put in "subject-positions," for instance. There also seems to be something like a
fear of inevitable ideological contamination if we dabble in the "always already" constructed field of language. Why else would MacCabe find himself wanting to identify the
possibility of producing knowledge with a "route, directly to the object, which is non-lin-
guistic" (142)? Perhaps we need to learn instead how to work with dirty tools.

forces that control history and society. For Petrey, it appears that realist language can be faithful to the second nature congealed in linguistically based social practice, and that the critic's own language can represent that practice. Yet at the same time *all* language is and must remain "pitilessly barred" from "a sociohistorical referent." Once again, the semiological hypothesis cannot account for its own insights, or for those of the works it discusses. Petrey's adherence to the semiotic barring of the referent short-circuits historical explanation that would extend beyond linguistic practices as such. It allows us to trace the ways language imposes power, but not to explain why certain practices have succeeded while others have failed. Petrey's analysis shows that it is important to take seriously the performative aspect of realist language; it also reveals that it is impossible to account for the part linguistic performances play in creating history if our notion of language recognizes *only* its performative aspects.

Petrey's thesis is that society creates its own ungrounded but constraining reality through conventions that control meaning. Hilary Putnam, speaking in a different context, suggests that "our knowledge, or any piece of it, is conventional relative to certain alternatives and factual relative to certain others. . . . *Everything* we say is conventional in the sense that we might have said something else, perhaps something verbally incompatible; and *everything* we say is factual in the sense that we could not have said just anything else."[48] Can Petrey's notion of society as performing itself apart from "the referent" explain why, when a society fixes its conventions, it "could not have said just anything else"? The French Revolution spoke, and there was no King of France; the Restoration spoke, and there was a King. Fair enough. But, to use an extreme but not an unfair example, could any society today create the Restoration by using the power of its performative utterances? A truly historical sense of temporality would render meaningless the choice Petrey offers between his vision of an entirely performative social language on the one hand, and of the referent as "a world *prior* to language" on the other. Only a grasp of the dialectical and historical relationships between language, actions in the world, and social conventions could allow us to explain how it is that when revolutions occur, prisons fall, heads are placed on pikes, and new conventions arise. If realist representation is pitilessly barred from "the referent," how is it to help us understand the limits within which speech acts have their efficacy?[49]

Petrey might well reply that the realist novel, especially as written in

[48]   Putnam, *Philosophical Papers*, vol. 3, 178–79.
[49]   Need I add that the total and indefeasible understanding of context Derrida believes Austin/Searle's system requires is not the issue here?

England, would appear to be aware of little else than limits, that the realist fascination with complex webs of social determination itself tends to
bring with it a feeling of helplessness in the face of history. His book
could be defended as an attempt to radicalize from within an inherently
conservative genre. If we take such a line, we find ourselves adding to the
term "literary realism" some familiar connotations, involving the cynical
tough-mindedness we associate with a certain brand of "realism" about
politics, the sort of realism that tells us that we really can't accomplish
much, given the overwhelming complexity of things, or the rottenness of
people, or both. This is a significant association, and one to which we'll
return in subsequent chapters. There's something very attractive about a
critical position that insists that the possibility for social and historical
change is always present, is built right into the language that fixes our social practices. By downplaying the possibility of objective knowledge, Petrey reminds us of the importance of dispositions of the will. A critical fixation on the epistemology of realism, whether "naive" or sophisticated, is
indeed misleading, because it ignores the central concern of realist fiction
with problems not of knowledge, but of will and action.

Barring the referent has been effective in emphasizing the workings
of ideology in representation: criticism, once largely oblivious to ideology, now seems aware of little else. But now that ideology has come out
of hiding, might we not dispense with this aspect of the semiological
hypothesis, in quest of a more useful way of theorizing the relationship
of language and the referent? The wish to prevent "direct" access to the
referent seems to reflect a fear that, once the bars are let down, reality
will appear completely unproblematic and the possibility of recognizing the infiltrations of ideology will vanish. This fear has some justification. Ideology has a quick volatility when reference to it is not fixed by
some expedient or other. But perhaps such matters can never be dealt
with once and for all. More than one set of recent events have shown
tragically that human beings make history in a situation not of their
own making—that, in Putnam's terms, you can't say *just anything*, that
there is an insistently "factual" basis to our sayings and doings. So we
return to the question of whether the realist novel is "pitilessly barred"
from the referent. There may be something to be said for providing access to a world we can know well enough, and feel sufficiently comfort-
able in, to render informed action possible. The price of yielding to one
version of "realism" may indeed be a helpless feeling that we are dominated by the objects around us. But the price of cutting ourselves off, in
advance and as a matter of theoretical necessity, from an active knowledge of the actual, objective historical relations obtaining between such
objects may be even higher. Barring "the referent" may have the unin-

tended consequence of denying us a vital resource in what must be a day-to-day struggle.

For Petrey, the language society uses to perform itself is constituted by its being barred from the referent. A dialectical interplay, productive of knowledge, between language and the world crosses the bar. I suspect that, for all his emphasis on the social making of meaning, Petrey conceives of society as a large version of the individual mind, caught in the situation of the individual observer. There would then be little room for learning, much room for acts of pure will and arbitrary nomination. But a dialogue between subjectivities has potentialities that transcend the dialogue of the mind with itself. The realist novel matters because it explores ways past the individual mind.

In *Bleak House*, Jo, the ignorant vagrant, looks up at the cross on the dome of St. Paul's cathedral in London, and the narrative voice sternly reminds us that Jo is able to make no sense whatever of the religious significance of that object. This is a moment when reference becomes an issue in several ways. It could become an issue for the theory of fictions, since the narrator breaks a certain fictional decorum by referring in his novel to an actual object in an actual city. More immediately, reference is an issue for Jo: he could refer to the cross under a more general name ("that bright thing up there"), but he can't make the cross refer to anything. Of course there is the possibility that he might learn to make the cross refer to something, if someone would only talk to him about it. A language exists for this purpose, but Jo has been excluded from it. If we turn to our own implication in the scene, we realize that Jo is our double in certain respects, though we are culpable in ways he is not. When the passage invites us to remember the times we have seen (or might have seen) the cross on the dome of St. Paul's, it is also inviting us to realize that it is entirely possible that, at the very moment when we saw the cross and properly coded it, a person like Jo might also have been looking at it, unable to understand it. Suddenly there emerges a connection between us and Jo, a connection we would normally be either unable or unwilling to make.[50] Like Jo, we haven't seen all the possible references of the cross—or more likely, unlike Jo, we have been unwilling to imagine them, though they are there, plain as day, plain as the cross itself. Of course, this is something that the objective *significance* of the cross, as a symbol of an event and of Christian doctrine (and in particular the Christian imperative of charity for others) could have told us all along, which is why this particular object is the per-

[50]   On the importance of making connections in this scene, see Ralph W. Rader, "A Comparative Anatomy of Three Baggy Monsters," *Journal of Narrative Technique*, 19 (1989), 49–69.

fect one for Dickens's purposes. The cross ought to make certain demands on us, but deadened by its familiarity as an object of perception,
and hardened by our unwillingness to face our implication in the poverty
of people like Jo, we ignore those demands.

Jo is "pitilessly barred" from the referent, as recent critical discourse
would have it, but his being barred is a matter of social neglect and oppression, not epistemological necessity; by the same token, readers are
likely to find it convenient to abstract themselves from the referent.
Dickens suggests that Jo's predicament is tragic and remediable, and
ours is inexcusable, not a condition of life in language. To be sure, the
referent here turns out to be something much more complicated than a
single physical object: it involves instead a complex web of actual and
potential relationships, a widely various array of paths to the referent
taken and not taken. The scene with Jo typifies the way in which realist
representation draws on our normal competencies, including our referential competence, to make sense of the world. It is also typical in its
demonstration of the sorts of things that can occur when we refer to the
world, and of the variety of linguistic operations that cohere to make a
fictional world seem "real." Our access to the referent, like Jo's, has
everything to do with intersubjective discourse; it has nothing to do with
the lonely situation of single-observer epistemology, a nice emblem of
which is Jo himself, who, in his ideological and linguistic predicament,
"don't know nothink."

Conclusion, with Reference to Austin

This chapter has made much of Ian Watt's attempt to define the language of realist fiction as performing a more largely referential function
than that of more traditional literary forms. It has tried to show that this
characterization of "formal realism" is inadequate to describe the end to
which language is used in realist novels. It has also suggested that Watt's
dichotomy between pure reference on the one hand and self-reference in
a variety of guises on the other, paves the way for views of realism that
can only be impoverishing. Watt's notion of realism's more largely referential use of language can easily slide into the notion that realism attempts to create an illusion of pure transparency in its language. This notion, in turn, proves very helpful to those who wish to scapegoat realism.
When the virtues of the preferred other of realism involve linguistic self-
referentiality, the realist project is made to seem dull; when they involve
a recognition of the power of the signified, the realist project is made to
seem positively and malignantly mystified. Watt himself senses the inad-

equacy of "formal realism" as the basis for permanently valuable literature, and he tries to redress it in the closing pages of *The Rise of the Novel*.
Adding "realism of assessment" as a supplementary category has the
virtue of pushing his analysis in the direction of the social, but the idea
that a stress on "realism of assessment" might simply be added, as a "balance" to his "formal realism," simply won't do. Incorporating "realism of
assessment" into his scheme would have required him to *reformulate* "formal realism," particularly with respect to the question of the relationship
between language and the world. What would be needed would be not
the addition of a supplement, but a radical reworking of the notion of formal realism itself.

In arriving at this conclusion, I have been anticipated by another critic,
none other than Ian Watt himself. In "Serious Reflections on *The Rise of the
Novel*," Watt sometimes may make it sound as if a fundamental problem
with his book was that the discussion of "realism of assessment" wasn't
long enough, because of the fact that he cut his original manuscript radically, sacrificing discussion of precisely those authors for whom realism
of assessment was central. In fact, he knows better than this. "Many problems about the two realisms," he tells us, "would have remained even if
there had been no cuts." The main reason why the problems would have
remained, he adds, is that his "treatment assumed it was somehow possible to separate the two kinds of realism in a novel's structural elements—
from the single word to the plot as a whole." But in fact, "though this separation may be legitimate as an analytic construct" it turns out to be
deeply problematic as an account of how realist language functions, because "as regards the smallest units—words and phrases—there is always a tension between the literal meaning, the bare denotation, on the
one hand, and the connotations of the word on the other, to say nothing
of its larger reference to the narration and to the whole pattern of the
reader's expectations."[51] Though Watt doesn't put it quite so baldly, what
this inseparability implies is that the notion of "formal realism" simply
isn't salvageable as an account of realist language, or even (his plea for it
as an "analytic construct" notwithstanding) as an independent part—
something that could be "balanced" by another part—of an account of realist language. For unless we adopt a notion of language that does not
recognize the possibility of "pure" referentiality, Watt's discussion of
"denotation" and "connotation" would simply internalize the split between "formal realism" and "realism of assessment" into language itself.
On a more positive note, it seems clear that an adequate account of realist
uses of language would find it very useful indeed to make "larger refer-

---

[51] Watt, "Serious Reflections," 98–99; hereafter cited in the text.

ence to the narration and to the whole pattern of the reader's expectations."

Why are there so many objects in realist novels? It seems unlikely that an adequate answer to this question could possibly arise from supposing that the primary and defining function of realist language is to create a situation in which we feel we're eavesdropping, one which reduces the realist language to a more largely referential function than that possessed by the language of other works. Instead, we'd need to ask (as Lukács does) why realism, using a very broad range of linguistic potentialities, focuses on "the object" in ways earlier literary forms hadn't found necessary.

At one point in "Serious Reflections," Watt wryly comments that some of the problems in *The Rise of the Novel* arose from following up "the commonest of all Receipts to make an Academick Book—'Get yourself a couple of poles and turn 'em loose' " (98). We've seen that Watt has not been alone among critics of realism in adopting such a procedure. Yet as it happens, at about the same time that Watt's seminal work appeared, a philosopher was demonstrating in his articles and public lectures that it is possible to begin with a pair of opposing linguistic categories, turn them loose, and then use what you've learned from them to reach a more adequate vision of how language puts us into contact with the social world. The philosopher was J. L. Austin; the lectures became *How to Do Things with Words.*

Austin does not discuss problems of reference in *How to Do Things with Words.* In his search for the performative aspect of language, however, Austin himself provides a model for how acts of reference can help to produce knowledge about the world. He enacts a process that recalls the dialectical process Putnam describes, in which knowledge is produced and extensions are refined as we refer over time to natural-kind substances.

Austin begins with a sense that received models of language fail to do justice to what occurs as human beings use language. He singles out a remarkable set of linguistic phenomena for which the vocabulary of propositions, truth values, and the like simply cannot account: when you christen a ship, you aren't reporting, you're doing. The right words uttered in the right circumstances christen a ship; they do not report that a christening has occurred. In pointing to the performative utterance, Austin achieves something like the discovery of an overlooked natural kind in the second nature that is our language. The task then becomes to explore, in ways always open to revision in the light of future discoveries, the extension of this phenomenon. The goal will be to make explicit sense of the implicit linguistic competence we employ when we make words perform. Referring to speech acts by using the tentative categories of "performative" and its defining opposite "constative" will serve as an initial step on what we can expect to be a winding path.

Difficulties quickly arise when Austin essays to distinguish performative locutions, which do things, from constative locutions, which make statements about the world. Before long, he announces that "at least in some ways there is danger of our initial and tentative distinction between constative and performative utterances breaking down."[52] Instead of resting content in proclaiming that this danger results from the essentially contested nature of language itself, however, Austin presses forward. Perhaps a supplementary distinction, one that opposes truth and success, will succeed in separating the performative from the constative. Constatives, which report on states of affairs, can after all be true or false; performatives, which do things, cannot. They do them successfully or unsuccessfully, happily or unhappily. To suppose that performatives *centrally* involve truth and falsehood is to mistake the words which christen a ship for a report that the christening has occurred. Yet Austin soon realizes that questions of a true or false "fit" to the world are raised by performatives, and that considerations of "happiness" arise when we make factual statements. He also finds it impossible to isolate a grammatical criterion that would solidify the distinction between performative and constative. At this point he announces that "it is time then to make a fresh start on the problem" (91).

Austin makes his fresh start by considering not two but three kinds of locutionary doing: uttering meaningful sets of words (the locutionary act: a physical utterance plus sense and reference); uttering a specific *kind* of locution conventionally recognized as such (the illocutionary act: the center of Austin's interest); and uttering a locution that happens to have one or another effect in the world (the perlocutionary act). The "fresh start" means a redefinition of the object of inquiry, a new view of the location of verbal doing. Instead of defining separate kinds of utterances, Austin identifies different dimensions of doing contained in utterances. Instead of distinct kinds of utterances, he seeks distinct "forces" *within* utterances. The locutionary act transmutes the phenomena he previously considered under the heading of the "constative"; the illocutionary act, those he previously discussed under the heading of the "performative." The perlocutionary act enters new territory—the world of contingent states of affairs in the world, a world it had been the traditional role of something on the order of the "constative" to describe. The perlocutionary extends

---

[52] J. L. Austin, *How to Do Things with Words*, 2d ed., ed. J. O. Urmson and Marina Sbisà (Cambridge: Harvard University Press, 1975), 54; hereafter cited in the text.

the utterance in the direction of *reception* but beyond the immediate speech situation, recalling the unpredictable things that can result when utterances enter the world. (A measure of the quality of Austin's mind is that this entry into the world involves the contingent, not the necessary: he maintains his distance from the logician's "proposition.") Austin fails to produce a fourth category to extend the utterance in the direction of *production*. He does add an emphasis, fertile in the production of ambiguities and of dissents from later theorists of the speech act, on "conventions" of meaning that make it possible for speakers to produce both the locutionary and the illocutionary forces of language.

There has been much loose talk to the effect that, in revising his search for the performative, Austin blithely and continually contradicts himself as he goes along, taking up and then discarding positions with Dionysian abandon. According to those who knew Austin, he hated to be proved wrong in argument, so much so that some have faulted him for hedging his bets, refusing to release an argument until it appeared unassailable. The notion that such a man would, on three separate occasions, parade an argument as it simply breaks down seems incredible. And then there's another report. Austin's prewar Rover had a way of coming to an unexpected halt every time he took an American friend for a ride in it. ("It just doesn't *like* you!" he once told the friend, with apparent conviction.) Austin would lift the hood, tinker, restart the car ("whatever it was he did, it worked every time"), and the voyage would continue.[53]

Austin's initial focus on explicit performatives, and his initial distinction between "performative and constative," are best seen as part of a first attempt to determine the extension of the performative, the field of phenomena to which the word refers. At this point, a simple dichotomy suffices, with the constative helping to organize that field by functioning primarily as that which the performative is not. Austin's discussion progresses through a series of attempts to clarify both the nature and the extent of the performative phenomenon. The referent here has a certain autonomy. We discover, after a good deal of labor, that our excavations have commenced at its edge, not its center; a clearer sense of extension then enables a substantial growth of knowledge.

At the end of this process, we are in a position to "place" the explicit performative that had provided us with our first approximation at fixing an extension for the performative in general. Petrey (intent on reducing the language of realism entirely to the performative by dropping out reference beyond the bar altogether) suggests that when Austin asks at this

---

[53] George Pitcher, "Austin: A Personal Memoir," in Isaiah Berlin et al., *Essays on J. L. Austin* (Oxford: Clarendon, 1973), 26.

point in his discussion what's left of the performative/constative distinction, his "implicit answer" is "Nothing worth thinking about" (36). This is a surprising conclusion, for Austin himself gives an admirably clear answer, made possible by his crucial shift of the terms of analysis from different kinds of utterances to different forces within utterances. The explicit performative is an abstraction of the "illocutionary" force, made for purposes of social convenience; the shadier "constative" is a similar abstraction made for the purposes of logicians.[54] Both are specialized, reflexive uses of linguistic potentialities. Such an explanation is eminently worth talking about on its own merits. It has the further merit of marking the distance we've traveled with Austin, providing a measure of what we've learned through the dialectical interplay of extension-fixing and revised understanding. Direct, static, "transparent" reference—the kind of reference realism supposedly trades in—would make such journeys impossible and unnecessary.

When Austin explains what has happened to his initial distinction between performative and constative, he suggests that the idea that both the performative and the constative involve self-reflexive uses of linguistic potentialities was what he "really . . . had in mind" when he framed the distinction in the first place (145). This bit of play with the reader deserves notice, and not only because it seems so novelistic. There is, to be sure, a sense in which Austin's redescription was indeed potentially there "in his mind" at the outset of his philosophical journey; if not, he couldn't have arrived. It was there in his mind because it is embodied in common language. But the gap between the point of departure and the destination, between implicit existence and explicit knowledge, remains vital. Hence Austin's slightly but only slightly apologetic tone, as his wry comment reminds us of the many pages we've had to read in order to discover what he "really" had in mind all along.

Austin's practice in *How to Do Things with Words* exemplifies the way reference and the fixing of extensions can help us learn about the world. The vision of language he develops provides a way past the sterile dichotomies that inevitably arise when one supposes that there could be a language of realism that approaches the "purely referential." Instead of suggesting that a supposedly purely referential language needs to be supplemented by another kind of language (as Watt does with "realism of assessment"), Austin's account recognizes that language always contains a variety of ways of mixing with the world. We should accordingly

---

[54] My characterization of the performative and even more of the constative would suggest that attempts to employ these categories as foundations for large speculative operations are, to say no more, un-Austinian.

expect the language of fictional realism to contain locutionary, illocution-ary, and perlocutionary components. We might also expect it to be em-ployed by realist authors as Austin employs language in his works: in an attempt, at once descriptive and persuasive, to produce an ever-clearer "fix" on reality, by beginning with realities that continually surround us but that will yield up their significance only if we take the time to attend to them in all their concrete complexity.

In trying to show how this process operates in Austin, I found myself giving a narrative. Perhaps the most interesting question that arises from placing Austin in the context of realist fiction is whether his own recourse to narrative is merely a pedagogical convenience, or whether the kind of knowledge Austin has discovered must involve the telling of stories. Some have said that *How to Do Things with Words* contains a breakdown and starts afresh because it records the path Austin happened to take "historically" in sorting out the problem that interested him. Might Austin be suggesting instead that to understand, you *must* follow a path?

His insistence on not proceeding too quickly, on moving at a walk and not a gallop, seems consonant with such a view. The strolls through the dictionary he sometimes recommends might also be seen as embodying an essentially narrative vision. No doubt a drive toward synchronic sys-tem can also be found in Austin, but it is remarkable how little such an impetus dominates his thinking if we compare him to many predecessors and followers. His thought, like the conception of the speech act he finally arrives at, contains a variety of forces. Yet his unwillingness to abstract from the specificities of the case at hand is marked; in this he also re-sembles the realist novelists. Perhaps only a narrative can stay so close to the things.

In an early attempt to rescue historical explanation from the clutches of those who would turn history over to the logic of propositions, truth functions, and covering laws, W. B. Gallie suggested that narrative has its own explanatory logic. He argued that when we listen to a story or watch a game, explanations may function primarily to aid us to follow the ac-tion further; the action isn't there to be reduced to explanations or to yield general laws.[55] The status of such things as explanations depends, as Austin might have put it, on what acts you were narrating under what circumstances. Not all philosophers, to be sure, have seen games in this light. John Searle is considered by many to be Austin's heir.[56] Searle's use

[55]   W. B. Gallie, *Philosophy and the Historical Understanding* (London: Chatto and Windus, 1964).
[56]   According to Petrey, Searle's work extends Austin "without violence" (13), and Der-rida's most telling refutations of Austin/Searle refute words employed and copyrighted by Searle.

of games is diametrically opposed to Gallie's: Searle sees games as a prime example of activities that can be precisely and synchronically codified. For Searle, Austin's own work, pioneering in more ways than one, can also be codified, and it ought to be. For those who find the aims and tone of Searle's speech-act theory fundamentally different from those of Austin, this different attitude toward games will suggest larger differences. Perhaps it will turn out that Austin himself was as much narrator as philosopher, that Austin was indeed a novel philosopher.

Literary critics—and philosophers as well—have found the heart of Austin's matter in the speech-act theory adumbrated in the lectures that became *How to Do Things with Words*. The other set of lecture notes that were expanded into a book after Austin's early death have received less favorable attention. The editor of *Sense and Sensibilia*, G. J. Warnock, has described them as the only extended batch of Austin's published philosophical work that is "almost throughout undeviatingly negative, critical, even polemically critical," since Austin doesn't reveal how the topics he shows others have mistreated should in fact have been handled.[57] Yet that negativity is telling. I've suggested in this chapter that Watt's appeal to Descartian single-observer epistemology has had unfortunate results, both for his own work on realism and for the more negative analyses of realism that have exploited the weaknesses mirrored in his formulation of "formal realism." As one recent observer has realized, the stakes of Austin's "purely negative" attack on traditional ways of doing epistemology are in fact very large: indeed, they involve "an overwhelming challenge to the entire Cartesian tradition."[58] It was this tradition that Austin finally had in mind when, in the "undeviatingly negative" *Sense and Sensibilia*, he insisted that "the right policy is not the one . . . of trying to patch it up a bit and make it work properly; that just can't be done. The right policy is to go back to a much earlier stage, and to dismantle the whole doctrine before it gets off the ground."[59] Taking seriously the implications of Austin's challenge to traditional epistemology could do much to undermine the linguistic basis of what have become the standard attacks on realist fiction.

In a memorable and often-cited comment, Austin suggests that "our

[57]   G. J. Warnock, *J. L. Austin* (London: Routledge, 1989), 11.

[58]   Antony Flew, review of *J. L. Austin* by G. J. Warnock, in *Philosophical Investigations*, 13 (1990), 285. A philosopher who has insisted throughout his career on Austin's importance and scope is Stanley Cavell. For a penetrating commentary on Austin and Derrida, see Cavell, *Philosophical Passages: Wittgenstein, Emerson, Austin, Derrida* (Oxford: Blackwell, 1995).

[59]   J. L. Austin, *Sense and Sensibilia* (Oxford: Clarendon, 1962), 142. This is a useful reminder in these days of theory wars, in which he who is most abstractly theoretical generally gets to start the ball rolling with the spin of his choice.

common stock of words embodies all the distinctions men have found worth drawing, and the connexions they have found worth marking, in the lifetimes of many generations: these surely are likely to be more numerous, more sound, since they have stood up to the long test of the survival of the fittest, and more subtle, at least in all ordinary and reasonably practical matters, than any that you or I are likely to think up in our armchairs of an afternoon—the most favoured alternative method."[60] Particularly when we think of Austin's work as in part a repudiation of the Cartesian tradition of basing epistemological speculation on the fiction of the single isolated observer, the essentially *social* view of Austin's philosophical enterprise becomes striking here. It's our "common" stock of words that will put us in contact with reality, not the ability of the individual, sitting alone, to devise distinctions. The idea that a certain faithfulness to the experience of the quotidian will bring us into contact with the real is one that realist fiction shares.

It is also one that rouses strong attack. Austin's scorn for theories spun out of the armchair evoked quick and predictable hostility, both from defenders of the dignity of traditional philosophical speculation, but also and perhaps especially from those on the left. Austin was attacked as being what would be called these days "anti-Theory." It was assumed that he was urging philosophy to restrict itself to a myopic view of the surfaces of actual social practices, and it was concluded that such a view could only ensure the continuance of things as they are, because it ruled out in advance any understanding of the deeper structures that controlled them. Such sentiments echo the attack on realist fiction as inherently conservative because it is fixated on the social surface. (This is the attack that Petrey's work is so skillfully designed to counter.) Now it turns out that those who attacked Austin for his alleged conservatism tended to play fast and loose with his texts, ignoring the qualifications of his position he himself carefully and explicitly introduced. Thus, as Antony Flew has pointed out, Austin is careful to tell us within a few pages that "ordinary language is *not* the last word: in principle it can everywhere be supplemented and improved upon and superseded. Only remember, it *is* the *first* word."[61] And indeed Austin goes further than this, allowing for a positive need for specialized language to describe what Habermas has called "distorted speech situations" and showing its value in his own coinages. Yet Austin's suggestion that ordinary lan-

---

[60] J. L. Austin, "A Plea for Excuses," in *Philosophical Papers* (Oxford: Clarendon, 1961), 130.

[61] Flew, in his review of *J. L. Austin*, 280–82, cites and contests the attacks on Austin by Ernst Gellner and Anthony Arblaster. He quotes here from "A Plea for Excuses," in *Philosophical Papers*, 133.

guage is the "first" word remains tendentious. One can always ask whether, if we habitually start with the sort of linguistic reality Austin recommends, we will ever progress beyond it. By the same token, we can wonder how much his preferred methods of operation could help us to fabricate new kinds of language for difficult situations. (Judging from the success of some of his neologisms, I'd say his record is rather good in this respect; judging from the ways in which his central terms have been misunderstood and misused, I might be tempted to second thoughts.) In raising such objections, however, we would at the very least have progressed beyond the point of assuming that any reference to the world has been barred in advance by the workings of language. We would instead find ourselves in a situation where it becomes necessary to consider what's actually "done" with respect to the world after a thinker—or a novelist—has made reference to it. To justify assuming this position—to suggest that it's anything but "naive" or "transparent"—has been the purpose of this chapter.

3

An Approach to Realist Narratives

> Historicism has nothing to do with eclecticism. . . . We cease,
> it is true, to judge on the basis of extrahistorical and absolute
> categories, and we cease to look for such categories, precisely
> because the universally human or poetic factor, which is com-
> mon to the most perfect works of all times and which should
> consequently provide us with our categories of judgment, can
> only be apprehended in its particular historical forms, and
> there is no intelligible way of expressing its absolute essence.
> —Erich Auerbach, *Literary Language and Its Public in Late
> Antiquity and the Middle Ages*

At the end of *Sense and Sensibilia*, J. L. Austin announces in no uncertain terms that certain kinds of philosophical argument require a
radical response. When a doctrine is based on "a question that *has* no answer . . . a quite unreal question," we shouldn't try to "patch it up a bit
and make it work properly; that just can't be done. The right policy is to
go back to a much earlier stage, and to dismantle the whole doctrine before it gets off the ground."[1] The dismantling I've attempted in the previous two chapters isn't intended to be quite so absolute; the doctrines I've
combated seem to me wrong, but a number of them are also enlightening.
Nonetheless, their influence in the discourse about realism needs to be
suspended before we can hope to grasp the nature of realist fiction. In my
first chapter, I argued that realist fiction is neither inherently repressive,
nor inherently liberating. It does not embody a closed "totalization," nor
does it provide a guaranteed escape from totalization by embracing a real
world of recalcitrant particulars. In the second chapter, I argued that realist fiction does not attempt "transparent representation" based on a more
largely referential use of language than one finds in other literary genres.
As a result, it is not stopped in its tracks by philosophical quandaries con-

---

[1] J. L. Austin, *Sense and Sensibilia* (Oxford: Clarendon, 1962), 142.

cerning the possibility of reference. Because it is primarily interested in connections, not objects, the kinds of referring it engages in needn't involve the high, "rigorous" stakes that certain kinds of philosophical accounts require. In this chapter, I shall offer a different view of realism, one that my first two chapters have from time to time gestured toward but haven't spelled out.

To do so, I shall make significant use of the work of Erich Auerbach, and especially of his magisterial work on the representation of reality from Homer to Woolf, *Mimesis*. I shall consider Auerbach's work in two lights—as an analysis of realism, and as a narrative text in its own right. I summon up this fifty-year-old book because no single work on realism since has achieved its critical "weight" and historical importance. (The nearest rival would probably be Barthes's *S/Z*.) As doctrine, I'll contend, *Mimesis* does not directly provide an adequate theory of realism. It does, however, suggest what an adequate theory of realism would look like, revealing the kinds of things it would need to take into account and the kinds of means it would employ to do so.

If we shift our focus from *Mimesis* as an account of realism to *Mimesis* as a text, as I shall do later in this chapter, the results are also valuable for the study of novels touched by historicism. Auerbach may not provide direct answers to all our questions; it's possible, however, to tease out of his practice as a narrator useful insights. His preferred mode of critical narration attempts a significant solution to the problem of imagining a noncoercive mode of telling a historical story (and imagining historical process), a mode in which plotting and telos do not wholly determine what we notice in individual moments and works. It does so by embodying a vision in which historical moments are knowable, but not because they are part of a deterministic, uni-directional chain, in which all meanings are construed in a way that will make the final link seem inevitable and good. Auerbach's mode of narration provides a suggestive parallel for the relationship between plot and local texture in realist novels. Beyond that, it is fully and subtly aware of the grand hermeneutical problem facing historicist realism: How is it that someone in the stream of history can have sufficient distance on other historical moments to give an account of them that achieves more than a simple reflection of his own historical moment? How are the claims of present and past to be weighed against one another, and what happens to the claims of historical representation when such weighing enters into it?

In the end, I shall be arguing, Auerbach's work finds its intellectual and aesthetic center in the novels of the nineteenth century. This is not to say that the works he most prizes or on which he writes with the keenest insight necessarily come from that period. It is to say that the habit of mind he brings to these works is one fundamentally influenced by the achievements and problems of that period. Auerbach's works accordingly have much to offer anyone with an interest in the habit of mind that I shall be arguing is central to historicist realism, if we are willing to draw upon and extend his insights, attending to the implications of his analysis and to his own practice as a narrator.

Auerbach and the Shape of Realism

Figural Realism and Modern Realism

In *Mimesis*, Auerbach is intent on isolating the different ranges of phenomena various authors and ages were willing to include in their representations of the real. The attitudes toward reality he describes embody complex attempts to make sense of the world, attempts informed and constrained by the movements of history and society. In principle, they are open to the sort of examination that would begin with theory; in practice, however, as with many other complex human activities, it is less cumbersome and less potentially misleading to describe them in action. Auerbach centers his discussions with detailed analyses of how relatively brief literary passages enact a particular attitude toward reality. He prefers common language over a specialized critical vocabulary, and it serves him well. When he writes of the lack of "tension" in the Homeric epic, for instance, he makes a stylistic point and at the same time suggests volumes about a certain kind of aristocratic ethos.[2] His distrust of abstraction (which distrust, as we shall see, is for him theoretically grounded) leads him to avoid terms of art; when he finds himself compelled to employ them, it's usually with a difference. The crucial concepts of the separation and mingling of styles, for instance, lead not to further abstract stylistic speculation, but back to the concretions of the text, and to the ideologies those texts concretely embody.

There is one moment in *Mimesis*, however, when Auerbach finds himself entirely at ease in providing an extended theoretical discussion of a seminal stylistic feature; indeed, should that discussion prove insufficient, he refers us to his previous work for further clarification. This involves the question of figural representation, of the "figura." Even here his eye is on the specific and the concrete. He wants his contemporary readers to understand figural realism, because the existing critical languages not only failed to understand figural realism, they actively pre-

---

[2]   Erich Auerbach, *Mimesis* (1946), trans. Willard R. Trask (Princeton: Princeton University Press, 1953), 4; hereafter cited in the text.

empted it, in favor of inappropriately allegorical interpretations or (more rarely) a too-simple "realism." Without a knowledge of the figura, we might take Dante's Beatrice to be either a character who abstractly and allegorically stands for church doctrine, or (in an outmoded, "romantic" mode) simply a girl who lived at a certain time and became part of Dante's earthly love-story. Understanding how figural realism works can take us beyond both these views.

According to Auerbach, figural realism arises from the Christian beliefs that history has a providential design, and that the lowly and everyday may be imbued with cosmic importance (a belief understandable enough as part of a religion in which God is physically born into the family of a laborer). In general, we might expect the representation of spiritual reality to emerge at the expense of the representation of the concrete specificities of specific historical moments, and vice versa; and indeed, in standard allegorical interpretations, that is precisely what happens. Figural realism is different. "In this conception, an occurrence on earth signifies not only itself but at the same time another, which it predicts or confirms, without prejudice to the power of its concrete reality here and now. The connection between occurrences is not regarded as primarily a chronological or causal development but as a oneness within the divine plan, of which all occurrences are parts and reflections. Their direct earthly connection [to each other] is of secondary importance, and often their interpretation can altogether dispense with any knowledge of it" (555). David was an actual historical king and at the same time a foreshadowing of Christ. Unlike allegorical interpretation, figural interpretation insists on the literal, concrete, historical existence of both figure and fulfillment. It locates and describes reality in history by specifying a method of viewing earthly occurrences that reveals their participation in a larger structure. This structure, in turn, makes reality real. Figural realism suggests that all parts of earthly life have the potentiality to be linked to the larger scheme of Christian history, and hence to participate in the ultimate human reality.

Figural realism is not our realism. We can, however, extrapolate from it a simple, general model of what any account of the realism of any period should look like, of the elements and relationships it should include. I believe that an adequate theory of literary realism must take the *general form* of Auerbach's description of figural realism. Attempts to theorize different kinds of realism must specify the field of mundane phenomena that have the potentiality to be revealed as participating in or constituting "the real." They must also specify a larger structure that has the potentiality to confer reality on the phenomena. Finally, they must specify the nature of the link between the larger structure and the mundane phenomena. For both figural and modern realism, I'll be arguing, the larger structure that confers reality has a particularly intimate connection with the mundane: this is one reason why figural realism has a significant affinity with modern realism, despite the fundamental differences between the two. It is also why the two share such a pivotal role in Auerbach's history of realism. But this need not be the case: one can imagine realisms in which that which confers reality on the mundane is entirely transcendent, instead of being, as the Christian story is, at once mundane and transcendent.

Conceiving of realism in this way has consequences for the critiques of realism we discussed in previous chapters. It renders incoherent the suggestion that realism involves creating the illusion of something called "direct" representation, or depicting reality as "natural." For according to our model, realism involves, on a fundamental level, structures and relationships, not the "immediate" presentation of objects or even situations. The model we have derived from Auerbach also, though perhaps less obviously, undercuts the attempt to describe realism in a purely formal way—as, for instance, Jakobson does when he suggests that the effect we call "realism" will occur whenever literary conventions are altered in certain ways. For the phenomenal content of our model does not have the status simply of neutral material that "motivates" a structure of relationships.[3] Our model of realism suggests that not just any kind of phenomenal content will suffice for realism: as a result, realism must involve more than literary convention, which presumably could be altered to suit any kind of content, in line with the thinking that demotes content to the status of "motivation" for form. In figural realism, for instance, that which can become real must be, in the requisite sense, historical. A larger point is involved here, which to their credit most of the attackers of realism, and especially those who fear its "totalizing" tendencies, grasp quite well. Literary realism always carries with it an ontological claim. It does not attempt to represent the world "directly"; it does claim to tell us what our world is really like. Even the subtlest attempts to set aside this claim do so at the cost of falsifying its nature.

If we wish to apply this general model to the nineteenth-century realist novel, we will need to describe the field of phenomena that realism promotes to the status of the (potentially) real. We'll also need to identify the

---

[3]   Roman Jakobson, "On Realism in Art," in *Readings in Russian Poetics*, ed. Ladislav Matejka and Krystyna Pomorska (Cambridge: MIT Press, 1971). Marshall Brown, in "The Logic of Realism: A Hegelian Approach," *PMLA*, 96 (1981), 224–41, makes the most sophisticated and stimulating attempt I know to define realism as "one literary mode among many, a structure of ordered negations perceived within the text quite independently of any relationship between the text and what is assumed to be its 'world' " (237).

structure that has the power to make these phenomena real, and to define the mechanism that connects the structure and the phenomena. I shall maintain that the peculiar predicament of modernity creates a situation in which both the structure that confers reality on particulars, and the particulars themselves, are located entirely in the sphere of the social and historical quotidian. Further, I'll suggest that the mechanism that unites structure and particulars is a dynamic metonymy, which operates both in the text and in the specified real world. To clarify what I'm driving at here, it will be useful to return to *Mimesis*, this time attending to the general shape of Auerbach's critical narrative. Auerbach's work will again prove suggestive, though uncovering its suggestions will require some digging.

Auerbach's critical narrative is many-layered, and its allegiance to historical particularity means that no simple pattern will emerge from it. It nevertheless has a peculiar coherence. The narrative moves toward two principal moments of achievement: the works of Dante and the nineteenth-century French realist novel. The juxtaposition of a single author against a century of novel-writing suggests a certain tension.[4] This feeling is enhanced when we consider the nature of the two climaxes in Auerbach's story. Even the first climax is inherently contradictory. Auerbach considers Dante's achievement double-edged: its clairvoyant vision of the realities of this world, which become luminously significant because of their part in the universal scheme, proves so piercing that it destroys the figural framework that allows it to occur. The "Christian idea of the indestructibility of the entire human individual" is at the basis of Dante's vision (199). When, after death, individuals find themselves indestructibly present for eternity, what's humanly essential about them gains a centered, fully expressed reality it could never possess in the temporal order of earthly existence. The love of life of Cavalcante and the stern republicanism of Farinata are no longer obscured by the shifting currents of mundane existence: they burn with a clear and unquenchable flame. But such is the genius of Dante that this very revelation of the essence of mundane life turns against the divine scheme that makes it possible: "by virtue of this immediate and admiring sympathy with man, the principle, rooted in the divine order, of the indestructibility of the whole historical and individual man turns *against* that order, makes it subservient to its own purposes, and obscures it. The image of man eclipses the image of God. Dante's work made man's Christian-figural being a reality, and de-

---

[4]   For an account that places the anticlimactic "plot" of *Mimesis* in a different light, see Timothy Bahti, *Allegories of History* (Baltimore: Johns Hopkins University Press, 1992), 137–55. Bahti provides a discriminating and massively informed critique of Auerbach and indeed of historicism itself along the lines of de Man's version of deconstruction.

stroyed it in the very process of realizing it. The tremendous pattern was broken by the overwhelming power of the images it had to contain" (202). There seems to be something, even in Dante's realism, that prevents the emergence of a stable, "totalized" vision for very long.

After Dante, a full realism comes into its own only in nineteenth-century French fiction. As Auerbach moves through his analyses of Stendhal and Balzac, one senses the potentialities of this new realism emerging. We are given, to be sure, no extended description of a representational technique like the figura; instead, there are more general references to the vision of historicism and in particular to the apprehension of "the present as history" (480). But these suffice, and we anticipate the emergence of another Dante. In Flaubert a new realism seems to flower. Stendhal had been too attached to an eighteenth-century view of man against society; Balzac had been too flamboyant, melodramatic, and eclectic in his intellectual underpinnings. Flaubert, however, achieves a truly serious depiction of everyday life, as Madame Bovary sits across from her husband at dinner and Flaubert's language allows the meaning of her existence to emerge. There is even an echo of the discussion of Dante's figural realism in Auerbach's mention of the "mystical-realistic insight" (487) informing Flaubert's view that any piece of reality, if described in a fully adequate language, "interprets itself and the persons involved in it far better and more completely than any opinion or judgment appended to it could do" (486). Language, used in accord with this insight, allows Flaubert to present his subjects "as God sees them, in their true essence" (487).

Yet when we come to Zola, we discover that Flaubert's "mystical-realistic insight" and the "objective realism" to which it leads have grave limitations. There were, to be sure, hints of deficiency even as Auerbach was describing Flaubert's greatness and the conditions from which it arose, for Flaubert's fictional world was depicted as possessing qualities that must give us pause: the lack of any narrative issue to the lives of the characters, the lack of any "common world" of intelligence that they might share, the lack of clear connections between characters and the historical stream. Indeed, in Flaubert's radically secular world the very "mystical" weight which language itself must bear seems incongruous and disquieting. But only the challenge of doing justice to Zola leads Auerbach to register the full significance of the differences between Flaubert and his predecessors: "When we compare Stendhal's or even Balzac's world with the world of Flaubert or the two Goncourts, the latter seems strangely narrow and petty despite its wealth of impressions" (505). The contrast with Dante, whose vision of earthly individuals becomes so intensely and grandly real that it breaks the mold from which it emerges, could hardly be greater.

The contrast is worth exploring. Auerbach provides an analysis of the writers' class affiliations that helps to explain the thinness of vision he deplores in Flaubert and the Goncourts. But the simultaneous success and failure of realism in the nineteenth century, the inability of all parts of the realist project to coalesce into a luminous whole, reminds us of another and even larger story, especially when seen in the light of Dante—the story of the rise of a modernity in which connections weaken and links break. It's surely significant that the source of Auerbach's vision of Dante was Hegel, a figure who, as Habermas has forcefully reminded us, heralded and theorized the coming of a modernity ruled by "diremption."[5] I suspect that Auerbach's picture of Dante has at least as much to do with the nineteenth century as it does with the thirteenth.

Auerbach's Dante, in the plenitude of his achievement, stands as a measure of what modern realism can no longer fully accomplish, because nothing like God's vision of an eternally present history is available to it. Auerbach's notion of the figural, then, may be a projection into the past of what realism ought to be able to do but cannot in its more recent form. There is surely a utopian ring to his description of the figural vision itself, with its remarkable mixture of a youthful vitality ("figural interpretation with its living historicity, though scarcely primitive or archaic, was assuredly a fresh beginning and rebirth of man's creative powers") and a mellow, wisely nostalgic age ("a great culture had to reach its culmination and indeed to show signs of old age, before an interpretive tradition could produce something on the order of figural prophesy").[6] Figural realism, thus characterized, seems to promise a renewal of energy but also to preserve a venerable cultural tradition. In its youthfulness, using the media of the visual arts, it can appeal to the illiterate medieval masses; in its maturity, it can appeal to the clerisy—and also to the historian who looks back on it. How poignant a dream for Auerbach, himself at the end of a rich European tradition, as he sat in Istanbul awaiting a coming "simplification" that would destroy the rich European literary tradition he was chronicling! What vision could more eloquently and compactly indicate by contrast the debility of the modern world? Dante, in becoming the poet of *earthly* existence and shattering the figural vision, figures the moment when an entry into modernity makes the grasp of totality no longer possible. To be sure, the compact definitiveness of the dramatic moment

---

[5] Jürgen Habermas, *The Philosophical Discourse of Modernity* (1985), trans. Frederick Lawrence (Cambridge: MIT Press, 1987). In his various commentaries on *Mimesis*, Auerbach says much about Vico and almost nothing about Hegel. There is a brief mention in "Epilegomena zu *Mimesis*," *Romanische Forschungen*, 65 (1953), 15, where he suggests that *Mimesis* would be "unthinkable in any tradition other than that of German Romanticism and Hegel" (my translation). For a stimulating discussion, see Timothy Bahti, "Vico, Auerbach, and Literary History," *PQ*, 60 (1981), 239–55.

[6] Erich Auerbach, " 'Figura' " (1938), in *Scenes from the Drama of European Literature* (Minneapolis: University of Minnesota Press, 1984), 56–57.

when Dante bursts the old paradigm is denied to the new age and the new realism, products and producers of the tentative and the anticlimactic. Modern realism is born not from a sense of plenitude, but from a sense of loss. For modern realism, plenitude of life or of meaning is a dream and would be an achievement; it is not something taken for granted, assumed, or posited.

In their different ways, then, Dante and Flaubert point to what we identified in Chapter 1 as the constitutive problematic of nineteenth-century realism, and to the historical situation that gives rise to that problematic. Whatever one might think of the objective validity of Auerbach's vision of Dante, his intuition that a definitive, "finished" realism never emerges in the nineteenth-century novel seems to me entirely accurate of the novelistic tradition with which I shall be directly concerned, the British novel, and of the other traditions with which I am familiar. What gives these works some measure of unity is not that they share a common achievement, but that they encounter common problems in pursuit of a broadly similar project, and that the nature of the problems is such that the best that can be achieved is a set of partial successes. At the most general level, the realist novel attempts to forge connections between the disparate elements of a reality seen as radically historical, and to place the reader in a fruitful relationship with the tentative totalities it creates.

Nineteenth-Century Realism and the Quotidian

Figural realism rests upon a well-articulated system of distinctions. Even though all the phenomena its operations link have a mundane aspect, the Christian story can be isolated from all other stories we might construct to make sense of the mundane world. If we attempt to apply the general model of realism we earlier extracted from figural realism to a world that is definitively "after Dante," the components of the model shift and become elusive. Figural realism, we recall, posits a mechanism that links certain aspects of the mundane world to a transcendent structure that renders them real. We might suppose that, with any recourse to a transcendent and timeless level of reality no longer possible for modern realism, the whole notion of constructing a realism through linking different levels of reality would become impossible. I'd like to suggest, however, that a recourse to a more fundamental level of reality persists, despite the collapse of metaphysical supports. The vision of reality does not collapse into a homogeneous quotidian. Instead, the quotidian itself splits apart into a seemingly endless set of possible levels, the identity and coherence of which are underwritten by a sense of historical structure and progression. That which makes reality real is immanent in the mundane itself; it is what orders and gives meaning to the epiphenomena of everyday life. What makes reality real is a process. The level of reality that becomes fundamental is the one most fully informed by that process.

Auerbach himself seems to have his eye on what confers reality on mundane phenomena in modern realism when he defines the workings of figural realism. The modern equivalent of the figura plays the role of defining opposite, when Auerbach remarks that "the connection between [mundane] occurrences is not regarded as primarily a chronological or causal development but as a oneness within the divine plan, of which all occurrences are parts and reflections" (555). Chronological and causal development are what modern realism depends upon; they lie at the heart of realism's sense of historical process. But just how they operate is understood differently by different authors, not to mention critics and theorists. As we shall see, it rarely involves what has come to be known as "providential history" or "simple teleology." For Lukács, for instance, the teleology is real enough, but it's anything but simple. For him, the direction in which history is moving determines what is most real, singling out the entities and events that help history on its way. Artists, according to Lukács, make us aware of the vectored movement of history by depicting, in the formulation Engels had made canonical, typical characters in typical circumstances. From other points of view, and in works in which the real is imagined in terms that are less directly historical (and less ultimately euphoric), structures like the "marriage market" or "the workings of Parisian society" play a similar role. There's a direct parallel here with what happens to the "separation of styles" that is key to so much of Auerbach's stylistic analysis. When a strict separation of styles is abandoned, as it is in the nineteenth-century novel, this does not mean that we are left with a single, undifferentiated style. Instead, what we might call a "mundane" style becomes enriched and diversified, even though certain extremes of style are denied it. At the same time, an attempt to identify authoritative styles and voices within the limits of the mundane becomes a central concern.

In figural realism, the real-world events joined in the figura exist on an equal plane in that they are all thought of as historical, but the divine story always has priority. For modern realism, questions of priority are rarely so clear-cut. We do not think of one event as the fulfillment of another. Further, it's difficult to capture a static pattern that underlies historical existence and then depict its fictional equivalent, in synecdochic form, because the patterns keep changing and are informed by historical particularities that are always different. Modern realism must capture the logic and texture of a process; it cannot produce pictures of a persisting form. It substitutes for the stasis provided by the divine incarnation a focus on movement and relationship as the ultimate realities; bereft of a definitive point of departure and return, it has an inherent bias to follow metonymical relationships moving in time.

In *S/Z*, Barthes analyzes Balzac's novella *Sarrasine* in an attempt to demonstrate that realism wishes to achieve an impossible plenitude, only to discover a terrifying absence that reveals the inherent nullity of the realist project. I believe that what Barthes has actually discovered is evidence of problems and maneuvers that are likely to arise when realism must find within the quotidian itself a structure that can determine what aspects of the quotidian are "real."

For Barthes, the necessary failure of realist representation is figured in *Sarrasine* by the death of the protagonist, the sculptor who gives the story its name—and especially by his doomed attempts to attain reality. Sarrasine, Barthes suggests, attempts to penetrate beneath the surface of quotidian experience and the text, but discovers to his horror either nothing—or simply a proliferation of further surface.

> [The] impulse, which leads Sarrasine, the realistic artist, and the critic to turn over the model, the statue, the canvas, or the text in order to examine its back, its interior, leads to a failure—to Failure—of which *Sarrasine* is in a way the emblem: *behind* the canvas Frenhofer [a painter in Balzac's *Lost Illusions*] envisions there is still nothing but its surface, scribbled lines, an abstract, undecipherable writing, the unknown (unknowable) masterpiece which the inspired painter ends up with and which is in fact the signal of his death: *beneath* La Zambinella (and therefore inside her statue) there is the *nothingness* of castration, of which Sarrasine will die after having destroyed in his illusory statue the evidence of his failure: the envelope of things cannot be authenticated, the dilatory movement of the signifier cannot be stopped.

Sarrasine cannot, then, give the social surface greater reality by connecting it to a realm beyond or beneath it, for no such realm exists. In a similar way, the realist world Balzac depicts in *Sarrasine* demands the impossible achievement of a total vision of society by connecting everything in the world with everything else: "all the cultural codes, taken up from citation to citation, together form an oddly joined miniature version of encyclopedic knowledge, a farrago: this farrago forms the everyday 'reality' in relation to which the subject adapts himself, lives. One defect in this encyclopedia, one hole in this cultural fabric, and death can result. Ignorant of the code of Papal customs, Sarrasine dies from a gap in knowledge."[7]

Nineteenth-century realism is in my view anything but oblivious to the fact that there is nothing behind the canvas, if what we expect to find there involves some sort of transcendental plenitude. Instead, it finds a more fundamental source of order and reality on the surface itself. The cultural "encyclopedia" to which Barthes refers is a "farrago" only to those for whom metonymy involves a constant slippage from one damn thing to another. If instead we take metonymy to involve the creation of a set of "contingent" (that is, historical) and systematic relationships, filling in the gaps as occasion serves and our needs require becomes a reasonable pastime, for metonymical systems function in and only in the realm of the concrete and historically specific.[8] The realist projects Barthes describes, then, may be seen as neither so compulsive nor so hopeless as he would make them.

Metonymy and Realism

I have argued that the levels of reality nineteenth-century realism brings into relationship are aspects of the quotidian. I have also suggested in passing that metonymy is the mechanism nineteenth-century realism employs to do this. It is now time to discuss this latter claim more fully. In making metonymy the organizing principle for what amounts to a worldview, I am invoking a line of analysis most fully developed by the historian Hayden White. White, following Kenneth Burke, identifies four tropes as "master tropes": metaphor, metonymy, synecdoche, and irony. For White, these tropes function somewhat in the manner of Kantian categories: they serve as "paradigms, provided by language itself, of the operations by which consciousness can prefigure areas of experience that are cognitively problematic in order subsequently to submit them to analysis and explanation. That is to say, in linguistic usage itself, thought is provided with possible alternative paradigms of explanation."[9] The

[7] Roland Barthes, *S/Z* (1970), trans. Richard Miller (New York: Hill and Wang, 1974), 122–23; 181; 184–85.
[8] Barthes makes it all but inevitable that the structure of society as expressed in its norms and customs will seem a "farrago" by defining what he calls the "referential" code in *Sarrasine* as a collection of clichés (205–6; 262).
[9] Hayden White, *Metahistory* (Baltimore: Johns Hopkins University Press, 1973), 36. Compare Jonathan Culler, "The Turns of Metaphor," in *The Pursuit of Signs* (Ithaca: Cornell University Press, 1981), 217, which suggests that such tropes are said to embody "common patterns of sense-making."

master tropes thus offer general descriptions of modes of interpretation and habits of thought, not linguistic decoration; accordingly, the presence of local metaphors in an extended passage need not imply that the overall mode of the passage is itself metaphorical.

Roman Jakobson made a pioneering contribution to the modern discussion of tropes with his celebrated analysis of metaphor and metonymy. He distinguished between metaphorical uses of language that organize the world through similarity, and metonymical uses that rest upon relationships involving various kinds of "contiguity." Jakobson grounds this distinction in the structure of language itself. He associates metaphor with the "paradigmatic" axis of language (the "vertical" axis on which, for example, any number of nouns can grammatically replace one another as the subjects of sentences) and metonymy with the "syntagmatic" axis (the "horizontal" axis on which we string words together in a row to produce a sentence).[10] Jakobson makes a point of considerable importance for our purposes when he subsequently associates realist fiction with metonymy, and poetry with metaphor. Realist fiction, in Jakobson's view, is content to reproduce "contingent" relationships found in nature and society, whereas poetry creates nongiven meanings through metaphorical juxtaposition.

I follow White's lead in considering the master tropes useful in formulating basic modes of apprehending and ordering the world (though I do not believe that the tropes *produce* those modes). I also concur with Jakobson's identification of metonymy with nineteenth-century realism. But here I would make a distinction. Jakobson and those who have built on his work tend to stress the note of "mere" contiguity and contingency when they discuss metonymy. (Another relationship traditionally identified with metonymy, the relationship of cause and effect, is less frequently mentioned.) My emphasis is different. In my view, the "contiguity" characteristic of nineteenth-century realism is "contingent" only if the word sheds the random, just-happening-to-be-there associations sure to crop up if we are operating under the assumption that our experience is really flux.[11] In a historicist view (which, I believe, is the one we currently find ourselves living with, either by assent or by negation), life in

[10]   Roman Jakobson, "Two Aspects of Language and Two Types of Aphasic Disturbances," in Roman Jakobson and Morris Halle, *Fundamentals of Language* (The Hague: Mouton, 1956). These axes are in turn grounded in the functioning of the brain, discovered through studying language disorders.

[11]   The notion that our experience is "mere flux" is generally produced in two ways: either by draining experience of its temporal and social aspects, or by employing inappropriately "high" philosophical standards to create a binary opposition between flux and nonflux. (Yes, it's certainly true that our experience does not come to us by way of analytically true propositions, but that doesn't make our experience "mere flux"!)

history is contingent (as opposed to logically or conceptually necessary) just because it is historical. But this doesn't imply that life in history is random, or that our experience is flux. Viewed in this light, metonymy involves significant real-world relationships, with cause and effect replacing contiguity as the typifying instance.

This line of argument has the following remarkable consequence: Auerbach's figural realism embodies *either metaphor or metonymy, depending on one's assumptions about the nature of reality.*[12] From a postmodernist point of view, figural realism would seem clearly *metaphorical* in nature, since its connections are ungrounded. A historicist point of view would draw the same conclusion on different grounds. Figural realism for a historicist involves comparisons made in defiance of what has become our normal sense of temporal progression, historical causality, and cultural specificity: it skips over large tracts of history, and interests itself in connections having nothing to do with the chains of causality that form the essence of the metonymical webs that make up our normal historical existence. Jonah's emergence from the belly of the whale has, from either point of view, no "real" connection with Christ's resurrection: the only connection is one made by a willful analogizing. Yet if we shift our ontological and metaphysical presuppositions, the picture changes. From its own point of view, figural realism evokes an important kind of "contiguity," provided by God's intention and the divine vision, which brings seemingly disparate pieces of mundane history into an ordered contact. To the extent, then, that we imagine ourselves back into a situation in which we can take seriously the claims of figural realism to capture the real, we find ourselves conceiving of the connections it makes as *metonymical* in nature. After Dante, figural realism appears to be founded in a species of metaphor—as does much of the literature we most prize. But that is because our culture's sense of the real has itself shifted. I draw from this the following moral, which extends Jakobson's contention that metonymy is the trope characteristic of nineteenth-century prose fiction: the defining trope of *all* realisms is metonymy—but it is metonymy *as defined in the light of the ontology to which a given realism appeals.*

If we return to our model of realism, then, I am suggesting that the

---

[12]   There's nothing new in the idea of a certain amount of play between tropes. Under the right conditions, it is argued, metaphor can "become" metonymy, or can be shown to depend on the making of metonymical connections, and vice versa. Yet what is usually demonstrated in this regard is that tropes can be made to slide into one another, if you apply the right kind of pressure: see, for instance, Jonathan Culler, *On Deconstruction* (Ithaca: Cornell University Press, 1982), 243–45. In the Appendix to this book, I suggest that the pressure in fact results from viewing one trope from the point of view of another, not from any inherent linguistic indeterminacy: instead of a slide, we find something more like a motivated and explicable gestalt switch.

mechanism that connects different levels in modern realism is a *historicist metonymy*. This metonymy assumes as many inflections as there are realist novelists. Its general character may be indicated by tracing its workings in a pivotal realist author.

In the second chapter of *Waverley*, Scott describes the effect on a north-of-England Jacobite of an eighteenth-century method of disseminating news. Sir Everard Waverley discovers that his younger brother has taken a series of steps (the "events" of the passage that follows) to accommodate himself to Hanoverian rule, in pursuit of governmental favors:

> Although these events followed each other so closely that the sagacity of the editor of a modern newspaper would have presaged the last two even while he announced the first, yet they came upon Sir Everard gradually, and drop by drop, as it were, distilled through the cool and procrastinating alembic of Dyer's Weekly Letter. For it may be observed in passing, that instead of those mail-coaches, by means of which every mechanic at his sixpenny club may nightly learn from twenty contradictory channels the yesterday's news of the capital, a weekly post brought, in those days, to Waverley-Honour [Sir Everard's country seat] a Weekly Intelligencer, which, after it had gratified Sir Everard's curiosity, his sister's, and that of his aged butler, was regularly transferred from the Hall to the Rectory, from the Rectory to Squire Stubbs' at the Grange, from the Squire to the Baronet's steward at his neat white house on the heath, from the steward to the bailiff, and from him through a huge circle of honest dames and gaffers, by whose hard and horny hands it was generally worn to pieces in about a month after its arrival.[13]

A certain kind of critic would be pleased to call this passage, and especially its self-proclaimed digression, mere "local color." In fact, it embodies a quality of historical representation central to Scott and his contribution to the realist novel in Europe. What's truly remarkable here is Scott's detailed dwelling on the hands, first metaphorical and then quite actual, through which *Dyer's Weekly Letter* passes. In another kind of novel such a description might act simply as a metaphor for the workings of Sir Everard's mind, which handles information with a slow repetitiveness that wears it to pieces, shorn of the drama that might rouse him to action. Scott's interest is richer than this—he's offering *Dyer's Weekly Letter* not as a freely chosen metaphor, but as part of a historical structure that in very

---

13   Scott, *Waverley*, ed. Andrew Hook (Harmondsworth: Penguin, 1972), 39.

fact existed. Sir Everard's mind, the mail service, the weekly newsletter, and all the people who receive it are for Scott parts of a complex and systematic whole in which personality, ideology, technology, and even geography all interact. Sir Everard lives in the north of England, and not in London, for a mixture of very good reasons, the most immediate of which is that, having refused to abandon his Jacobitism, he is persona non grata to the Hanoverian government. Yet subtler issues than direct governmental pressure are also involved. Staying in the economically and socially archaic north allows him to maintain his political allegiances; at the same time, it tends to neutralize his political potency and indeed to guarantee that it will diminish with time, which is precisely why the government tolerates him, so long as he keeps his distance. The government, which allows him and his party to calcify in the north, knows that it can count on the more supple generation epitomized by his turncoat brother to cooperate and move into the future, leaving Sir Everard and his like behind as historical curiosities. The mail service is a causal agent in this process. Its inefficiency helps to ensure that Sir Everard will stay insulated from the current of action: it keeps him in a state of political (and perhaps more important, of mental) suspended animation, where issues never quite come to a head. The mail service, then, isn't a metaphor for Sir Everard's mind: it *is*, to a certain determinate extent, his mind, and both it and his mind, through Scott's description, find a place in history.

In a relatively early, untheoretical and "humanist" version of the attack on realism, some critics dismissed Scott because his "local color" did not come in the form of what they called "spiritual symbols," symbols representing timeless aspects of the mysteries of human personality and destiny. Their idea seemed to be that a novelist has unlimited choice among milieus with which to surround a character, and that in all cases a novelist should choose to portray milieus designed to reveal timeless truths. Scott's novels seem to me valuable and interesting precisely because of their distance from such an aesthetic, with its basis in romantic notions of the symbol as an ultimate metaphor, piercing to the heart of things by dissolving the metonymical relationships that inform history and our normal experience. The revelation that the conjunction of Sir Everard and the mail service creates has nothing to do with hidden personal depths or with eternal truths. It's very much on the surface. To read the passage is to experience the unfolding of a complex and proliferating surface network, not the dropping away of the surface to reveal unexpected depths. The passage, then, is *not* centrally informed by metaphor. It *is* informed by metonymy. But how?

Returning to the passage, we can see that the level of the individual sentence or phrase cannot be relevant here. The most conspicuous local trope in the passage is not a metonym, but a laboriously introduced metaphor describing how the pieces of information "came upon Sir Everard gradually, and drop by drop, as it were, distilled through the cool and procrastinating alembic of Dyer's Weekly Letter." We could, to be sure, lavish time and ingenuity on this metaphor. We might discover that it figures the workings of the passage, acting as a metaphor for metonymy or even for figurality itself.[14] What sort of alembic is Scott employing as he distills history, here and throughout the novel? Is it an ancient, magical, transformative (and thus metaphorical) device, or as Lukács would have it, a modern, scientific apparatus that purifies and transmits real essences in a metonymical fashion?

It would be a mistake to limit ourselves to this level of analysis, which comes so readily to mind and pen. If we use "metonymy" to describe the passage as a whole, we must be working on a higher level of generality, referring to a habit of mind that, like the "dominants" of Russian Formalism, transforms the nature of subordinate fictional structures. Scott's metonymy would then involve a play of mind over a web of systematic historical and cultural connections, often causal in nature, among phenomena existing at all levels of our experience—phenomena ranging in this case from technological modes of distributing information, to political systems, to individual minds and dispositions, to physical and unique newsletters. Metonymy would impute to these phenomena and the ways in which they are connected an existence and validity independent of the mind observing them: it would claim to represent what we might call "real-world connections." This is why Scott, in selecting his metonymical descriptions, has a range of choice more limited than is available to the producer of metaphorical descriptions.

In suggesting that metonymy involves a "habit of mind," I'm extending Donald Davidson's valuable commentary on the workings of the trope critics most readily discuss, metaphor. Davidson suggests that metaphors don't convey a special kind of cognitive content, a deeper meaning hidden beneath a literal meaning. Instead, a metaphor works by bringing two objects together and telling us to compare them: it doesn't stipulate the kind of result that will follow, it simply tells us to compare and see what happens.[15] In suggesting that metaphor involves a process

[14]   I owe the hint that Scott's extended metaphor might itself be a metaphor for metonymy to Mark Seltzer: the reading of the metaphor I've given here is, however, my own, and extends an earlier analysis in Harry E. Shaw, *The Forms of Historical Fiction* (Ithaca: Cornell University Press, 1983), 133–34.

[15]   Donald Davidson, "What Metaphors Mean," *Critical Inquiry*, 5 (1978), 31–47; compare Hayden White, "The Historical Text as Literary Artifact" (1974), in *Tropics of Discourse* (Baltimore: Johns Hopkins University Press, 1978), 91: "The metaphor does not *image* the thing it seeks to characterize, *it gives directions* for finding the set of images that are intended to be associated with that thing."

with certain limits, not a closed formula, Davidson has produced a description of how many tropes behave. (Auerbach's figura is, I believe, no exception: its function is not to reveal abstract truths but to create a universe by engaging us in the unfolding of a certain kind of story.) Tropes select certain phenomena and ask the mind to perform a range of procedures with them: they offer a series of procedures according to which we may select and organize experience.

The passage describing Sir Everard invites us to set our minds to work in certain ways over certain kinds of materials. It involves us in a practice of thinking, a mode of drawing connections, that Scott would claim puts us in contact with the way history itself works. On the simplest level, reading through the passage (and others like it) teaches us to attend to the importance, oddness, unpredictability, and yet ultimate rationality of chains of cause and effect. Beyond that, we learn to recognize the complex intermeshing of the individual consciousness with larger technological, social, and political structures. And when we read a number of such passages, dispersed through the narrative, all different in content but similar in the mental operations they evoke from us, we realize that Scott's novel provides a way of processing historical reality in general—or more precisely, since history "in general" doesn't exist for a historicist like Scott, of processing each historical conjuncture as it comes along. This passage is extremely pure and concentrated in its demonstration of the working of Scott's characteristic mode of historical representation—it would strike one as a tour de force, if one supposed that Scott interested himself in demonstrations of technique as such. Usually the metonymical mode doesn't find such compact expression in Scott. Yet the insistence that there is a web of causality informing our situations in history, that we are part of our time in a sense that is concrete, specifiable, and representable—this is a quality that fills Scott's works and gives them whatever vitality and interest they possess. It is also a quality we find in the realist novels that follow his. At its most ambitious, realist fiction offers us the possibility of participating in the workings of a mind capable of following the unfolding of that most real of modern phenomena, the workings of history itself.

Georg Lukács, as we saw in the first chapter, has suggested that Scott's historical fiction acted as a necessary prelude for modern realism. The novel learned to represent historical process where (after the rise of historicism) it could hardly be avoided, in attempts to represent the past; it then applied what it had learned to capture "the present as history." As a piece of "conjectural history" that helps to clarify an important literary development, Lukács's account has much to recommend it. For more local purposes, it requires adjustment. The shorthand image Lukács provides can make it seem that a historicist consciousness suddenly precipitated in Scott's works in a lump sum, which was then passed on to other novelists to spend as they would. If we wish to tell a heuristic story about the development of the nineteenth-century novel, placing Scott at its pivot, we might better imagine a series of uneven developments in response to, and sometimes in opposition to, Scott's discovery of the fictional means to represent history seen in the mode of historicism. However that may be, Scott's metonymical representation was the key to his contribution to European realism, a source of pleasure for readers and an expansion of the European consciousness.

The nineteenth-century novel's characteristic exploration of the inner life has a crucial relationship to the development of historicist representation, as a fascination with the inner lives of individuals and with the structure of societies spur each other on. One can hardly develop a historicist vision of other societies unless one can maintain a certain distance from one's own society, and the sense of possessing an interiority under siege from the outside world would seem an excellent candidate for producing the necessary distance. In *Persuasion*, for instance, a deepened sense of the power of individual memory, and an attempt to base a sense of individuality on the shaping of memories, accompanies an awareness of historical change as an ongoing process. *Persuasion* explores Anne Elliot's consciousness of the past with a richness unparalleled elsewhere in Austen's works; it also resonates with a sense of the need for her society to put its past behind—and a hint that the results could be bracing and exciting.[16] The connection between these two aspects of the past is not made explicit. The emergence of both in this early nineteenth-century novel is, however, suggestive.

Thus far, we've been speaking of metonymy as it informs social and historical representation. Its logic of connection-making, however, also makes itself felt with regard to the relationship between reader and text, especially through the agency of the narrative voice. It would be absurd to claim that realism is alone in attempting to create an affective bond

---

[16] This is not to say that *Persuasion* itself directly depicts such a change, certainly not the simple replacement of one class by another—a phenomenon that rarely occurs in history, except perhaps by massacre. Perhaps a better formulation would be that Austen's depiction of the barrenness and stultification of the gentry (and token aristocrats) in this novel leads her to produce a wish-fulfillment fantasy of escape and renewal, which fantasy resonates with (but is not identical with) changes actually occurring socially, for which she has no name. For a dismissal of the idea that *Persuasion* depicts actual class change, or even a defective ruling class, see John Wiltshire, *Jane Austen and the Body* (Cambridge: Cambridge University Press, 1992), 157–59. In a deft revelation of signs of mutual influence between Scott and Austen, Jane Millgate remarks that what "distinguish[es] *Persuasion* from its predecessors in the Austen canon is precisely its heightened sensitivity to the temporal dimension of the lives of its characters" ("*Persuasion* and the Presence of Scott," *Persuasions*, no. 15 [16 December 1993], 188).

with its reader. What does need stressing, however, especially in the light of the "passive/duped reader" implications of the notion that realism deals in "transparent representation," is the complexity of the bond realist narrators create with their readers. Such a bond is not unique to realism; I hope to show, however, that the essence of the bond in question has much to do with involving the reader in imagining realist metonymical connections. As a result, what we might call the "texture" of our relationship to the narrator becomes entwined with our sense of reality as the novel construes it. This doubling may add to the unwelcome sense some readers feel that realism has totalizing designs on them.

Auerbach as Narrator

Auerbach's practice as a narrator of the history of realism is at least as suggestive as his commentary on realism. The vision of history his narration embodies and the rhetorical relationship it creates with the reader are both instructive. I am not suggesting that Auerbach's narration is just like the narration of a novelist, or that it could be. I am suggesting that the habit of mind embodied in his narration is in crucial respects comparable to the habit of mind realist novels wish to evoke. In this section, I shall be claiming that *Mimesis* shows that narration can be "directed" without being "closed" or "providential," and that though historical narratives are inevitably inflected by our present-day concerns, they need not be overwhelmed by them.

Narrative itself has been placed under rigorous scrutiny and found wanting on these scores and others. What we can for convenience refer to as "traditional" narratives—roughly speaking, narratives which relate a series of connected events (or several overlapping strands of internally connected events) under the control of an implied author—have been viewed with particular suspicion. I believe that the shape of novelistic plots is more likely to energize a novel's realist vision than to embody or control it, and in the chapters that follow I will pursue this issue further. Here, I shall concentrate on what I consider the prime and originating instance of the alleged trouble with "traditional" narratives—the issue of their being "teleological" in the sense that they culminate or eventuate in an ending, finding themselves directed by their endings or at least impelled toward them.

An important part of the critique of traditional narratives has focused on what they leave out. As the work of the *Annales* historians has made apparent, traditional narrative is not well suited to register aspects of history that persist—or that change, if at all, only gradually over very long periods of time. One of Auerbach's most stimulating critics has found the critical narrative of *Mimesis* blind in just this way. Bruce Robbins, in his remarkable study of servants in Western literature (a study much involved with the nature and limitations of realism), suggests that for Auerbach, European realism until very recently simply excluded servants and the rest of the lower classes from serious representation. According to Robbins, however, servants have played a more positive role in literature. Perhaps most important, they have consistently gestured toward normally untapped possibilities for human solidarity and community, creating what Robbins memorably refers to as moments of "abridged, transient utopia." Auerbach misses this, according to Robbins, because the kind of progressive, "providential" story he's telling, with its denouement at the end (in which a place for the lower classes finally begins to emerge), cannot pause to register it. As Robbins puts it, "providential history . . . devalues and suppresses premature or untimely manifestations of that which it reserves for the end. There exist resources of political precedent that cannot be perceived at all if they cannot be neatly placed in an upward trajectory. Inattentive to the contingency of history, this vision squanders its available energies."[17] It seems to me, however, that it is possible to discriminate between ways in which different forms of narrative tend toward their endings, and to suggest that in different kinds of narrative progression the influence of the ending may produce qualitatively different results.

When we speak of "providential history," few names come so readily to mind as that of Macaulay. Macaulay is eminently capable of producing narratives that march toward a better world, looking neither to the right nor to the left. A reasonably simple set of rhetorical maneuvers assists him. He is a master at creating vivid contrasts, especially in the form of stylistic antitheses, designed to preclude the thought that other positions might lie between them. Once he has accomplished this, his main work is done. It's then easy enough to weight the scales toward one pole, the "progressive" one:

> History is full of the signs of this natural progress of society. We see in almost every part of the annals of mankind how the industry of individuals, struggling up against wars, taxes, famines, conflagrations, mischievous prohibitions, and more mischievous protections, creates faster than governments can squander, and repairs whatever invaders can destroy. We see the capital of nations in-

[17]   Bruce Robbins, *The Servant's Hand* (New York: Columbia University Press, 1986), 32, 33.

creasing, and all the arts of life approaching nearer and nearer to perfection, in spite of the grossest corruption and the wildest profusion on the part of rulers. . . . Now and then there has been a stoppage, now and then a short retrogression; but as to the general tendency there can be no doubt. A single breaker may recede, but the tide is evidently coming in.[18]

In his description of literary representations of the Highlanders—he's thinking primarily of Scott here—Macaulay produces another set of ringing antitheses: "Whatever was repulsive was softened down: whatever was graceful and noble was brought prominently forward. . . . Artists and actors represented Bruce and Douglas in striped petticoats. They might as well have represented Washington brandishing a tomahawk, and girt with a string of scalps."[19] Having established the truth about romanticized depictions of the Highlanders (and given Scott what appears to be intended as a knock-out blow in the process), Macaulay can then go on, in the manner of one writing an epitaph, to praise the virtues of Highland life Scott had praised before him, without having to fear that readers might imagine he's telling a story tempered and diffused by the sort of ambivalence about progress Scott consistently betrays.

A more subtle case is provided by J. G. Frazer, in the grandiloquent close of *The Golden Bough*. He too is telling a story of progress, or at least of what seems empirically to be a certain progression:

We may illustrate the course which thought has hitherto run by likening it to a web woven of three different threads—the black thread of magic, the red thread of religion, and the white thread of science, if under science we may include those simple truths, drawn from observation of nature, of which men in all ages have possessed a store. Could we then survey the web of thought from the beginning, we should probably perceive it to be at first a chequer of black and white, a patchwork of true and false notions, hardly tinged as yet by the red thread of religion. But carry your eye farther along the fabric and you will remark that, while the black and white chequer still runs through it, there rests on the middle portion of the web, where religion has entered most deeply into its texture, a dark crimson stain, which shades off insensibly into a lighter tint as the white thread of science is woven more and

[18] Macaulay, "Southey's Colloquies on Society," in *Selected Writings*, ed. John Clive and Thomas Pinney (Chicago: University of Chicago Press, 1972), 76.
[19] Macaulay, *History of England*, in *The Works of Lord Macaulay*, ed. Lady Trevelyan, 8 vols. (London: Longmans Green, 1866), vol. 3, 51.

more into the tissue. To a web thus chequered and stained, thus shot with threads of diverse hues, but gradually changing colour the farther it is unrolled, the state of modern thought, with all its divergent aims and conflicting tendencies, may be compared. Will the great movement which for centuries has been slowly altering the complexion of thought be continued in the near future? or will a reaction set in which may arrest progress and even undo much that has been done? To keep up our parable, what will be the colour of the web which the Fates are now weaving on the humming loom of time? will it be white or red? We cannot tell. A faint glimmering light illumines the backward portion of the web. Clouds and thick darkness hide the other end.[20]

Frazer's argument by image is in every way more supple than Macaulay's argument by antithesis. The "providential" end has become an aspiration, not a certainty—something that, though it would complete the image nicely, does not seem inevitable. (The rhetoric of hope and uncertainty is of course intended to make us *wish* for the proper ending—or at the very least, to emphasize the importance of what the ending will be.) We might, for instance, just imagine an extension of the image that answered Frazer's question, "will it be white or red?" with "Neither—it will be black." The image does however produce a certain kind of orderliness, akin to the insistent order produced by Macaulay, and it suggests a clear set of preferences and values. The introduction of a third term, however, leaves its destabilizing mark, as does the openendedness of metaphor itself.

The story Auerbach tells in *Mimesis* bears little resemblance to Macaulay's single-filamented fiber-optic cable, in which impurities may impede but cannot long prevent the progress of the light. Its structure is more like Frazer's twisted web. As we saw earlier in this chapter, though, Auerbach's narrative is structured around two climaxes, provided by the works of Dante and of the nineteenth-century French realist novelist, and these climaxes are oddly asymmetrical. The achievement of the great French realists is somehow deficient and lacking, each time in a different way. When the common man comes to the fore in nineteenth-century French realism, this does not occur in the works of Flaubert, whose quasi-mystical belief in the power of the detail to rise to the universal recalls most clearly the artistic and philosophical basis of Dante's figural realism. Instead, it occurs in the works of Zola, whose achievement as a whole we

---

[20]   J. G. Frazer, *The Golden Bough*, abridged ed. (1922; London: Macmillan, 1963), 933–34.

can hardly consider the culminating step in a triumphal, ascending, "providential" history. What Auerbach provides, then, is a pattern of seeming repetition with qualitative difference. In *Mimesis*, Auerbach sets in motion a variety of narrative strands, braided together by the repetition of certain motifs to form a metonymical network much like that I have ascribed to realism in general and to the historicist vision of historical causality.[21] His extreme sensitivity to particular historical contexts prevents him from "flattening out" the narrative of history in the way that would produce the "providential" history Robbins has in mind.

In fact, providential history, in which everything significant strives toward a single controlling end, denies all that is most fundamental in Auerbach's vision. In the most extended discussion of his assumptions and methods available in English, Auerbach describes the ontological and epistemological nature of the kind of reality he seeks to capture through his version of historicism: "Historicism has nothing to do with eclecticism. . . . We cease, it is true, to judge on the basis of extrahistorical and absolute categories, and we cease to look for such categories, precisely because the universally human or poetic factor, which is common to the most perfect works of all times and which should consequently provide us with our categories of judgment, can only be apprehended in its particular historical forms, and there is no intelligible way of expressing its absolute essence."[22] Auerbach, working in the tradition of German hermeneutics, balances an attempt to "free" individual historical moments so that they can be seen in their own terms, with an attempt to avoid depriving them of all continuity with one another and with our own present (which would mean depriving us of any chance of understanding them and engaging with them). So that it begins to seem that the large story Auerbach is telling exists in the service of the particular moments, and not the other way round. The end of the narrative is, to be sure, important for Auerbach—it's unsurprising that most of my examples have been drawn from his book's final chapters. But this is because his allegiance to particular moments is so pronounced that he is largely unwilling to generalize about them until they have all been experienced with as little generalization as possible. ("If it had been possible, I would have used no general expressions at all, but would have conveyed the thought [of my book] to the reader entirely through the presentation

---

[21] Auerbach's complexly braided narrative is described by W. Wolfgang Holdheim, "Auerbach's *Mimesis*: Aesthetics as Historical Understanding," in *The Hermeneutic Mode* (Ithaca: Cornell University Press, 1984), 211–25, a book dedicated to Auerbach's memory.
[22] Erich Auerbach, *Literary Language and Its Public in Late Latin Antiquity and in the Middle Ages* (1958), trans. Ralph Manheim (Princeton: Princeton University Press, 1965), 13.

of a series of individual examples.")[23] In subsequent chapters, I'll be arguing that this valuation of the local is also characteristic of realist narratives that take the shape of novels. In the works with which we'll be concerned, as in Auerbach's critical practice, reality resides in specific moments and local textures. The plots of these novels are there not to control our access to the real, but to enable it; they exist in the service of fantasy and desire, providing the energy that enmeshes us in and propels us through the minute-by-minute reading experience. Especially for those who doubt the existence of "the universally human or poetic factor" that Auerbach believes can reveal itself only in particular historical incarnations, his attempt to tell its story may well seem an enabling fiction, not a controlling telos. At any rate, it is clear that allowing the telos of the story to select examples and to determine their significance in advance would place him exactly where he doesn't want to be—he'd find himself telling a story in which generalities are more real and more intelligible than historical particularities. His focus on the concrete instance is intended to give each work he studies the freedom to be itself—which, for a historicist like Auerbach, means in part achieving a living connection with the larger course of history, but not being simply or entirely constrained by that course. It also provides a large measure of imaginative freedom for Auerbach as a realist narrator, allowing his mind to move purposefully but without coercion among historical moments.

At one point in *Mimesis*, Auerbach states that "only through a disposition, and active will, to give the world a form does the gift of understanding and rendering the phenomena of life acquire the power to transcend the narrow confines of one's own life" (259). In the concluding pages, it may, despite all I've argued to the contrary, seem that his attempt to "give the world a form" has finally overwhelmed his fidelity to the particular. He suggests that the concern for undifferentiated reality that characterizes the modernist novelists heralds an impending "simplification" that will return us (though, as always with Auerbach, with a difference) to the undifferentiated reality of Homeric epic:

> It is still a long way to a common life of mankind on earth, but the goal begins to be visible. . . . So the complicated process of dissolution which led to fragmentation of the exterior action [in literature], to reflection of consciousness, and to stratification of time seems to be tending toward a very simple solution. Perhaps it will be too simple to please those who, despite all its dangers and catastrophes, admire and love our epoch for the sake of its abundance of

[23]   Auerbach, "Epilegomena zu *Mimesis*," 16.

life and the incomparable historical vantage point which it affords. But they are few in number, and probably they will not live to see much more than the first forewarnings of the approaching unification and simplification. (552–53)

Even in this passage, however, one hears a cadence rather different from that of the brisk, lively, forward-looking Macaulay. Creating a cyclical return to the beginning may, it is true, seem just as blinding and constraining as creating a march toward the ineluctable future. Yet, as with the way in which the nineteenth-century French novel does and does not echo Dante, Auerbach nowhere suggests that the modern lack of differentiation is just the same as the ancient, or is a sublation of the ancient. The only thing approaching a privileged moment or "end" here would appear to be the incomparable historical vantage point which Auerbach's own cultural moment affords him. But this doesn't come at the end of the story, and it doesn't guide the story. Instead, it seems to be an unexpected by-product of a process that itself moves in surprising ways—and that will brush aside the very historical moment Auerbach prizes.

The turn of the story Auerbach has been tracing toward "a very simple solution" cannot be entirely welcome to him. He faces the coming "simplification" with a dignified, this-worldly heroism; he confronts complex, disheartening forces far beyond his control without fear or reproach, and with a regret that is quiet and well controlled. In part because of the democratic impulse Robbins so perceptively isolates, he refuses to engage in a rhetoric of despair. He rests content with suggesting that perhaps the coming simplification "will be too simple to please those who, despite all its dangers and catastrophes, admire and love our epoch for the sake of its abundance of life and the incomparable historical vantage point which it affords" (553). Beneath the mourning here, there may also be an undertone of relief. Auerbach writes very much as a modern intellectual, fully aware of the human costs that have been borne to create the human variety and the summits of artistic achievement he so much admires. He knows cultural guilt. No doubt there are many reasons for his melancholy acceptance of what looks to be the inevitable destruction of the conditions of possibility for his own vision and narrative practice. Among them could there be a wish to escape an Olympian position "above" the particularity he chronicles, an attempt to subject even that position more fully to the contingency of history?

Auerbach's tenuous vantage point brings us to a topic centrally important to the practice of nineteenth-century realist novelists—the question of how narrators are positioned, of the space they occupy, how they came to be positioned there, and what kinds of power, authority, and vision their positioning affords them. The remarkably fluid positioning of Auerbach's narrative voice—a fluidity we also find in the great nineteenth-century realist novels—is well exemplified in another passage wherein he discusses the coming "simplification." As we turn to consider this passage, I ask the reader to ignore for the moment the square brackets I've inserted at its beginning and its end:

> [What takes place here in Virginia Woolf's novel is precisely what was attempted everywhere in works of this kind (although not everywhere with the same insight and mastery)—that is, to put the emphasis on the random occurrence, to exploit it not in the service of a planned continuity of action but in itself.] And in the process something new and elemental appeared: nothing less than the wealth of reality and depth of life in every moment to which we surrender ourselves without prejudice. To be sure, what happens in that moment—be it outer or inner processes—concerns in a very personal way the individuals who live in it, but it also (and for that very reason) concerns the elementary things which men in general have in common. It is precisely the random moment which is comparatively independent of the controversial and unstable orders over which men fight and despair; it passes unaffected by them, as daily life. The more it is exploited, the more the elementary things which our lives have in common come to light. The more numerous, varied, and simple the people are who appear as subjects of such random moments, the more effectively must what they have in common shine forth. [In this unprejudiced and exploratory type of representation we cannot but see to what an extent—below the surface conflicts—the differences between men's ways of life and forms of thought have already lessened. The strata of societies and their different ways of life have become inextricably mingled. There are no longer even exotic peoples. A century ago . . .] (552)

In reading this passage, if we omit the material enclosed in square brackets at the beginning and the end, it appears to record Auerbach's own, "transparent" views, presented as eternal verities.[24] If, however, we read

[24]   One reason why I shall linger over this passage is that it has been taken, not only by Robbins, to be a direct report of Auerbach's own views—and as such has been used as evidence of a simplistic, providential vision of history ("We modernists have discovered the culminating truth of Western society, as Macaulay mistakenly thought he had"). For a discriminating discussion of Auerbach's complex relationship to modernism, see Geoffrey Green, "Erich Auerbach and the 'Inner Dream' of Transcendence," in *Literary History and the Challenge of Philology*, ed. Seth Lerer (Stanford: Stanford University Press, 1996), 214–26.

the passage in its entirety, our sense of its status shifts. (The shift increases as we fit the passage into larger stretches of Auerbach's chapter—and his text as a whole.) We discover Auerbach submitting himself for a time to the mind of the movement he is describing—allowing himself to act as the medium through which that movement voices its own beliefs. It isn't completely wrong to see Woolf and her generation as intermingled with Auerbach's own position, and with his own narrative positioning; it's crucial to the rhetorical effect of such writing, however, that in this passage and others like it Auerbach never entirely merges his narrative voice and discursive position with the voices he seeks to bring to life. But this begins to suggest that Auerbach is writing in a mode that's like the novelist's Free Indirect Discourse (or, for convenience, FID), which, according to its traditional description, is also characterized by a shifting, elusive interplay of the voices of narrator and depicted character.[25] I shall argue that Auerbach's discourse here is indeed, mutatis mutandis, a close critical counterpart to FID—or perhaps better, that both exemplify a common impulse. Free Indirect Discourse has often been considered a synecdoche for larger matters, among them Bakhtinian dialogism, literariness, and the essentially citational nature of all discourse.[26] I shall make the more limited claim that FID, which is generally recognized as a centrally important representational mode in nineteenth-century realist novels, itself typifies a mode of making contact with history central to the realist mind.

One of the attractions of Free Indirect Discourse is that it allows the critic to move effortlessly from theoretical generality to grammatical and stylistic specificity. FID makes its presence felt in ways that can be specified with some grammatical precision. The most important of these are that, in representing speech or thought, FID (1) omits such "tags" as "he said that" or relegates them to the status of "comment clauses" that are parenthetically interspersed in the speech or thought of a character but never introduce them; (2) refers to the character whose speech or thought it reports in the third person; and (3) subjects the verbs in the report to a temporal "back-shift" in comparison to how they would be expressed in direct discourse. Thus Free Indirect Discourse ("He hoped he would get a gift") is often said to blend characteristics of Direct Discourse (" 'I hope

---

[25] There are many conflicting accounts of Free Indirect Discourse. The common (and I believe correct) notion that FID involves a blending of voices, which I here invoke, has, for instance, been strongly attacked. A useful overview is provided by Shlomith Rimmon-Kenan, *Narrative Fiction: Contemporary Poetics* (London: Methuen, 1983), 106–16. Brian McHale's, "Free Indirect Discourse: A Survey of Recent Accounts," *PTL*, 3 (1978), 249–87, gives an excellent critical account of different views through the mid-1970s. Monica Fludernik, in *The Fictions of Language and the Languages of Fiction* (London: Routledge, 1993), sets a new standard in this and related areas of narrative poetics.

[26] Thus, as Rimmon-Kenan reports, FID has been considered "a miniature reflection of the nature of both mimesis (in the broad sense of representation) and literariness" (114).

I'll get a gift,' he said") and Indirect Discourse ("He said that he hoped he would get a gift").[27]

It's possible to make the case that, according to these strict grammatical criteria, the part of the long passage from Auerbach I've cited that's not in brackets is written in FID. Clearly enough, it contains no "tags." We aren't told that someone or something believes that x or says that y. So the first criterion poses no problem. To meet the second and third criteria is more complicated. To begin with, we need to identify the "person" whose thoughts are being reported, so that we can see whether this person is referred to with first-person pronouns. In the passage, the "person" could only be an "entity"—namely one aspect of the mind of the age Auerbach seeks to describe. If we accept the idea that FID can represent the thoughts of such an entity, then we find ourselves in a position to say (unsurprisingly) that the mind of the age isn't referred to as "I" or "We," and the second criterion has been met. (The only first-person pronoun that exists in the German original of the passage is the "our" in "our life"; this seeming exception will be dealt with shortly.)[28] But the final criterion, involving a "back shift" in tense, raises difficulties. The passage begins with a past-tense verb, which is promising, in the sentence "And in the process something new and elemental appeared" (*"sichtbar wurde"*). After that, however, Auerbach uses the present tense. This might seem fatal to the claim that the passage is in FID. In fact, it isn't. In FID, what is called the "gnomic present" can be employed for general statements of timeless truths.[29] (If the first sentence of *Pride and Prejudice* were embedded in a passage of FID, it would still be the case that "It *is* a truth universally acknowledged, that a single man in possession of a good fortune, must be in want of a wife.") We can account for the use of the first-person pronoun I mentioned above ("The more it is exploited, the more the elementary things which our [*unser*] lives have in common come to light") as another aspect of this "gnomic" style.

A telling confirmation that Auerbach is indeed employing a "gnomic" style here emerges when we compare his evocation of the world of Woolf with his evocation of the world of Dante:

[27]   This descriptive genealogy is a handy pedagogical tool; much recent work, however, denies that FID is actually linguistically derived from either Direct Discourse, Indirect Discourse, or both.

[28]   For the German versions of the passages I shall be concerned with, see Auerbach, *Mimesis: Dargestellte Wirklichkeit in der abendländischen Literatur* (1946), 3d ed. (Bern: Francke, 1964), 513–14; 185.

[29]   This includes, of course, truths a particular character believes to be timeless. See Günter Steinberg, *Erlebte Rede* (Göppingen: Alfred Kümmerle, 1971), 225–35. See also F. K. Stanzel, *A Theory of Narrative* (1979), trans. Charlotte Goedsche (Cambridge: Cambridge University Press, 1984), 196–97, and Gérard Genette, *Narrative Discourse Revisited* (1983), trans. Jane E. Lewin (Ithaca: Cornell University Press, 1988), 53.

For it is precisely the absolute realization of a particular earthly personality in the place definitively assigned to it, which constitutes the Divine Judgment. (193)

It is precisely the random moment which is comparatively independent of the controversial and unstable orders over which men fight and despair. (552)

In the first passage, about Dante, we have what we might call a "historicized gnomic" style. Auerbach is voicing what seems a timeless truth *from the point of view of Dante's age*, but certainly not from his own. In the second passage, I believe that we face precisely the same phenomenon—except that Auerbach happens to be voicing an attitude that exists in his own age. This is why it's easy to take the second passage as a simple transcription of his own beliefs.[30]

Some would find it superfluous to make a grammatical case that the long passage we have interested ourselves in is in Free Indirect Discourse. Bakhtin and others have suggested that in the final analysis FID cannot be pinned down to a set of grammatical specifications. What matters is the orientation of an utterance, in a given context, to other utterances—or to put it another way, the number of voices we hear as we read it.[31] Following this account, we might say that in the central part of the passage, Auerbach, so to speak, "lowers" his habitual voice, allowing the voice of the other to emerge for a moment, instead of describing it from the vantage point from which he marshals his total narrative. If we miss this shift of voice at the opening of the passage, it becomes clear on the way out, as we hear the words, "In this unprejudiced and exploratory type of representation we cannot but see. . . ." These words are unmistakably those of Auerbach as narrator and disposer. When we read them, we realize that what we've been listening to is the simulation of a set of beliefs characteristic of a limited historical moment. We've heard a "historicized gnomic," not a timeless or universal gnomic. Auerbach thus opens

[30] Manheim's translation makes these two passages appear exactly parallel in verbal detail as well as in nature and function. In fact, Manheim (quite properly) translates two different words as "precisely" here: *"eben"* appears in the passage on Dante, while *"gerade"* appears in the passage on Woolf.

[31] In "The Problem of Speech Genres," in *Speech Genres and Other Late Essays*, trans. Vern W. McGee (Austin: University of Texas Press, 1986), 60–102, Bakhtin grounds this view in a distinction between "sentences" (which can be adequately dealt with by using formal systems such as grammar) and "utterances" (which, just because they occur in specific life contexts and form part of larger dialogic patterns, cannot). For an enlightening discussion of the relationship between Bakhtin's views on FID and those of his compatriot Volosinov, see Gary Saul Morson and Caryl Emerson, *Mikhail Bakhtin* (Stanford: Stanford University Press, 1990), 123–71.

up a space between the modernist project and his own—which, to be sure, values unprejudiced (or "random") elements, but which, in its narrative form, discovers a historical form that unites them.[32] Ultimately, we realize that the passage uses FID to voice such a moment, because movements in and out of FID for this purpose are typical of *Mimesis* as a whole. We recognize this rhythm because we've seen it before. By bringing us to recognize such effects, Auerbach ultimately adds another layer to his book, as *Mimesis* itself becomes a historicized account of historicized moments.

The difference between the "gnomic present" in the two sentences I've cited above is intriguing. Precisely where is Auerbach with respect to the differing mentalities he is representing? In the first sentence, he seems to be playing a disappearing game, in which he effaces himself almost entirely, to become the voice of Dante's Christianity. In the second, the situation is more equivocal. We cannot believe that a twentieth-century critic could in fact embrace Dante's world view as true and self-evident; we can just believe that such a critic might himself embrace the views he attributes to Virginia Woolf. In my view, Auerbach here enacts a problem that

[32]Auerbach's prominent use of the concept of "randomness" in *Mimesis* can lead to misunderstanding. (Among other things, it can seem to identify his work with certain modernist assumptions that do not underlie it.) He speaks, for instance, of how "Stendhal and Balzac took random individuals from daily life in their dependence upon current historical circumstances" (*Mimesis*, 554) as the basis for their realism. The *selection* of individuals made by the novelists may be presented as "random"; the *lives* of the characters are hardly random, for they are embedded in a specific and indeed a constraining historical milieu, which works in anything but a random manner and is itself a product of a historical development with its own inner logic. By the same token, Auerbach suggests that he himself chose the texts on which *Mimesis* is based "at random, on the basis of accidental acquaintance and personal preference rather than in view of a definite purpose" (556). Again, what gives "random" its meaning here is primarily that to which it is opposed. In terms of a deductive or scientistic standard, Auerbach's choices are "random"; there is nothing *logically* necessary about what he happens to have read or happens to value. But this randomness isn't random at all from another point of view, that of the story of his own life, which in turn itself has a determinate relationship to institutions of learning and finally to the culture whose artifacts he is studying. Auerbach's randomness has little to do with the epistemology of the subject, stranded in an instant and showered by discrete sensory impressions; it has everything to do with, and is entirely compatible with, the notion of a reality constituted by a rich web of social narratives and a general embeddedness of the individual within history. We may associate two kinds of claims with Auerbach's concept of the random. The *methodological* claim suggests, negatively, that thesis-ridden selections of material for study will falsify historical reality; positively, it suggests that large cultural movements will be present, in however differential a form, in all significant works of art produced at a given period. What we might call the *ontological* claim involves the principle that the most basic and significant human realities can be apprehended only as a historically linked set of concrete moments, not as abstractions or instances of a larger law we can adequately state in general terms—the sort of law that would allow us to select (logically) "necessary" examples of its workings.

must inescapably arise given the sort of story he's telling and the beliefs about narrative and reality that undergird that story. Is Auerbach "in" or "above" the ideology he depicts? Or is he somehow occupying both positions, either simultaneously or in rapid succession? This problem of the narrator's positioning reflects hermeneutical puzzles that are part and parcel of the rise of a historicist point of view. So all ages are equally immediate to God, because each has its own unique and systematically coherent view of reality? How, then, if you belong to such a society, could you possibly enter the mind of another cultural or historical moment? How could you escape the modes of understanding peculiar to your own?

In my view, Auerbach is neither "in" nor "above" the views of reality he represents for very long.[33] By using such techniques as Free Indirect Discourse to support his realist critical narrative, he manages to oscillate between these positions (a movement that fixed-frame epistemologies will miss). Some have found in Free Indirect Discourse the ultimate expression of the most sinister aspects of realism, the most definitive example of realism's attempt to make its disciplinary activities seem natural—or nonexistent. (In FID, the argument runs, the narrator fixes the meaning of a character's speech or thought, while simultaneously giving the impression of not being there at all, of acting simply as a mouthpiece.) But at its best, Free Indirect Discourse is not limited to such coercive functions. Precisely because the narrator's voice in *Mimesis* goes in and out of FID, the technique models a serious and promising attempt to know and depict the other, not to override the other. In the realist novel, as in *Mimesis*, nonprovidential narratives can solve problems that seem insoluble when viewed in synchronic terms. The possibility that such narratives might be efficacious is crucial to the account of realism I am offering, for they are the ideal means of involving the reader in the process of following the metonymical chains of relationship that, for modern realism, are at the heart of historical reality.

My claim is not that there is something inherently or necessarily efficacious about the narrative forms Auerbach employs in *Mimesis*. The attempt to make such a claim would be self-defeating: we'd find ourselves back in the world where artistic forms have inherent ideological forces.

---

[33] Others differ. Claus Uhlig, "Auerbach's 'Hidden' (?) Theory of History," in *Literary History and the Challenge of Philology*, 43, for instance, believes that Auerbach places himself in an unearned position above history: "Dante, not unlike God Himself, may well be able to pass judgment on all history, but when Auerbach, centuries later, with evident sympathy shares this view of the world, he, as an earthly human being who certainly does not occupy the seat of umpire Providence, appears to be much closer to the tenets of an unhistorical existentialism than to those of a theoretically sound historicism."

What I do claim to have demonstrated is that the notion that Auerbach's narration takes the form of a "providential narrative" simply won't do. Auerbach doesn't position himself at the end of a cumulatively "rising" tide of improvement, and he doesn't align himself with the winners of his development. (Whether the course his narrative charts produces winners is itself deeply problematic.) He oscillates from a position above the narrative to one within it, but he never streamlines his narrative so that it will place him in a secure position, safely at its end. Auerbach's narrative mode has the same status in my argument as does the philosophical narrative pursued in J. L. Austin's *How to Do Things with Words*. Each exemplifies a path along which productive encounters with reality can occur. Different though they are, these two paths seem to me to suggest some conclusions about realist narratives in general. Among them is the conclusion that the meaning and effect of realist narratives are unlikely to be entirely determined by any univalent shape eventuating in a dominating ending. In Auerbach as in Austin, what matters most is the path taken. In realist novels, too, the local texture, the moment-by-moment reading experience is more likely to be where the vision of reality lives. (This is a problem I will have more to say about in the next chapter, as I discuss Jane Austen and her plots.)

In demonstrating the insufficiency of the notion that Auerbach has produced a "providential narrative," I have not demonstrated that his more complex approach to the historically other succeeds, much less that it defines a method that guarantees success. There nonetheless seems something promising in a narrative stance so richly responsive to the hermeneutical problems that must accompany any attempt to grasp the historically other. And it's enlightening to observe how important to his efforts is the general narrative context he accumulates—the context that, for instance, allows us to hear his narrator's commentary on Dante behind the commentary on the modernist novel. By such means he creates a mode in which he can depict his own position as one involving both historical perspicacity and also an inevitable (and enabling) historical positioning. Yet there is no way to determine in advance how successful he will be in grasping historical moments other than his own (and indeed in grasping his own historical moment). We simply have to wait and see, judging the results by employing the realist techniques of understanding available to us in our own historical situation. From the point of view of this study, this is an expected and welcome situation. Once you suppose that you can determine in advance and as a matter of theoretical or philosophical necessity the success or failure of an attempt to grasp reality, you've entered a path that, especially in the present intellectual climate, is likely to lead to the conclusion that realism cannot possess the quality of open-endedness it requires, and hence that realism can't work. (Some matters *can* be predicted in advance, and this is one of them.)

The situation here parallels the situation of realist reference, in which it is just as crucial to maintain the possibility of an open-ended relationship to things in the world (especially when those "things" are structures and relationships). My account in the previous chapter attempted to do this in two complementary ways. Acceding for the moment to the fashion of treating reference as a synchronic, non-narrative phenomenon, I suggested that reference is best viewed as open-ended and potentially productive—which is to say that the important work occurs after we've referred to something; it's not presupposed in the act of the reference or contained in that act. My account left open the possibility that reference might be productive by denying (as I've just denied in the case of Auerbach's narrative techniques) that we can determine in advance what it can accomplish (or, on a more basic level, whether it is possible). If, however, we think of a diachronic *process* of reference and not of single referential moments, we can give a stronger account, in which reference becomes inherently recursive and therefore fitted (though not certain) to produce ever-richer knowledge about the objects it embraces. This would not be possible if the kinds of results reference could lead to were settled in advance, or if narratives such as Auerbach's could be reduced to the form of providential narratives. My accounts of realist reference and of Auerbach's realist narrative converge in stressing the centrality of a supple hermeneutic practice.

The open-endedness I'm insisting on here seems inherent in the process of making metonymical connections. Engels celebrated it when he spoke of the "triumph of realism"—of the way Balzac found himself revealing radical truths about the old order denied by his consciously conservative ideology. Realism seeks to involve us in a certain kind of attention to a certain range of phenomena, but the results can be unexpected. To exemplify this potentiality of realism, I'd like to return to the passage, analyzed earlier in this chapter, involving Sir Everard and the mail service. When Scott describes the process by which news reaches the north of England, I argued, he is describing how a material practice shapes, indeed constitutes, a form of consciousness that (as he elsewhere puts it) could not have existed either forty years earlier or forty years later. His metonymical representation reveals in action the conditions of historical possibility for such a mentality, allowing the reader to reconstruct it and thereby providing a model for how other historical mentalities and actions might be reconstructed. Ultimately, our participation in such imaginative recreation should lead us to view our own societies and our own historical selves as "other," as products of history, not nature.

Yet precisely by employing the mode of forming connections the passage invites us to share, we may find ourselves unwilling to acquiesce entirely in its sunny geniality. The passage celebrates the way in which *Dyer's Weekly Newsletter* "was regularly transferred from the Hall to the Rectory, from the Rectory to Squire Stubbs' at the Grange, from the Squire to the Baronet's steward at his neat white house on the heath, from the steward to the bailiff, and from him through a huge circle of honest dames and gaffers, by whose hard and horny hands it was generally worn to pieces in about a month after its arrival." But what if we place the emphasis, not on Sir Everard's mentality, but on the hands that wear the newsletter to pieces? Scott appears to take a certain satisfaction in the hardness and horniness of the gafferian hands, finding it entirely appropriate that they hold the newsletter after the softer hands in the larger houses do. He takes no interest whatever in evoking pathos or rousing indignation at the hands as symbolic of expropriated labor—or indeed, of promoting any part of his description to the status of the sort of symbol that might transcend or reverse the meaning of its context. If he has a "transient utopia" in view here, its nature is profoundly conservative. Does his interest in "the other" here involve a certain kind of social and historical policing? Does he wish to embed the dames and gaffers in an ineluctable historical framework, the better to contain their latent energies?

Virtually everything Scott wrote suggests that he views the metonymical links in the chain described in this passage as organic bonds of a particular, conservative kind. The description of the progress of *Dyer's Weekly Newsletter* celebrates the way in which a traditional, organic society is able, for a charmed and charming moment, to neutralize a technology that will in the long run become an agent of change. The dames and gaffers are given a ritual relationship with the newspaper. We may imagine them poring over it, perhaps repeating names and phrases with hushed knowingness, or perhaps with an ironical knowingness that doesn't really know. We cannot really imagine their learning anything useful from it, as their counterparts might in later years have learned, say, from Cobbett. Whatever their relationship to the news, it certainly won't eventuate in political action. In Scott's vignette, the medium that appears simply to disseminate "news" in fact articulates and even refreshes a very old chain of subordination. Indeed, the image of the hard and horny hands reducing the newspaper to simple materiality (by way of reducing it to nonmateriality, "wearing it out" physically) would appear to enact a wish-fulfillment. Isn't Scott gleefully seeing to it that the newspaper (which after all provides a link back to venial London and to the low cunning of Everard's "modern" brother) gets its just deserts? Isn't there a certain suspension of history here, to be sure entirely appropriate for the historical backwater Everard inhabits, but also with the special attraction of being effected by those who, from one point of view, might have the most to gain from the coming of modernity? But if this is true, might we not suspect that there's much about Scott's brand of realism which is inherently quietist in its politics? Historicism takes great pleasure in assuming an attitude that views all historical realities as equally immediate to God, equally valuable, equally apt to promote aesthetic pleasure as objects of contemplation. Yet what are we to say, finally, of such a seemingly catholic habit of mind? Doesn't it erect a binary opposition between, on the one hand, all those equally valuable historical objects, and on the other, us as historicist observers? And won't this in the end always mean that we will value ourselves more and the objects less? In more general terms, won't we find that in the very process of bringing the dames and gaffers into focus as objects of attention, we are complicit in a process with epistemological and ideological consequences that demean them?

These are issues we will pursue in the second part of this book. What needs to be said here is that the questions arise not as part of unmasking the text by bringing our superior wisdom to bear on it (from an unexplained platform of authority), but by working through its grain, employing methods and materials it itself has furnished. The questions arise from a hermeneutical encounter with the text, to which we inevitably and properly bring our own historical moment. To understand is not always to forgive: understanding can allow us to condemn the more definitively. Engaging in the sort of encounter I'm describing does, however, remind us that we too are creatures of history. Encounters involving this hermeneutical awareness can be productive in unexpected ways, as I trust this chapter's encounter with Auerbach has been.

4

Austen: Narrative, Plots, Distinctions, and Life in the Grain

> You should have distinguished.
> —Anne Elliot to Frederick Wentworth

> I was going on, but he was pleased to withdraw, leaving me [kneeling before him] on the floor, saying that he would not hear me thus by subtlety and cunning aiming to distinguish away my duty.
> —Clarissa Harlowe, describing her father

> Now, as I said, the way to the Celestial City lies just through this town, where this lusty fair is kept, and he that will go to the city, and yet not go through this town, must needs "go out of the world."
> —John Bunyan, *The Pilgrim's Progress*

To introduce her richly nuanced reading of *Persuasion*, Adela Pinch recounts how as a girl she would read that novel through again and again, so that she could reach the scene in which Wentworth writes his letter to Anne Elliot.[1] Sometimes, she tells us, simply reading the scene itself would suffice, but not always or even usually—which suggests that even when she read the scene by itself, the cumulative force of the plot made its contribution. A memory of the impetus of plot seems to have lingered, sometimes needing to be refreshed, sometimes waiting to be tapped.

Pinch's account reminds us that realist plots are, for readers, primarily a matter of developing affect, not of objective structural patterning. Pinch didn't contemplate the design of the plot or find in it a meaning, she drew

---

[1] Adela Pinch, "Lost in a Book: Jane Austen's *Persuasion*," *Studies in Romanticism*, 32 (1993), 97–117.

upon its energy. Plots are cumulative: in memory, they have the power to gather up and concentrate the moment-by-moment experience of reading a novel. But this happens as part of an unfolding temporal process. We can't simply rely on a general memory of a plot to energize a climactic scene. One reason for this is that a central function of plots is to get us into the grain of a novel. Our developing pattern of hopes and fears for the characters as the plot proceeds needn't necessarily involve vicarious identification with them; following the plot offers us a place at their level and in a temporal frame like theirs. Our participation in the plot facilitates our ability to imagine what it would be like to be affected by the forces that impinge on the characters, even though we know full well we are reading a novel, not living it. This may, indeed, be the most important reason why a reader might choose to prepare for a scene like the letter scene by reimmersing herself in the plot. To be sure, the letter scene offers an image of transcendence, as Anne leaves her apprehensions and the grain of her society behind. In this respect, the plot might seem simply to offer a lift-off mechanism that must be jettisoned when the proper altitude is reached. But the power of this gesture toward release itself depends upon the firmness with which *Persuasion* has hitherto avoided going "out of this world"—a stance that reasserts itself after the effect of the scene dissipates.

In the letter scene, there's an impulse to escape speech and articulation altogether; when Wentworth's pen drops, it says more than speech could ever say, as does his look of "glowing entreaty" as he hands her the letter.[2] But even these moments are prepared for and ignited by language, most dramatically by Anne's speech to Captain Benwick and in the wording of the letter itself. The fantasy fulfilled by the scene, for characters and readers alike, does not centrally involve finding a moment that transcends language; it is a fantasy of achieving perfectly adequate articulation and communication, through speech, gesture, the written word, and silences made full by the language that surrounds them. If we read through the letter repeatedly, it is to reexperience the perfectly voiced and articulated communication that following the plot has led us to desire to hear in it. The letter scene, drawing upon the cumulative force of *Persuasion*'s plot, extends and fulfills our wish for a silence that would leave social codes behind, but in doing so, it places that wish in relation to what the novel takes to be the inescapable prose of life. We stay in the grain.

This chapter will explore the place of the plot in the realist novel. I shall

---

[2]   Austen, *Persuasion*, ed. D. W. Harding (Harmondsworth: Penguin, 1965), 239; hereafter cited in the text.

be interested in the extent to which plots shape meanings, and kinds of plots have meanings. More broadly, I shall be concerned with the telling of stories in realist novels, whether this activity is performed by narrators or characters. The previous chapter's discussion of whether Auerbach offers a "providential narrative" in *Mimesis* touched upon the issue of whether realist plots are imaginatively or ideologically coercive; the discussion of this issue will continue here. I shall begin by offering a general assessment of the nature and function of realist plotting, and indicate how this assessment relates to the ideas about realism offered in the first part of the book. Next I shall discuss some significant views that betray a suspicion of plots in general, arguing that this suspicion rests heavily upon the rejection of a narrative process that depends upon the progressive creation of a web of distinctions. Because plot involves temporal ordering, larger questions of temporality are central here, including the suspension of normal temporality that occurs in moments of the sublime. Finally, I shall turn to the uses of plot in Austen's first and last complete novels, *Northanger Abbey* and *Persuasion*.

Thus far, I have been employing the term "plot" in an inclusive fashion. It will be helpful at this point to distinguish. For my purposes, plot as a static structure or pattern has little usefulness; accounting for realism requires that we think of plot as a temporal ordering that is part of the dynamic, developing transaction between narrator and reader (that is, part of the narrative itself, which includes much more than plot). This is the sense of plot on which we'll focus. Thinking of plot in this way already suggests that there are limitations to a now common conception of plot, to which we'll nonetheless need to attend: the notion that literary plots act as templates with a pre-given ideological meaning, and that they are drawn from a limited repertoire. We usually don't think of templates as dynamic or as evolving; they repeatedly impose the same pattern. A conception of plot as template seems a valid tool for assessing the ideological effects produced by a culture's novels in the aggregate. It can have considerable power in accounting for ideological constraints authors face: the classic case here would be the paucity of ways of plotting women's lives available in traditional fiction, a subject explored by such critics as Nancy K. Miller and Rachel Blau DuPlessis.[3] It is less useful in exploring how plots actually function in the reading experience of individual novels, for we don't read in the aggregate. The other kind of plotting that will concern us involves the act of shaping and thereby making sense of individual experiences, sequences of events, and lives. I'll normally refer to

[3]   Nancy K. Miller, *The Heroine's Text* (New York: Columbia University Press, 1980); Rachel Blau DuPlessis, *Writing beyond the Ending* (Bloomington: Indiana University Press, 1985).

this activity as "story-telling" and to the narratives that result from it as "stories." What distinguishes stories of this kind from dynamic plots and plots as templates is that, even in third-person narratives, they are typically produced by a novel's characters. The incidents shaped come from a character's past, which is viewed as the actual, limited past of an individual, not the past of narration in general ("In that part of the western division of this kingdom which is commonly called Somersetshire, there lately lived . . . "). And we see the shaping at work; it's something we are called upon to contemplate, which is to say that it's "thematized." We can also use the notion of "story-telling" to describe an activity engaged in by the narrator, especially a dramatized narrator. Here too we employ the concept when our interest is in how a human intelligence makes sense of life from a position within it. It would be possible to use this sense of "story" to describe how a narrator fills out an ideological template, but the usage would seem odd. Among other things, with templates, the shaping is done by the template.

Plots in their various guises, I shall be arguing, are not the key to realism, or its cornerstone. Their primary function is not to embody or impose meaning, but to lend force to our imaginings. The continuing and pervasive force of plots is to move us through the world of a novel. Sometimes they throw us up against an unwelcome reality.[4] They perform these functions by creating what Ralph W. Rader has aptly called an "objective fantasy," which involves us in a pattern of hopes and fears, which as readers we tacitly realize is based on our projected desires.[5] This can involve another aspect of what's often called "identification" with a character, which we've already seen is aided by the way in which plots place us in the grain of a story. We fully and dynamically imagine the situation of Dorothea Brooke because in following the plot of *Middlemarch* our hopes and fears are aroused on her behalf. Plots are primarily involved in the mobilization of the will; they are in this sense "rhetorical," for they call upon the reader to respond. They give force to our experience of the local texture of novels—the aspect of a novel which, as we saw in the previous chapter, most forcefully bears the signs of its involvement with reality. Plots remain subservient to our experience of a novel's texture: our place in the plot influences how we will take a scene in, but this is primarily because of the power of plot to accumulate our previous, local ex-

[4]   Compare Fredric Jameson's analysis of how Balzac's desire throws him against the texture of the realities of French society, in *The Political Unconscious* (Ithaca: Cornell University Press, 1981), 151–84.
[5]   Ralph W. Rader, "Defoe, Richardson, Joyce, and the Concept of Form in the Novel," in William Matthews and Ralph W. Rader, *Autobiography, Biography, and the Novel* (Los Angeles: William Andrews Clark Memorial Library, 1973), 31–72.

periences of the text. No doubt when we recognize that the plot of a novel we're reading is assuming the shape of a tragedy, this too shapes our expectations, but the meaning we're looking for in realist novels involves *this* tragedy and the social web that surrounds it and makes it possible. We can go further: when we read a realist novel, we expect that, even if the plot takes a tragic way, it will not turn out to be "tragic" in a classical or even a Shakespearean shape; it will be too weighted by a sense of the modern mundane. This indeed is a prime source of pathos—and of one familiar sense of the real. In *The Heart of Midlothian*, Scott has to assure us that David Deans is *like* a classical hero—which of course means that he isn't one. When Hardy insists that his novel is depicting a true, archaic tragedy, he's playing against our recognition that novels don't and can't do this.

The view of plot I've outlined here has been anticipated in the first part of this study. In the previous chapter, for instance, I was at pains to show that what Auerbach involves his readers in is not a "providential" narrative. One of the problems with the notion of the providential narrative is that it tends to reduce "narrative" to "plot." Any movement that leads to an end is taken to be controlled by that end. Now of course it's possible to adjust all the parts of a narrative to celebrate a triumphal march forward—which, in the terms we've been using, would mean to place all the resources of a work's narrative at the service of a certain kind of linear plot. Macaulay does this. This possibility, however, doesn't justify the identification of all kinds of linearity, much less of narrative coherence, with providential history. I therefore argued that Auerbach's narrative provides a significant way of coming to grips with history, one that transcends providential history. In Auerbach narrative isn't simply plot, and narrative doesn't by its shape mimic the actual movement of history. The movement of the narrative is, in the first instance, a movement of understanding—a path of approach, and way of taking in and making sense of historical process and what it has left behind. So too with realist novels. Our narrative experience of a novel may occasionally seem to us an experience of the movement of history itself—a reader of *War and Peace* may feel this way. But this is a second-order phenomenon, which has at least as much to do with the texture of the novel's vision of history as with its plot. We feel a sense of scope, complexity, and depth of judgment, along with a sense of movement, involving both the movement of our own minds as we confront the story and the narrator's movement between scenes dispersed in time and space.

My way of defining historicism, the key ingredient of modern realism, has reflected the notion that plot serves texture. I've suggested that historicism is based on two perceptions—a sense of the systematic wholeness and otherness of different cultures in time, and a sense that despite difference, we can encounter them in a productive manner. This account leaves out entirely what many would consider the hallmark of historicism, the idea that all significant historical moments, however disparate, can be formed into a single progressive story. Historicism thus *becomes* "providential history"—especially with respect to evaluation. For Karl Popper, historicists emplot history in a way that seems to them so logical and linear as to enable them to predict the future.[6] Even for the less tendentious, massively well-informed historian of ideas Maurice Mandelbaum, "the thesis of historicism . . . demands that we reject the view that historical events have an individual character which can be grasped apart from viewing them as embedded within a pattern of development."[7] Here, too, the pattern of development (or, for narrative history, the plot) calls the tune and sets the meaning, in a way that recalls our notion of "plot as template." Such formulations have the advantage of terminological precision and unambiguity, but in my view they mistake a single possibility for the norm.

The idea that we need plots primarily to propel us through the texture of a novel is also consonant with the view I have presented on how reference works in realist fiction. I have been at pains to deny that realist fiction has any use for "transparent representation." Instead, I've argued, realist novels create imaginative experiences that elicit the mental operations necessary to confront the world they identify as real. This line of argument shifts realism's claims from fulfilling the impossible (and incoherent) task of "direct" representation to providing a mode of grasping life in history. Yet, as I've pointed out, the shift doesn't mean leaving the particular objects and conditions of the historical world behind. Realist novels don't need to engage in "direct representation," but they can train our minds to apprehend historical reality only if they contain the right kinds of representations, the right grist for the mill. If we recall Auerbach's dictum that the kind of reality whose story he wishes to tell can be grasped only with reference to a series of concrete incarnations, and not as an abstract pattern, we can see why not just any content will do for realism, even if we conceive of realism as centered on the making of connections and the probing of relationships. Plots are different. Realist novels don't need to contain the right kind of plotting. Plots are instrumental;

[6] Karl Popper, *The Open Society and Its Enemies* (Princeton: Princeton University Press, 1950).
[7] Maurice Mandelbaum, *History, Man, and Reason* (Baltimore: Johns Hopkins University Press, 1971), 43. Mandelbaum continues, "What is, then, essential to historicism is the contention that a meaningful interpretation or adequate evaluation of any historical event involves seeing it as part of a stream of history." These are statements I could subscribe to, if "pattern of development" is expanded to include the kind of movement Auerbach describes, in which the meaning of the pattern cannot be grasped abstractly but only in specific incarnations.

as we've seen, they needn't be imagined as having some essential connection with the ways history actually progresses through time.

Austen's plots have recently come under scrutiny. A good deal has been written, pro and con, about the significance of her use of the "marriage plot" (which is, simply put, a plot that ends in a marriage).[8] Some critics have suggested that employing a marriage plot is always suspect, on the assumption that such plots in and of themselves reinforce the notion that heterosexual marriage and the mores surrounding it should be the focus of women's intelligence and desire. Other kinds of relationships are possible, it is argued, and other roles for women should exist. Sometimes, though not always and not necessarily, the attack on the marriage plot is an attack on marriage as an institution, or more generally on traditional ways of imagining the relationship between men and women. All of this has not gone unanswered. Readers, it is claimed, are not so passively malleable as is assumed by those who deplore what they see as the inevitably negative effects of the marriage plot. Readers can contest values of all kinds, and novels themselves can critique and contest the values of marriage even if they end in a marriage—or perhaps especially if they end in (a bad) marriage. And isn't there something suspect about what, echoing E. P. Thompson in a very different context, we might refer to as this "enormous condescension of posterity" with regard to the social and sexual mores of our forebears?[9]

Whatever their other differences, however, critics on both sides of the issue tend to endow the marriage plot with the power to fix meaning and effect. Thus in a canny assessment of the state of play in such criticism, accompanied by a partial defense of the marriage plot, Laura Mooneyham White suggests that marriage plots define in novels a certain kind of "narrative closure," where closure is conceived of as an "achievement of psychic identity" which when accomplished is "signaled, *represented*, by the act of comic closure." She follows this immediately, however, by stating, "In comedy, we achieve—or feel that we have achieved—psychic integration through the power of wedding bells at a narrative's close." White objects to those who assume "the *prima facie* injuriousness of romance plots"; she does not contest the notion that plots

---

[8] Or is it? Perhaps better, a "conventional" marriage? The use of the term "marriage plot" can suggest that all marriages are essentially the same—indeed in some hands, this seems one of the purposes of using the term. In *The Country and the City* (London: Chatto and Windus, 1973), Raymond Williams uses the term "inheritance plot" to cover much the same selection of novels. In *Pursuits of Happiness* (Cambridge: Harvard University Press, 1981), Stanley Cavell has written on a twentieth-century filmic variant he calls "the Hollywood comedy of remarriage." These terms are useful as heuristics: they urge you to attend to certain thematic issues. In the present critical climate, it's hard not to hear them as provocative variations on the default "marriage plot."

[9] E. P. Thompson, *The Making of the English Working Class* (New York: Vintage, 1966), 12.

and their endings are powerful enough to *be* injurious.[10] The wedding bells retain their power.

The distinctions I have offered among different meanings of "plot" can help us to clarify the issues at stake here. The assumption that marriage plots are by nature potentially or actually dangerous assorts best with the notion of plot as template. But fundamental objections arise to that notion when we are considering individual novels and how they are likely to be read, as White herself points out. The best way to make the "template" argument plausible is in reference to the reading of novels in the aggregate; it works best with respect to the institution of novel-reading. In this frame of reference, we might plausibly suggest that if all novels are based on marriage plots, the ideological force of marriage as a woman's only and best career would be considerable. For in the aggregate, the force of the general pattern would separate off from the treatment of marriage in each individual novel: at this level of analysis, even the most critical of novels might be "complicit" in the general ideological work of the marriage plot. What is most persuasive about this sort of argument is its implicit stress not on what we do within a framework of possibilities, but on the framework itself and what it allows us to do, the choices it offers. Yet if we extend this important form of argument, reversals can occur. Novel-reading has not been the only institutional support for prevalent views of marriage. In the heyday of the realist novel, institutional support was pervasive, involving any number of society's central discourses. But in the face of such pervasive support, half-empty may turn to half-full. We may come to value any possibility of contestation, not to deplore the fact that partial contestation or conflicted contestation isn't total—indeed, we may begin to wonder whether the best site (or perhaps the only site) on which to stage one's analysis might not be one that appears to be within the grounds of the ideologically hegemonic. Thinking along these lines, we may further conclude that the species of plotting as what I've called "story-telling" is particularly promising, just because it depicts the creation of narrative meaning as occurring right there before us, as a character tells her story, which invites us to imagine the needs and interests that feed into it. Then too, writing always has the chance of being seen as writing. We may add that arguments about the effect of novels in the aggregate invoke a realm to which literary criticism cannot penetrate; in eliding questions of quality and kinds and degrees of affective power, they also presuppose that the experience of reading one novel by Jane Austen

[10]   Laura Mooneyham White, "Jane Austen and the Marriage Plot: Questions of Persistence," in *Jane Austen and Discourses of Feminism*, ed. Devoney Looser (New York: St. Martin's, 1995), 71–77. White discusses Cavell on the "plot of remarriage." She is also interested in the relationship between plot and identity, an issue I touch on in a different way below.

could not redefine the meaning of our experience of reading a hundred novels by lesser authors.

To deal adequately with the effect of the marriage plot in individual novels, we need to turn to a conception of plot as a temporal ordering of incidents that is part of a dynamic, developing transaction between narrator and reader. For affect is the bearer of ideology in any work of art. To make arguments against the marriage plot work in these terms, critics generally (and I believe necessarily) stress the importance of the *ending* of the plot, arguing that its "closure" or "telos" snaps together the rest of the plot, making the experience endorse marriage. There is a certain amount of ambivalence about just what role the plot's ending plays in such a process. The quotation from White cited above contains two significantly different possibilities (one, to be sure, attached to the workings of the "comic" plot in general). To say that the "achievement of psychic identity" is "signaled, *represented*, by the act of comic closure" suggests a gathering up of cumulative effect. To say that "in comedy, we achieve—or feel that we have achieved—psychic integration through the power of wedding bells at a narrative's close" suggests that this kind of ending has an inherent, independent power. With both formulations, however, an interest in the temporality and duration of plot seems lacking. In fairness, we should note that dealing specifically and substantively with the temporality of novels is one of the most difficult tasks a critic can face; static patterns are quick to reassert themselves at every level of generality, including the level at which we find ourselves discussing the formal experiments with time novels are said to enact. I do not wish to claim too much for my own procedures in this regard, but I will claim that some sense of ongoing temporality is maintained by my emphasis on our moment-by-moment encounters with the texture of a text, and my stress on the recursive way in which those encounters form our sense of what it would mean to encounter reality (including the reality represented in the novel one is reading) in an adequate way.

One way to deal with the marriage plots in Austen's novels is to suggest that since, given the conventions of novel-writing in her age, Austen could hardly avoid using them, they don't mean anything special to or about her. Doubtless there is some truth to this view, but it shouldn't be extended so far as to suggest that her plots are somehow detachable from her other fictional practices or that they and their effects are negligible. I believe that those who are uneasy with the marriage plot in Austen are on to something, but that the real issue involves the way Austen's plotting is involved with the web of distinction-making that informs her texts, giving them their characteristic imaginative texture. Suspicions of the "marriage plot" echo a complex distrust of narrative itself, a distrust that forms a central component in some of the most powerful literary and cultural criticism produced in this century. It is to this distrust that I now turn.

Distrusting Narrative Distinctions: The Fragmentary and the Sublime

Consider the following viewpoints. First, two views of history. Walter Benjamin suggests that since narratives about history are always written to celebrate the victors, we need to blast apart the continuities of the story by allowing the past to enter the present in a moment of explosive illumination. Hayden White declares that the only liberating history would need to be written in the mode of the sublime: revealing the meaninglessness of the past would spur us on to create meaning in the present. Next, two views of Austen. Claudia Johnson finds that Henry Tilney in *Northanger Abbey* is at base just like his father, and that both are just like John Thorpe. And Marilyn Butler contrasts the closed, conservatively plotted novels of Austen with the formally and ideologically looser novels of Scott.[11] What do these four viewpoints share? An immediate similarity is this: all are in their different ways suspicious of the "official" plots and story-telling, and all seek ways to get beyond the official, surface story. I'd like to suggest another similarity, on which I believe the first is founded: all four distrust the power of a network of metonymic connections to defuse our moral vision and our political will. (With this similarity goes yet another: all these positions are connected to the two criticisms of realism with which this study began—realism is totalistic, and realism depends upon creating the illusion of "transparent" reference.) In a celebrated dictum, Walter Benjamin tells us that the "materialist critic" engages in brushing history against the grain. A distrust of "the grain" unites these four positions: those who hold them want to read and write against the grain.

For critics of literature and culture, the notion of "reading against the grain" of a literary work has become a commonplace. It provides the title, for instance, for a collection of Terry Eagleton's essays. Eagleton's use of the phrase derives from his work on Walter Benjamin; indeed, Benjamin's

[11] Walter Benjamin, "Theses on the Philosophy of History," in *Illuminations*, trans. Harry Zohn (New York: Schocken, 1969), 253–64. Hayden White, "The Politics of Historical Interpretation: Discipline and De-Sublimation," in *The Content of the Form* (Baltimore: Johns Hopkins University Press, 1987), 58–82. Claudia L. Johnson, *Jane Austen: Women, Politics, and the Novel* (Chicago: University of Chicago Press, 1988), 28–48. Marilyn Butler, *Romantics, Rebels, and Reactionaries* (Oxford: Oxford University Press, 1981), 94–112. Subsequent references to these works will appear in the text.

"Theses on the Philosophy of History" are likely to come to the mind of any literary or cultural critic when the phrase is employed.[12] Benjamin's own reference to brushing history "against the grain" appears in the Seventh Thesis, following hard upon perhaps his best known aphorism:

> There is no document of civilization which is not at the same time a document of barbarism. And just as such a document is not free of barbarism, barbarism taints also the manner in which it was transmitted from one owner to another. A historical materialist therefore dissociates himself from it as far as possible. He regards it as his task to brush history against the grain. (Thesis 7; 256–57)

One of the purposes of Benjamin's "Theses on the Philosophy of History" is to attack what he considers to be the "historicist" view of history, a view of history as smooth and uniform progress. A few sentences before the passage that I've just quoted, he condemns such a view of history as a triumphal procession whose chroniclers always side with the victors. Indeed, Benjamin seems unwilling for history to be given any fixed plot, because he thinks that the victors will inevitably write it. Instead, he wants us to imagine connections between present and past that flare up in disruptive, fleeting moments. Eagleton associates the notion of reading against the grain with images of smashing and exploding, and there is ample warrant for doing so in Benjamin himself, who speaks of how for Robespierre "ancient Rome was a past charged with the time of the now which he blasted out of the continuum of history" (Thesis 14; 261). For Benjamin, "brushing history against the grain" creates sudden, explosive flashes in which certain possibilities, loosed from normal temporal continuity, intrude themselves into the present. This emphasis on violently disrupting our normal, linear vision of the world by forging unexpected correspondences links Benjamin's thought and practice to the other critical positions I've just mentioned. (Does it also provide a link to every other political reading of art and life? Perhaps, but only in a weak sense. To be sure, all critique can be—not quite accurately—described as "disrupting our normal vision," but not all critique involves contesting linear progression and the making of distinctions.) Thus Johnson shows that the careful "surface" distinctions between characters that fuel the plots of Austen's novels hide ideological identities, especially with regard to male characters, who are all the bearers of patriarchal authority, and Butler (in a way that's less complimentary to Austen) demonstrates how Austen's

---

[12]   Terry Eagleton, *Against the Grain* (London: Verso, 1986) and *Walter Benjamin, or Towards a Revolutionary Criticism* (London: Verso, 1981).

marriage plots smooth over actual injustices and make alternative poss-
bilities disappear. And Hayden White suggests that giving history any
coherent surface story falsifies not a buried meaning, but a crucial lack of
meaning: what really needs to be revealed is not that history has a hidden
meaning, but that history is meaningless.

White's vision of history as meaningless echoes Benjamin's own image
of the angel of history's standing transfixed by the growing rubbish heap
at her feet—but Benjamin's image doesn't necessarily suggest that there's
nothing but chaos in the heap. The chaos may be the result of the fact that
the angel's vision itself is trapped. Embodied in the angel's predicament,
however, is a characteristic antinomy. On the one hand, our "normal"
world and mode of perceiving the world are seen as bewilderingly and
overwhelmingly "full." History may be a rubbish heap, but it's a *big* rubbish heap; the spectacle of its meaninglessness is enough to freeze the
mind and belittle the will. On the other hand, the sense of time which history's victors seek to impose on the rest of us is, as Benjamin puts it,
"empty," involving arid repetition; the only truly "full" temporality is
what Benjamin calls the "now-time"—which is to say the time created by
disrupting ordinary historical time. With respect to realism, this antinomy may be usefully seen as running in parallel with the antinomy provided by the two kinds of attacks on realism with which this book began,
which argue that realism seeks to create coercive, wall-to-wall totalities,
but brings those totalities into being through creating the illusion of an
arid, referentially "transparent" relationship between us and the world.
Here too we have an overwhelmingly full picture, and an empty frame.
And in both cases, the function of construing realism as both full and
empty is, I believe, the same. It allows the critic to register a radical dismay at what seems an inescapable vision of the world, while at the same
time rendering the logic and the claims of that vision meaningless. In my
own view, this involves taking what I've been calling the web of
metonymical connections constituted by real-world relationships at once
too seriously and not seriously enough.

I shall refer to criticism that participates in the mode of thought I've
been describing as "sublime criticism." To allow for the various degrees
in which this thinking is drawn upon, we may also usefully speak of sublime moments within a critical practice. Sublime criticism operates
metaphorically, often by discovering hidden likenesses, and so it may
have an innate antipathy to realism and its metonymical nature. I don't
consider it farfetched to conceive of the disruptions of Austen we've
touched upon as offering a moment of the sublime. When Claudia Johnson tells us that Henry Tilney, General Tilney, and John Thorpe are at
base the same man, her audacity is breathtaking, and it's meant to be.

What better way to evoke the pervasiveness and invisible power of patriarchal ideology? The mind stops in its tracks and then readjusts, with respect and considerable pleasure. For the critics of Austen's marriage plot,
it's useful to stop Austen's plot in its tracks. What's vital is to produce a
striking, clear-cut, liberating discontinuity with what ideology has made
the norm. This expedient can be memorably effective: it has certainly
proved its worth with respect to gender relations. A powerful inaugural
image for popular American feminism was what *Ms.* magazine called
"clicks"—freeze-frame moments when women perceived structures of
power at work beneath the surface of "ordinary" experience. "Clicks"
were prized because they called for action, and enabled it: they yielded
insight into the structure of what needed to be opposed, and they provided energy and a sense of power (one hallmark of the sublime). Pierre
Bourdieu has taken a distrust of the grain in another direction, demonstrating the thoroughness with which fine distinctions of taste in food,
art, music, and the like can be employed to create and enforce class distinctions.[13] Faced with this, one wonders whether *distinction-making itself*
doesn't ultimately solidify class injustice. On a more general level, it's not
entirely unreasonable to fear that entering the grain of a situation will
mean losing the forest for the trees and encourage an eventual failure of
energy. After the student uprisings at Harvard in 1969, a committee was
formed.

The link between the sublime and action, however, can itself be vexed.
When Hayden White advocates sublime historiography, he wants it to
lead to action, but his mode of conceiving of the sublime raises problems.
In the classic accounts, the mind freezes when it confronts the sublime;
but to engage in action in the world, the mind will need to unfreeze, returning to metonymic actuality. For White, however, the sublime vision
of history reveals that it is chaotic and meaningless; thus though experiencing the historical sublime may spur us to action, nothing in the sublime experience can provide a guide to how we need to act. Unlike the
"click," this version of the sublime doesn't burn a concrete and potentially reversible structure of injustice into our consciousness. Like the sensations that supposedly stream in on us according to certain epistemologies, history is revealed as essentially chaotic. Sublime history is meant to
impress upon us this intolerable truth and thereby to goad us on to give
history a meaning by engaging in "visionary politics" (72), but no species
of historiography, it appears, can play a positive and substantial role in
guiding action.[14] White debunks history that is "domesticated" by those

13   Pierre Bourdieu, *Distinction: A Social Critique of the Judgment of Taste* (1979), trans.
Richard Nice (Cambridge: Harvard University Press, 1984).
14   White takes a number of courageous political chances in "The Politics of Historical Interpretation." It seems hard to believe that, in his stress on the necessity of preserving for

who try to write objectively and dispassionately—a stance reminiscent of Hume's demonstration that truly disinterested action could never happen (without an impetus in one or another direction, the mind would simply rest). But (remembering the "click") isn't a certain kind of domestication of history precisely what we require—a return of sublime energy back to the world of our everyday experience? Turning from White to Benjamin, we realize that the latter's disruptive flashes evoke a different world altogether. The relationship between those flashes and action is complex and murky—which is perhaps unsurprising, given the discomfort Benjamin's own relationship to action in the world has raised in some distinguished commentators.[15] The flash accompanying the moment when one rips open the continuity of history has the feel of an illumination which is more than fireworks; it's not the negative preamble to the making of meaning but an emergence of meaning that has to be made good on. Do we return from the full "now-time" to a "real world"? Or does the "now-time" make the world real? If we extend the allusion to Robespierre's relationship to ancient Rome, it would seem that the moment of illumination itself provides a blueprint for action, assigning roles, ethos, and the activity that stems from them. But can you live in the "now-time"?

We might have raised these issues simply by considering the metaphor of brushing history against the grain itself. (Doing this may not involve brushing the metaphor against its grain.) The German expression "gegen den Strich zu bürsten" commonly refers to brushing hair against the grain; here *den Strich* means "stroke," as in "give your hair a hundred strokes." If we take this as a live metaphor, we find ourselves contemplating the image of historiography as coiffeur, of the historian as hairdresser—who, to be sure, might produce wild or unseemly locks. The expression can also mean to brush a plush fabric against its grain.[16] Now the implications of even these two referents for the metaphor are slightly dif-

---

mankind the sense of historical "meaninglessness that alone can goad living human beings to make their lives different for themselves and their children" (72), he is not recalling the final words of another critique of "historicism" which proceeds from very different political assumptions—Popper's injunction, in concluding *The Open Society and Its Enemies*, that we assume responsibility for giving history the meaning it itself does not possess.

[15] For a critique of such misgivings, see Françoise Meltzer, "Acedia and Melancholia," in *Walter Benjamin and the Demands of History*, ed. Michael P. Steinberg (Ithaca: Cornell University Press, 1996), 141–63.

[16] Benjamin had a liking for such metaphors. He speaks also of history's having "a thousand loose ends that hang down like unravelled braids, none of them [having] its appointed place until all of them have been taken up and braided into a headdress," and of the eternal as "at all events the ruche [embroidered fringe] of a dress rather than an idea." I owe these quotations to Irving Wolfarth's splendid "On the Messianic Structure of Walter Benjamin's Last Reflections," *Glyph*, 3 (1978), 172, 182.

ferent. If hair is what Benjamin has primarily in his sights, it must be long hair; there would be no point in giving a crew cut "a hundred strokes." But such hair usually lacks a grain in the strong sense of the word: it will, within limits, go where you want it to. So that brushing history against the grain here would tend to mean brushing it against the way it has always been brushed. We find ourselves a short step from the notion of historical accounts that are totally malleable, that can be cast in any form the teller wishes. If we take up the notion of brushing against the "nap," however, the picture changes. Velvet has a grain, and the results of brushing against that grain are predictable. To brush against the grain of history would then become to reveal an alternative, normally overlooked side of a relatively stable entity.

In *The Philosophical Discourse of Modernity*, Jürgen Habermas also wishes to revive lost, ignored, and fading voices from the past. This interest is obvious from the very design of his book, which conceptually begins with a moment when Hegel, having discovered something that looks a lot like Habermas's "ideal speech situation," then backed away from it and opted instead for the "philosophy of the subject." Habermas wants to amplify the voice that Hegel allowed to die away. But where Benjamin imagines discrete moments of explosive insight, Habermas is interested in the possibility of alternative possibilities within continuities and traditions. In the opening chapter of *Philosophical Discourse*, Habermas provides a reading of Benjamin's "Theses" that suggests that Benjamin "twists the radical future-orientedness that is characteristic of modern times in general so far back around the axis of the now-time that it gets transposed into a yet more radical orientation toward the past."[17] Again, attention to metaphor is rewarding. The metaphor of "twisting" is significantly different from the sudden "flashes" of which Benjamin speaks. If you are to "twist" something, there must be something persisting to twist, hence continuity. In an earlier essay, Habermas points out that Benjamin's discounting of tradition prevents him from achieving the materialist critique of culture he essays. In the critique of ideology, by contrast, "cultural tradition is established methodologically as part of social evolution and becomes accessible thus to materialist interpretation. Benjamin has fallen behind this concept."[18] Benjamin refuses to allow for

[17]   Habermas, *The Philosophical Discourse of Modernity* (1985), trans. Frederick Lawrence (Cambridge: MIT Press, 1987), 12.
[18]   Habermas, "Consciousness-Raising or Redemptive Criticism: The Contemporaneity of Walter Benjamin" (1972), trans. Philip Brewster and Carl Howard Buchner, *New German Critique*, no. 17 (Spring 1979), 50. Habermas goes on to criticize Benjamin's view of tradition for ignoring possibilities offered by the critique of ideology: "A critique that appropriates the history of art with a view to redeeming messianic instants and preserving an endangered semantic potential [that is, the "mimetic" capacity of language] can but comprehend itself as identification and *repetition* of emphatic experiences and utopian con-

the possibility that there might be not potentially redemptive moments, but potentially redemptive traditions in the past, on which we could draw for our present needs. In questioning Benjamin's view of our cultural inheritance, Habermas implicitly defends the powers of narrative itself, making space for narrative possibilities that elude the simple binary opposition between timeless moments of "open" illumination on the one hand, and a "closed" and "totalistic" narrative progression on the other.

The different spins Benjamin and Habermas put on the redemption of moments in the past derive, I think, from sources that are at once historical and ethical. Throughout the "Theses on the Philosophy of History," Benjamin is intensely interested in avoiding "complicity" with the Nazi "victors" who had brushed German history and culture into the form that confronted him. Avoiding complicity is, however, a task that, he rightly sees, is all but impossible, even for him—especially since he refuses to congratulate himself for *admitting* his complicity. Habermas, a member of the generation in Germany that tried to pick up the pieces after the military defeat of the Nazis, has something rather different in mind. In interpreting Benjamin, he speaks not of "complicity" but of a "guilt" before the past, evoking "the liberating power of memory . . . to contribute to the dissolution of a guilt on the part of the present with respect to the past."[19] One reason why I find Habermas preferable to Benjamin on this score is that I consider the burden of an ineluctable complicity in the suffering of the past too great for conscientious human beings to bear. Guilt seems a more productive inheritance.

The metaphor of "brushing against the grain," then, reveals its own

---

tents—and not as reflection in a formative process" (50). Habermas's critique has been contested. For a different view, which holds that both Habermas and his opponents in this debate have missed the point of Benjamin's relationship to tradition, see John McCole, *Walter Benjamin and the Antinomies of Tradition* (Ithaca: Cornell University Press, 1993).

[19] Benjamin: "Die Betrachtung . . . sucht einen Begriff davon zu geben, wie *teuer* unser gewohntes Denken eine Vorstellung von Geschichte zu stehen kommt, die jede Komplizität mit der vermeidet, an der diese Politiker weiter festhalten" (*Illuminationen* [Frankfurt: Suhrkamp, 1977], 256). "Our consideration . . . seeks to convey an idea of the high price our accustomed thinking will have to pay for a conception of history that avoids any complicity with the thinking to which these politicians continue to adhere" (Thesis 10; 258). Habermas, discussing Benjamin: "Hier soll die befreiende Kraft der Erinnerung nicht, wie von Hegel bis Freud, der Ablösung der Macht der Vergangenheit über die Gegenwart gelten, sondern der Ablösung einer Schuld der Gegenwart an die Vergangenheit: 'Denn es ist ein unwiederbringliches Bild der Vergangenheit, das mit jeder Gegenwart zu verschwinden droht, die sich nicht als in ihm gemeint erkannte' (5. These)" (*Der philosophische Diskurs der Moderne* [Frankfurt: Suhrkamp, 1985], 25). "Here the liberating power of memory is supposed not to foster a dissolution of the power of the past over the present, as it was from Hegel down to Freud, but to contribute to the dissolution of a guilt on the part of the present with respect to the past: 'For every image of the past that is not recognized by the present as one of its own concerns threatens to disappear irretrievably' (Thesis V)" (15).

complexities if brushed. I have dwelt upon them partly precisely because references to reading "against the grain," which gain saliency and scope from their resonance with Benjamin's phrase, have become so common and automatic. It seems important to remember how many issues about the redemptive remembering of the past and indeed about the nature of history itself the metaphor of "brushing against the grain" leaves open. Putting pressure on the metaphor opens the possibility that there may be many routes to this goal—and in particular, that the dichotomy "with the grain/against the grain" may not exhaust all the possibilities.

Further complications arise when we apply Benjamin's metaphor of brushing history against the grain to the process of reading a text. Just where is the grain of a text, anyway? When Gillian Beer warns us against "reading [a text] only along the grain of our pressing cultural and personal needs," she's locating the grain in us.[20] When by contrast Eagleton refers to reading against the grain, he seems to be talking about the grain of the work. But of course these two possibilities need not be mutually exclusive. A strong sense, positive or negative, of cultural tradition can make the two grains coalesce: those cultural forces that silenced past voices continue to work in our present. Indeed, locating "the grain" solely in the work and the past would seem to give the reader an unearned privilege. Not subject to a grain himself, the reader sits there, happily rasping the grain of the works that come under his inspection.

I'd like to suggest that appeals to liberating discontinuities have been oversold in criticism, especially in criticism bent on showing the bankruptcy of realism. There is of course no question of trying to proscribe appeals to the sublime, or of eschewing metaphorical attempts to pierce beneath a misleading surface to discover essential and disruptive connections to replace "empty" continuities. Relying on sharp dichotomies here would be as unwise as granting the notion that our only choices are to read with or against the grain. But with regard to the impenetrable Jane Austen, this chapter will suggest that blasting one's way into meaning may have limited value. To bring the discussion back to the agent of continuity and coherence known as the novelistic plot, I'd like to return to my earlier statement that the primary function of plot is to push us through the texture of a novel, to energize our response. (This recalls the very function of the sublime we've been discussing; the crucial difference is that here the energy is ongoing and cumulative; it's doesn't involve a moment in which the mind freezes and distends. It is thus a "domestication" of the sublime.) In the densely imagined world of Austen's novels, plot in this sense can help to bring alive the possibility as well of

[20]   Gillian Beer, *Arguing with the Past* (London: Routledge, 1989), 6.

what might be called "co-plots," continuities and implications at the periphery.

Both Benjamin and Habermas are interested in giving voice to moments in the past that have fallen silent or been silenced, and in both this involves either disrupting or bending the course of a certain kind of teleology. A criticism that draws on such thinking with the purpose of redeeming past textual voices would therefore contest the notion that novelistic teleology should specify what voices we ought to listen to in a novel. This means rejecting the notion that novelistic plots have the power to define, once and for all, the ideology of the works they inform. Marilyn Butler determines that Jane Austen is a straightforward conservative largely on the strength of what seems to her the import of Austen's "fables"; Alexander Welsh chides critics who don't consider Scott a Burkean for ignoring the defining power of plot.[21] We would have to disagree. Instead of reading for the end, we'd read for the middle. Instead of reading for or against the grain, we'd want to read through it. In particular, we'd want to encounter the network of possibilities opened up by the existence of the grain, so that we can thread our way through the different stories the grain allows.

Lionel Trilling, Henry Tilney, and Finding Yourself in the Grain

In previous chapters, I've noted that on a general level, the claims of realism are likely to make readers uneasy. There's something about realism that can easily turn claustrophobic. The quality of Austen's world can also be intimidating, making it seem that the only choice is total acceptance or aggressive rejection, that we must read her either with or against the grain, and there's something about positing, or seeming to posit, the existence of a grain that can make you want to go against it. Behind much suspicious Austen criticism lies, I believe, the experience of being drawn into Austen's linguistic orbit, only to feel rebuffed. Or perhaps more accurately: the critic, faced with what seems an impenetrable surface, feels compelled to create a situation in which the linguistic circuit can be bro-

---

[21] In a recent critique of Lukács, this view (which is central to Welsh's earlier, seminal *Hero of the Waverley Novels*, originally published in 1963) is made quite explicit: see "History and Revolution in *Old Mortality*," in *The Hero of the Waverley Novels: With New Essays on Scott* (Princeton: Princeton University Press, 1992), 210–11. A similar belief in the power of plot undergirds Marilyn Butler's *Jane Austen and the War of Ideas* (Oxford: Clarendon, 1975). In a preface to the 1987 reissue of this pathbreaking book, she has changed her view of how central the marriage plot is to *Mansfield Park*, *Emma*, and *Persuasion* (xlii–iii), but continues to find it the driving force behind Austen's earlier novels and indeed behind "the commonest type of late eighteenth-century novel" (xxxii).

ken, in which the inevitable becomes contingent, the familiar strange. (The experience of writing on Austen thus becomes a miniature version— on two inches of ivory?—of the experience of trying to write "against the grain" of a totalized and totalizing culture.) Austen's language provides, or seems to provide, a complete, systematic mechanism whereby the reality she presents can and must be processed. Her language seems to grant itself the power to make a set of discriminations that fully "map" reality and in the process to preclude the critic's ability to make decisive imaginative leaps that unmask a reality hidden beneath the surface of the text. What texts could be more "readerly" than Austen's novels? The problem of writing about Austen is the problem of finding a way to remain engaged with, but unmastered by, her mode of processing reality.

In his essay on *Emma*, Lionel Trilling (echoing Falstaff) remarks that it is impossible to know "where to have" that novel.[22] Is a fear embedded in the aspect of this statement that rings as a joke—the fear that *Emma*'s creator will not only remain impenetrable but will thereby "have" (a male) us? Trilling himself had, in an earlier essay, identified a "male's revulsion" felt by Mark Twain and others toward Austen, arising from "a man's panic fear at a fictional world in which the masculine principle, although represented as admirable and necessary, is prescribed and controlled by a female mind."[23] One maneuver that allows us to "have" Austen is to produce a twin for her, who yields herself up more easily. Providing an escape from the web of distinctions Austen creates, the twin fixes its meaning as a whole. The classic example of this maneuver is the furious Austen, filled with "regulated hatred," evoked by D. W. Harding.[24] But perhaps the most telling example of a critic's attempt to "have" Austen is provided by Trilling himself. Trilling's essay on *Emma* takes elaborate care to demonstrate its awareness of the problems involved in coming to grips with Austen. The essay is repeatedly concerned with the question of how much of Trilling's own contemporary concerns it is importing into Austen's world. (The degree to which Austen's world might not be ours was a topic of lasting interest for Trilling: it appears prominently in the very last essay he wrote for publication.) The essay on *Emma* nonetheless focuses on two problems that are perhaps more resonant for Trilling than for Austen: the question of the problem of "modern" selfhood (Trilling claims that, in her recognition of this problem, Austen

[22]   Introduction to *Emma*, ed. Lionel Trilling (Boston: Houghton Mifflin, 1957), viii; hereafter cited in the text.
[23]   Lionel Trilling, *"Mansfield Park"* (1954), in *The Opposing Self* (New York: Harcourt Brace Jovanovich, 1979), 183.
[24]   D. W. Harding, "Regulated Hatred: An Aspect of the Work of Jane Austen," *Scrutiny*, 8 (1940), 346–62.

shows herself to be the first "modern" novelist), and the presence in the novel of what Trilling calls the "idyllic" and we would probably call the "utopian," especially as it involves the possibilities and trials of something Trilling calls "mind." In producing and exploring both of these cruxes, Trilling engages in the process of discovering a "true" Austen underneath Austen's language or discriminations. He finds an Austen who moves in a capacious vista of intellectual history, a vista that opens as a result of a shift in registers of generality, from Austen's specificity to the luminous, broad generality of "mind" as such, and as discussed by the likes of Hegel and Schiller. What are we to make of this shift?

If our present is one in which an awareness of historically specific injustice is a commodity we believe ourselves to have recently purchased through struggle, then Trilling's talk of "mind" may seem to reflect the avoidance of that struggle. Trilling turns to a spuriously universal and safely abstract "mind" so that he can avoid the specificities of Austen's own time, and of his own. "Mind" allows him to abstract himself from McCarthyism. [25]

It would be possible to construct another story. We might suppose Trilling to be acutely aware of historical moments, including his own, and we might consider his own intellectual priorities and mentors. Trilling wrote often and well about a falsely immediate materiality that his American contemporaries and their ancestors tended to mistake for "reality in America." The voice of Trilling in this account would be a voice always speaking in opposition, always reminding us of what the current brand of intellectual slovenliness wishes to gloss over. [26] The work of the critic would then become precisely to remind readers that other kinds of reality exist besides "reality in America." If you can show that "mind" is also real in Jane Austen's eminently real world, you've done something, per-

[25] Lionel Trilling, "Mind in the Modern World" (1973), in *The Last Decade: Essays and Reviews, 1965–75*, ed. Diana Trilling (New York: Harcourt Brace Jovanovich, 1981), 100–128, can be seen as "hypocritical" evasion in voicing objections to affirmative action—despite (or from one point of view especially because of) its measured qualifications. See Daniel T. O'Hara, *Lionel Trilling* (Madison: University of Wisconsin Press, 1988), 282–85. The abstractions Trilling finds himself reaching for seem to me to stem precisely from his sense of the concrete as something with endlessly proliferating nuances; at their best, they serve as stays against confusion, and their very abstractness demands that we engage them with concrete historical content if they are to have any meaning at all. Of course, there is indeed always the danger that such abstractions will be pressed into the opposite cause, as a refuge from the complexities and specificities of a given historical conjuncture. This is the possibility to which Butler and O'Hara are responding. The problems arising from an attempt to inhabit positions both in and above one's own culture form a central concern of the following chapter.

[26] As Mark Krupnick nicely puts it in his valuable study *Lionel Trilling and the Fate of Cultural Criticism* (Evanston: Northwestern University Press, 1986), "it's always possible to catch the drift of Trilling's criticism if we keep in mind that it is reactive" (66); he also speaks of Trilling's "allergy to closure" (188).

haps even something political. Criticism working in this mode would know itself to be inherently partial and contingent; for all its reference to a generalized "mind," it would aspire to affect its own moment and in that aspiration would inevitably become "complicit" (or at least connected) with it.

Such a stance invites misunderstanding. The following comment from Trilling's essay on *Emma* shows how:

> Women in fiction only rarely have the peculiar reality of the moral life that self-love bestows. Most commonly they exist in a moon-like way, shining by the reflected moral life of men. They are "convincing" or "real" and sometimes "delightful," but they seldom exist as men exist—as genuine moral destinies. We do not take note of this; we are so used to the reflected quality that we do not observe it. It is only on the rare occasions when a female character like Emma confronts us that the difference makes us aware of the usual practice. Nor can we say that novels are deficient in realism when they present women as they do: it is the presumption of our society that women's moral life is not as men's. No change in the modern theory of the sexes, no advances in status that women have made, can contradict this. The self-love that we do countenance in women is of a limited and passive kind, and we are troubled if their self-love is as assertive as man's is permitted, and expected, to be. Not men alone, but women as well, insist on this limitation, not simply, and not without qualification and exception, not without pleasure when the exception appears, but in general and with the quiet effectiveness of an unrealized, unconscious intention. (xi)

When we read this passage, it's tempting to conclude that Trilling is reporting on something he considers an unchangeable aspect of the human condition and indeed approves of—or shrugs his shoulders at, in what can be an infuriating way for those who feel their own objections have thus been swept aside. His use of "our" rings with particular oddness here. But can this lack of self-awareness really be true of an author who insists on describing in super-conscious detail one of "our" culture's "unconscious" assumptions? Aren't we invited to see that there's something fishy and factitious about this assumption from the moment Trilling's description of it employs the hackneyed association between women and the moon? And isn't his use of "we" and "our" a provocation for the reader to admit complicity or provide a defense?[27]

---

[27]   William M. Chace, in *Lionel Trilling: Criticism and Politics* (Stanford: Stanford University Press, 1980), 146–47, notes the bivalent possibilities of Trilling's use of "we" with reference to his *Sincerity and Authenticity*. Chace honors "a 'we' whose best side—informed curios-

What is Trilling's "real" voice as he writes on Austen: a voice attempting to create an opposing vision in a subjectively understood historical framework, or a voice that, responding to forces and powers of which it is unaware, raises certain issues but crucially neglects others? Are we to take Trilling at his word or his silences? I suspect that both these approaches are unsatisfactory. Is there a way of refusing to throw the bipolar switch that would either decide to honor the "real" Trilling by simply taking him at his word, or attack the even realer but hidden Trilling by pointing out what he leaves out or demonstrating that his words betray more than he realizes? We can elude this dichotomy by seeing Trilling as a critic who has self-consciously chosen to work *within* the grain of his culture, but who is also trying to work *through* that grain toward an alternative set of cultural possibilities. Such a position has its problems and its blindness; by reading through the grain of Trilling's own writings, we might however find ourselves able to define them with something approaching his own subtle shadings, without in the process losing a sense of his virtues.

From Lionel Trilling to Henry Tilney has become but a short step. In a recent review article, Alistair Duckworth paused to ask whether Henry is really "quite the bully and misogynist he is now being painted?"[28] If we assume that the hidden voices in texts must be redeemed by reading against the grain in an explosive fashion, the answer is likely to be "yes." As we've seen, one of Austen's best critics suggests that the principal male characters in *Northanger Abbey* are all really the same, all bearers of a patriarchal ideology that tries to silence Catherine Morland and her Gothic imaginings at every turn. The discovery of this sameness is meant to allow Catherine to speak despite history's official shapers and custodians.

Though I respect such a goal, I'll have to admit that the idea that Austen is an author whose works are, at any level, built on structures of coalescence and identity doesn't accord with my own sense of the texture of her novels, which seems instead to involve the creation of an intricate web of linguistic and ideological differences. Of course this dissonance is just what one might expect from a reading against Austen's grain; it hardly proves that such a reading is simply mistaken. But what if we fol-

---

ity, patience, wise understanding and invulnerability to surprise—constitutes the compliment Trilling seductively had paid to his readers for years," but notes that this "strategy is both generous and insidious. It is the same in this book as it has been in his others: to argue by means of an abstract terminology whose meaning is presumed to be accessible to everyone but that is actually something the author alone controls and whose separate units he introduces and partially defines as the appropriate occasions arise."

28   Alistair Duckworth, "Jane Austen and the Construction of a Progressive Author," *College English*, 53 (1991), 87.

lowed Habermas's way of redeeming lost voices, with his greater emphasis on tradition and continuity? What would happen if we read Austen's
text "through the grain"—that is, in a way that took fuller account of the
web of distinctions that, in my view, *give* Austen's text its characteristic
grain? We might then wish to preserve a crucial distinction between
Henry and his father, in which Henry would turn out to be not the understated and therefore more efficient bearer of the patriarchal power
General Tilney represents in excess, but a character who is marked by patriarchal discourse but who, by finding some play in a complex system,
escapes from being wholly determined by its ends or end. We might then
conclude that Austen is willing to imagine him as a character who is at
once a partial conduit for establishment values, but at the same time limited and desirous of escaping them—a character immersed in and bene-
fiting from repressive social codes who makes them bear a charge for
which they are not officially designed.

In a celebrated scene in *Northanger Abbey*, Henry, his sister, and Catherine take a walk together, and the two Tilneys begin using the vocabulary
of the picturesque to describe the panorama of Bath that spreads beneath
them from the top of Beechen Cliff. Catherine feels ashamed of her igno-
rance of this aesthetic discourse, but the narrator tells us she shouldn't:

> She was heartily ashamed of her ignorance. A misplaced shame.
> Where people wish to attach, they should always be ignorant. To
> come with a well-informed mind, is to come with an inability of
> administering to the vanity of others, which a sensible person
> would always wish to avoid. A woman especially, if she have the
> misfortune of knowing any thing, should conceal it as well as she
> can.
>
> The advantages of natural folly in a beautiful girl have been al-
> ready set forth by the capital pen of a sister author;—and to her
> treatment of the subject I will only add in justice to men, that
> though to the larger and more trifling part of the sex, imbecility in
> females is a great enhancement of their personal charms, there is a
> portion of them too reasonable and too well informed themselves
> to desire any thing more in woman than ignorance. But Catherine
> did not know her own advantages—did not know that a good-
> looking girl, with an affectionate heart and a very ignorant mind,
> cannot fail of attracting a clever young man, unless circumstances
> are particularly untoward. In the present instance, she confessed
> and lamented her want of knowledge; declared that she would give
> any thing in the world to be able to draw; and a lecture on the pic-
> turesque immediately followed, in which his instructions were so
> clear that she soon began to see beauty in every thing admired by

him, and her attention was so earnest, that he became perfectly satisfied of her having a great deal of natural taste. He talked of foregrounds, distances, and second distances—side-screens and perspectives—lights and shades;—and Catherine was so hopeful a scholar, that when they gained the top of Beechen Cliff, she voluntarily rejected the whole city of Bath, as unworthy to make part of a landscape. Delighted with her progress, and fearful of wearying her with too much wisdom at once, Henry suffered the subject to decline, and by an easy transition from a piece of rocky fragment and the withered oak which he had placed near its summit, to oaks in general, to forests, the enclosure of them, waste lands, crown lands and government, he shortly found himself arrived at politics; and from politics, it was an easy step to silence. The general pause which succeeded his short disquisition on the state of the nation, was put an end to by Catherine, who, in rather a solemn tone of voice, uttered these words, "I have heard that something very shocking indeed, will soon come out in London."[29]

Catherine's dramatic statement generates a set of confusions. She's thinking of the appearance of a new horror novel, while Miss Tilney supposes her to be talking of political unrest. Henry perceives the misunderstanding immediately and teases both with a series of outrageous statements about the limits and confusions of female understanding, as when he remarks that "no one can think more highly of the understanding of women than I do. In my opinion, nature has given them so much, that they never find it necessary to use more than half" (101).

Is Henry Tilney bullying Catherine, his sister, and by inference the reader and women in general in this scene? This is a story that's worth finding in the scene; it embodies one intention of patriarchal discourse nicely. Even though it happens that Catherine is already silent at this point, and even though in the scene as a whole Henry seems to enjoy leading her to speak, there's an important way in which patriarchal discourse *does* seek to silence Catherine, by reminding her of her proper sphere and role—politics is, after all, a taboo subject for her as a proper lady. In this sequence taken as a whole, however, something else appears to be occurring as well. For the *reader*, Henry's statements about the limits of the female understanding, for instance, counter the narrator's earlier ironic attack on the proclivity of "the larger and more trifling part" of *men* to value absolute female stupidity. This is *not* to say that any latent misogyny on Henry's part is thereby simply canceled out: it is to say that,

[29] Austen, *Northanger Abbey*, ed. Marilyn Butler (Harmondsworth: Penguin, 1995), 99–100; hereafter cited in the text.

in our experience of the text, Henry does not pass unanswered.[30] And even on the level of interactions among the characters themselves, other possibilities arise.

If we take Henry to be the perfectly efficient custodian of patriarchal discourse and hence at one with his father in the project they both forward, then it's fair enough to suggest Henry is engaged in a play of power that aims to reduce Catherine to silence. If we take a different view, however, we may decide that there's another person Henry wishes to silence in this passage, namely *himself*, so that he can shut up and enjoy the view—as well as the affective charge that's flowing between Catherine and him. And he succeeds—or rather, something succeeds. "He shortly found himself arrived at politics; and from politics, it was an easy step to silence." There's a wonderful subtlety here in the specification of agency: we feel the flow of discourse directing the speaker, as it finds conscious paths for unconscious desire. Henry wants to slip out of the role of instructor, though he must code this wish in a language of being considerate to Catherine, mindful of the pupil's limitations. The public language of aesthetic appreciation has done its part in promoting an affective exchange between him and Catherine, and now it's time for a delicious moment of silence. It's therefore entirely appropriate that Catherine should break the silence by returning to the affective/sensual register that is engaging both her and Henry, by referring to what is for her the type of affective/sensual imaginative experience: not the theory of the picturesque, but one of its practical applications, the Gothic novel. Henry's sister, who has not participated in this affective dynamic, quite reasonably supposes that when Catherine speaks of "something very shocking indeed" that "will soon come out in London," she is continuing in the political mode Henry earlier employed to drop speech altogether: she fears a riot. Henry, by contrast, instantly recognizes that Catherine is indulging in voluptuous Gothic imaginings involving a new novel from the London presses. If, when he makes the "easy step [from politics] to silence," he hasn't entered an affective, perhaps even an erotic mode, it's hard to see how even he, with all his quickness, could immediately identify the imaginative register Catherine adopts when she breaks the silence. Within the discussion on Beechen Cliff, then, language allows alternative possibilities, and silencing can mean different things. But this depends on maintaining the possibility of a significant distinction between Henry and his father, instead of assuming that Austen has simply made them *look* different, the better to surprise us with their essential similarity. To put it another way,

---

[30]   The issue of whether narrators can enter "story space" is canvassed in Chapter 6. Here I'll simply suggest that the realist project has a tendency to involve narrators in at least seeming encroachments on story space.

we need to suppose that Austen's web of distinctions allows for finer and more multifarious possibilities than that Henry is simply a kinder, gentler patriarch.

By the same token, it's important to deny that a simple coalescence occurs between Henry and the narrator. Henry may express certain ideas or sentiments that seem in consonance with those of the novel's implied author, but his voice never has narratorial authority. He is allowed some measure of the narrator's linguistic virtuosity, but there's no substantial merging here. Indeed, the opposite is closer to the truth. Henry Tilney is depicted as young, limited, "strange," and therefore winning—in religious parlance, he is "creatural." It's worth dwelling on Henry's "strangeness" and the charm it brings with it. His strangeness is pronounced enough to lead Catherine, in another scene, not to be silenced, but to achieve the silence at the edge of what one's speech and cultural conventions permit one to say: " 'How can you,' said Catherine, laughing, 'be so—' she had almost said, strange" (26). Catherine's reaction comes in response to Henry's knowing discussion of muslins and silks with Mrs. Allen. It is one of many points in the novel where romantic affect emerges at the edge of expected norms. Catherine edges up to impertinence, as Henry dances on the edges of a stereotypically female sphere.

It would seem an impoverishment to place Henry squarely in the middle of the picture, directing things and silencing people. The very visual imagery of the scene should prevent this: we see a landscape with figures, not a single figure blotting out the landscape. Henry is, to be sure, removed from the naive absorption that fills Catherine when she begins to find her way into the discourses of the Gothic or the Claude Lorraine glass. It's obvious enough that in certain respects, though Henry is hardly in the center of the picture, he is a step ahead of Catherine, on somewhat higher ground. Part of the framework of the scene on Beechen Cliff, part of the armature that allows its affect to flow among the characters, is its enactment of a cultural rule stated directly nowhere by Austen but given flatfooted expression by Scott's third-person narrator in *Redgauntlet*: "The relative situation of adviser and advised, of protector and protected, is so peculiarly suited to the respective condition of man and woman, that great progress towards intimacy is often made in very short space; for the circumstances call for confidence on the part of the gentleman, and forbid coyness on that of the lady, so that the usual barriers against easy intercourse are at once thrown down."[31] Aesthetic advising, to be sure, is not quite the same thing as the life-and-death advising that the characters in

[31] Scott, *Redgauntlet*, ed. Kathryn Sutherland (Oxford: Oxford University Press, 1985), 389.

Scott's scene believe themselves to be engaged in, but the underlying stereotype is unmistakable. But to recognize such a stereotype is for Austen the beginning, not the end of analysis. It remains necessary to determine its function in this particular context, to gauge what it does and what is done with it by the characters, and indeed what other kinds of agency besides cultural agency are also operative.

Austen's novels embody the recognition that, though the idea that we could somehow escape history or stand over and against it is a fantasy, there may nevertheless be a certain amount of play *within* the systems that constitute history and society. The contradictions working between different systems within the social totality, and the incoherencies these contradictions produce, leave room for at least a limited amount of innovation and spontaneity of action, for an individuality sufficiently well developed to assume the function of agency, if not entirely alone, then in concert with others. But any such action must be imagined, and those imaginings must be communicated (if only by the self to the self), before they can be realized in practice. Such realizations must, for any age, result in part from its own reading practices; such reading practices, themselves the product of history, must draw upon the powers of language, conceived of as operating in interpersonal ways, to release the latent, unspoken potentialities of both the present and the past. When Raymond Williams speaks of how Austen's language finally appeals to a set of values that are not simply the foregone conclusions of the ideology of her class, he is appealing to this linguistic potentiality: "What happens in *Emma*, in *Persuasion*, in *Mansfield Park*, is the development of an everyday, uncompromising morality which is in the end separable from its social basis and which, in other hands, can be turned against it."[32]

The Henry Tilney we have lately encountered in Austen criticism is a perfectly centered, enviably efficient bearer of a male discourse of power; he concentrates in himself all that is overbearing and coercive about "patriarchal society." He merges with his father and even with the boorish John Thorpe because he *includes* them, plays the understated realist whole to their exaggerated, comic parts. The Henry Tilney I find lurking in the novel's pages is rather different. He is young; and as Catherine notes, he is "strange." His role-playing includes a fascination with such aspects of the feminine sphere as the durability of muslins. Why is he attracted to Catherine? During an early encounter, she testifies to her unquenchable delight in Bath: "If I could but have papa and mamma, and the rest of them here, I suppose I should be too happy!" she tells him. Henry replies to her exclamation, "Oh! who can ever be tired of Bath?"

---

[32]   Williams, *The Country and the City*, 116–17.

with an effusion of his own: "Not those who bring such fresh feelings of every sort to it, as you do. But papas and mammas, and brothers and intimate friends are a good deal gone by, to most of the frequenters of Bath— and the honest relish of balls and plays, and every-day sights, is past with them" (72). The full force of his statement emerges only later in the novel, when we learn of his mother's death and what it has meant to him, and to his sister. But Henry not only talks disparagingly about those for whom an "honest relish" is gone, he mimics them and their small talk: this is part of the "strangeness" that so intrigues Catherine. Does his ability to play the mimic rank him too with those for whom an "honest relish," in the sense of something immediate and spontaneous, is no longer possible? We might then take Henry's praise as backhanded condescension, delivered from the other side of the line it draws. But doesn't his mimicry also momentarily allow him to share the energy and fun that have, until now, simply been "given" to Catherine by her youth and inexperience? The fun here includes aggressiveness, and I shall be arguing that its ultimate target is not polite society in general, but Henry's papa, the redoubtable General Tilney. In this context, it's worth pausing to ask why Henry praises Catherine to her face in the first place. Does he simply wish to evoke blushes; is this a way of paying court, perhaps an imposition of a certain kind of "male" discipline that would seek to transform Catherine into a conscious producer, on demand, of such artlessness for Henry's enjoyment? Henry later says that Catherine's feelings should learn to know themselves ("Such feelings ought to be investigated, that they may know themselves" [180]), but can they know themselves and remain themselves? Or is this just what excites him: does he hope that Catherine might possess a force that could withstand the aspects of society he mimics—and, more particularly, could stand up against the General? (Can such motives be definitively untangled, and would the "negative" ones cancel out the "positive"?)

At the end of the novel, Austen's narrator explains that Henry's "affection" for Catherine *"originated* in nothing better than gratitude, or, in other words . . . a persuasion of her partiality for him had been the only cause of giving her a serious thought" (212; my emphasis). The full dimensions of Henry's gratitude can be measured only when we recognize the release Catherine's artlessness represents from the life of calculation the General imposes. Henry's "strangeness" is hardly surprising in one seeking to make room for himself in an atmosphere of claustrophobic restraint. And it's well not to forget the sensual possibilities opened up by Catherine's artlessness, which allows her to transport into real-world situations the affect that fills Gothic novels. One of the triumphs of recent criticism of Austen has been to reveal in her texts such things as the erotic nature of the exchange between Henry and Catherine when she suggests, in the Gothic mode, that the General may have murdered his wife. The moment before his rationality reasserts itself in talk of "voluntary spies," the moment when Catherine raises her eyes and looks him in the face, sharing a frisson with him, is full of delicious confusion: "Dearest Miss Morland, what ideas have you been admitting?" (172)—and what ideas of my own might you admit, and express, for me!

In the event, Catherine has even more to offer than the admission of forbidden ideas. She provides Henry the joy of opposing the General in a socially irreproachable way, a way entirely befitting a proper young clergyman.[33] The dream that hovers around the edges of *Clarissa*—the dream that you could find an ideal father whose will would coincide with and authorize your own, against the wishes of your actual father—gains ironic fulfillment in *Northanger Abbey*, with Catherine Morland playing, against all probability, the ideal paternal role. The Henry Tilney with whom we are becoming acquainted edges into the light as the novel draws to its close. He forgets things. He blushes. This blushing is of a piece with the affect-sharing that occurs during the scene in his mother's bedroom: "Henry, in having such things to relate of his father, was almost as pitiable as in their first avowal to himself. He blushed for the narrow-minded counsel which he was obliged to expose" (215). How delicious to be *obliged* to say these things about the General, to be *obliged* to reduce him to his place, having in a cloud of righteous indignation absented oneself from the place he inhabits! The completeness of this reversal could exist only in a social setting with a normative grain. Catherine joins the game of playing the system when she rejoices that Henry asked for her hand before he told her of his father's opposition to the marriage, thereby relieving her "from the necessity of a conscientious rejection" of his suit (212). Henry's forgettings are rich. He neglects to tell Catherine about the General's having forbidden their marriage until after she's given her promise. Earlier, he had passively observed his father preparing for his own discomfiture. Both he and his sister "had seen with astonishment the suddenness, continuance and extent of [the General's] attention [to Catherine]; and . . . latterly, from some hints which had

---

[33] Judith Wilt, in *Ghosts of the Gothic* (Princeton: Princeton University Press, 1980), 147, speaks of Henry as the "real culprit" in his "glee in the enjoyment of the joke he has foisted on his father and on Catherine. If his joke turned real, his abbey legitimately 'horrid,' and his father into a true ogre, serve him right! And it did serve him well, for faced with a Montoni-[like]father, Henry turned into a genuine Valancourt." When Henry praises Catherine for having a "mind . . . warped by an innate principle of general integrity, and therefore not accessible to the cool reasonings of family partiality, or a desire of revenge" (191), doesn't the list at the end of the compliment pay covert tribute to her ability to activate less noble impulses in others (that is, him)?

accompanied an almost positive command to his son of doing everything in his power to attach her, Henry was convinced of his father's believing it to be an advantageous connection" (214). No doubt the General is not a man to argue with; yet why did Henry do nothing to disabuse him of his erroneous estimation of the pecuniary advantages Catherine would bring as a wife? Didn't he want to give his father enough rope to hang himself?

At this point Catherine's feelings are described in a celebrated passage. The narrator tells us that in listening to Henry's explanation of his father's mercenary motives, first in courting her for his son and then in ordering her out of the house, Catherine "heard enough to feel, that in suspecting General Tilney of either murdering or shutting up his wife, she had scarcely sinned against his character, or magnified his cruelty" (215). Some have vindicated Catherine by going her several better and assuming, on the slimmest evidence from the text, that the General's cruelty was in fact the "real" cause of his wife's death. Does this really do Catherine a favor? Isn't the point of the scene that both Catherine and Henry find themselves able to define and defy the General for exactly what he is? From the moment of Catherine's visit to the Tilneys' lodgings in Bath and probably before, *we* realize that he is a vain, stifling bully. The signs that reveal the General's character are clear, for those who can interpret the requisite cultural codes. In the early portions of the novel, Catherine doesn't: she's too busy reading Gothic novels. To be sure, her time is not entirely wasted. Though the Gothic does not help her to clarity or insight, it does add affective force to her perceptions and judgments. This is by no means a trivial contribution: given the cultural codes that seek to govern Catherine's own behavior, a good deal of affective force is required to get her to make any judgment at all of a male authority figure, and to keep that judgment alive. But by itself, affective force leads precisely nowhere. The distinction I'm making here is honored in Austen's text, which speaks of her "feelings" and then gives them a cognitive overlay in her judgment that she had "*scarcely* sinned against his *character.*" And Catherine hasn't been wasting her time as far as Henry is concerned, either. On some level, Henry knows his father, but the fullness of this knowledge is something that the discourse of Christians and gentlemen can hardly register. At the very moment when Henry, quite properly, reminds Catherine of what is probable in England (given its neighborhoods of "voluntary spies"), the errant imaginings he's putting in their place are activating his own tacit knowledge, helping to bring it near the boil. When the General breaks the gentlemanly Christian code, the knowledge will boil over into action.

I am aware that praising Catherine for the energy of her imagination (and the realist plot for its capacity to energize readers) may seem a backhanded compliment, particularly when matters of gender are in the air. Isn't this all too redolent of the kind of patronizing the General indulges in when he praises Catherine for the "elasticity of her walk" (92)—though now, to be sure, I've moved to a realm that would appear to praise something on the order of an energetic "feminine intuition" that can be made useful by (and only by) masculine ratiocination? By the same token, don't my attempts to put what I've called "sublime criticism" in its place cast me in the role of a critical Henry Tilney? Well, you can of course make such connections—especially if you're working in the mode of sublimely metaphorical critique—and they have their uses. Working in the metonymical mode, however, one would want to make a distinction between historical developments and future possibilities. That women have regularly been identified with matter and anarchic energy, and men have been identified with form and rational control, doesn't mean that such identifications are necessary or inevitable, for those who have learned to distinguish. Nor does it follow that the notion that energy will at some point have to be put under the control of reason to effect change is itself inherently sexist, simply because this view can be and has been coded in ways that mean that women should submit to men. In the order of what has been, sublime criticism fueled by many kinds of interests has often played an indispensable role, and no doubt it will continue to do so. My own understanding of both Catherine Morland and Henry Tilney could hardly have formed without the stimulus of such criticism of Austen, which has made it impossible to forget that gender matters. Yet the example of Austen's vision, as I construe it, still leads me to embrace the practice of making distinctions and accepting hierarchies of value as a necessary part of coming to grips with the real.

I earlier suggested that the primary function of plot in the realist novel is to energize our encounters with its imaginative texture as revealed in local moments in the text. Catherine's Gothic imaginings may serve as an allegory for this function. Realist plots don't create or fix the boundaries of meaning. They give imaginative power to the meanings that arise from the local texture of the fiction. Shouldn't we rejoice that Catherine begins to judge the General correctly, not because she has finally learned to believe in the reality of Gothic metaphors, but because she's learning to find her way in the web of connections that make up her world? Don't we want her to be able to use the energy released by the Gothic, instead of being used by it?

I have been describing a Henry Tilney who does not univocally (and monotonously) embody the forces of a male privilege. If a modern woman may activate a self in Catherine Morland that would strongly object to certain aspects of Henry Tilney, a modern man may find in Henry

Tilney someone facing powerful codes and norms with which he feels hardly identical, though in which he is implicated and from which he ineluctably draws privilege. Issues of gender, and also of class, race, and education arise here. I am Henry Tilney. Are you? A novel or a mode of novel-reading might do worse than encourage readers of all sorts and conditions to find affective moments that provide models of partial disengagement from the forces that seek to speak for them. Such possibilities are offered by the grain of Austen's writing in two ways. First, establishing the mode of a continual making of distinctions prepares us to expect a certain level of complexity in the situation of a character like Henry. Second, Austen's fine-grained metonymical imagination creates a work in which we can infer the existence of unmentioned narrative possibilities, of proliferating plots. There's more than one way of weaving one's way through the grain of an Austen novel, even though the grain itself stays the same. Austen's discourse needn't be brushed before it can be worn.

Extricating Catherine and Henry from sublime criticism does not mean ignoring situations of gender oppression in the novel, it places them, making them clearer, less clichéd, and more interesting. The story about Henry we've found in the grain of Austen's text has a moment of relative freedom, but it also involves a battle between two men; as so often, the battle takes place, as they say, "over the woman's body." But Austen has given Catherine a role in the battle more substantial and self-centered than that phrase would imply. When the General's perfidy and Henry's resistance are revealed to her, her "feelings" are said to have "hardened into even a triumphant delight" (212). What is involved in this hardening? To begin with, it's an affectionate joke. There's something piquant about the notion of the mild, naive Catherine suddenly attaining a steely self-assertion; that she has to harden herself, has to become "tough" to admit such ideas is a measure of the difficulty she has in imagining ill of others. But reminding us of Catherine's hitherto normal self cuts both ways, making her "triumphant" delight all the more an achievement, and also suggesting that, given the difficulty she's had in seeing certain aspects of others, she must here be experiencing the sort of gestalt switch that sticks. We feel a sense of power here, one that's reinforced by the use of "harden" to describe the process of making plants and children hardy and robust and, at least for us, by the sexual connotations of "harden."[34]

A hardened judgment is a judgment capable of taking a stand, drawing the line, talents called upon in readers and characters alike throughout Austen's works. In opposing the theatricals at Mansfield Park, Edmund

---

[34] The OED cites Beddoes (1793) as writing "It is not true . . . that cold hardens children as it hardens steel."

Bertram points out that the company assembled there is incapable of "good harden'd real acting."[35] Hardened actors can tell the difference between the imaginative world they create on the stage and the real world beyond it. They may vary their interpretations of a part, but they stay with the script. Unlike the Bertrams and Crawfords, they do not slip between acting and living, because they act for a living. They stay in the grain of their fiction, and they stick to their lines. Nor would they mistake a Gothic play—or novel—for the life they lead on the other side of the footlights.

Neither Catherine nor the reader of *Northanger Abbey* would profit much from learning that Gothic novels are "right" in that they point to broad underlying truths that override surface distinctions. Hardened actors know when to act and when not; they can *use* the codes of acting instead of being used by them, or collapsing all of life into acting. Catherine's "hardened" pleasure is a pleasure of discrimination; for her and for us, it's a pleasure to be able to say that she had *scarcely* sinned against the General's character in her Gothic imaginings. We might say both that Catherine sinned in a way that requires imaginative and erotic energy, and also that she can now fully savor her sin retrospectively, since she can place it. Then again, her ability to draw the proper lines contains but does not cancel out the naive energy that led her to condemn the General in the first place: "scarcely" can mark an exclamation as well as marking judgments of degree.

It's important that we give full weight to Catherine's articulations; otherwise, we might suppose that her freshness is used to create a dichotomy between rigid linguistic and cultural codes on the one hand, and a realm of silence and freedom that eludes them. At the play in Bath, when she insists to Henry that he had given her an offended look, he "replie[s]" simply by sitting next to her and talking about something else (85), and I've already commented extensively on the silence achieved on Beechen Cliff. No one knows better than Austen that there are things that can hardly be expressed, especially in public. But we also find Catherine finding ways to use linguistic distinctions to place General Tilney; her feelings do come to "know themselves." In this, we see in operation a re-

---

[35]   Austen, *Mansfield Park*, ed. Kathryn Sutherland (Harmondsworth: Penguin, 1996), 104. Edmund says that he is quite willing to "see real acting, good harden'd real acting; but I would hardly walk from this room to the next, to look at the raw efforts of those who have not been bred to the trade,—a set of gentlemen and ladies, who have all the disadvantages of education and decorum to struggle through"—which is to say that the set of distinctions that govern their normal behavior plays against their making the sorts of distinctions you need to make if you're going to accomplish real, hardened acting. For a brilliant reading that erases any hard line between "hardened" acting and other acting on stage and off, see David Marshall, "True Acting and the Language of Real Feeling: *Mansfield Park*," *Yale Journal of Criticism*, 3 (1989), 87–106.

deeming side of language asserting itself, at the service of desire, against the stultification and mendacity on which the General relies, and beyond the ability of any single character to control. The General thinks otherwise. He acts as if his voice simply is the voice of patriarchal authority; his comeuppance is the more complete because he has been "accustomed on every ordinary occasion to give the law in his family, prepared for no reluctance but of feeling, no opposing desire that should dare to clothe itself in words" (215).

Our discussion of *Northanger Abbey* began with the scene in which Henry, Eleanor, and Catherine survey Bath from the top of a hill. Judging Henry's discussion of politics to be an attempt to reduce Catherine to silence is an excellent example of reading Austen's text against the grain. Catherine may be silent already, and she may be depicted as feeling anything but oppressed; nonetheless, brushed against the grain, Henry's talk can rightly be seen to echo and reinforce a set of cultural norms intent on reducing women to order. And in this way he can be made to seem at one with characters as "superficially" different from him and from each other as General Tilney and John Thorpe. I've been arguing, though, that the cost of reading only against the grain of Austen's representation may be high. For Austen, nothing is ever essentially the same as anything else. She is always making distinctions; we can think of her linguistic practice as constituting a "difference machine." Dealing with language means evolving an ever more finely tuned and articulated instrument for measuring disparate realities, not by conflating them, but by putting them in their (slightly different) places. Then too, for some, sublime criticism can feel anything but liberating. Not too long ago, a female critic published in a prestigious journal an article that indicted "the feminists" for supposedly creating an oppressive climate in Austen studies. As Catherine supposedly is silenced, so are those young, untenured critics who do not agree with the new reading of Austen, the argument ran.[36] In those who feel that the grains of works they love (or, for that matter, their own grains) are being brushed the wrong way, this kind of reaction seems predictable. Reading Henry Tilney against the grain leaves him no room to maneuver; he's just like his father, and that's that. He has one "subject-position," and he's trying to push Catherine into another. Being put in one and only one place is what the critic who leveled her accusation at "the feminists" objected to; unfortunately but predictably, she defended herself by assigning a single and oversimplified place to them. The model of ferreting out the true, hidden political self of critics and fictional characters has its uses. It also has its limits. We might want to think twice

---

[36] Julia Prewitt Brown, "The Feminist Depreciation of Austen: A Polemical Reading," *Novel*, 23 (1990), 303–13.

about overriding a novelistic discourse that allows for the emergence, within limits, of a series of potential selves that, under the right circumstances, could become part of a larger dialogue.

What does plot mean to Henry Tilney? Well, he can use fictional plotting to excite Catherine Morland, but in a world in which he is participant, not creator, his role is less powerful. Throughout most of the novel, he simply waits, observing how the plot of his father's infatuation is working itself out to his own psychic advantage. At the same time, he participates in a love plot his father does everything he can to create. When the decisive moment of rectitude and defiance arrives, he is ready for it. Indeed, his adroitness throughout the novel gives him the air of somehow orchestrating the whole thing. It is worth mentioning that he contrives to extract as much enjoyment as he can from the plots that develop around him, from which we may gather the moral that plots are for pleasure. For his sister, the norms of society are a more serious matter, given what society expects from a woman by way of obedience and resignation. Her eventual release from her father's orbit by the entrance of "the most charming young man in the world" (218) is, in respect to plots and plotting, a nice parody of Henry's all-too-easy mixture of spectatorship, escape, and mastery, revealing (if by this point in the novel it needs to be revealed) the element of readerly fantasy that lies behind our acceptance of Catherine and Henry's achievement of perfect felicity. When the plot has run its course, the large problems concerning the fates and proprieties of men and women remain as they have unfolded; they are energized by the workings of the plot, not solved or "solved" by its ending.

Telling and Ending Stories in *Persuasion*

Captain Frederick Wentworth is given to strong emotion and sometimes betrays a narrative imagination without nuance. When he sees Anne Elliot after eight years of separation, he judges her changed beyond recognition, imagining himself part of a plot that has contained a sharp and unchangeable reversal. When he falls back in love with her, he tells her that, in his eyes, she never has changed and never could. One suspects that Wentworth returns to England a rich and successful naval officer because his simple, linear plotting focuses his attention and his will, so that he makes his plots come true. His passion certainly energizes readers, who may find themselves repeatedly riding the novel's forward momentum so that they can see him write a letter which, in his eyes, will determine his fate forever. Even Anne Elliot can be touched by this sort of story-telling about the past and the future. Wentworth's letter is infectious; she too develops fears that something may happen to prevent him from discovering her feelings about the letter. What if (as in *Romeo and Juliet*) the mail doesn't get through? Of course, she has sense enough to realize that in the grain of Austen's world, different moments for various kinds of communication are there to be taken advantage of, yet doubts and anxieties assail her, and even the more confident reader, who in the words of *Northanger Abbey* realizes that "we are all hastening together to perfect felicity" (217).

In general, however, Anne resists Wentworth's kind of plotting, despite its sublime possibilities. An important moment in her growing ascendancy over him occurs when he is in the midst of telling the story of his doubts and fears that her "friends" might persuade her now to marry her cousin, as they had eight years ago persuaded her to break their engagement. Anne replies, "You should have distinguished . . . You should not have suspected me now; the case so different, and my age so different. If I was wrong in yielding to persuasion once, remember that it was to persuasion exerted on the side of safety" (246) and so on. What a wonderful way of reassuring Wentworth that she has always loved him! At this point in their mutual reconstruction of the true story of their past, Anne is willing to concede that she was "wrong" in allowing her friends to dissuade her from marrying Wentworth. She is not willing to allow her own specific stance in the larger social texture to be swallowed up by the narrative of Wentworth's fears.

Throughout the novel, making distinctions is intimately associated with Anne's singularity and especially with her escape from being subsumed by the mores of those around her. At the heart of her distinction-making lies an attempt to create and protect a certain version of the self. Early in the novel, Austen appears to thematize the issues involved, as Anne comes to grips with the Musgroves' entire lack of interest in the doings at Kellynch-hall:

> She acknowledged it to be very fitting, that every little social commonwealth should dictate its own matters of discourse; and hoped, ere long, to become a not unworthy member of the one she was now transplanted into.—With the prospect of spending at least two months at Uppercross, it was highly incumbent on her to clothe her imagination, her memory, and all her ideas in as much of Uppercross as possible. (69–70)

Here we see combined a moment of attempted identification (it is "incumbent" upon her to try to fit in), yet at the same time an inevitable moment of difference-making, figured as an ironic and partly involuntary withdrawal which involves both loss (she cannot be a "real" member of this community) and the avoidance of loss (she does not really want her finer sensibility to be entirely subsumed by it anyway, and it turns out to be a relief to escape from the mores of Kellynch). This is a historicist moment par excellence. A moment of loss and gain results from recognizing that a social milieu has its own customs and its own consciousness, a recognition that can come only from feeling oneself separate from that milieu. It is typical and fitting that Anne should employ the metaphor of "clothing" to evoke a network of social customs that makes objective demands but can, in the right circumstances, be shed. Scott uses the metaphor of clothing in this way, and so does George Eliot, though neither entirely believes in the shedding: their sense of historicity implies that differentiating clothes and the skin beneath them is a formidable task. In a less historicist vein, of course, Austen's own sense of the complex social network means that anything approaching a radical break from society, a true lighting out for the territory, is never an issue. For all three authors, though in differing ways and degrees, the moments of identity-making and difference-making are the *same* moments; they are mutually reinforcing. Individuals become individual precisely when they find themselves aware of alternative cultural textures. The power to recognize the different ways in which cultures function sparks a recognition of how they shape their members, but at the same time it distances the recognizer from the shaping. Anne would lack as deep an individuality in our eyes if we did not see her making judgments on the necessity of merging with Uppercross. Distinguishing, then, helps to carve out a place to be oneself in the interstices of a seemingly all-encompassing social network. That Anne is capable of calling upon Wentworth to make distinctions ought to reassure him about her independence from the pressures of her friends.

At the end of *Persuasion*, Anne Elliot and Frederick Wentworth review the past that has finally led them to their present happiness. The very circumstances in which they speak of the past may serve as an emblem of the interstices and multiple possibilities that exist in even the most seemingly rigid grain of social conventions and conventional plots. Their reminiscing occurs in the midst of an unknowing social gathering, during which they contrive from time to time to find themselves alone together in the conservatory:

> It was in one of these short meetings, each apparently occupied in admiring a fine display of green-house plants, that she said—
> "I have been thinking over the past, and trying impartially to judge of the right and wrong, I mean with regard to myself; and I must believe that I was right, much as I suffered from it, that I was perfectly right in being guided by the friend whom you will love

better than you do now. To me, she was in the place of a parent. Do not mistake me, however. I am not saying that she did not err in her advice. It was, perhaps, one of those cases in which advice is good or bad only as the event decides; and for myself, I certainly never should, in any circumstance of tolerable similarity, give such advice. But I mean, that I was right in submitting to her, and that if I had done otherwise, I should have suffered more in continuing the engagement than I did even in giving it up, because I should have suffered in my conscience. I have now, as far as such a sentiment is allowable in human nature, nothing to reproach myself with; and if I mistake not, a strong sense of duty is no bad part of a woman's portion." (248)

Telling the story of the past leads Anne to take back her previous admission that she had been wrong to break her engagement. We might have expected her story-telling to dwell on how the bliss of marrying Wentworth effaces the sufferings of the past; it doesn't. She insists on a continuity with her past, not a break from it. Her ability to distinguish allows her to achieve a metonymical relationship between her present and past selves. She refuses to allow a love-story capped with the acquisition of Wentworth to exhaust the possibilities of her former self and to silence her earlier voice, the voice that said "no" to him. Her story is fully articulated, though (recalling the uses of silence in *Northanger Abbey*) it gains force by verging on the ineffable: when asked whether she would have married Wentworth had he returned for her earlier, " 'Would I!' was all her answer; but the accent was decisive enough" (248). She maintains solidarity with her past self, with Lady Russell, and through Lady Russell with the memory of her mother, refusing to belittle female relationship. All of this becomes possible through the making of distinctions, major and minor.[37] Her happy ending has a difference: it is not simply the ending of a traditional comedy in which an older blocking figure is finally got round. She distinguishes between roles and times, insisting that she would *never* give advice like Lady Russell's . . ."in any circumstance of tolerable similarity." Before our very eyes, Anne Elliot reads her past through the grain.

But what are we to make of the end of Anne's speech? Don't her closing

---

[37]   Distinction-making provides room to maneuver for heroines drawn by other authors, as some oppressive males come to realize. One of the lowest blows her father deals Clarissa is his insulting charge that she aims to "distinguish away [her] duty"—see Richardson, *Clarissa*, ed. Angus Ross (Harmondsworth: Penguin, 1985), 65. This is not to say that, in other power relations, the making of distinctions can't be used as an instrument of a less admirable avoidance. One case against the realist mind-set I have been describing is that it distinguishes away its present political duty.

words deliver the entire speech, scene, and novel over to the "bad" marriage plot, where every ounce of the heroine's seeming independence is suddenly canceled by her willingness to smother herself in a marriage? "If I mistake not, a strong sense of duty is no bad part of a woman's portion," she tells Wentworth. In offering her "sense of duty" to Wentworth as what seems a kind of a dowry or marriage portion, isn't she handing over the rest of herself as well? The expression Anne uses, however, is "a *woman's* portion." "Portion" is a complex word, and its complexities help create the kind of room for movement and distinction-making that allows Austen (and realism) purchase on the prefabricated meanings associated with the marriage plot (or any other plot as template).[38] At root, "portion" means "part" or "share"; it also means "fate or destiny." The word, then, makes room for a range of issues involving the justice of shares and the inevitability of fate; it does this even though (or perhaps because?) it often carries with it a sense of an *appropriate* share or of a *deserved* fate (and even fate as merited punishment).

In Anne's reference to a "woman's portion," the meaning of "portion" as "inheritance" comes into play. She is reminding Wentworth of her own full value; at the same time, for those who have attended to her distinction-making with regard to Lady Russell's advice, the idea of portion as inheritance also evokes a female line of inheritance that passes from Anne's mother, through Lady Russell, to Anne herself.[39] Wentworth has his own way of asserting his worth. It is not clear to me that Austen's contemporaries would have found as jarring as we are likely to do the note of acquisition sounded in his comment that pride had prevented him from returning years earlier to ask for Anne's hand "as what could alone crown all [his] other success" (248). In a pinch, one might argue that he is really laying all his triumphs at Anne's feet: she both is the crown and wears it. Yet it's hard to deny that he's also laying all the triumphs, including Anne, at the feet of an image of his own self-sufficient mastery. By the end of the scene, however, he finds himself qualifying his pretensions to mastery, admitting the force of circumstances as he tells the story

[38]   I am tempted here to associate the word "portion" itself directly with metonymy, since one of its basic meanings is "any part of a whole." But this won't quite do, at least for the kind of metonymy I find at the base of modern realism—a metonymy that takes the form of an articulated system of differences. "Portion" tends to mean a part of a *continuous* and *uniform* whole.

[39]   For an inspiring discussion of the Greek word *moira*, a cognate of "portion" that parallels the English word quite closely in its ranges of meaning, see Bruce Robbins, *The Servant's Hand* (Durham: Duke University Press, 1993), especially chap. 1. Robbins is particularly illuminating on the radical, egalitarian possibilities of the word, and on its association with a certain kind of social order threatened by the historical developments surrounding it.

of the part he has played. "I have been used to the gratification of believing myself to earn every blessing that I enjoyed. I have valued myself on honourable toils and just rewards," he tells Anne. "Like other great men under reverses" he then adds with a smile, "I must endeavour to subdue my mind to my fortune. I must learn to brook being happier than I deserve" (249). In granting himself this ironic place in the company of Great Men, he is undercutting his claims to such mastery. Anne continues to find a way of maintaining her selfhood in the interstices of social reality, as she has done throughout the novel. (In this, she recalls Henry Tilney.) Wentworth feels a brake on his will to mastery and sense of entitlement. Anne finds pleasure in keeping her particular hold on the past. Wentworth, softened by pleasure, loosens his hold on a stereotypical story about manly heroism, and decides to accept a happiness he does not deserve. There is nothing simple about their marriage plot.

An Evasion of History?

What sort of contribution does *Persuasion* make to historicist realism? To ask this question is not to ask whether Austen's novels can be read as embodying aspects of the ideology of her time and symptoms of societal strain and contradiction. Of course they can. The issue here involves what modes of intelligence and imagination her novels make available to the project of grasping historicist reality.

In the previous chapter, I noted that in *Persuasion*, Austen explores with a new richness certain areas that cluster around the historicist view of historical process, which in the realist novel develops for a time in tandem with an enriched awareness of human interiority. The most striking way in which she develops her depictions of the inner life in *Persuasion* involves simple sensation—the buzzings and semi-perceptions that impinge on Anne (as in her inchoate sensation—which is at once emotional, visual, and tactile—that Wentworth must be lifting her into the Crofts' cart). Yet, as we've seen, Austen also explores the uses an individual can make of memory. In a similar fashion, though a sense of social process is always there in Austen, in *Persuasion* we feel the impetus toward social change and motion viewed as a rich and potentially liberating process, not simply as a moral necessity. Finally, the form in which Anne makes use of the powers of memory recalls a central historicist insight. Scott can capture the historical and cultural specificity of the Highlands only at the moment when it's at the verge of disappearing. Anne Elliot can redeem her past—indeed, possess her past and, in the fullest sense, "live" its experiences—only when time and repetition have attenuated the link between her present and past selves to the point where she needs to assert that there *is* a link. Her very assertion of continuity itself marks a vivifying distance between older and younger selves. The presence of such echoes and parallels tempts one to claim that *Persuasion* is feeling its way toward the historicist vision—or perhaps that this novel marks a moment when a dynamic historicism begins to have its effect on Austen's vision.

What can be claimed with certainty is that Austen's fiction makes a crucial contribution with respect to what I've called the texture of its representation. Metonymy, I've argued, is the trope on which modern historicist realism depends. Austen's powers of metonymical representation are remarkable and exemplary. As we have seen throughout this chapter, Austen immerses her characters and readers in remarkably fine and nuanced processes of distinction-making. The web of differences with which characters and readers must cope draws upon and captures the form of the mental movements that will be needed to make sense of history: it helps install a grammar adequate for understanding the texture of historical existence. Following and participating in the exacting mental processes Austen involves us in, we begin to learn what would be required to take in present realities and to connect them with our pasts, and we taste the pleasure open to minds capable of such distinction. In these ways, Austen's world shadows and is shadowed by the subject of the following chapter, the fictional world of Scott, who famously believed that Austen outdid him in producing "the exquisite touch which renders ordinary common-place things and characters interesting from the truth of the description and the sentiment."[40]

It remains possible to contend that Austen turns her back on history, nowhere more so than in her use of the marriage plot. The charge would be that she engages in privatization, promoting a retreat from the public sphere to what we used to call bourgeois interiority. Don't Austen's novels get us into the habit of thinking that we can solve the underlying problems of our society by improving our selves? Here is where Austen may look weakest and the claims of sublime criticism seem most compelling. Don't we require some rousing and goading? Doesn't Austen's ironic response to life provide a bad example, lulling readers into imagining that irony in and of itself does something? Such questions seem inescapable when you imagine yourself moving in the grain of history and society; indeed, the insistence with which they arise is itself a legacy of the realist habit of mind. I hope to have shown that Austen's novels are entirely aware of such problems; it is true, however, that she doesn't worry them

[40] Scott, *The Journal of Sir Walter Scott*, ed. W. E. K. Anderson (Oxford: Clarendon, 1972), 14 March 1826.

to the extent that we might. Austen's contemporary Scott feels the weight of these problems very heavily; in his novels, the grain of society and history is very stiff, and we see his characters knocking into it constantly, in ways that can be both entertaining and deeply threatening. But for Scott, the issues involved have quite different contours. On the one hand, he directly confronts historical differences as such; on the other, he never discovers individuality in the way that Austen does. We shall see in the next chapter that the issue of what freedom exists in the grain is supremely important to Scott, but also that the problem takes for him a quite different shape than it does for Austen. Another path leads from Austen and Scott to Eliot. Eliot's novels are permeated with a sense of the historicity of life in society, to the point that a fascination with its workings no longer suffices. Within her fiction arises the rhetorical appeal that we do something about reality, which we may miss in reading Scott or in making our way through the plots of Jane Austen.

5

Scott: Realism and the Other

Is the notion of a distinct culture (or race, or religion, or civilization) a useful one, or does it always get involved either in self-congratulation (when one discusses one's own) or hostility and aggression (when one discusses the "other")?

—Edward Said, *Orientalism*

Sam Johnson was a Tory
And Walter Scott a dope
—Terry Eagleton, "The Ballad of English Literature"

Scott brought history, a full historicist history, into the novel, in the place of thin evocations of exotic lands that happened to be located in previous eras. He influenced writers across Europe, and the best of these responded, not by adding a historical coloring to their works, but by creating coherent historical milieus. He made possible the fictional depiction of what Hegel calls "the present as history." George Eliot's art is unthinkable without him.

Criticism in this century has nonetheless accorded him marginal attention. He has been neglected for a complex of reasons, including what seems an inevitable reaction to his status as a cultural icon for nineteenth-century British culture, a broader revolt against "the burden of history," a view of the development of the novel focused on techniques and values left undeveloped in his work, and a host of more local critical views and needs as well.[1] The effect of ignoring him has been unfortunate, nowhere more so than in the critique of realism. If criticism had made a significant attempt to come to grips with Scott, it would have found the denigration of realism I've charted much harder to sustain. It's no surprise that for

[1] I use the phrase "the burden of history" partly to recall the seminal essay of that name by Hayden White, reprinted in his *Tropics of Discourse* (Baltimore: Johns Hopkins University Press, 1978), 27–50. For Scott's critical reception, see James T. Hillhouse, *The Waverley Novels and Their Critics* (London: Oxford University Press, 1936), and John Henry Raleigh, "What Scott Meant to the Victorians," *Victorian Studies*, 7 (1963), 7–34.

Georg Lukács, Scott remains an obligatory stop on the literary timetable. To be sure, it's possible to write valuably about realism even if one lacks a substantial grasp of what Scott's novels involve. Auerbach gives a throw-away description of Scott as a purveyor of "romantic Historism," and then moves on to his debtor Balzac.[2] Only a critic so thoroughly steeped in the historicist tradition could make such an omission without damage to the rest of his project.

Scott's novels are of exceptional interest for any study of British realism, and not simply for their palpable contributions to the development of the metonymical historicist representation that is central to the realist project. They are also useful because they have an ambiguous relationship to the fiction that followed them. Scott's novels find form for much that would become central to nineteenth-century realism, but they were written before it had fully established its norms, and they depart from those norms in significant ways. They offer critical leverage, providing a sense of alternative possibilities and helping to calibrate the course of later realism.

In an earlier book, I countered a range of critical assumptions, espoused by friends of Scott as well as foes, that seemed to me to obscure the nature of his achievement. There appeared to be a large measure of agreement that novels ought to be, first and foremost, about the inner lives of characters. Some of Scott's defenders had attempted to show that, appearances to the contrary notwithstanding, his were too; many of his detractors suggested, more plausibly, that his novels lacked such depiction and were therefore negligible. I agreed with the description provided by the detractors, but not with their value judgment. Scott's characters, I maintained, do tend to lack interiority, but this lack turns out to be a positive virtue, for it enables his novels to focus centrally on how cultures move through history. I tried to shift attention from the inner lives of characters to the inner logic of cultures, insisting that critics of all persuasions were making a grave mistake in assuming that the virtues of Scott's fiction were or should be the virtues of what they took to be The Novel (that is, the side of the Victorian novel that culminates in James and Woolf). Instead, we needed to find ways of approaching Scott's fiction, seen as an Other that had to be met on its own terms. This endeavor would run in parallel with Scott's own project—or at least the part of his project that interested me—which is itself an attempt to bring to living representation cultures and mentalities that are interesting precisely because they elude our own cultural norms.[3]

---

[2] Erich Auerbach, *Mimesis* (1946), trans. Willard R. Trask (Princeton: Princeton University Press, 1953), 477.

[3] Harry E. Shaw, *The Forms of Historical Fiction* (Ithaca: Cornell University Press, 1983).

In making my case for Scott, I realized soon enough that what I had initially taken to be an essential difference between Scott and, say, George Eliot was actually much more an essential difference between Scott and the way a dominant tradition of modern critics had read George Eliot (and other novelists). I thus became aware that Scott might provide a way of allowing us to discover that Eliot herself resists that tradition. But to pursue such a line of argument would have required another book. I elected to emphasize Scott's singularity, believing (as I still believe) that if the differences are ignored, Scott's fiction isn't very interesting.

The strict separation of sheep and goats I engaged in would now seem less necessary than it was fifteen years ago. Practical criticism of the novel based on the assumption that an exploration of individual interiority is the novel's central achievement is on the wane. (To be sure, it had been severely attacked on theoretical grounds much earlier.) Criticism has become more hospitable to the historicity of fiction in general. One needn't be a Lukácsian to feel a lively interest in the shape and shaping of the past. One needn't propose (as I do here) that prose fiction can claim to represent an objective historical process, to find significant the problems a novel is likely to encounter if it attempts to make good on such claims.[4]

As one might expect, however, new challenges have arisen to Scott's novels, and also to the terms in which I sought to define his achievement. What if the attempt to see earlier periods and other cultures as interesting because they differ from one's own is itself suspect, and is in fact likely to have oppressive cultural consequences in direct proportion to the extent to which it succeeds in representing cultural and historical difference? Does my vision of Scott's fiction merely deliver him over to a more fundamental critique?

My sense that Scott's interest in the culturally Other might have a sinister side came from recognizing the full implications of Edward Said's critique of Orientalism. Cultural critiques gain credibility not so much because they win a theoretical argument as because they suddenly bring a set of particular phenomena into focus in a way so compelling as to make us willing to consider a shift in our basic assumptions. What persuades is the union of a general theoretical framework that seems plausible and provocative, with a powerful explanation for a field of phenomena we

---

[4]   This is not to say that critics of Scott have universally or even mainly come to focus on his novels as representations of history. Currently the dominant trend is to view Scott in the context of his own age, often as a purveyor of its ideology. In an overview of Scott criticism with particular reference to the past forty years, I argue that this emphasis is in consonance with the long-standing view of Scott as a "projective" creator of romances, not novels: see the Introduction to *Critical Essays on Sir Walter Scott*, ed. Harry E. Shaw (New York: G. K. Hall, 1996).

care about. Said's *Orientalism* has just this quality. As it happens, Said mentions Scott only in passing, and as I'll suggest in a moment, in an anecdotal way that's quite misleading. Nevertheless, taking seriously the case made by *Orientalism* as a whole should make any admirer of Scott— and anyone impressed with the claims of realist fiction to represent the cultural and historical Other—uneasy.[5]

When you open a Scott novel and give it the careful, active reading it deserves, you find yourself in the presence of a mind that invites you to experience the workings of historical moments quite different from your own. Scott's vision offers an exhilarating revelation of new fields of human possibility hidden in the past, balanced by a recognition that historical process involves inevitable, tragic loss. In describing Scott's works in this way, I'm painting the picture of an intellectual achievement characterized by intelligence, generosity, and unsparing honesty. These are the characteristics the admirers of the realist novel—of Austen or Eliot or Thackeray—have always claimed for it. They are also the characteristics of at least one vision of the academy.

Said's study reveals that, in historical fact and nowhere more than in the academy, what may seem simply to be knowledgeable attempts to understand the Other can be anything but generous in their motivations, and anything but liberating in their effects. Europeans who have come into contact with what they call the Orient have consistently created pictures of it that advance European interests. Said argues that the very notion that the Orient is Other from Europe has been a prime instrument in European political and cultural domination, for the category of the Other always implies a hierarchical ordering. He produces instance after instance in which attempts to capture the Other in a seemingly value-neutral way turn out to embody habits of thought that put the Other at a disadvantage, ensuring that what the observer sees is what he wishes to see. By attempting to understand a culture as "distinct" from one's own, by making it an object of study, we deprive it of its own subjectivity. We render it passive: we see it as "that which we study and understand," not "that which can understand itself." If Said failed to show that European visions of the Orient have in actual historical fact repeatedly been used in the service of domination, his analysis might be less persuasive. But he does show this, and so persuasively that it's difficult to resist imagining that the dynamic behind the Orientalist practices he describes involves an

---

[5]   I shall be using the word "Orient" and related locutions in the evaluative context Said's work provides, without making special rhetorical or typographical attempts to dissociate myself from the ideology they represent. Similarly, I will simply capitalize "Other." This typographical convention is not intended to add an aura of absolute inaccessibility to the Other.

epistemological necessity—difficult for the reader, and also for Said himself. "Is the notion of a distinct culture (or race, or religion, or civilization) a useful one," he asks, "or does it always get involved either in self-congratulation (when one discusses one's own) or hostility and aggression (when one discusses the 'other')?" I shall return to this formulation, questioning the terms in which the alternatives are drawn up, and their status as mutually exclusive choices. But it seems important to face the issue Said raises here.[6]

Said's analysis makes us wonder about the pleasure we take as we read Scott and find ourselves delighted with a world that is historically Other. It not only undercuts the concrete, moment-by-moment texture of the vision of history Scott invites us to share, it also calls into question another major aspect of Scott's achievement, his powerful evocation of the movement of history and the losses that movement entails. Orientalist thinking, Said reveals, regularly has viewed the Orient in terms that contrast a glorious past with a colorless present. The *real* Egyptians built the pyramids; the Egyptians who happen to be living near the pyramids in the present are unreal. By grace of his expert knowledge, the Orientalist possesses a more authentic kinship with the real, Ancient Egyptians than do their modern, degenerate descendants. The interests of the present-day Egyptians can accordingly be justly ignored by Orientalist and Imperialist alike. Now Said himself doesn't make this point, but in describing the myth of a "full" past versus an "empty" present, he is describing Scott's novels. The past is always fuller than the present in Scott. Because of his enormous influence on the mentality of nineteenth-century Europe, and particularly on literature and historiography, Scott must have played a significant role in accustoming the literate public to think of the present and past in these terms. This means that, no doubt inadvertently, Scott helped pave the way for the acceptance of the fundamental Orientalist assumption that modern Orientals don't matter. Scott's fiction helped to ac-

---

[6] Edward Said, *Orientalism* (New York: Pantheon, 1978), 325; hereafter cited in the text. Subsequent work has made the project of imagining Others seem increasingly suspect. Johannes Fabian, in *Time and the Other* (New York: Columbia University Press, 1983), for instance, explores the problems that arise when anthropologists treat contemporary societies as if they embody "earlier" stages of the development of (their own) culture. Aijaz Ahmad's *In Theory* (London: Verso, 1992) has not been alone in turning the charge of an objectifying and demeaning Othering against Said's own work. However justified some of the objections may be, the spectacle of Said's being attacked for ignoring cultural complexity, in a book that placed at the center of critical discussion the ways in which the West has ignored the complex specificity of the East, threatens an infinite regress. As I will suggest below, the only remedy seems to me to embrace one's own historical and social position knowingly, which involves among other things recognizing that one has a psychic (even perceptual) need to essentialize, and that discourse itself needs to essentialize, and then to mitigate the problems that result.

custom educated Europeans to think deeply and with feeling about the inaccessibility of past cultures and the sadness of their gradual, inevitable extinction by modernity. But those who formed this kind of affective bond with the Orient, Said tells us—Lawrence of Arabia is a good example—tended to lose sight of the Oriental Other because they focused instead on their own feelings *about* the Other, on the pathos arising from their very conviction that the Orient really was inaccessible. The passage to the Orient became everything; the Orient itself faded from view.

Two opposed theoretical positions about speculations concerning the cultural Other seem to me compatible with Said's analysis of the historical workings of Orientalist thought. One would be that the very attempt to imagine the cultural Other as different will always bring with it blindness and denigration: we'd respond with a resounding "Yes" to Said's question of whether "the notion of a distinct culture (or race, or religion, or civilization) . . . always get[s] involved either in self-congratulation (when one discusses one's own) or hostility and aggression (when one discusses the 'other')?" We might, however, come to a different assessment. We might conclude that, however bad the historical record of attempts to know the Other has been, employing "the notion of a distinct culture" might nonetheless prove fruitful, given the right circumstances, assumptions, and intellectual procedures.[7] (It's worth adding that a fruitful approach to the Other wouldn't need to depend upon the assumption that we could in any simple sense tell the *whole truth* about the Other. The

[7] Christopher Herbert's *Culture and Anomie: Ethnographic Imagination in the Nineteenth Century* (Chicago: University of Chicago Press, 1991), which gives a valuable, sobering account of the pitfalls accompanying the rise of the concept of culture in the nineteenth century, nonetheless reminds us that "to represent the theory of culture purely as an adjunct or expression of an impulse of domination would be seriously incomplete. . . . it often was employed in precisely the opposite manner. To learn to think of an alien society as a seamless web of institutions with its own inherent 'law and order' is at least potentially to confer on it an integrity not legitimately to be violated by outside interventions" (44). For a powerfully and subtly argued case that Scott does the work of English imperialism by totalizing Scottish culture into a single and therefore manageable Other, however, see James Buzard, "Translation and Tourism: Scott's *Waverley* and the Rendering of Culture," *Yale Journal of Criticism*, 8 (1995), 31–59. Buzard suggests that my earlier work ignored "the very pointed fashion in which Scott's work puts forward particular things as ethnographic symbols" (55–56, n. 19). His critique has its validity, though I was primarily interested in denying that Scott's novels are or should be in the business of making historical milieus sources of "spiritual" symbols for the inner life of characters, and though the stress on ideological symbolism he favors had long been so amply represented in the criticism of Scott (though without his rich ethnographic slant) that suggesting its limitations seemed necessary. My focus rested on determining what aspects of Scott's mode of representation are most vital and promising. I attempted to recover (to borrow a concept from the Russian Formalist) the "dominant" of his form. In any case, I trust this book makes it clear that I do not believe that Scott's metonymical representation is limited to what Buzard describes as "the 'microhistorical' wish to preserve what is passing."

truth might instead figure as a regulative ideal, a goal to be approached in asymptotic fashion.) These two positions reflect different assumptions concerning the extent to which our perceptions, lives, and actions are predetermined by epistemological structures. If indeed we must (independently and "totalistically") construct the Other as an object of knowledge before we try to know it, and if our very modes of construction are bound to produce an entity to which we will inevitably condescend and over which we will try to wield power, then who could doubt that the very attempt to imagine the Other is poisoned from the start? If, by contrast, we believe that our relationship with the Other might involve a mutually constituting dialectic or mutually informative dialogue, the project of trying to know the Other will seem more promising. Orientalism may not wish to know the Other, but since all approaches to the Other need not be Orientalizing, the possibility for a more productive dialogue would remain open. And if we believe that Scott's fiction promotes a habit of mind capable of entering into a dialogue with the past, the sense his fiction projects that the past is more alive than the present could turn out to be heuristically useful, in the right hands. The problem with the Orientalists would then be that they picked up on only one part of Scott's vision.

The opposed positions I have outlined here easily translate into positions concerning subjectivity and agency.[8] Are we "positioned" as subjects so that we will always do epistemological violence to that which we perceive as the Other? Working along Habermassian lines, Amanda Anderson has made a cogent distinction between "systemic" and "participatory" notions of the subject. She is suspicious of what she terms the "systemic anti-cogito that characterizes the poststructuralist sensibility ('The system thinks me, therefore I am not')." Anderson believes that such a view of subjectivity produces "an utterly atomized social field, one that precludes entering into the standpoint that is assumed by subjects in non-reifying encounters."[9] The reading I shall be giving of Scott's attempt to represent the Other will emphasize a dialectical play between subject and

[8]   In retrospect, it has become clear that *Orientalism* takes two divergent views of subjectivity, agency, and our ability to know the truth. Sometimes, drawing on certain poststructuralist arguments, Said places the subject so fully at the behest of larger cultural discourses that knowing and acting on the truth seem impossible; simultaneously, however, he himself claims to have discovered the truth about European distortions of the Orient, which implies that he also knows the truth about the Orient itself. For a stern critique of such contradictions, see Ahmad, *In Theory*. This problem recalls the problem of the narrator's privileged position in the realist novel, which will form a major theme in this and the following chapter. In my view, it's inaccurate to suggest that Said isn't aware of this problem in his own work: his discussion of Massignon and human finiteness (271–74), for instance, is an impressive attempt to negotiate it.
[9]   Amanda Anderson, *Tainted Souls and Painted Faces* (Ithaca: Cornell University Press, 1993), 221–22.

system at every turn and level. The subjects involved in this play include not only those represented in the fiction, but the narrator and reader.

It seems clear that Scott's influence inadvertently helped to create a climate in which Orientalism could flourish. And are there aspects of Scott's realism that, if they had been attended to, might have challenged Orientalist thinking? Realism posits an evolving, reciprocal relationship between forms of thought and the external realities that they organize for us, a vision which renders suspect any notion that a form of thought can determine in advance all the perceptions and arrangements that derive from it. I've suggested earlier that realism is valuable because of the habit of mind it can foster. Is the habit of mind evoked by Scott's realism sufficiently complex to supplement a passive delight in historical otherness with more active, reciprocal modes of analysis and engagement?

Changing Places: *The Talisman* and *The Journal*

In the opening pages of *The Talisman*, the protagonist, Sir Kenneth, is on a crusade led by Richard the Lionhearted. He comes upon an Emir, who is in fact Saladin in disguise, at an oasis, and fights an impromptu tournament with him. (Saladin's penchant for disguising himself is something we'll return to.) When the tournament ends in a stalemate, the two talk with each other, and (as Said nicely puts it), "the Christian discovers his Muslim antagonist to be not so bad a fellow after all" (101). As a result, when Sir Kenneth suggests during their conversation that the Muslims couldn't possibly continue to withstand the Crusaders if they weren't in league with the Devil, he adds a sentence to let the Emir know that he shouldn't take this observation personally. "I speak not thus of thee in particular, Saracen," he says, "but generally of thy people and religion" (3, 62; chap. 3).[10]

In his only substantive commentary on Scott in *Orientalism*, Said gives a pointed account of this vignette. Part of his discussion suggests that in depicting Sir Kenneth as bigoted about Islam, Scott is engaging in a "feeble historicism" (101) that makes the scene exotic, entertains modern readers, but finally lets them off the hook. By allowing Sir Kenneth to at-

[10]   No reliable, readily available edition of the *The Talisman* exists. (The Everyman paperback is defective.) I therefore cite volume and page numbers (followed by the chapter numbers found in one-volume editions) from the first edition of *Tales of the Crusaders*, 4 vols. (Edinburgh: Constable, 1825), in which *The Talisman* comprises volumes 3–4. For a reading of *The Talisman* that touches on Said but views the novel from the perspective of Scottish identity, see Caroline McCracken-Flesher, "The Recuperation of Canon Fodder: Walter Scott's *The Talisman*," in *No Small World*, ed. Michael Carroll (Urbana, Ill.: NCTE, 1996), reprinted in *Critical Essays on Sir Walter Scott*, 202–17.

tack his Muslim opponent's religion with a crude naiveté, Scott invites his European readers to falsely assume that they themselves don't share such prejudices. Said's analysis has much to recommend it, particularly when he comments on the larger ideological usefulness of the kind of "courtesy exception" Sir Kenneth makes in favor of the Emir. What's most interesting for our purposes, however, is how quickly he rises to the level of the *forms* of thought implied by the passage. The particular insult to Islam Sir Kenneth voices, Said implies, matters little in comparison with the larger mental operation in which he is engaging, and in which the fiction invites us to engage as well, on another and more general level. The implication seems to be that such a passage embodies a form or style or template of thought powerful enough to override the importance of *any* content whatever, in a way that recalls the notion of plot as a template with an overriding significance we encountered in the previous chapter. I too am interested in forms of thought, but I believe they need to be understood as potentially responsive to unexpected or disruptive particularities.

Said's analysis suggests that in this brief vignette, Scott places Sir Kenneth wholly within his cultural and historical moment. In this I believe Said to be entirely correct: for most of the novel, Sir Kenneth is indeed depicted as being (as the narrator subsequently comments) "superior in no respect to the ideas and manners of his time" (3, 128; chap. 5). Said is, however, mistaken when he implies that Scott's text invites its readers to assume a position of secure superiority to Sir Kenneth. Said's notion that it does echoes the well-known view that the narrative voice in realist novels always, from its position of authority, smooths over any ideological dissonances that emerge within a novel. I'd suggest, by contrast, that our cathexes with the limited mentalities of characters in Scott's novels, and in most of the realist novels we prize, are much too strong to allow this. In fact, Scott wishes the reader to take both a more conscious *and a more favorable* attitude toward Sir Kenneth's prejudices than Said's discussion would suggest. I'd like to add, at the risk of evoking misunderstanding and perhaps even indignation, that this indulgent attitude toward prejudice may be no bad thing. To explain what I mean here will require a digression on the larger issues involved.

Humanist criticism has been attacked for pretending to rise above its own cultural position, almost as often as the realist novel has been attacked for believing in transparent representation. And of course spurious universalism and transparent representation can be made to walk hand in hand. Too often, what results is a parade of straw men. Though erecting one's own historical situation into "the human condition," transparent or opaque, is a practice that deserves our suspicion, it is facile to assume that all concepts of universalism can be equated with this pseudo-universalism, and unhelpful to place pseudo-universalism in a circularly defined relationship with "humanism." If an easy slide toward a universality that ignores the particularities of our cultural positions is a hallmark of humanism, the novelists with which this book deals are not of the humanist persuasion. Pseudo-universalism rests on the assumption that, at the level that matters most, "we" are all the same. This suggests that, in the end, local particularities don't matter, except perhaps as a source of the picturesque. Scott would have found such a notion repellent, as we shall see more fully in a moment. No doubt enthusiasm for one's own culture—or even a recognition that one is, for better and often for worse, bound up with one's culture—has its problems. It's nonetheless possible to argue that a firm, self-conscious embeddedness in one's own culture provides the best available standpoint from which to encounter the Other. Attempts at an immediate universalism, recent discussions have taught us, have a way of backfiring, but so do hasty denigrations of one's own cultural position. It may turn out that, especially in an imaginative work, an *initial* assumption of difference as superiority is necessary as a way of creating a sufficiently firm sense of cultural security to allow the mind to imagine something different. At the *end* of such a process, one hopes that a considerably more nuanced view will emerge, in which the claims of the Other, seen in their full complexity, will be balanced by our allegiance to our own culture, which after all provides the only lived means whereby we can grasp what it would mean to belong to *any* culture. Hilary Putnam has written some interesting words on the problem of being able to value, or perhaps even love, someone for whose political opinions you have "something akin to *contempt*."[11] This is an extreme case of a common predicament. Do we require a neutrality of values, or a deracination of cultures, to live with one another?[12]

But do we really have cultural positions? And how are we to understand what it would mean to be "self-conscious" about our embedded-

[11]   Hilary Putnam, *Reason, Truth, and History* (Cambridge: Cambridge University Press, 1981), 165.
[12]   Since *Orientalism*, Said has worried this problem further, in his elaboration of the "secular criticism" announced in the Introduction to *The World, the Text, and the Critic* (Cambridge: Harvard University Press, 1983); see also his *Representations of the Intellectual* (New York: Pantheon, 1994). For an illuminating critique of other recent attempts to grapple with these issues, see Amanda Anderson, "Cosmopolitanism, Universality, and the Divided Legacies of Modernism," in *Cosmopolitics*, ed. Pheng Cheah and Bruce Robbins (University of Minnesota Press, 1998), 265–89. For what it's worth, as a reader I noted Scott's dealings with such issues some time before the New Cosmopolitans published their analyses of them—a tribute, of course, to Scott, not to me.

ness in them? Recent work in postcolonial studies can help here.[13] From the point of view of cultures that have experienced colonialism, the question becomes "How can we construct an oppositional cultural heritage to reinforce our struggle against domination?" Now it's crucial to recognize from the outset that the realist novels we are discussing do not and cannot in any simple sense find a place in oppositional discourses of this kind. British realist novels of the period with which we are concerned are, first and foremost, part of the dominant discourse with respect to questions of colonialism, just as Henry Tilney is a member of the patriarchal ruling class with respect to the question of gender domination in England. Given their cultural positioning, these novels have neither the ambition nor the right to think of themselves as taking on the work of the colonially oppressed—which is not to say that their techniques and the modes of thinking they induce might not be pressed into service (or shall we say "articulated"?) for such ends.[14] Postcolonial theorizing can nonetheless prove suggestive in our attempts to understand how realist novels operate, particularly because of its stress on the necessity to *construct* a notion of the culture one will then claim a place in. Finding a place in one's culture, whether that culture is dominant or subaltern, must always be an act of constructive imagination, one that's necessary to give substance to such insights as that "men make their own history, but they do not make it just as they please; they do not make it under circumstances chosen by themselves, but under circumstances directly encountered, given and transmitted from the past."[15] It is too easily assumed that the fascination with distinctive expressions of a national culture, past or present, which we find in Scott and Eliot reflects simple nostalgia, laced with an ideologically motivated apology for the power relations of the present. It seems important to keep open the possibility that rehearsals of the specificity of cultural identities may also help readers take responsibility for where they are in their cultures, and where their cultures are.

The argument can be made that for those living in our own period at

---

[13]   Throughout this section I draw in selective ways on Stuart Hall's discussions of ethnicity and articulation. Hall's views on these and related subjects are conveniently collected, and discussed by others, in *Stuart Hall: Critical Dialogues in Cultural Studies*, ed. David Morley and Kuan-Hsing Chen (London: Routledge, 1996). For a compact summary of a range of recent concerns about the Other, see David Morley's essay in this collection, "EurAm, Modernity, Reason, and Alterity: or, Postmodernism, the Highest Stage of Cultural Imperialism?," 338–40.

[14]   Achebe, to give a well-known example, either draws upon or reinvents Waverley techniques. This of course raises the specter that his fiction too may be essentially repressive, if we decide that Scott's is by its very form.

[15]   Karl Marx, *The Eighteenth Brumaire of Louis Bonaparte* (New York: International Publishers, 1963), 15.

least, the notion of rootedness in separate cultures is illusory. One way of weakening the oppressor's claim to superiority is to point out that his own culture is in fact already polyglot and hybrid, shot through with the traces of the cultures he dominates politically. This can be a salutary reminder, but it doesn't lessen the need for those in politically dominant cultures to take seriously the task of imagining their own cultural places—indeed, from one point of view, it reinforces it. And one must add that recent discussions have tended toward a consensus that a pervasive hybridity obtains only in specific cultural formations (above all, the Caribbean).[16]

Another way of throwing into question the existence of national or even local cultures does so by reference to a new and sinister universalism. In the age of multinational capitalism, the idea that individuals belong to different national or ethnic cultures is said to be a powerful ideological illusion, which distracts us from the fact that none of us are rooted any more, except in a transnational power structure whose interests are reinforced when we relax (or agitate) into an empty tolerance for a diversity of illusory cultures. As Slavoj Žižek puts it, multiculturalism then becomes a "new racism" which "empties its own position of all positive content (the multiculturalist is not a direct racist, he doesn't oppose to the Other the *particular* values of his own culture), but nonetheless retains this position as the privileged *empty point of universality* from which one is able to appreciate (and depreciate) properly other particular cultures— the multiculturalist respect for the Other's specificity is the very form of asserting one's own superiority."[17] Being in a position to tolerate the particularity of another culture means that you're superior to that culture, which couldn't appreciate you in the same way, being of a simpler mind. You manufacture a spurious particularity for the supposed Other, so that you can look down upon it in the guise of tolerating or even lauding it. You affix the Other to a pedestal, so that you can look down on it from a multicultural crane manufactured by a multinational corporation.

Žižek follows Jameson (and many others) in supposing that postmodernism marks a change every bit as important as the change from premodernity to the modern. Indeed, the postmodernist moment means the complete dissolution of holdovers from premodernity into modernity.

---

[16]   See, for example, the editors' commentary for the section titled "Hybridity" in the student anthology *The Post-Colonial Studies Reader*, ed. Bill Ashcroft et al. (London: Routledge, 1995), 183–84.

[17]   Slavoj Žižek, "Multiculturalism, Or, the Cultural Logic of Multinational Capitalism," *New Left Review*, 225 (September/October 1997), 44; hereafter cited in the text. In contesting Žižek's views, I do not mean to deny that there are serious problems with the way in which multiculturalism is often imagined and championed.

Every vestige of *gemeinschaft* vanishes: the world has become so completely disenchanted that it can now play a game of pretending to reenchant itself. One name of this game is "multiculturalism." It is pernicious, because it diverts attention from those who are systematically excluded from the benefits of postmodern, late-capitalist society, and whose exclusion constitutes a symptom of its true nature, those who are erroneously thought of as "today's 'exceptions'—the homeless, the ghettoized, the permanently unemployed" (46). Instead of playing the game of openness to other so-called cultures, we ought to adopt the "procedure of *identifying with the symptom*," in which "one pathetically asserts (and identifies with) *the point of inherent exception/exclusion, the 'abject,' of the concrete positive order, as the only point of true universality*, as the point which belies the existing concrete universality" (50), which universality is the reality of multinational capitalism. According to Žižek, one example of such pathetic assertion would be to say, in the face of the atrocious treatment of one group of "exceptions," that "We are all immigrant workers." Another is "the recent pathetic statement of solidarity 'Sarajevo is the capital of Europe' . . . an exemplary case of such a notion of exception as embodying universality" (51). Žižek's discussion of pathetic identification allies it to the "productive" reference I described in Chapter 2, for it is rhetorical in the sense of hoping to make something happen in the reader and in the reader's world. "When we say, 'We are all citizens of Sarajevo,' we are obviously making a 'false' nomination . . . however, precisely as such, this violation gives word to the injustice of the existing geopolitical order" (51).

I find it impossible to agree that postmodernity marks a break on the order of the one that inaugurated the rise of modernity. I follow Habermas in finding the rise of modernity the central hinge of "recent" history, employing a model that is bipolar, not tripartite.[18] Nor do I believe that we have "really" left our specific cultures behind, however much cultural homogenization has occurred and continues to occur in the world. The ways in which culture inflects our situations as we encounter the increasingly powerful forces of hybridization and a multinational economy still matter. At the very least, they remain potential resources; they also seem to me constraints. Doubtless, as Žižek suggests, we have left an integral, un-

---

[18]   I touch here on a web of voluminously and hotly debated issues, involving the magnitude of the break marked by the "post" in such terms as postmodern and poststructuralist, and also the extent to which various "posts" synchronize and correspond—a concern nicely indicated by the title of Kwame Anthony Appiah's article "Is the Post- in Postmodernism the Post- in Postcolonial?," *Critical Inquiry*, 17 (1991), 336–57. In siding with Habermas, I part company with Stuart Hall, who seeks to steer a course between Habermas and Lyotard: see "On Postmodernism and Articulation: An Interview with Stuart Hall," in *Stuart Hall*, 131–35.

mediated place in "traditional society" behind—but as I've suggested repeatedly, historicism tells us that we did so very early. The process began at the instant when we became able to conceive of traditional society (or any other kind of society) at all. For all the increasing pace of change, I doubt that in this instance a change in quantity has as yet become a change in quality. As a result, I don't feel inclined to avail myself of an opening which analyses such as Žižek's would allow for Scott, if not for us. Scott's times were hardly postmodern: we might therefore argue that he at least had a specific culture available in which to immerse himself. I'd argue instead that a place in Scottish culture was something Scott too had to construct, even at his relatively early date, though materials for construction may have been more ready to hand for him than they are for us. Ready to hand, but various and themselves contradictory, as no one realized more acutely than he did. To represent the Scottish nation during a visit of its Hanoverian king, Scott swathed the Lowlands in Highland Tartan (itself a partial fabrication, devised by commercial interests on the basis of imperfectly preserved tradition and scattered artifactual remnants).[19]

To say that Scott had to construct a place for and in his culture is not to say that he thereby was creating an illusion built from nothing objective, or that his reconstruction did not itself have culturally local and specific determinants. I believe that we are in a similar position now. Accepting the task of imagining a place for our own culture can help to render knowable, and therefore susceptible to critique, forces that continue to act on us. The effort to conceptualize how our culture intersects with and is itself inflected by global forces may render those forces, which are efficient in part because of their very elusiveness, more visible to us. Honoring the existence of our own cultures, and of our places within them, may also allow us to avoid certain kinds of bad faith. For there are inescapable respects in which we do not and cannot feel the pain of others, in which I am not a migrant worker, nor is Sarajevo the capital of the world. We require ways of coming to grips with the gaps here—though to be sure stating with a willed, creatively self-conscious hyperbole that we are migrant workers is preferable to wringing our hands about our "complicity" in the structures of power that oppress them.[20] Claiming a place in our own culture may

---

[19] For another perspective on Scott's Highland pageantry, and a wealth of information about Tartan, see Hugh Trevor-Roper, "The Invention of Tradition: The Highland Tradition of Scotland," in *The Invention of Tradition*, ed. Eric Hobsbawm and Terence Ranger (Cambridge: Cambridge University Press, 1983), 15–41. The classic biography of Scott by his son-in-law J. G. Lockhart views Scott's role in the royal visit with a remarkably complex mixture of irony and respect.

[20] Žižek provides a characteristically brilliant analysis of the bad faith often involved in such hand-wringing in *Tarrying with the Negative* (Durham: Duke University Press, 1993), 213–14.

help to define it. Seen more clearly, our culture may provide some useful material in bridging the gaps, just because it isn't simply a pre-given, homogenous, and inescapable entity that simply claims us. As a visiting student in England, I remember being told by a friend that England would be better off if someone blew up the cathedrals. Surely other uses can be made of them. If we obliterate cathedrals (or decide that they have already self-destructed so far as we are concerned), we preclude the possibility of drawing upon the energy which created them (and which the purposes of those who had them built cannot entirely contain), and of taking advantage of the perspectives their heterogeneous history may open for us.

Scott's cultural position was remarkably complex and conflicted. Though he was intensely attracted by the claims of the regional, he spent enormous energy in bolstering the idea that Scotland had a distinctive national culture, powerful enough to unite those he referred to in his Introduction to "Tales of My Landlord" as "His Loving Countrymen, whether they are denominated Men of the South, Gentlemen of the North, People of the West, or Folk of Fife."[21] As a Scottish patriot dedicated to preserving the uniqueness of this complex, multivalent cultural heritage, he found himself playing the role of the colonized, as he opposed specific instances of English cultural imperialism (for example, moves to deracinate the Scottish legal and banking systems). Yet he was at the same time tragically persuaded that a politically independent Scotland was historically doomed, for past and present reasons. Faced with what he perceived as Napoleon's attempt to homogenize all of European culture, Scott felt compelled to sacrifice Scottish independence in the name of preserving the possibility of saving any cultural particularity at all, and not just in Scotland.[22] A Great Britain large and strong enough to frustrate Napoleon's ambitions was required. Scott the Scottish patriot thus found himself in league with the English colonizer, as an apologist for the Union between England and Scotland that had occurred a century before. Cultural critics who interest themselves in Scotland, from Hugh MacDiarmid

---

[21]   Scott, Dedication to "Tales of My Landlord," reprinted in *Old Mortality*, ed. Angus Calder (Harmondsworth: Penguin, 1975), 49. "Tales of My Landlord" is a series of Scott novels that began with *The Black Dwarf* and includes, among other major works, *Old Mortality* and *The Heart of Midlothian*. I have checked the text here against P. D. Garside's edition of *The Black Dwarf* (Edinburgh: University of Edinburgh Press, 1993), a volume in the new Edinburgh Edition of the Waverley novels (editor-in-chief, David Hewitt), without finding variants that would alter my analysis.

[22]   For evidence, see Harry E. Shaw, "Scott, Scotland, and Repression," *Cencrastus*, 1 (Summer 1980), 26–28. Scott was no political theorist; I have drawn my conclusions about his general views on such matters by teasing out the implications of his novels and his wide-ranging nonfictional prose.

to the present, have tended to see him as one who greased the wheels for English hegemony over Scotland, by consigning Scottish cultural particularity to a picturesque past seen through the lenses of celebration and mourning.[23] He may be more usefully viewed as a man whose life and works dramatize and lend insight into the complexities of cultural identity in the modern world.

Before I turn to what Scott's fiction makes of these complexities, I want to pause a moment to observe his mind at work on them in his own experience, as recorded in the *Journal* he began shortly after he completed *The Talisman*. (The entry in question was made as financial ruin impended; hence the reference to forces that threaten his *peculium*.) Scott is meditating on the life of Chief Commissioner William Adam, head of the recently created Jury Court in Scotland:

> It is high treason among the Tories to express regard for him or respect for the Jury Court in which he prescribes. I was against that experiment as much as any one. But it is an experiment, and the establishment (which the fools will not perceive) is the only thing which I see likely to give some prospects of ambition to our bar which has been diminishd otherwise so much. As for the Chief Commissioner I dare say he jobs as all other people of consequence do in elections and so forth. But he is the personal friend of the King and the decided enemy of whatever strikes at the constitutional rights of the Monarch. Besides I love him for the various changes which he has endured through life and which have been so great as to make him entitled to be regarded in one point of view as the most fortunate in the other the most unfortunate man in the world. He has gaind and lost two fortunes by the same good fortune and the same rash confidence which has raised and now threatens my *peculium*. And his quiet, noble and generous submission under circumstances more painful than mine, for the loss of world's wealth was aggravated by the death of his youngest and darling son in the West Indies, furnishd me at the time and now with a noble example—So the Tories and Whigs may go be damnd together as names that have distracted Old Scotland and torn asunder the most kindly feelings since the first day they were invented. Yet d———n

[23] MacDiarmid accuses Scott of fostering "the paralysing ideology of defeatism in Scotland" in *Lucky Poet* (1943; Berkeley: University of California Press, 1972), 202. Scott was attacked for his allegedly reactionary politics from the beginning; a memorable early example is Hazlitt's essay "Sir Walter Scott" in *The Spirit of the Age* (1825).

them they are spells to rouse all our angry passions, and I dare say notwithstanding the opinion of my private and calm moments I will open on the cry again so soon as something occurs to chafe my mood. And yet God knows I would fight in honourable contest with word or blow for my political opinions but I cannot permit that strife to 'mix its waters with my daily meal,' those waters of bitterness which poison all mutual love and confidence betwixt the well disposed on each side, and prevent them if need were from making mutual concessions and balancing the constitution against the Ultras of both parties. The good man seems something broken by these afflictions.[24]

In this passage, we see Scott attempting to work out a stance—or a series or perhaps a narrative of stances—that will allow him to register contradictory aspects of his situation. Through much of the passage, we seem to be in fairly familiar waters, with Scott balancing the (private) self against the "world," and finding reasons to prefer the self. His interest in the complex particularity of worlds present and past plays its part here, by repeatedly revealing that things are more complex than they might appear to be. William Adam may "job" at elections for personal and party gain (and thus undermine the constitution), but he is after all the personal friend of the king (and therefore can be counted on to support, because of this very personal consideration, the constitution). The Jury Court looked to be a bad thing, an invasion of the liberties of Scotland; but in fact, given the actual historical situation of Scottish legal institutions, it has turned out to have its merits—and anyway, it's there. The list could be extended. This careful balancing act, however, remains precarious, and so at the end of the passage, Scott raises the specter of the "Ultras of both parties," against whom moderate men of whatever party should band together. The problem of personal and political differences is solved by focusing on "radicalism," the threat of action by political extremists. It begins to seem that Scott's invocation of a common humanity may involve little more than an attempt to forge a shared political center.

Were this all the passage contained, it would simply exemplify a familiar movement of nineteenth-century political ideology. What's striking in the passage, however, is the effort Scott feels he needs to expend in solving what, according to that ideology, is rather a simple problem. The twists and turns of Scott's musings are remarkable. He damns the names of Whigs and Tories, but in the next sentence adds, with what looks like a

---

[24]   Scott, *The Journal of Sir Walter Scott*, ed. W. E. K. Anderson (Oxford: Clarendon, 1972), 20 Jan. 1826. I have corrected Scott's spelling of "afflictions."

certain embarrassment, that these names will surely rouse his passions in the future: "notwithstanding the opinion of my private and calm moments I will open on the cry again so soon as something occurs to chafe my mood." Yet the very next sentence celebrates his desire to "open on the cry," before it swerves to assert the importance of nonetheless maintaining areas in life that will not be "poisoned" by party opinion. We see Scott, in short, appealing to a common humanity (to be sure within "moderate" limits), yet at the same time valuing himself because he knows that in the future he will respond to narrower promptings. He is admitting—with pride at not being *too* reasonable and tame—that though he may be rational, he's sometimes uncontrollable. His insistence that he'd "fight in honourable contest with word or blow" suggests a value for a certain lack of control, a wish to be found in the midst of the melee. (This part of his attitude has its precedents: even Sir Charles Grandison proves his manliness by pointing out *how close he has come* to losing his temper.) Wise moderation is all very well, but Scott would be less of a man, less valuable in all respects, if he didn't find himself rising to party names, heedlessly and immediately. He admires this aspect of himself: that's the reason his admission of what might seem mere weakness or irascibility is so quickly followed by evocations of the rhetoric of chivalry, of fighting in honorable contest with word or blow. The narrative of this passage, then, enacts a movement between promise of direct engagement and calm removal, between being in the fray and rising above it. Scott celebrates a consciousness apt to lose itself but then apt to find itself again. Indeed, his narrative, journal-keeping consciousness, as it balances this set of possibilities, goes a step further: it seems to have the capacity to be aware of, and to value, both possibilities at once. It takes its position simultaneously in and above the activities it describes.

Scott also builds the possibility for being both in and above a social world into the most conspicuous structural component of the Waverley novels. Few critics of Scott have failed to note that the Waverley hero is informed by what Lukács, following Goethe, calls "necessary anachronism."[25] The Waverley hero is, famously, more "modern" in sensibility, sentiments, and values than the characters who surround him. Explanations for this peculiarity have been various. Some have said that by being relatively modern, the hero translates older societies into terms we can understand, acting as our bridge to them and our representative within them. Others have suggested that his modernity allows the Waverley hero to import the values of the present into the past and thereby to con-

[25] George Lukács, *The Historical Novel* (1937), trans. Hannah Mitchell and Stanley Mitchell (London: Merlin, 1962), 61–63.

struct a past that will reinforce the political beliefs of the present. (Here the anachronism is *ideologically* necessary.) I'd like to add a further explanation that encompasses both possibilities, by setting them in a dynamic relationship to each other that extends to hero, reader, and Scott himself. In my view, the fundamental cause for Scott's creation of a "modernized" Waverley hero is to activate for the reader an oscillation between experiencing a historically specific society from within, and viewing that society from above. It all depends upon which of these characteristics a given scene stresses.

Scott's novels sometimes thematize this dual focus as part of the experience of the hero himself. The Englishman Edward Waverley, for instance, having renounced his allegiance to King George, finds himself marching with the Jacobite army out of Edinburgh as it begins its invasion of England. Characteristically, he starts a bit late, and has to catch up. He first sees the army from above and at a distance. From this point of view, it is exhilarating and picturesque—feelings that spread to characterize his own sense of his role in the rebellion. When he descends to join the ranks, however, prospects alter: "a nearer view, indeed rather diminished the effect impressed on the mind by the more distant appearance of the army."[26] In the battle on the following day, spectacle turns to nightmare:

> It was at that instant, that, looking around him, he saw the wild dress and appearance of his Highland associates, heard their whispers in an uncouth and unknown language, looked upon his own dress, so unlike that which he had worn from his infancy, and wished to awake from what seemed at the moment a dream, strange, horrible, and unnatural. (333)

Waverley has involved the reader in such rude awakenings before. After his first, seemingly apolitical visit to the Highlands, he is attempting to return to his English regiment when he's suddenly arrested—for high treason! When he's examined by a local magistrate, what had seemed innocent Highland tourism takes on an ominous logic. We know that Waverley didn't intend treason by his visit to the Highlands, but as the magistrate builds a case against him, the desultory actions he has engaged in snap together into a damning constellation. The meaning of his actions and his life undergoes a sudden metamorphosis, because of the ways in which they appear to fit in with larger historical forces (here, the Forty-

---

[26] Scott, *Waverley*, ed. Andrew Hook (Harmondsworth: Penguin, 1972), 323; hereafter cited in the text.

Five) of which he had been entirely unaware. History itself seems to have lowered the boom on our hero, and as readers we feel considerable discomfort. It's not that we're fundamentally worried for Waverley: we feel for him, but we know all along he's the sort of character who won't and can't be executed. Our discomfort, it seems to me, is primarily on our own behalf: we have been drawn into reading the novel's events with picaresque ease, and it's unsettling to see how wrong this has been. Indeed, it's more than unsettling, it's threatening—history has lowered the boom on Waverley, and it might serve us the same when our turn comes. Again, though, this insight hardly achieves tragic intensity, because at the same time we are viewing Waverley's situation from above. From that vantage point, it is grimly amusing to look back and see the feckless Waverley, like a hapless stage tramp, cheerfully heading toward the banana peel and the open trapdoor beyond it. We feel the pleasure of identifying, from above, with the imperturbable, inexorable historical forces that put him on the spot. The sudden clarity of structure feels wonderful; finally something has come to a point in this novel! But this is *just* a moment. There's plenty to draw us back on a level with Waverley, at risk in the midst of the fray—which indeed is where we mainly are when, subsequently, the Highlanders surrounding him seem part of a nightmare.[27]

It's worth adding that such imaginative oscillations in literature are by no means Scott's own invention.[28] Narrators of all sorts and periods have moved between positions within and above the fictions they narrate, and invited readers to do so as well. First-person narrators reminisce about the past from a position in the present. Third-person narrators can (like Sterne) make us reflect on our reactions to the fictional world before us, even as we're reacting. Or they can lull us into sharing the viewpoint of a character, only to jerk us out of that viewpoint. Situating the reader simultaneously in and above a situation can also define certain kinds of voyeurism and pornography.[29] And so on. What differs in the kind of realism Scott helped to inaugurate is the use for which these potentialities are employed. In inventing modern historical fiction, Scott habitually drew upon traditional fictional methods and effects to serve an altered content; in the process, the nature of the methods and effects themselves often changed. We might, for example, describe our grim pleasure in Wa-

[27]   For a different reading of the scene of Waverley's arrest, by a distinguished critic of Scott, see Alexander Welsh, *Strong Representations* (Baltimore: Johns Hopkins University Press, 1992), 76–99.
[28]   On one level, my discussion recalls the exploration of the dynamic involving "sympathy" and "judgment" memorably explored in Wayne Booth's *Rhetoric of Fiction* (Chicago: University of Chicago Press, 1961). My claim is to have historicized this issue.
[29]   On Richardson's use of this structure, see Tassie Gwilliam, *Samuel Richardson's Fictions of Gender* (Stanford: Stanford University Press, 1993), 38.

verley's discomfort as a form of classical dramatic irony, but we'd have to add that the forces revealed have no supernatural aura and that we see Waverley as "normal" in a way that Oedipus can never be. Scott's narrator here also recalls Fielding's, except that we are led to identify the process that led to Waverley's situation with our own conditions of historical possibility much more closely than we identify with the less historicized situation that seems ready to bring about Tom Jones's hanging. In similar fashion, Scott almost certainly drew his model for the disguising that pervades *The Talisman* from Shakespeare's comedies, but disguises in *The Talisman* are meant to reveal the truth about historical positions. They don't produce pastoral enlightenment. This may simply be to say that the situation of Scott's characters is ultimately a secular one, with ritual providing ways of coping with history instead of alternatives to it.[30] An oscillation between positions in and above "real" worlds, fictional and actual, becomes a necessary and inevitable part of the kit realism provides for making a certain kind of sense of our lives in society and history.

The oscillation Scott enacts in his novels is relevant to the problem of encountering other cultures. It raises a central hermeneutical and epistemological dilemma that faces any representation informed by the insights of historicism: the problem of how, given the historicist notion that we are embedded in culture, we can nonetheless achieve and transmit a view of life that transcends it. Reality for the historicist always involves a radical particularity as an indispensable element and perhaps as its keynote; but once you've given the specific and "contingent" this kind of status, the problem of emerging from it to a larger view becomes vexed. The formal category where this problem makes itself most obviously felt in prose fiction must involve narrative focus or point of view—the space the narrator occupies, the space he allocates to his characters and to us, and the relationship between these. We find ourselves, in short, faced with the question of the position characters, narrators, and readers assume with regard to the fictional text and ultimately to history itself. My final chapter will be largely occupied with such issues, and especially the problem of the realist narrator's seeming privilege of standing apart from history. For now, I will content myself with general considerations.

In describing the workings of metonymy in the previous chapter, I suggested that the metonymical representation characteristic of historicist realism imitates the motions of a mind that, in its ideal form, would be adequate to understanding historical process itself. The question that now

---

[30]   But see Judith Wilt, *Secret Leaves* (Chicago: University of Chicago Press, 1985). Wilt makes the case that, especially in his medieval novels, Scott's interest in history extends to nothing less than the fate of "Christendom."

arises is precisely where we might expect such a mind to reside, how we might expect it to position itself. It would be natural to expect such a mind to take its position above the world for which it is trying to account. How else could it see it whole? How else could it take in more than one culture? Yet we might also expect it to be embedded in a culture, not to float above it. After all, doesn't historicism insist that mentalities gain their saliency from belonging to larger historical structures? Thus the mind that imagines history would need to be in two places at once.

From what Anderson calls a "systemic" point of view, the paradox would appear to be insoluble. Indeed, in the end, the notion that "two" positions are involved would collapse. If you imagine that you are "above" your culture, you delude yourself; the judgments you make from such a supposed position will all the more surely flow from the fact that you are "in" your culture. If, however, we move beyond a "systemic" view to include the possibility of productive uses of narration over time, answers to the paradox become available. In my view, the most plausible are associated with the doctrine of "emergence," which holds that as human consciousness develops, over time, certain skills and aptitudes and systems emerge that are no longer wholly bound by the conditions that bring them into being.[31] (Without some such dynamic at work, a historicist vision could itself never have arisen in the first place.) The most significant of these systems would be the system of language itself, which by its very nature introduces an element of generality and therefore of potential mobility into our perceptions of the world. Whenever we use language, we are both in and beyond the situation at hand. And the same dynamic is at work in those larger systems of interpretation and understanding we erect by means of the use of language, which exploit our ability to participate in discursive dialogue.

All this may be true—indeed, I believe it to be true. Yet essaying a movement between cultural positions is a perilous and difficult enterprise, as I think we feel even in reading Scott's impromptu comments in the *Journal*. The last line of the entry I've quoted above seems something of a non sequitur. It certainly marks a break in tone from the reasoned compromise for which Scott has been striving. Scott had initially painted Adam as surmounting his troubles with a "quiet, noble and generous submission." Yet his final comment, in its unexpected return to the person of Adam, suggests that such submission exacts a price: "the good man seems something broken by these afflictions." It's hard to avoid sensing a strong identification between Scott and Adam. We may infer

[31] For discussions of "emergence" (in George Henry Lewes among others), see Maurice Mandelbaum, *History, Man, and Reason* (Baltimore: Johns Hopkins University Press, 1971), 379, n. 48.

something like covert self-pity in this final comment, when we think of the financial disaster that threatened Scott as he wrote these lines. I'd like to suggest, however, that Scott's sensitivity to Adam's "brokenness" may involve a projection of his own difficulties in areas that are not entirely financial. Adam endures violent oscillations of fortune, and he does so with grace, but at a cost. Perhaps a similar cost attaches to attempting to be both in and above the fray, and thereby bereft of the support simple participation brings with it. Being one of the "Ultras" would appear to be easier than sharing their passion but seeing beyond it. If this is so, one can imagine the lure of an imaginative setting in which inhabiting different and even contradictory positions simultaneously would produce not difficulty and exhaustion, but ease, exhilaration, and pleasure (not to mention the financial plenty that would allow you to build a "place" of your own, say in the Borders of Scotland). Scott's novels characteristically embody this freedom in their narrators and invite the reader to share it, even though its limits never entirely disappear. One of the fascinations of reading Scott is seeing the different modes and proportions in which the fantasy and reality principles here coexist.

Let's return now to Sir Kenneth and the Emir who turns out to be "not so bad a fellow after all." I would argue that Scott wishes us to react to Sir Kenneth's prejudice in the scene at the oasis in a rather more complex way than Said allows. We are meant to enjoy his prejudice, as a playing out of a certain set of historical probabilities.[32] We enjoy Sir Kenneth, as we enjoy a bluff English nobleman in the novel who is elaborately and vocally prejudiced against Scots like Sir Kenneth, yet who grudgingly comes to appreciate him. (The suggestion here would seem to be that you can only come to know the Other through a series of one-on-one encounters—certainly a problematic position, but a more interesting one than Said's analysis allows for.) There are, one must add, strict limits set to the kind of *behavior* stemming from such prejudice that Scott's novels will tolerate. The novels understand that prejudice can lead to murder—as, later in their encounter, it nearly does in the case of Sir Kenneth and the Emir. By the same token, Scott in the *Journal* knows that, in the future, he'll allow his political beliefs to possess him and control his actions; at the very moment when he voices this knowledge, however, he asserts

---

[32]   The reader may have noticed that I am using Scott's text to play out the Gadamer-Habermas debate on questions of prejudice, tradition, and the possibility of critique. Thus far, I have been stressing the aspects of Scott that are most in accord with Gadamer's insistence that we are inescapably bound to our cultural horizons. In my discussion of "The Two Drovers," I supplement this emphasis by stressing the disruptive effect of relations of power, recalling Habermas's interest in forces that distort our communications and interpretations.

(prays?) that his actions will not take a shape that would "poison" his domestic ties and affections.

However culturally rooted they are, the characters in Scott's novels with whom the reader forms anything approaching an identification are generally allowed at least one moment of transcendence of their constitutive prejudices. These moments gain poignancy precisely because of the extent to which the novels refuse to make their characters, in normal circumstances, vehicles for the expression of eternal value or of a timeless human essence. Said, then, is mistaken: Scott never wishes us simply to assume that we wouldn't act in prejudiced ways against the culturally Other. Instead, his novels help us to realize that we always act from our own cultural positions, but also that we sometimes can reach through those positions to a larger sense of our common humanity. There is, by the way, little sentimentality in Scott's view. He has a vivid sense of all the forces working against the emergence of anyone from a position "in" their culture to a position above it. The obstacles can be severe. The dispersal of events by means of time and narrative can prove useful in dissipating animosities, but it can also raise problems. A member of one society may offer to rise above his prejudices, but do so in a way that offends a member of another, provoking a response that quickly extinguishes any wish for transcendence in the first. If later the offended party finds himself moved to seek a reconciliation, it may turn out that he no longer has the power to effect one, perhaps because a third person in a position of power finds considerations of political expediency powerful enough to override quixotic notions of forgiving an enemy.[33] The impetus to transcendence may be there, but the conditions need to be just right for it to have any concrete results.

The conditions prove to be right in a sequence in *The Talisman* that mingles romantic exoticism with Scott's historicist concerns in an outlandish way. Sir Kenneth has been condemned to death for failing to defend Richard's royal standard, only to be reprieved and led off (as a slave) by Saladin, who is disguised as "El Hakim," an Oriental healer who has vis-

---

[33] I am here describing the outlines of a remarkable sequence in *The Betrothed*, the novel Scott wrote directly before *The Talisman* and published with it. In that sequence, a Welsh bard who has sworn to kill a Norman knight and has attached himself to him in disguise, hoping for an opportunity, is so impressed by the Norman's fortitude that he impulsively seeks to grasp his hand and become his true servant. But the Norman rebuffs him, on the grounds of social class. The Welshman subsequently tries to kill the Norman, but kills the wrong man. When this act and its aftermath reveal the Welshman's plan to the Norman, he in his turn rises above his cultural prejudices and attempts to save the Welshman from execution, on the historicist grounds that the Welshman was after all acting according to his own cultural priorities. But this attempt proves futile, because the King sees compelling political grounds for doing away with the bard. The importance of disguise throughout this sequence provides another link to *The Talisman*, as we shall see more fully in a moment.

ited the Crusaders' camp and saved Richard's life. As they return to the Moslem camp, El Hakim issues the call to prayer, and Sir Kenneth finds himself—much to his own surprise—joining it (though, as always with Scott, with a difference):

> Even Sir Kenneth, whose reason at once and prejudices were offended by seeing his companions in that which he considered as an act of idolatry, could not help respecting the sincerity of their misguided zeal, and being stimulated by their fervour to apply supplications to Heaven in a purer form, wondering, meanwhile, what new-born feelings could teach him to accompany in prayer, though with varied invocation, those very Saracens, whose heathenish worship he had conceived a crime dishonourable to the land in which high miracles had been wrought, and where the day-star of redemption had arisen. (4, 183–84; chap. 22)

This is hardly ecumenical (Sir Kenneth's "wonder" here is telling), but it is an unexpected development. Its emergence requires extreme status confusion and deprivation (from European knight to the slave of a Moslem) and a journey through utterly unfamiliar surroundings. (Alternatively, one could read a realist novel.) Now some of the language here gives the impression that the narrator is carefully undercutting any chance that an unwary reader might begin to imagine that the Moslem religion is as good as the Christian. Just what does the phrase "reason at once and prejudices" mean—what are the proportions of narrator and character ownership of the thoughts in this passage? Such an impression may be reinforced by the narrative commentary that immediately follows:

> The act of devotion, however, though rendered in such strange society, burst purely from his natural feelings of religious duty, and had its usual effect in composing the spirits, which had been long harassed by so rapid a succession of calamities. The sincere and earnest approach of the Christian to the throne of the Almighty, teaches the best lesson of patience under affliction; since wherefore should we mock the Deity with supplications, when we insult him by murmuring under his decrees?—or how, while our prayers have in every word admitted the vanity and nothingness of the things of time in comparison to those of eternity, should we hope to deceive the Searcher of Hearts, by permitting the world and worldly passions to reassume their turbulent empire over our bosoms, the instant when our devotions are ended? There have been, and perhaps

are now, persons so inconsistent, as to suffer earthly passion to re-
assume the reins even immediately after a solemn address to
Heaven; but Sir Kenneth was not of these. He felt himself com-
forted and strengthened, and better prepared to execute or submit
to whatever his destiny might call upon him to do or to suffer. (4,
184–85; chap. 22)

Surely this is the voice of Europe protecting its universal and timeless
values from Moslem infection, one might conclude. Well, perhaps not
quite so surely as all that. The richest reading of such passages would see
in them Scott creating a narrator's voice proper to himself and his readers
as nineteenth-century Europeans, in the full consciousness that he's so
doing. This passage is in the optative: it itself is a kind of prayer—an evocation by Scott of a nonsectarian, undogmatic "best self" of Christianity.
This is how middle-ground religious sentiment in Scott's own age would
like to imagine and draw upon a Christian past more authentic than the
violence of the Crusades.

The passage describing Sir Kenneth contains local signs of a historicizing presence. The content of this authorial intervention, for instance, isn't
something we can imagine Sir Kenneth or the other characters in the
novel thinking or saying, and a reference to Scott's present is built into
the passage, with its reminder that "there have been, and perhaps are
now, persons" so inconsistent as to forget that they've been praying. The
narrative language here also sounds an ecclesiastical note through a
slight archaism (for example, in the reference to "the Searcher of Hearts"),
but this language sounds archaic only with respect to Scott's own contemporary language (and ours), but not with respect to the language spoken by Sir Kenneth. The power of such language to invoke known and
habitual religious practices arises only from a modern perspective and
against a modern linguistic background, and the narrator takes self-conscious pleasure in speaking his way into a devout tradition. Its very spe-
cialization of language, which implies a differentiated, compartmental-
ized status for religious experience, itself helps to attach the religious
sentiments here expressed to the present: in Sir Kenneth's world, as the
novel shows us, religion, love, war, and statecraft run together.

The effect of historical self-consciousness is largely a matter of the narrator's voice and intonation. If we hear a quality of historical self-posi-
tioning in the narrator's voice, it is primarily because we've heard it before—at the end of *The Heart of Midlothian*, for instance. *The Heart of
Midlothian* winds up its narrative with the following moral: "Reader—
This tale will not be told in vain, if it shall be found to illustrate the great
truth, that guilt, though it may attain temporal splendour, can never con-

fer real happiness," and so on.[34] Some have taken this to be a platitudinous and fatuous moral of the story served up to us directly by Scott. In fact, this moral is consciously couched in a literary decorum entirely appropriate to the moment of its dramatized speaker, a late eighteenth-century schoolmaster and man of feeling. It therefore serves as yet another example of the historically rooted imaginative grammar on which the effect of Scott's novel depends. (Which is not to say that Scott would repudiate its gist if pressed on the matter.) To be sure, Scott wasn't ventriloquizing the mind of his own age when he created the "moral" that ends *The Heart of Midlothian*, as I've said he does in the account of how Kenneth joins the Saracens in prayer. But, as we'll see, there is a figure in *The Talisman* who does self-consciously ventriloquize a variety of cultural personas from his own age—Saladin. In voicing a nineteenth-century view of the true Christian heritage, then, the narrator of *The Talisman* would be following Saladin's example.

Sir Kenneth is extravagantly rewarded for this fleeting transcendence of his reason and prejudices. When the Templars allied to King Richard dishonorably attack El Hakim's party, Sir Kenneth finds himself quite literally transported beyond conflicts of loyalty and culture, as the disguised Saladin puts their (Arabian) horses into a gallop of such irresistible speed as to deprive Sir Kenneth of any independent volition—and indeed, of anything but an amazed semi-consciousness: "the motion, . . . as easy as it was rapid, seemed more like flying through the air than riding on the earth, and was attended with no unpleasant sensation, save . . . awe" (4, 191; chap. 22). Here, too, we're historically in and above the world of the fiction, taking in an Enlightenment explanation for tales of Eastern flying carpets as we ride on one. Sir Kenneth gains a libidinal release also. Exhausted and feverish, he is put into a soothing, healing sleep by the benign use of opium; as he drifts off, he dreams of fame, glory, and the winning of his lady's hand: "A state ensued, in which, still conscious of his own identity and his own condition, the knight felt enabled to consider them not only without alarm and sorrow, but as composedly as he might have viewed the story of his misfortunes acted upon a stage, or rather as a disembodied spirit might regard the transactions of its past existence" (4, 196; chap. 22).

Sir Kenneth subsequently wakens on a soft Oriental couch, in a tent resplendent with the luxuries of the East. This is followed by an elaborate game of shape-shifting. Sir Kenneth hears the voice of "El Hakim" outside his tent, asking admittance. He replies that, since he is El Hakim's

---

[34] Scott, *The Heart of Midlothian*, ed. Tony Inglis (Harmondsworth: Penguin, 1994), 531; hereafter cited in the text.

slave, permission to enter need hardly be sought. The Moslem replies that he does not consider himself Sir Kenneth's master; Sir Kenneth returns that physicians always have a right of entry. The dialogue continues:

> "Neither come I now as a physician," replied El Hakim; "and therefore I still request permission, ere I come under the covering of thy tent."
> "Whoever comes as a friend," said Sir Kenneth, "and such thou hast hitherto shown thyself to me, the habitation of the friend is ever open to him."
> "Yet once again," said the Eastern sage, after the periphrastical manner of his countrymen, "supposing that I come not as a friend?"
> "Come as thou wilt," said the Scottish knight, somewhat impatient of this circumlocution,—"be what thou wilt—thou knowest well it is neither in my power nor my inclination to refuse thee entrance."
> "I come, then," said El Hakim, "as your ancient foe; but a fair and a generous one."
> He entered as he spoke; and when he stood before the bedside of Sir Kenneth, the voice continued to be that of Adonbec the Arabian physician, but the form, dress, and features, were those of Ilderim of Kurdistan, called Sheerkof. Sir Kenneth gazed upon him, as if he expected the vision to depart, like something created by his imagination. (4, 201–2; chap. 23)

The content of this vignette provides something of an allegory of the attitude toward otherness I've been arguing Scott strives to embody in his fiction, with Saladin offering friendship and maintaining difference and even enmity at the same moment. Even the dull Sir Kenneth finds himself experiencing the truth that such a confrontation must begin with the imagination, though it cannot end there. Most telling, however, is the way the scene engages the reader's imagination. From the beginning, we as readers recognize and enjoy the "Eastern" decorum of ornate question and answer. As a result, we enjoy the historicist comedy of Sir Kenneth's impatience at all this circumlocution. He doesn't know that he's in an Oriental tale, but we do, and we enjoy his restiveness because it enacts a cultural particularity with which we ourselves are to some extent identified, creating a joke at his expense and also at ours. In the end, we cannot fully enjoy the scene without holding in suspension multiple viewpoints: that of Saladin–Ilderim–El Hakim, that of Sir Kenneth, and that of ourselves. We are invited to imagine our way into putative Eastern and Western conditions of cultural probability within the scene; simultaneously, and as a necessary condition for doing so, we must maintain our own historical perspective above it, though not entirely above its cultural implications and identifications.

Saladin's mastery of disguises provides a figure for this complex imaginative positioning. Indeed, there are times in the novel when he seems to take on the role, not simply of a series of Moslem types, but of the Author of Waverley himself. For this is not the only moment in the novel when Saladin deliberately creates a situation in which different cultures are set in conflict, the better to reveal their differing natures. After Saladin reveals his various disguises, Sir Kenneth mildly accuses him of dishonesty. He notes that, although Saladin as Saladin has just offered iced drinks to his guests, Saladin as Sheerkof the Kurd denied the very possibility that ice could exist during their encounter at the oasis. (Sir Kenneth had suggested that the nearby Dead Sea would have frozen over in winter had it been in his country, Scotland; Saladin, playing the part of a son of the desert, was incredulous.) Saladin's answer reflects a grasp of the importance of entering fully into a cultural mentality:

> "Wouldst thou have an Arab or a Kurdman as wise as a Hakim [that is, a sage or healer, Saladin's second disguise]?" said the Soldan. "He who does on a disguise must make the sentiments of his heart and the learning of his head accord with the dress which he assumes. I desired to see how a brave and single-hearted cavalier of Frangistan would conduct himself in debate with such a chief as I then seemed; and I questioned the truth of a well-known fact, to know by what arguments thou would'st support thy assertion." (4, 354; chap. 28)

We may regret the cruel necessity that throws Scott upon the expedient of using such words as "Frangistan" to reflect Saladin's own cultural difference, but there's more to the passage than that. I earlier suggested that the Waverley novels offered Scott the ability to negotiate, with various degrees of ease, between positions in and above his own constitutive prejudices and cultural positioning. By making Saladin his covert double within the fictional world of *The Talisman*, with its unusually prominent element of self-conscious play and fantasy, Scott puts himself very much at ease.

Said asks whether the very project of thinking of a culture as Other won't by its very nature produce self-satisfaction on the part of the viewer, and denigration of the viewed. In *The Talisman*, we've found other dynamics at play. I think we'd want to reply to Said that, yes, an attempt

to imagine the Other is likely to begin with self-assertion and self-satisfaction, but that it needn't end that way. On both thematic and formal
levels, Scott's narrative attempts to give a model of what it would mean
to pass beyond a self-satisfaction that denigrates other cultures. It shows
us characters who do this, however fleetingly and imperfectly. And our
own imaginative experience of the novel involves inhabiting shifting
points of view that disrupt an easy settling into the point of view of our
own culture. Whether the promise these mechanisms hold is strong
enough to counter Said's demonstration of what has been effected by
those who exploited the elegiac view of the past Scott helped give cur-
rency to is a difficult question to answer. It's hard to know what would
count as conclusive evidence for an assessment of the potentialities of
Scott's realism. I would, however, suggest that Scott's imaginative world,
if fully entered into, might help prepare us to encounter the Other in
ways that would lead to further understanding on something like equal
terms. At the very least, I hope to have demonstrated the dubiousness of
supposing that, even in a "light" novel like *The Talisman*, Scott's fiction
doesn't know that such problems exist.

"The Two Drovers"

In *The Talisman*, Saladin, adept at playing multiple roles and inhabiting
multiple disguises, acts as a cultural middleman. Structurally this means
that he assumes many of the functions usually reserved for the Waverley
hero, which in turn allows Scott to embed Sir Kenneth more firmly in his
own age than is usual for a Waverley hero. Saladin is less tied to a single
culture than any other character in the novel; indeed, he seems to know
the minds of his European antagonists better than they do themselves. At
the end of the novel, he nonetheless resumes his place in his own society,
with conscious, deliberate dignity. Richard the Lionhearted, eternally
adolescent, burns to meet Saladin in a duel. Saladin replies that however
much he would have relished such an opportunity in his persona as the
Kurdish Emir who did battle with Sir Kenneth at the oasis, his duties to
his people prevent him from needlessly imperiling his life—as if he actually becomes another person when he dons or doffs his disguises! Here
again Saladin reveals his supernatural ability to inhabit multiple cultural
spaces, reinforcing our sense that he is the supreme expression of Scott's
fantasy of an easy, painless oscillation between them. Yet in the end, even
he returns to his place.

In "The Two Drovers," a piece of short fiction written two years after
The Talisman, Scott takes a less sanguine view of the possibility of emerg-

ing from the mentality of one's own society. As short fiction, "The Two Drovers" is and must be more end-driven and linear than is the norm with Scott's novels. Perhaps partly as a result, imaginative movements beyond the confines of a single culture are few, and the story's single gesture toward cultural transcendence occurs in an aside, a digression from the plot. Like Saladin, the protagonist of "The Two Drovers" acts as a cultural middleman, with a foot in each of two societies and even two eras. Robin Oig, however, has a stake in the cultures he bridges that is more organic, substantial, and concretely historical than is Saladin's. As a Highland cattle-drover, he is linked in metonymic fashion to the forces of modernization that in the late eighteenth century were delivering the Scottish Highlands over to the power of England. The roads he travels were created to subdue the Highlands militarily: they allowed English troops to penetrate the Highlands efficiently and at will. They also promoted economic and cultural assimilation. Initially, Robin seems to be a beneficiary of the changes the roads have made possible. His business is thriving.

In the Waverley novels, Scott's middlemen normally survive their encounters with different cultural forces, and usually profit from their dual allegiances. In "The Two Drovers," acting as a cultural middleman brings death. The story's opening scene shows Robin torn between the old world and the new. As he prepares to leave his native village to meet Harry Wakefield, an English drover with whom he plans to take his herd to market, his aunt stops him so that she can walk the Deasil around him. In the midst of this ancient ceremony, she suddenly tells him that she sees "English" blood on his hand and his dirk, and implores him not to journey south that day. At this point in the story, Robin seems, for all his Highland pride, primarily a creature of the new world, for he reacts to his aunt with that definitive emotion of modernity, embarrassment, mixed to be sure with a chagrined love for his relation. He refuses to stay home, but placates his aunt by giving up his dirk to the keeping of a Lowland drover. But by the story's end, he reveals that his "Highland" side is deeply ingrained. When he and his English friend have a misunderstanding, the Englishman demands that it be adjudicated through a fistfight, and punches Robin when he refuses to partake in what Robin considers a form of strife beneath the dignity of a Highland "gentleman." Robin loses his temper, tries to strike back, and is soundly beaten. Highland tradition suggests that such a beating leaves an indelible mark, which can only be purged with blood. Smarting with his disgrace, Robin recalls passing the Lowlander who is keeping his dirk earlier that day on the high road. He walks for an hour, retrieves the dirk, and returning to the inn where he and Wakefield fought, kills Wakefield. He is subsequently tried, convicted, and hanged. Lest we miss the fact that Robin's death is a result of his position as someone with a foot in two cultures, we are informed that, as a point of law, he would not have been hanged had he killed Harry Wakefield during their initial fistfight. But his long walk to retrieve his knife gave him time to calm down; thus according to English law, his crime is not manslaughter, but murder in cold blood. If he had listened to his aunt, he would never have come to England in the first place; if he had ignored her completely, he would have carried his dirk, used it immediately, and been guilty only of manslaughter. His attempt to find a compromise between the old and the newer ways dooms him.

Further issues involving cultural embeddedness are elaborately explored by the story's succession of narrative voices. The story is officially narrated by Chrystal Croftangry, the most fully developed of Scott's many frame-narrators, a genteel Scotsman trained as a lawyer. In the story's opening pages, Croftangry seems as much English as Scots. His proper English narrative language contrasts strongly with the lower-class dialects spoken by both Scottish and English characters. He makes a few stock jokes about the Highlanders, emphasizing their parsimony and acquisitiveness. At best, he seems to be trying to create a sense of solidarity with the genteel reader by poking gentle fun at the Highland yokels, so that he can then go on to show that they really do have their own proper dignity, that even a drover can participate in a tragedy. In the opening paragraphs of the story, his narration is studded with Gaelic nouns followed parenthetically by their English meanings, as in this description of Robin's exit from his native village: "All cried—'Good luck travel out with you and come home with you.—Give you luck in the Saxon market—brave notes in the *leabhar-dhu*' (black pocket-book) 'and plenty of English gold in the *sporran*' (pouch of goatskin)."[35] The heaping up of Gaelic vocabulary here does nothing to promote a sense that certain Gaelic words encapsulate a mode of cultural perception or practice unavailable to us in our own language. When Scott, writing the notes to his first major publication, *The Minstrelsy of the Scottish Border*, glosses the Scots word "haugh," he invites us to imagine a way of taking in a landscape that is worth trying to understand and to share.[36] The collection of quickly trans-

---

[35] Scott, *The Two Drovers and Other Stories*, ed. David Cecil (Oxford: Oxford University Press, 1987), 226; hereafter cited in the text. For a reading of this story alive to its social and economic resonances, see W. J. Overton, "Scott, the Short Story and History: 'The Two Drovers,' " *Studies in Scottish Literature*, 21 (1986), 210–25.

[36] "The Scottish language is rich in words expressive of local situation. The single word *haugh* conveys to a Scotsman almost all that I have endeavoured to explain in the text, by circumlocutory description" (Scott, *Minstrelsy of the Scottish Border*, ed. T. F. Henderson, 4 vols. [Edinburgh: Blackwood, 1902], vol. 2, 208).

lated items of Gaelic vocabulary Croftangry produces has nothing of this force: he seems interested in them only because they sound exotic and denote exotic objects. Words become labels; the web of associations that would make it possible for them to convey cultural meaning is lacking. We might call this sort of language "dead metonymy."

In this depiction of local color in the Highlands, however, we find a brief passage describing Robin which, though it begins with "English" condescension, comes to evoke a complex grasp of the disparate elements comprised by cultures and mentalities:

> He was a topping person in his way, transacted considerable business on his own behalf, and was entrusted by the best farmers in the Highlands in preference to any other drover in that district. He might have increased his business to any extent had he condescended to manage it by deputy; but except a lad or two, sister's sons of his own, Robin rejected the idea of assistance, conscious, perhaps, how much his reputation depended upon his attending in person to the practical discharge of his duty in every instance. He remained, therefore, contented with the highest premium given to persons of his description, and comforted himself with the hopes that a few journeys to England might enable him to conduct business on his own account, in a manner becoming his birth. For Robin Oig's father, Lachlan M'Combich (or *son of my friend*, his actual clan-surname being M'Gregor), had been so called by the celebrated Rob Roy, because of the particular friendship which had subsisted between the grandsire of Robin and that renowned cateran. Some people even say that Robin Oig derived his Christian name from one as renowned in the wilds of Loch Lomond as ever was his namesake Robin Hood, in the precincts of merry Sherwood. "Of such ancestry," as James Boswell says, "who would not be proud?" Robin Oig was proud accordingly; but his frequent visits to England and to the Lowlands had given him tact enough to know that pretensions, which still gave him a little right to distinction in his own lonely glen, might be both obnoxious and ridiculous if preferred elsewhere. The pride of birth, therefore, was like the miser's treasure, the secret subject of his contemplation, but never exhibited to strangers as a subject of boasting. (224–25)

As this passage progresses, the situation of the Highland Drover becomes not a set of amusing clichés, but something problematic, an example of what Auerbach calls the serious representation of everyday life. The details of Scott's description evoke not local-color minutiae but the components of a metonymical historical structure reminiscent of the description of the mail service in *Waverley*. The reference to Boswell helps to signal a deepening of perspective. This cultural cliché (that the Scottish people have an inordinate pride of ancestry) cuts across class lines instead of drawing them.[37] The one moment in the description that might seem to involve mere local color, the reference to the "renowned cateran" Rob Roy McGregor, is sufficiently obscure and complex to prevent it from functioning in the way the tags earlier in the story do. As readers of Scott's earlier novels would know, the McGregors, from an early time, were a "broken" clan. Their clan was legally denied the use of its own name, and they therefore had to proceed in disguise, under aliases—as Robin himself has to proceed, we will see, in more ways than one.[38]

In this context, the place that money might play in Robin's mental horizon becomes more than an ethnic joke. Does Robin's concern for his "reputation" reflect simply a canny business sense, or does it reflect the pride that is "the secret subject of his contemplation"—or can we really make a distinction here? Would such a distinction occur to Robin? Robin's connections with Rob Roy "*still* gave him a *little* right to distinction in his own lonely glen." It is only a "little" right, because the heroic, violent career Rob Roy himself followed has become archaic and impossible with (among other things) the coming of the Highland roads. The very conditions that allow Robin Oig the chance of gaining money and the "distinction" it brings by being a drover are those that have diminished his family glory. Is this too part of his consciousness? Such considerations change the ring of the jokes made earlier about the Highland heart being "made glad" by the abundance of English money. Why did he make them so glibly, and how did we laugh at them so easily? It's not simply that Robin's situation is more complex than we had imagined. We sense a different mental world from ours, one in which money has a substance and

---

[37]   The comedy latent in Boswell's characteristic self-delight helps here, as does the deftness of the parallel Scott creates between Robin Oig and Boswell's name-fixation. For readers who recall the passage, Robin's fixation here is likely to seem less foolish than Boswell's, for the latter jumps upon the opportunity of a passing mention of his four-month-old daughter's Christian name Veronica to boast in a footnote that the blood of the Bruce flows in his own veins: "The saint's name of *Veronica* was introduced into our family through my great grandmother Veronica, Countess of Kincardine, a Dutch lady of the noble house of Sommelsdyck, of which there is a full account in Bayle's Dictionary. The family had once a princely right in Surinam . . . " and so on, with twists and turns back to Robert the Bruce, and the winning conclusion, "Of such ancestry who would not be proud? And . . . who would not be glad to seize a fair opportunity to let it be known?" (*Johnson's Journey to the Western Isles of Scotland and Boswell's Journal of a Tour to the Hebrides*, ed. R. W. Chapman [London: Oxford University Press, 1970], 175 n. 1).

[38]   On the history of the McGregors, see Scott's extended Magnum Opus Introduction to *Rob Roy* (1829). The novel itself (1817) makes the "broken" nature of the clan clear.

aura derived from its ability to summon up and continue a past family glory built on very different grounds from those of modern, anonymous commerce. In this context, the metaphor of the hoard which for the miser provides "the secret subject of his contemplation" has a powerful and eerie effect. Money is alive for a miser in a way that it isn't for us. This image attaches mana to Robin's nexus of dealings with money, honor, and selfhood—something archaic, obsessive, and alien to us. We feel like intruders who have carelessly broken into the miser's contemplation, or tourists who have stumbled into part of a village we are not meant to see.

This effect is repeated in a different key with the entrance of Robin's aunt Janet. The Lowlanders in the scene are uneasy, fearing her supernatural powers over the herds, and they reassure themselves that Robin is clever enough to have taken precautions. Croftangry glosses their conversation by remarking for our benefit, "It may not be indifferent to the reader to know that the Highland cattle are peculiarly liable to be *taken*, or infected, by spells and witchcraft; which judicious people guard against by knitting knots of peculiar complexity on the tuft of hair which terminates the animal's tail" (226). One purpose of this superciliousness is to help us identify with Robin's own embarrassment at his aunt. But Janet's entrance has a power, and raises issues, that cannot be so easily dismissed. One sign of this power lurks in a simple statement Robin makes to his aunt, which includes a Gaelic word Scott significantly does not gloss. When Janet takes his dirk from him, telling him she sees English blood on it, Robin replies: "You cannot tell by the colour the difference betwixt the blood of a black bullock and a white one, and you speak of knowing Saxon from Gaelic blood. All men have their blood from Adam, Muhme" (228). We understand the notion of a universal brotherhood of man conveyed by the reminder that all men have their blood from Adam, but what could "Muhme" mean? The juxtaposition of universalistic sentiment and a recalcitrant linguistic particularity is striking. It enacts the central dynamic of the story, for Robin and for us—an attempted movement beyond the culturally particular to the universal which inevitably and tragically returns to the very particularity it sought to avoid. If "all men" really had their blood from Adam, if difference were not the source of cultural definition and animation, then Robin Oig would not die at the end of the story. But if cultural difference were not fundamental, the story itself would not live. To the extent that we transcend Croftangry's moments of simple cultural stereotyping and use our own imaginations to enter the metonymical web of Highland culture, we have an investment in believing that cultural differences matter. We thus become imaginatively complicit in a crucial aspect of the situation that causes Robin's death. To conclude that we thereby become in some sense personally "responsible" for his death would, however, be to indulge in an unearned moment of the interpretive sublime. What we are shown to be complicit in is history. The possibility that the mind-set the story promotes might allow us more freedom of thought and agency than the story's characters possess remains open.

As the story progresses to its tragic climax, its characters are increasingly spoken by the logic and language of their cultures. Harry is singing an English folk song with his friends when Robin enters the inn and calls to him to "stand up" and face him. When he naively tries to patch things up with the man who, having retrieved his dirk, has returned to the inn to kill him, his initial attempt to speak beyond his local prejudices falters, he laces his language with insults, and Robin follows suit. Harry begins by speaking of hearts and hands, things as common to all men as the blood of Adam, but he ends with language that draws invidious boundaries of nationality and sex:

> "Harry Waakfelt," repeated the same ominous summons, "stand up, if you be a man!"
>
> There is something in the tone of deep and concentrated passion, which attracts attention and imposes awe, even by the very sound. The guests shrunk back on every side, and gazed at the Highlander as he stood in the middle of them, his brows bent, and his features rigid with resolution.
>
> "I will stand up with all my heart, Robin, my boy, but it shall be to shake hands with you, and drink down all unkindness. It is not the fault of your heart, man, that you don't know how to clench your hands."
>
> By this time he stood opposite to his antagonist; his open and unsuspecting look strangely contrasted with the stern purpose, which gleamed wild, dark, and vindictive in the eyes of the Highlander.
>
> " 'Tis not thy fault, man, that, not having the luck to be an Englishman, thou canst not fight more than a schoolgirl."
>
> "I *can* fight," answered Robin Oig sternly, but calmly, "and you shall know it. You, Harry Waakfelt, showed me to-day how the Saxon churls fight—I show you now how the Highland Dunnièwassel fights." (250–51)

From his own viewpoint, Harry doubtless considers himself to be, as the disguised Saladin had put it, an "ancient foe . . . but a fair and a generous one," since he has no conception of what the beating signifies to Robin. Robin stabs him to death, and even in death the Englishman preserves a "smile of good-humoured confidence in his own strength, of conciliation at once and contempt towards his enemy" (252). The scene seems a grim parody of Scott's normal cultural translation and mediation, and also of the oscillation we noted in Scott's *Journal* between his passionate engagement with his own historical moment and an ability to transcend party feeling in the interest of preserving the kindly feelings of a universalizing friendship. When Robin kills Harry, the only thing that can evoke a cross-cultural response is the "sound" of "passion," which imposes awe on the bystanders and evokes a fatal response.

Robin's last words as he gazes at his dead friend are "He was a pretty man!" (253). Even this attempt at appreciating an antagonist is tinged with a cultural irony, for the use of "pretty man" to refer not to a fop but to an able warrior is a distinctly Scottish locution which evokes war, not prizefighting. One wonders what the "Saxon churls" make of this locution; indeed, one wonders whether Robin speaks it in English or Gaelic. We begin to doubt that any speech, any language, can reliably transcend its cultural base. To be sure, Croftangry's own narrating voice, partly by the very way in which it expresses prejudice, seems designed to incite us to transcend prejudice—as he himself sometimes seems to do, especially when his voice melts into the narrative voice that habitually takes over in Scott's novels when their individualized frame-narrators fade from view. This is a voice we as readers have a stake in. If we have read earlier fiction by Scott, we count on it to translate and mediate, rendering intelligible such phrases as "pretty man" and the cultures from which they arise.

After the murder, we expect a quick wind-up to the tale; instead, we're faced with a report of the "venerable" English judge's charge to the jury which convicts Robin. This charge extends over several pages and includes speculations on the American Indians as well as a careful explanation of the seventeenth-century law that excluded murderers who used short weapons from the Benefit of Clergy. The judge is clearly part of the historical moment that contains both Robin and Harry, but he nonetheless demonstrates an ability to rise above it, doubling what we take to be the implied author's own viewpoint, while remaining within the fiction. For the heart of the judge's charge involves explaining to the jury that Robin, in murdering Harry Wakefield, was not acting in a cowardly or underhanded manner, but was instead responding to the dictates of his own culture. It is as if the plot line's refusal to end with cultural understanding demands that someone within the frame of the story voice more hopeful possibilities.

The judge does not act simply as a disembodied voice of reason. At several points he inadvertently and amusingly provides proof that anti-Scottish prejudice is not the property of the English lower classes alone. He opines, for instance, that Robin's part of Scotland "was, in the days of many now alive, inaccessible to the laws, not only of England, which have not even yet penetrated thither, but to those to which our neighbours of Scotland are subjected, and which must be supposed to be, *and no doubt actually are*, founded upon the general principles of justice and equity which pervade every civilized country" (257–58; my emphasis). Such laborious good faith is disarming, but also telling. Yet this is a venial slip. The judge puts an impressive amount of effort, good faith, and penetrating intelligence into the task of understanding Robin's deed from the point of view of Robin's own culture. With the judge, then, we begin to feel that the possibility of being both wholly and passionately "in" one's society, yet also able to stand "above" it, may yet be achieved. Even when he feels called upon to demand that the jury find Robin Oig guilty and amenable to the penalty of death, he evokes an immediate and timeless sympathy: "The venerable judge thus ended what, to judge by his apparent emotion, and by the tears which filled his eyes, was really a painful task" (259). To be sure, Scott's normal, external narration, which tends to eschew direct reports on the consciousness of characters, leaves the state of the judge's mind in doubt, referring only to his "apparent" emotion; but who can doubt the reality of his tears? The story provides a corroborating witness. Though we haven't seen a first-person narrative comment for pages, Croftangry reemerges as a personified narrator: "I shall never forget the charge of the venerable judge to the jury, although not at that time liable to be much affected either by that which was eloquent or pathetic" (253).

Yet even the judge's learned and humane attempt to represent the voice of a reason cognizant of cultural difference proves ultimately brittle. During the trial, the prosecutor had suggested that, like a "cowardly Italian," Robin killed Harry Wakefield because he was afraid to "submit to the laws of the ring" (255). The judge quite properly finds such a line of argument unsatisfactory. Though he happily employs the category of the "cowardly Italian," he calls attention to the ethnocentric bias that blinds the prosecutor to the fact that Robin, coming from another culture, has no reason to submit himself to "the laws of the ring." The judge buttresses this argument with the following commentary:

"Gentlemen, as to the laws my brother talks of, they may be known in the bull-ring, or the bear-garden, or the cockpit, but they are not known here. Or, if they should be so far admitted as furnishing a species of proof that no malice was intended in this sort of combat, from which fatal accidents do sometimes arise, it can only be so admitted when both parties are *in pari casu*, equally acquainted with, and equally willing to refer themselves to, that species of arbitrament. But will it be contended that a man of superior rank and education is to be subjected, or is obliged to subject himself, to this coarse and brutal strife, perhaps in opposition to a younger, stronger, or more skilful opponent? Certainly even the pugilistic code, if founded upon the fair play of Merry Old England, as my brother alleges it to be, can contain nothing so preposterous. And, gentlemen of the jury, if the laws would support an English gentleman, wearing, we will suppose, his sword, in defending himself by force against a violent personal aggression of the nature offered to this prisoner, they will not less protect a foreigner and a stranger, involved in the same unpleasing circumstances." (255–56)

The case is admirably and equitably argued here. Yet in the midst of this measured legal rhetoric there occurs a moment of excess, when the judge insists that a certain outcome would be not unfair or unreasonable, but "preposterous." This hyperbole is significant. Our sense of what is preposterous is likely to depend upon our sense of what is natural. "Preposterous" is a word designed to preclude further discussion. The discussion here precluded, the facts here made self-evident, involve historically specific class relations. *Of course* a gentleman should not have to submit to the "coarse strife" engaged in by his social inferiors—any of them, for though the judge's example adduces a strong young ruffian attacking a reverend elder gentleman, its logic suggests that it is in the nature of things that a strapping young gentleman need not engage in a fistfight with an older and weaker lower-class opponent. Need I say that my purpose here is not to assess the justice of the judge's views on the laws of the ring? What interests me is what seems immediately obvious to him, and why. It would appear that the judge sympathizes with Robin, and strives to understand his cultural predicament, not entirely on the basis of a shared universal humanity, but also as the duty of one "gentleman" to another. Robin had indignantly asserted his status as a Highland "gentleman" before the fistfight began, to the amusement of the English boors in the tavern; the judge, however, is enough of a historicist to recognize a gentleman when he sees one.

The judge repeats the word "preposterous" a few paragraphs later, this time in comparing Robin's mentality to that of the *ancien régime*: "Those laws of the ring, as my brother terms them, were unknown to the race of warlike mountaineers; that decision of quarrels by no other weapons than those which nature has given every man, must to them have seemed as vulgar and as preposterous as to the noblesse of France. Revenge, on the other hand, must have been as familiar to their habits of society as to those of the Cherokees or Mohawks. It is indeed, as described by Bacon, at bottom a kind of wild untutored justice" (258). Here again, Scott creates a nicely ironic mixture of the culturally fixed and the humanely universal. In this part of his charge, the judge anchors a claim that certain possibilities would be "preposterous" in a single class living at a given historical moment, and he makes reference to other cultures and times. But in the end, his doing so only serves to emphasize the extent to which he himself is caught in time and class.

The judge has a reason for spurning any comparison between Robin and a "cowardly Italian": "as I would wish to make my words impressive when I point his real crime, I must secure his opinion of my impartiality, by rebutting everything that seems to me a false accusation. There can be no doubt that the prisoner is a man of resolution—too much resolution—I wish to Heaven that he had less, or rather that he had had a better education to regulate it" (255). The judge's charge, then, is an attempt to supply such education, after the fact. This attempt fails. Robin's notion of justice and the judge's never meet. Robin's remains "primitive," more like that of the Cherokees than that of the "noblesse of France." In agreeing to the justice of the judge's sentence of death, Robin evokes legal practices much older than English law: " 'I give a life for the life I took,' he said, 'and what can I do more?' " (259). After reading this, the closing line of the story, one wonders whether the judge has understood Robin at all.

It might hardly matter, except that providing such understanding is the central claim of Scott's fiction, and that the judge uses his powers of understanding to ensure that the jury puts Robin to death. They are, Croftangry informs us, initially much impressed by his exposition of cultural relativism—much, perhaps, as we might imagine that the early audiences for Scott's fiction were swayed by the glimpses it gave of life in history, of men and not protocols, as Carlyle would have it.[39] Indeed, they are so swayed that they are inclined to release Robin. But this the judge cannot permit. He knows Robin; he knows his culture; he is therefore in a position to know, name, and demand punishment for his "real crime." That crime is, in English law and language, *premeditated* murder. Robin walked for an hour to retrieve his dirk from the drover named Morrison, and walked another hour to return to the inn. He thus had time to cool off and to engage in "premeditation." On this point, however, the story knows better than the judge. During the depiction of Robin's walk, something odd occurs. After an external view that measures the time with a pedestrian precision, we suddenly find ourselves in the present tense:

[39]   Carlyle, review of *Memoirs of the Life of Sir Walter Scott, Baronet*, vols. 1–6, in *London and Westminster Review*, 6 (1838).

When Robin Oig left the door of the ale-house, seven or eight English [!] miles at least lay betwixt Morrison and him. The advance of the former was slow, limited by the sluggish pace of his cattle; the last left behind him stubble-field and hedge-row, crag and dark heath, all glittering with frost-rime in the broad November moonlight, at the rate of six miles an hour. And now the distant lowing of Morrison's cattle is heard; and now they are seen creeping like moles in size and slowness of motion on the broad face of the moor; and now he meets them—passes them, and stops their conductor. (247)

Whose present tense informs the last sentence here, if not Robin's? The sudden, timeless immediacy here suggests that time simply hasn't passed for him, since the moment he was beaten. There has been no "cooling off" and no premeditation—such "English" categories simply don't apply. Robin's resolve to kill Wakefield was the work of an instant. It involved not premeditation, but a shift into the mythic, "second-sight" temporality that allows his aunt to "see" in the present objects and events which our ordinary notion of time place in the inaccessible future. After his beating, Robin exclaims, "the dirk—ha! the English blood!—My Muhme's word—when did her word fall to the ground?" (246). The temporality Robin here enters forecloses the ordinary open-endedness of our normal sense of time, the sense of time that lies behind the telling of historicist stories.[40] From the moment when Robin places himself in the category of someone who has been beaten by the hands of another, there remains no story for him to inhabit, just an ending. It's worth noting in this regard that Scott's sudden narrative transition to the present tense does not "directly" or "transparently" mime the alternative temporality Robin enters, for it cannot in any simple sense be represented in our language and with our cultural grammar. Instead, it alerts the reader to the possibility of alternate forms of temporal being. As usual with Scott, it's up to us to try to imagine the conditions of possibility of such a temporality, using the raw materials he has placed at our disposal.

Even if the judge's cultural relativism had revealed to him the insufficiency of the notion of "premeditation" to describe Robin's actions, he could hardly have acted upon this knowledge. The judge's informed imagination has allowed him to assess events with an impartiality rare for any character in Scott's fiction, but his job is to mold events as well as react to them. In demanding and obtaining the death penalty, he makes

---

[40] Compare Saree Makdisi, "Colonial Space and the Colonization of Time in Scott's *Waverley*," *Studies in Romanticism*, 34 (1995), 171, who believes that even in *Waverley*, Highlanders in general are imagined as occupying a "spot of time" from which there is no escape.

history, to the advantage of history's winners, the English society whose law has "not yet" fully overtaken the Highlands. The judge's plotting recalls the "providential history" Bruce Robbins describes.[41] With it vanishes the space for the kind of self-conscious mobility within and between cultures I've been at such pains to reveal in *The Talisman*. In the end, the safety of the new form of English society, whose laws have not yet penetrated fully into Scotland, demands Robin's death. The judge's final words on the matter are decisive: "But his crime is not the less that of murder, gentleman, and, in your high and important office, it is your duty so to find. Englishmen have their angry passions as well as Scots; and should this man's action remain unpunished, you may unsheath, under various pretences, a thousand daggers betwixt the Land's-end and the Orkneys" (259). It is grimly instructive to see how the judge's earlier generous attempt to understand Robin's motivations now contracts to talk of "angry passions" and "pretences."

Tears fill the judge's eyes as he passes sentence, and Croftangry is moved by them. As this circle of pity extends, the implied author, Croftangry as narrator, and the judge—figures who have been kept separate as part of Scott's overall narrative strategy—begin to merge, and the reader merges with them. Yet this doesn't negate the story's suggestion that the tales we tell about history may function as exercises of power at the expense of the Other and that our knowledge of cultural difference, and our sympathy for it, may grease the wheels for a certain kind of "progress." The invitation to share in the judge's tears marks a point beyond which Scott's vision of history can hardly proceed. The story comes to a close.

This is not, however, quite the whole story about the sense of possibility that emerges from "The Two Drovers." Realism, as we've seen with Austen, finds its home in middles at least as much as in endings. The first of the story's two chapters ends with the following reminiscence:

> It is difficult to say how Harry Wakefield and Robin Oig first became intimates; but it is certain a close acquaintance had taken place betwixt them, although they had apparently few common subjects of conversation or of interest, so soon as their talk ceased to be of bullocks. Robin Oig, indeed, spoke the English language rather imperfectly upon any other topics but stots and kyloes, and Harry Wakefield could never bring his broad Yorkshire tongue to utter a single word of Gaelic. It was in vain Robin spent a whole

---

[41] In Chapter 3, I argue at length against Robbins's wish to extend the notion of "Providential History" to Erich Auerbach's plotting of the history of realism. The notion of "transient utopias" that disrupt providential history employed below is drawn from Robbins.

morning, during a walk over Minch Moor in attempting to teach his companion to utter, with true precision, the shibboleth *Llhu*, which is the Gaelic for a calf. From Traquair to Murder-cairn, the hill rang with the discordant attempts of the Saxon upon the unmanageable monosyllable, and the heartfelt laugh which followed every failure. They had, however, better modes of awakening the echoes; for Wakefield could sing many a ditty to the praise of Moll, Susan, and Cicely, and Robin Oig had a particular gift at whistling interminable pibrochs through all their involutions, and what was more agreeable to his companion's southern ear, knew many of the northern airs, both lively and pathetic, to which Wakefield learned to pipe a bass. Thus, though Robin could hardly have comprehended his companion's stories about horse-racing, and cock-fighting or fox-hunting, and although his own legends of clan-fights and *creaghs*, varied with talk of Highland goblins and fairy folk, would have been caviare to his companion, they contrived nevertheless to find a degree of pleasure in each other's company, which had for three years back induced them to join company and travel together, when the direction of their journey permitted. Each, indeed, found his advantage in this companionship; for where could the Englishman have found a guide through the Western Highlands like Robin Oig McCombich? and when they were on what Harry called the *right* side of the Border, his patronage, which was extensive, and his purse, which was heavy, were at all times at the service of his Highland friend, and on many occasions his liberality did him genuine yeoman's service. (231–32)

As we would expect with Scott, this lyric moment remains part of the mundane world, tethered most obviously by its recognition of the ties between economic realities and the rest of life. It nevertheless offers a "transient utopia," in which the cultures that define Harry and Robin coexist and mingle without dilution.[42] The two men discover, without rancor and

[42]   In speaking of utopian possibilities arising from coexisting musical lines, we rejoin the work of Said, in a mode of at least partial harmony. In *Musical Elaborations* (New York: Columbia University Press, 1991), for instance, Said suggests that "Glenn Gould . . . understood the potential interest in this essentially contrapuntal mode—that is, you think of and treat one musical line in conjunction with several others that derive from and relate to it, and you do so through imitation, repetition, or ornamentation—as an antidote to the more overtly administrative and executive authority contained in, say, a Mozart or Beethoven classical sonata form" (102); he subsequently identifies this mode as "utopian" (105). *Musical Elaborations*, however, tends to associate narrative with "administrative and executive authority"—see, for instance, the commentary on Messaien as "an anti- or non-narrative alternative to the mainstream tradition" (99). *Orientalism*, by contrast, finds in narrative the power to liberate the Oriental Other from the freezing view of the Occident (240), in a way more in consonance with my own speculations here. I am indebted to

indeed much to their mutual amusement, that they will never master each other's languages. But they can share the resonances of those languages in other ways. Harry Wakefield sings English songs; Robin Oig McCombich whistles "interminable" Highland pibrochs. Both enjoy each other's native music. Then something remarkable occurs. They find a way of singing in counterpoint to one another, each using elements of his own native music.[43] Neither attempts to assimilate the music of the other, and their voices blend, an echo of the aspirations of Scott's own art. Robin and Harry experience their moment of cultural harmony as they journey through the Scottish Borders, not far from the house where Walter Scott wrote the words that describe their actions, the region where his salvaging of Scottish culture had begun, when as a young man he set about collecting the ballads that became *The Minstrelsy of the Scottish Border*.

Even in "The Two Drovers," cultures fleetingly intermingle, and the Other is honored without being engulfed, through a wordless counterpoint which the reader must bring to imaginative life. This structure recalls our theoretical description of realism as a kit that provides you with concrete materials to work with, and a set of examples that train you in the skills required to put it together. But to experience a way of imagining the Other is not necessarily to solve the problems of the Other in history.

When Robin and Harry journey through the Scottish Borders, we hear two voices. When the judge sentences Robin, and when he delivers his charge to the jury, his is the only voice heard in the courtroom. It is easy to sentimentalize the need for dialogue. The judge's monologue is preferable to any number of dialogues we can imagine, including the one that occurs before Robin stabs Harry. Everything about "The Two Drovers" seems to demand the entrance of a single voice that can adjudicate the issues it raises. Everything, that is, but the very quality of our delight in the opposition between different cultures that is the basis of the story's interest, and that persists in its one moment of utopian harmony.

No doubt the harmony the men achieve is transient and, as the rest of the story demonstrates, easily broken. The music that Robin and Harry make lacks any shared linguistic content, rich as it is in cultural reference. The meeting of cultures it creates is procedural, not substantive. But there is surely a need for utopian imaginings of what it would mean for two cultures to coexist in a state that requires neither to give up its essence so that it can be translated into the terms of the other. "The Two Drovers"

Krishna Lewis for pointing out to me the relevance of Said's writings on music to my reading of "The Two Drovers."

[43] The expression "northern airs" is equivocal here. If it refers to the Scottish ballads, not the English, then the language Scott himself used best and which is proper to neither Harry nor Robin may be acting as a mediating force between them. In the reading I prefer, such mediation comes solely from the geographical placing of their singing bouts.

uses artistic means to create a utopian vision and make it desirable, even as it reveals all that stands in the way of its realization, and indeed shows how our very interest in other cultures as "exhibits" may itself become an accessory to their obliteration. The judge finds Robin interesting as a reflection of a knowable culture, and he is certain that he can define the nature of Robin's crime. His ability to react to Robin's plight with feeling, in a way that mixes the ethical and the aesthetic, seems admirable, yet it also helps to render his demand that the jury find Robin guilty the more peremptory. Realism claims to help us understand the workings of human societies in history. Scott's realism, in this story at least, is anything but naive about the limited efficacy of cultural understanding, especially when we feel called upon to defend the conditions, social and personal, that underpin our ability to make sense of things. "The Two Drovers" reveals a problem more challenging than the familiar notion that somehow we'll never see beyond our own cultural grid. "The Two Drovers" demonstrates that we can often see far beyond our own cultural grid, but that our vision may in the end have little effect on our actions. The deepest problems realism uncovers involve not epistemology, but the will.

The Voice of the Other: Jeanie Deans

In "The Two Drovers," when the boundaries between cultures begin to seem permeable, Scott's representation moves toward the pictorial and perhaps even the ineffable. A song arises in a landscape. Robin's doomed temporality flashes before us in the mist. There are of course moments in any reality where words don't seem to suffice, but in realism, especially as practiced by Scott, a sustained transcendence of the prose of everyday life is an illusion. The ineffable gains definition and significance from the world of history. When Robin Oig embraces a mythic temporality, no place remains for him in that world, but that world still defines the no-place he inhabits—at least for us. The counterpoint Harry and Robin briefly achieve depends upon setting aside words in favor of music, but it wouldn't be the counterpoint it is if their mingling musical lines didn't gain separate definition from the rich freighting of specific cultural tradition each bears. One reason why these moments seem to leave the habitual language of realism behind is that they draw so heavily on the powers of the reader, whose work is not inscribed on the page.

Certain aspects of the historicist vision do, however, put what can seem an impossible strain on the language of realist narration. This is particularly true of the narrative representation of speech and thought, when the speech and the thought belong to those who are culturally Other. Speech is the more obvious problem. With a character like Saladin (and with Scott's medieval and Renaissance figures in general) there's simply nothing to be done but to create an artificial substitute for language that can hardly be recovered and would be intelligible only to specialists even if it could. Scott was entirely aware of this problem: he discusses it in the introductory material he added to *Waverley* toward the end of his life, for the Magnum Opus edition. The representation of thought has similarities, but it can take subtler forms, especially as the setting of a novel begins to approach the author's own present. Further complexities can arise when the crossing of class boundaries is involved.

Scott's fiction deals most richly with the thoughts of the Other in *The Heart of Midlothian*.[44] Nothing places the novel's protagonist, Jeanie Deans, in history more clearly than the Scots vernacular language she speaks. But what is the narrator's relationship to that vernacular, and what attitude are we encouraged to assume with regard to it? There's always a tendency for vernacular speech to provoke amused condescension. For readers of Scott's day, vernacular speech as part of artistic representation was familiar chiefly as it involved the stage, where "stage Irish" or "stage Gaelic" could be counted on to produce a ready laugh. (Here we find ourselves back with Said's hunch that attempts to imagine someone as belonging to a culture definitively different from our own bring with them hostility and self-satisfaction.) Vernacular language, redolent of her cultural and historical place, would seem to offer the perfect medium for depicting the thoughts of such a character as Jeanie Deans, but it would also be compromised from the start.

The most thorough study to date of Scott's language points out that vernacular never enters the Author of Waverley's narrative voice; its author concludes that this implies a demotion by the narrator of vernacular speech, the kind of demotion that seems likely to occur whenever genteel speakers compare dialect with their own proper language.[45] The description is accurate, but the conclusion seems unwarranted. It is possible that Scott's narrator, by avoiding the vernacular himself, is not so much demoting the vernacular Other as attempting to avoid overwhelming it in advance. Scott was faced with the problem of how to encourage readers to recognize in vernacular speech not a cue for laughter, but signs of a

---

[44]   For further examination of these issues, see Harry E. Shaw, "Scott's 'Daemon' and the Voices of Historical Narration," *JEGP*, 88 (1989), 21–33. A discerning treatment of literary uses of Scottish vernacular is Emma Letley, *From Galt to Douglas Brown: Nineteenth-Century Fiction and Scots Language* (Edinburgh: Scottish Academic Press, 1988).

[45]   Graham Tulloch, *The Language of Walter Scott* (London: André Deutsch, 1980), 181: "If Scots is not used for all purposes whereas English is (Scott uses English in dialogue as well as narrative) then, however interesting it is, it must *appear* inferior."

mental world different from their own—a world which, with the help of the context provided by the novel and their own linguistic resources, they might be able to feel their way into. To bring the reader this far, he watered down the thickness of Scots vernacular, so that difficulties with syntax and lexicon would not obscure the sense of a passage, and perhaps more important, do not obscure the fact that people have lived who were able to think in such a language as naturally as we think in ours. The hope would be that sufficient cultural saliency would remain to function as a point of departure. Such a procedure would exclude from the outset the fantasy of allowing readers simply to "be" the Other, or even to view the Other without regard to their own places and interests. The goal of a historicist mode of representation like Scott's is not to attempt the impossible task of insulating the past from the interests and determinations of the present, but to make possible a dialogue between past and present, by staving off the demands of the present for a moment. Scott seeks to create a space in which the past can emerge, before present interests reassert themselves.

Scott's characters often voice their thoughts to themselves or to the empty air in set speeches that resemble nothing so much as stage soliloquies. This expedient allows him simply to avoid the tricky business of representing thoughts in the mind: his habit of imagining his characters from the skin out is so pronounced as to make set speeches appear to him a plausible medium for what we would call "inner" thoughts. Thus he depicts Jeanie Deans speaking her thoughts aloud to herself when she receives a letter from her errant sister:

> What Jeanie least liked in the tone of the letter was a smothered degree of egotism. "We should have heard little about her," said Jeanie to herself, "but that she was feared the Duke might come to learn wha she was, and a' about her puir friends here; but Effie, puir thing, aye looks her ain way, and folks that do that think mair o' themselves than of their neighbours.—I am no clear about keeping her siller," she added, taking up a 50 l. note which had fallen out of the paper to the floor. "We hae aneugh, and it looks unco like theft-boot, or hush-money, as they ca' it. . . . " (478)

Scott's eagerness to give Jeanie's Scots the form of direct speech is amusingly apparent here, as she herself improbably glosses a word likely to puzzle an English reader ("theft-boot, or hush-money, as they ca' it"). Yet this bit of awkwardness seems a small price to pay for a language that resonates with the cultural and historical specificity we would miss if her ruminations were reported in the more colorless language of the narrator.

A richer mode of reporting the thoughts of a character filters concrete examples of a character's vernacular speech through a medley of reportorial forms, including direct quotations, assertions that the character thought or felt something, and language approaching free indirect discourse. This mixture of modes directs us as readers to create a voice for the content of a character's thoughts, to imagine that we are hearing them in the character's vernacular idiolect—or at least to assume that they were or could be thought in the vernacular. In the process, the vernacular loses its potentially comic or quaint nature: because we imagine its possibility but do not hear its actuality, it gains the "natural" respectability of our own inner language. If my own experience is any guide, a reader tends to remember such passages *as* free indirect discourse in the vernacular, but in turning to the text discovers they are nothing of the kind.

An inner debate, of which I shall quote only a small part, concerning whether Jeanie Deans should save her sister Effie from execution by betraying her seducer, George Staunton, exemplifies this technique. Staunton in disguise headed the mob that executed a government functionary named Porteous, and the government would gladly grant a pardon for Effie in return for learning his identity and whereabouts:

> But Jeanie, in the strict and severe tone of morality in which she was educated, had to consider not only the general aspect of a proposed action, but its justness and fitness in relation to the actor, before she could be, according to her own phrase, free to enter upon it. What right had she to make a barter between the lives of Staunton and of Effie, and to sacrifice the one for the safety of the other? His guilt—that guilt for which he was amenable to the laws—was a crime against the public indeed, but it was not against her.
>
> Neither did it seem to her that his share in the death of Porteous, though her mind revolted at the idea of using violence to any one, was in the relation of a common murder, against the perpetrator of which every one is called to aid the public magistrate. . . . With the fanaticism of the Scotch presbyterians, there was always mingled a glow of national feeling, and Jeanie trembled at the idea of her name being handed down to posterity with that of the "fause Monteath," and one or two others, who, having deserted and betrayed the cause of their country, are damned to perpetual remembrance and execration among its peasantry. Yet, to part with Effie's life once more, when a word spoken might save it, pressed severely on the mind of her affectionate sister.

"The Lord support and direct me," said Jeanie, "for it seems to be his will to try me with difficulties far beyond my ain strength."

While this thought passed through Jeanie's mind, her guard, tired of silence, began to show some inclination to be communicative. (356–57)

The skill with which Scott here entices us to recreate in our own minds the movements of Jeanie's, to imagine them as having a separate but valid existence in a language not our own, is remarkable. Some of the reported language here resonates with earlier, spoken formulations of the same material, giving this passage the feel of culturally specific vernacular language. When we read that "a word spoken" might save Effie's life, for instance, we recall (among other moments) Effie's own angry reminder of Jeanie's refusal to save her from condemnation as a child-murderer by lying during her trial: "What signifies coming to greet [weep] ower me . . . when you have killed me?—killed me, when a word of your mouth would have saved me . . . me that wad hae wared body and soul to save your finger from being hurt!" (255). The mention of the "fause Monteath" and the sentence directly quoting Jeanie's thoughts reinforce this aura, which comes to suffuse the passage as a whole, so that the reader hears more than is printed on the page. Scott does not try to set before us a transcript of Jeanie's vernacular mentality; he creates a cumulative fictional context that leads us to participate in a dynamic reconstruction of the workings of her culturally inflected inner voice. What we imagine is in the end a set of interlocking, metonymical forces sufficient to create the thought of a character like Jeanie, not the fixed substantiality of that thought, which because of its very historical difference must always finally elude us.

In the passage I have quoted, Scott engages us in the act of creating a voice for Jeanie Deans on her terms, using the resources of her culture he has made available to us. The passage thus epitomizes much of what I wish to claim for Scott's mode of historicist representation. At its best, that mode involves the reader in an active re-creation of the historical Other. We have a sense of the limitations of that re-creation, but we also feel a joy in engaging in it, and a wonder at the rich cultural integrity of a character like Jeanie Deans. The feeling here can easily shade into nostalgia, with all its questionable ideological associations, but nostalgia too can have its positive uses. Experiencing such a character certainly evokes a sense of loss: her integrity may seem something which the very historicist consciousness that allows us to recognize also prevents us from sharing. There is, however, some compensation in our conviction that a representative of a culture has been enabled to speak to us—and our wish that others might be similarly enabled.

The turn to the inner life in the passage we have been considering has much to reveal about the nature of Scott's realism, but its pretensions are modest if we view it in the light of later developments. There's little here that evokes the ebbs and flows of emotion and sensation, the subtle textures of moment-by-moment consciousness. In the novelists who follow Scott, a growing interest in human inwardness poses problems for the metonymical representation of history for which Scott's own representational techniques are inadequate. Yet Scott's emphasis on reader involvement and the creation of a dynamic sense of historical milieu remains significant even for such a master of the depiction of the inner life as George Eliot, as we shall see in the following chapter.

6

Eliot: Narrating in History

> But I am not poised at that lofty height. I am on the level and
> in the press with him, as he struggles his way along the stony
> road, through the crowd of unloving fellow-men.
> —George Eliot, *Scenes of Clerical Life*

> Rhetoric . . . seeks to perfect men by showing them better ver-
> sions of themselves.
> —R. M. Weaver, *The Ethics of Rhetoric*

The narrator is the key to nineteenth-century realist fiction. A significant challenge to the realist narration employed by Austen and Scott
arises from the interest in exploring human interiority and inwardness
that gains momentum as the century proceeds. The exploration of the
inner life is doubtless one of the chief glories of nineteenth-century fiction, but it has also functioned as a time bomb. It encouraged a tradition
of critical praise that turned to attack as the individual, seen as a locus of
timeless values, became "the subject." It also strained the resources of realist representation. This chapter will concern itself with George Eliot's
response to the problem of narrating human interiority in history. I shall
begin by considering her versions of the external depiction of character
that I've shown characterizes Scott, particularly for characters meant to
be seen as Other (for our purposes, this will mean rural folk). I shall then
consider an exemplary sequence in which Eliot's exploration of the inner
life threatens to lose contact with historical and social processes altogether. Finally, I'll suggest that the dynamic behind Eliot's realism leads
her to attempt to make even her narrator subject to history. By placing her
narrator as well as her characters under the constraints of history, she
hopes to gain ethical authority as she invokes her readers' own responsi-
bilities as historical beings.[1]

---

[1] The critical literature on Eliot is vast. In dealing with the problems that are my central
concern in this chapter, I have found the following books particularly useful, though I
don't always agree with them. On various aspects of Eliot's narrative voice: Suzanne

Eliot and External Characterization

Eliot is masterly in her ability to place characters in a living relationship with a social and historical milieu. For all her interest in the inner
life, such depiction often recalls Scott's external characterization. We
have examined Scott's depiction of the mind of the Scottish peasantry in
the person of Jeanie Deans. The closest analogue with which I am familiar
to this sort of representation in Eliot occurs in an address to the reader
that probes the issue of Adam Bede's typicality:

> Adam, you perceive, was by no means a marvelous man, nor, prop-
> erly speaking, a genius, yet I will not pretend that his was an ordi-
> nary character among workmen; and it would not be at all a safe
> conclusion that the next best man you may happen to see with a
> basket of tools over his shoulder and a paper cap on his head has
> the strong conscience and the strong sense, the blended susceptibil-
> ity and self-command of our friend Adam. He was not an average
> man. Yet such men as he are reared here and there in every genera-
> tion of our peasant artisans—with an inheritance of affections nur-
> tured by a simple family life of common need and common indus-
> try, and an inheritance of faculties trained in skillful courageous
> labour: they make their way upward, rarely as geniuses, most com-
> monly as painstaking honest men, with the skill and conscience to
> do well the tasks that lie before them. Their lives have no dis-
> cernible echo beyond the neighbourhood where they dwelt, but
> you are almost sure to find there some good piece of road, some
> building, some application of mineral produce, some improvement
> in farming practice, some reform of parish abuses, with which their
> names are associated by one or two generations after them. Their
> employers are the richer for them, the work of their hands has worn
> well, and the work of their brains has guided well the hands of
> other men. They went about in their youth in flannel or paper caps,
> in coats black with coal-dust or streaked with lime and red paint; in
> old age their white hairs are seen in a place of honour at church and

Graver, *George Eliot and Community* (Berkeley: University of California Press, 1984), and
Elizabeth Deeds Ermarth, *Realism and Consensus in the English Novel* (Princeton: Princeton
University Press, 1983), 65–92, 222–56 (though for me the narrator is somebody, not "nobody"). On Eliot and realism: George Levine's work, especially on Eliot's use of hypotheses, inaugurated in "George Eliot's Hypothesis of Reality," *Nineteenth-Century Fiction*, 35
(1980), 1–28, and related work by David Carroll, including *George Eliot and the Conflict of
Interpretations* (Cambridge: Cambridge University Press, 1992). The best reason I know for
taking a line on Eliot based on presuppositions foreign to my own is provided by Neil
Hertz's essays on Eliot, soon to appear in book form.

at market, and they tell their well-dressed sons and daughters, seated round the bright hearth on winter evenings, how pleased they were when they first earned their twopence a-day. Others there are who die poor, and never put off the workman's coat on weekdays: they have not had the heart of getting rich; but they are men of trust, and when they die before the work is all out of them, it is as if some main screw had got loose in a machine; the master who employed them says, "Where shall I find their like?"[2]

The narrator here is not, to be sure, inviting us to participate in imagining Adam's conscious thoughts on a particular occasion, and she does not draw on vernacular speech, as Scott's depiction of Jeanie Deans's thoughts does. Instead, an intertextual resonance involving a special kind of language invites us to participate in imagining Adam's mentality in general, as it is informed by his culture.

This resonance makes itself most decisively felt in the closing lines of the passage. The passage begins with Adam, passes to the gnomic realities of what men like him mean to their communities, and then tells their stories as individual histories, things that have been. Following hard upon this come the words "Others there are," which make us aware that the diction of the passage has become increasingly solemn, that it rings of the King James Bible. This turn to elegiac and elevated solemnity, coupled with the subject being discussed, recalls a similar elegiac celebration in *Ecclesiasticus*, where the work of men remembered and men forgotten is also compared. "Others there are who die poor . . . but they are men of trust" in Eliot quietly echoes "And some there are, that have left no memorial . . . but these were men of mercy" in a well-known passage from the Apocrypha:

Let us now praise famous men, and our fathers that begat us. The Lord hath wrought great glory by them through his great power from the beginning. Such as did bear rule in their kingdoms, men renowned for their power, giving counsel by their understanding, and declaring prophesies: Leaders of the people by their counsels, and by their knowledge of learning meet for the people, wise and eloquent in their instructions: Such as found out musical tunes, and recited verses in writing: Rich men furnished with ability, living peaceably in their habitations: All these were honoured in their

---

[2]   Eliot, *Adam Bede*, ed. Stephen Gill (Harmondsworth: Penguin, 1980), 258–59; hereafter cited in the text.

generations, and were the glory of their times. There be of them, that have left a name behind them, that their praises might be reported. And some there be, which have no memorial; who are perished, as though they had never been; and are become as though they had never been born; and their children after them. But these were merciful men, whose righteousness hath not been forgotten. With their seed shall continually remain a good inheritance, and their children are within the covenant. Their seed standeth fast, and their children for their sakes. Their seed shall remain for ever, and their glory shall not be blotted out. Their bodies are buried in peace; but their name liveth for evermore. The people will tell of their wisdom, and the congregation will shew forth their praise. (*Ecclesiasticus* 44.1–15)

Adam Bede, we learn two sentences before the passage we have been concerned with occurs, "had read his Bible, including the apocryphal books" (258). The passage from the Apocrypha helps us grasp how such reading could inform his own emergent humanity in a historically particular time and place, how the praise for work, remembered and forgotten, could ring in his ears and strengthen his steps.[3] *Ecclesiasticus* helps provide Adam with an ideology, which is to say a mental way of being in the world; what he makes of that ideology and what it makes of him are subjects the rest of the novel explores. This mode of depiction is qualitatively different from the creation of thematic parallels to the Bible (Adam as the first Adam), because it invites us to imagine metonymical processes at work in the world of the novel, not to code the meaning of that world using a procedure that verges on the allegorical.[4] It is a realist appropriation of the Bible. We are invited to imagine a set of social structures and connections at work, with Adam in the midst of them. Eliot here draws, with characteristic subtlety, on realism's basic impetus—putting things in juxtaposition and leading the reader to imagine the web of relations that connects them, the conditions of possibility for a given aspect of social reality.

[3]   Eliot was attached to this passage: Mrs. Garth movingly alludes to it in praising her husband Caleb (Eliot, *Middlemarch*, ed. Rosemary Ashton [Harmondsworth: Penguin, 1994], 403; hereafter cited in the text). It would be pleasing to imagine Adam Bede hearing the passage, year in and year out, as the lesson for All Saints Day (which it is today). Unfortunately, in the nineteenth century, it was simply a reading for Evening Prayer on a weekday (November 15).

[4]   The classic interpretation of *Adam Bede* along what I'm calling "allegorical" lines is Ulrich Knoepflmacher, *George Eliot's Early Novels: The Limits of Realism* (Berkeley, University of California Press, 1968), 89–127.

The impulse to present characters as parts of a historical milieu is strong in Eliot. It crops up in places where we might not expect it. In several of her novels, for example, she employs traveler or visitor figures to ease us into a scene—the man on horseback who observes Dinah preaching in *Adam Bede*, for instance, or the Renaissance Florentine whose spirit revisits modern Florence in the Proem to *Romola*. Now of course the Florentine is bound to function as a historical exhibit to some extent (though the final sentences of his prologue stress the timeless human emotions he shares with present-day Florence, and with us). We might, however, expect more recent figures to function, after they catch our attention, as transparent lenses. Yet even they are touched by history, in ways that can affect the meanings of the material they introduce. *Felix Holt* opens with a "happy outside passenger" seated on the box of a coach traveling through (mainly) rural England thirty-five years before the writing of the novel (which is to say, at the time of the novel's action). His place on the box, next to the coachman, allows him to gather up "enough stories of English life, enough of English labours in town and country, enough aspects of earth and sky, to make episodes for a modern Odyssey." He travels through rural poverty and rural plenty, and from the countryside through occasional towns and cities. Through his eyes we observe a "manufacturing town, the scene of riots and trades-union meetings," but soon after find ourselves in "a rural region, where the neighbourhood of the town was only felt in the advantages of a near market for corn, cheese, and hay, and where men with a considerable banking account were accustomed to say that 'they never meddled with politics themselves.' "[5]

Raymond Williams, still the most distinguished critic to have concerned himself with the ideology of Eliot's representation of the British countryside, considers this journey a source of mystification. It makes town unrest seem unnatural in comparison to stolid, apolitical country life. By filling us with hazy nostalgia for a peaceful countryside set in relief by city squalor and chaos, it obscures the vital connections that in fact exist between country and city, and existed both in Eliot's own day and in the period during which *Felix Holt* is set. Eliot creates this ideological effect, according to Williams, by making us identify with the traveler, whose judgments these are.[6] Now Williams seems importantly right

---

[5] Eliot, *Felix Holt, The Radical*, ed. Lynda Mugglestone (Harmondsworth: Penguin, 1995), 3, 7; hereafter cited in the text.
[6] Raymond Williams, *The Country and the City* (London: Chatto and Windus, 1973), 180, 178; hereafter cited in the text. For a stimulating brief commentary on his general conception of realism, see Jon Thompson, "Realisms and Modernisms: Raymond Williams and Popular Fiction," in *Views beyond the Border Country*, ed. Dennis L. Dworkin and Leslie G. Roman (London: Routledge, 1993), 72–88.

about an influential ideological pattern that can be created by drawing upon the elements in the picture Eliot paints. But he is on shakier ground when he suggests that the novel uses the traveler simply to invite us to assent to that pattern. To call upon Gérard Genette's classic narratological distinction, Williams is confusing who sees with who speaks. The traveler may serve as the narrative focus in that, mainly, we see what he sees. But we also see him. His isn't the only voice we hear during the journey; another voice puts him in perspective. The traveler is not Eliot's transparent mouthpiece, and we as readers are not expected to merge our judgment with his. The voice of a narrator quite separate from the passenger weaves in and out of our focal attention, and at times this narrator's voice becomes so firmly established that it comes as a mild shock when we are reminded that what's being described are the things the passenger sees and thinks. Even when we're most "with" the traveler, the presence of the narrator persists. The phrase "riots and trades-union meetings" in the description of the town, for instance, has the ring of a zeugma; as such, it provides amusement and distance, and also a nice encapsulation of a certain mentality. The full significance the zeugma creates cannot be the conscious product of a traveler who finds their conjunction natural.

The complication of perspective becomes full historical objectification a few sentences after the description of the contented, apolitical farmers:

> The busy scenes of the shuttle and the wheel, of the roaring furnace, of the shaft and the pulley, *seemed* to make but crowded nests in the midst of the large-spaced, slow-moving life of homesteads and faraway cottages and oak-sheltered parks. Looking at the dwellings scattered amongst the woody flats and the ploughed uplands, under the low grey sky which overhung them with an unchanging stillness as if Time itself were pausing, *it was easy for the traveller to conceive* that town and country had no pulse in common, except where the handlooms made a far-reaching straggling fringe about the great centres of manufacture; that till the agitation about the Catholics in '29, rural Englishmen had hardly known more of Catholics than of the fossil mammals; and that their notion of Reform was a confused combination of rick-burners, trades-unions, Nottingham riots, and in general whatever required the calling-out of the yeomanry. *It was still easier to see* that, for the most part, they resisted the rotation of crops. . . . (7; my emphasis)

With Eliot, viewpoints that are "easy . . . to conceive" are always suspect, particularly when balanced against a description of what it was "easier to see," and it's clearly unwise to feel secure in supposing that the reasonableness of one judgment implies the reasonableness of others. Though the traveler's conclusion about the rural knowledge of "Catholics" may contain grains of truth, there's a clear hint that his conception that there was still no real connection between country and city rests on shakier grounds. It's *too* easy for him to conceive this idea. As it happens, the novel will go on to provide glimpses of an evolving set of connections. Its heroine couldn't choose between country and city if there weren't a bridge for her to walk on between them. Its villain, Matthew Jermyn, may be despised (and perhaps scapegoated) as among other things a violator of sexual and economic boundaries, but he paved the way for this viola-tion by encouraging a process of modernization which, the novel shows us, brings country and town together economically and even socially. Is Transome Court a country house, or is it suburban? We are not meant to collude in the traveler's too easy perceptions but to recognize that, though they had in their own setting a certain reasonableness, subse-quent developments have shown them to be wrong.

Nostalgia does of course attach itself to the traveler. He himself is the object of nostalgia: no doubt we're meant to feel a certain nostalgia for a time when even someone intent on making sense of the land and society around him didn't have to worry issues that have since emerged. Still, the traveler appears to be trying to make sense of what he sees. This differen-tiates him from the men in the passage who have big bank accounts, who lack this element of an inwardness we as readers share with him. In this respect, the traveler does indeed function as our surrogate, and we re-spect him even as we recognize his limitations.

In her underplayed suggestion that the traveler on the coach box may be wrong about the lack of connection between country and city, Eliot leaves a marker for the reader, something to follow up. What makes it possible for this marker to emerge is Eliot's realist interest in what I have been calling external representation. The traveler may serve as a lens, but he is also a historical exhibit. Our recognition of this latter role is what gives us some purchase on the nostalgic ideology with which he is associ-ated, raising the possibility that Eliot may not be connecting (or discon-necting) the parts of the picture she's painting in quite the way he does, and we may be tempted to do.

It's true that Eliot's narrator doesn't *develop* this possibility in the direc-tion Williams would require, and it's true that, as we saw in the previous chapter, problems can arise whenever one looks back upon the past and finds in it a vitality and interest that no longer exist in the present ("the *real* Egyptians are the ancient Egyptians"). But announcements concern-ing the particular ideological work novels and the scenes within them ac-complish can be premature. Passages don't do work; they sit there on the page. Readers work. Experiencing the grain of Eliot's fiction is meant to set our minds in a motion attentive to the shifting nature of historical meanings and connections. Instead of joining the traveler in a world of knowing illusion, Eliot's fiction leads us to expect that an ever-changing web of concrete historical distinctions and potential connections will come into view with every turn of the road.

Eliot may draw on external depiction with great skill, inviting us to imagine Adam Bede's self-formation through a rich intertextuality and making the passenger in *Felix Holt* a historical exhibit, not a reader-surrogate to whose views we automatically assent. But of course her representational mode extends in other directions as well, to include a powerful focus on the inner life of characters. Not all characters, however, and not to the same degree. As part of his critique of Eliot's representation of the life of the countryside, Williams claims that Eliot habitually swerves away from representing country folk as what, in a formulation in which every word tells, he calls "the active bearers of personal experience" (168). When in the final section of *Adam Bede*, for instance, Eliot's narrator turns away from depicting the inner life of Hetty and renders her an object acted upon by external forces (not least in the form of Dinah), Williams believes that she creates a situation in which narrator, reader, and such characters as Arthur and Dinah are allowed to share an interior life and agency from which Hetty is excluded. (Williams's objection to the narration that opens *Felix Holt* would also appear to focus on this dynamic of exclusion, in which the narrator and the reader share a level of human interiority that some, but not all, of the depicted characters lack.) This objection to Eliot's depiction of the rural Other runs parallel to objections we discussed in the previous chapter to historicist treatments of historical and cultural Others. What I have called the external depiction of character can look like domination.

With Eliot, such problems become very complex. Her stress on the inner life can translate into an interest in charting stages of individual moral evolution in a way that parallels eighteenth-century "stages of society" arguments and the schematism of Comte. She is fascinated by the possibility that in "organic" society, mental life might be quite different from her own: the idea of a moral evolution allows her to preserve connection and intelligibility while exploring radical difference. The problems involved in notions of moral evolution remind us (if, in the present critical context, we need further reminding) that in its first flush of excited discovery, historicism may have overrated and underread the foreignness of what were then the hitherto neglected pockets of cultural distinctiveness in the world around it. And there can be little doubt that freezing the population of the countryside in the past can conduce to the political mystifications Williams deplores. Can we really speak of nineteenth-century rural England as constituting a culture separable from that of the rest of the island? (Then again, Scotland was and remains part of the island too; does this mean that it lacks cultural separateness?) What ideological interests are served by making such distinctions? I choose to view these complications as potentially productive, and to favor a mode of reading through the grain of Eliot's fiction that makes them so.

Behind Eliot's view of Hetty Sorrel lies, for good and ill, the legacy of historicism. Eliot doesn't depict Hetty as an active bearer of personal experience because she believes that someone in Hetty's historical situation wouldn't have been an active bearer of personal experience. Eliot wants to explore the possibility that there have been times and places in our own tradition that have produced rural folk who *simply don't think in the ways her implied readers do* (which is just what Williams objects to). I would argue that she does this from the beginning of the novel, in the places where Hetty might seem most fully a bearer of personal experience. Hetty Sorrel's mind as Eliot depicts it is largely composed of a specular fascination with her own beauty and a congeries of inchoate images of what it would be like to be a lady. Hetty (like an even more extreme case in *Adam Bede*, Chad's Bess) has an immediacy of experience that isn't confined to moments of self-absorption before a dimly lit mirror. It's not that she is unaware of her self *as* a self, it's that she has a wordless grasp of herself merging with the roles she plays and might play, and that this grasp lacks the sense of integrity and control one supposes Williams has in mind when he talks of being an active bearer of one's own experience. Her depicted self-awareness when she makes butter, for instance, has a tactile, kinesthetic feel to it—habitual motions, contours of clothing and body, a feeling of eyes upon her. Even the moral or quasi-moral resonances of the scene reduce themselves to a sense of being in place—a safe, cool, enclosed feeling of doing what is known and proper mingling with fleeting images of other possibilities roused by Arthur Donnithorne's eyes upon her. Why does Hetty lack conscious moral agency? Dinah has gained it, through her experience of Methodism. Mrs. Poyser has access to a rudimentary equivalent of it, through her largely unconscious immersion in certain traditional values. Hetty has remained immune, largely because her beauty and her quick social instinct have kept her from needing and seeking it. Hetty, then, is never depicted as a fully active bearer of personal experience; her self isn't coherent enough for that.

Eliot does not reserve a place in the ranks of those who fail to be active bearers of personal experience only for members of the English rural lower classes. In *Middlemarch*, the French actress Laure fits her stage roles in a way that is immediate to the point of seeming semi-human. Who can say what is "in the mind" of this woman from the south of France, what she means by "meant" when she declares that she "meant" to kill her husband (153)? And of course there's Laure's counterpart Rosamond Vincy, who "even acted her own character, and so well, that she did not know it to be precisely her own" (117) and whose crystalline images of what being a lady entails function in a way surprisingly like Hetty's vaguer notions. We must admit, then, that for Eliot, moral consciousness doesn't always evolve step-by-step up the social scale, or journey from country to town. It's also true that active moral worth doesn't correlate in any simple way with the keenness of one's inner awareness. Even the tendency for women to occupy the lowest (and highest) rungs on the ladder of improvement isn't quite so pervasive as my examples might seem to indicate. The limit case of Eliot's representation of alternative modes of consciousness must be Silas Marner, who lives in the country but who is by no means a countryman. The web of connection between Marner's mind and the inanimate objects that surround him is remarkable. Until he is touched by need and grace, his mind simply is his loom and his gold. His depiction is a striking example of Eliot's fascination with the idea that particular conjunctions of ideology and social relations can create minds that aren't like hers or her putative reader's. It seems significant that Marner's culturally and spiritually retrograde situation is produced by the forces of modernity, and also that it can be solved only by Eliot's creating a fairy-tale magic—a magic that can, however, be explained within the logic of metonymic everyday life. In the face of this, it's hard to escape the conclusion that Eliot was well aware of the stakes involved in her kind of historicism.

It is nonetheless clear that, in Eliot, your chances for becoming a consciously active bearer of personal experience markedly increase as you move forward in time, come to grips with the problems of city life, or mount the social scale. At this point, the sort of historicist thinking that produces providential narratives seems to make itself felt, and one recalls Bruce Robbins's dismay at the way in which such narratives can sap the latent powers of the past and dissolve possible solidarities between present and past. One may well want to question the political implications of this pattern—and, as Williams does as well, its objective historical accuracy—just as one may want to question possible uses of Scott's celebration of cultural otherness and Austen's secure distinction-making. Then again, one may also want to ask whether Eliot isn't simply facing squarely certain intractable implications of the problem of modernity.

I would not, however, maintain that objections to Eliot's treatment of minds in the countryside are simply mistaken. Eliot's realism can have and indeed has had the effects Williams isolates, in complicity with one aspect of her own mind. And, as Williams helps us see, there were surely kinds of minds in the countryside Eliot's depiction omits and, insofar as it implicitly claims to be giving a complete picture of country life, may obscure. The question then arises of whether Eliot's characteristic modes of narrative intelligence depend upon what would thus become strategic omissions. This is a complex and delicate matter—unless we are content to solve it by invoking a notion of ideology as a closed system of entirely homogenous false consciousness. How contingently and on what level does a work depend on ideological omissions? In the case of Austen, as we've seen, Williams is willing to grant the possibility that an author's works can call into life a "morality which is in the end separable from its social basis and which, in other hands, can be turned against it" (116–17). I believe that we need to keep open the possibility that Eliot's realism sets dynamic forces in motion between narrator and reader that can lead in many directions—that Eliot's metonymical vision of the texture of society, consistently applied, would among other things reveal, to readers placed differently in history than was Eliot, gaps in her own texts.[7]

Some aspects of Eliot's vision may indeed become so powerful that they lead us to neglect other possibilities it offers. The demand that all of Eliot's characters, including Hetty Sorrel, be accorded the status of "active bearers of personal experience" arises not least because Eliot has a way of making interiority and ethical agency seem so vital that we neglect the less exalted relations between human consciousness and the external world her fiction defines and explores. At this point in my argument, of course, a decentered reader may be only too ready to agree that in his concern for Hetty's status as an active bearer of personal experience, Williams has been taken in by Eliot's humanistic belief in individual human agency: Williams and Eliot thus turn out to be members of the same bad tradition.[8] (From such a point of view, the representation of Hetty Sorrel as I've described it ought to be of more than passing interest.) One notes, however, that Williams draws just this sort of conclusion with respect to the relationship between F. R. Leavis and Eliot: as Williams sees it, the way in which Leavis uses Eliot to support his views

[7]   The terms in which, in a celebrated essay, Eliot praises W. H. Riehl's depiction of the German peasantry seem relevant—particularly in light of our discussion in Chapter 2 of the open-ended, creative potentialities of reference. She praises him for deepening and making more accurate "the images that are habitually associated with abstract or collective terms"—in this case, the "peasantry" as employed in the phrase "the German peasantry." See "The Natural History of German Life" (1856), in *Essays of George Eliot*, ed. Thomas Pinney (New York: Columbia University Press, 1963), 267.

[8]   For perhaps the most uncompromising anatomy of Eliot as a purveyor of bourgeois ideology, see Daniel Cottom, *Social Figures* (Minneapolis: University of Minnesota Press, 1987).

of British society is itself proof of the wrongness of Eliot's vision of the countryside. From my own vantage point, much of Williams's critique of Eliot seems right on target—if the target is the George Eliot whom Leavis constructed. I've been suggesting, however, that instead of assimilating Eliot to Great Traditions, we explore the complex logic and the branching potentialities of her depictions of how human beings relate to societies, keeping in mind Chad's Bess as well as Dorothea Brooke.

Dorothea in and out of Place

Hetty Sorrel's lack of a full inner life raises questions about the scope of Eliot's realism. No one could say that Dorothea Brooke lacks inwardness; no one could deny that she is an active bearer of personal experience. Yet her inner life may raise a more fundamental problem. The claim that realist novels have played an important role in promoting a bourgeois turning away from history and society has persisted. Problems of individual conduct and destiny simply are not identical with larger social problems, it's argued; novels promote mystification by suggesting that they are.[9] Isn't there something threatening to *all* metonymic representation when the attempt to depict the inner life of characters from whatever classes becomes a dominant concern in a novel? Retreating to the depths of the individual seems likely to cut interior experience from that web, making privileged characters seem actual centers that give social experience meaning, and not the apparent centers produced, say, by holding a candle to a pier glass. The links among inner thoughts and feelings are fleeting, effervescent, hard to pin down, which suggests that metaphor will be required to make them intelligible. To be sure, one can use the word "metonymy" to describe the free juxtapositions and slippages of consciousness, particularly when they are represented as a stream of consciousness. But metonymy in this sense differs crucially from the metonymy central to historicist realism. Stream-of-consciousness metonymy is metonymy as defined from the viewpoint of metaphor— metonymy in two dimensions, as "one damn thing after another," or next

[9]   To deal with this issue, one needs to distinguish. In *The Forms of Historical Fiction* (Ithaca: Cornell University Press, 1983), my attempt to show that one cannot represent all the different levels of human generality at once failed to bring into focus the significant difference between two objectives: (1) the attempt to make human interiority model the movements of historical process, which places the two in a synecdochic relationship, and (2) the attempt to show how a given historical milieu informs human inwardness at a given time. The problems inherent in the first enterprise still seem to me practically insuperable, and this is the issue I was in fact dealing with in *The Forms of Historical Fiction*. The second can be managed, as I trust my discussion of Dorothea below will demonstrate.

to another. Such metonymy involves relationships that are precisely not what I've called "real-world" relationships.

Problems involving the meshing of inner and outer worlds don't arise at this level for either of the other two realist novelists on whom we have focused. Scott's primary interest in individuals "from the skin out" means that representing inner experience in relation to an external world rarely becomes a problem. It is entirely natural for him to represent the mind of Jeanie Deans externally, without an aura of deep subjectivity. The problem he faces in rendering her thoughts involves dealing with two different languages and cultures, not negotiating between inner and outer worlds. Austen's representation is less resolutely external, but her language of moral judgment applies to inner lives and outer lives with equal authority. Austen's novels are, as Raymond Williams reminds us, about conduct, and conduct as she conceives of it provides an entirely adequate meeting place for inner and outer worlds. In *Persuasion*, Austen may depict buzzes of sensation that escape her normal modes of intelligibility; in the end, however, these become adjuncts to the dominant language, markers of emotion and physicality that enrich without essentially altering the meaningful experience language conveys. In the end, Anne Elliot masters pain and perceptual confusion with a definitive statement of the shape and meaning of her past: "I have been thinking over the past . . . and I must believe that I was right, much as I suffered from it, that I was perfectly right in being guided by the friend whom you will love better than you do now."[10] To be sure, we might have expected this robust response from her earlier commentary on the pleasures of Lyme: "One does not love a place the less for having suffered in it, unless it has been all suffering, nothing but suffering—which was by no means the case at Lyme" (193). For Eliot, by contrast, the relationship between internal and external worlds is a seminal problem for her central characters, and for herself as a novelist.

At times, Eliot deals with this problem by insisting on a metaphorically oriented mode of coalescence and even identity between the interior and the external. In *Romola*, the problem of obedience divides the mind and spirit of the heroine. But in a flash of insight, Romola recognizes that her problem is essentially the same one that Savonarola faces in his dealings with the church and the world of Florentine politics. For Scott such identities do not exist, even though his characters have inner worlds that are rudimentary in comparison to those of Eliot's characters. When in *Old Mortality* Henry Morton discovers that his internal conflicts and the polit-

---

[10]   Austen, *Persuasion*, ed. D. W. Harding (Harmondsworth: Penguin, 1985), 248; hereafter cited in the text.

ical problems of his country are identical, that his problems can serve as a metaphor for the problems of Scotland and vice versa, the narrative makes it clear that he's engaging in self-mystification. The difference between Austen and Eliot in this regard is less dramatic, but it comes into focus if we consider how inadequate Austen's vocabulary of "conduct" would prove in formulating, much less solving, Romola's quandaries about obedience. However it may stack up against the norms of earlier realism in Eliot's fictional world, Romola's flash of insight has its limits: flashes illuminate that world but do not change it. Romola finds herself in very much the same situation after her discovery of this identity.[11]

With Dorothea Brooke, Eliot takes a more complex path, one more in consonance with the realism this book has explored. In the sequence with which we will be primarily concerned, Dorothea is depicted as at once a socially detached observer (like the traveler in *Felix Holt*), and a consciousness endowed with a deep and problematic interiority. When we dive into Dorothea's individual yearnings, we might expect to leave behind anything approaching a substantial, articulated sense of historical existence, as we do (or have been taught to think we do) in the works of later novelists. I shall be arguing instead that in presenting even Dorothea's inchoate internal feelings and intuition, Eliot's narrator maintains in the reader's mind a sense of metonymical interplay between psychological depths and historical determinants, on the level of affect as well as of implied analysis. We see Dorothea trying to make sense of her feelings by using the external world as an expressive metaphor for them, but that world remains, for us, part of history. Without reference to her place in history, we cannot indeed grasp the precise nature of Dorothea's psychological situation or participate in it. (Let me make clear that I'm not speaking here of an ability to read Dorothea's state as a symptom of ideology, which ideology the analyst can then relate to historical forces beyond the ken of the novel in which she appears.) Even when the focus lies most powerfully on deeply subjective aspects of Dorothea's life, the narrator never allows the external, historical world to become simply an expressive metaphor for them in our eyes.

Here is part of the scene in *Middlemarch* which recounts Dorothea's re-

---

[11] As Felicia Bonaparte has skillfully shown in *The Triptych and the Cross* (New York: New York University Press, 1979), such flashes do allow Eliot to adumbrate a large allegorical scheme concerning the progress of Civilization. This seems to me the sort of dealing with history likely to fall prey to the objections Robbins raises against "providential narratives"; it echoes the aspects of historicism about which I have the greatest misgivings, and seems to me to undercut the force of what I take to be a more useful historicist tradition. I provide a full discussion of these issues with regard to Romola and to Henry Morton in *The Forms of Historical Fiction*, 106–9, 192–97.

actions to glimpsing Peter Featherstone's funeral from a window of her manor house:

> But for her visitors Dorothea too might have been shut up in the library, and would not have witnessed this scene of old Featherstone's funeral, which, aloof as it seemed to be from the tenor of her life, always afterwards came back to her at the touch of certain sensitive points in memory, just as the vision of St. Peter's at Rome was inwoven with moods of despondency. Scenes which make vital changes in our neighbours' lot are but the background of our own, yet, like a particular aspect of the fields and trees, they become associated for us with the epochs of our own history, and make a part of that unity which lies in the selection of our keenest consciousness.
>
> The dream-like association of something alien and ill-understood with the deepest secrets of her experience seemed to mirror that sense of loneliness which was due to the very ardour of Dorothea's nature. The country gentry of old time lived in a rarefied social air: dotted apart on their stations up the mountain they looked down with imperfect discrimination on the belts of thicker life below. And Dorothea was not at ease in the perspective and chilliness of that height. (326)

This passage hovers between metaphorical and metonymical modes of understanding, with metaphor more overtly at play. In the second paragraph, Dorothea's situation is itself described by the use of an extended metaphor; in the first, an as yet unspecified relationship is depicted between her feelings and a scene from the world around her. Dorothea senses and we soon recognize that the scene of the funeral resonates with her own feeling of entrapment in the stillborn world of Mr. Casaubon. The funeral provides an ideal expressive metaphor for Dorothea. She finds it a "blot on the morning" because Featherstone died unlamented and she "cannot bear to think that any one should die and leave no love behind" (328). Her sense of being cut off from people of Featherstone's class intensifies the aura of hopeless, listless privation.

It's hard to imagine an engaged reader who would not respond to Dorothea's feelings here. In some forms of romance, this is all we would be called upon to do. But not in *Middlemarch*. We don't entirely merge with Dorothea; we also observe her transmuting the external environment into a subjective symbol. A great deal occurs in the scene that keeps our own minds working along nonmetaphorical lines. (The point here is precisely not that the scene has to be "really" either metaphorical or metonymical: Mill was right when he discovered that rainbows can be truly said both to be examples of the refraction of light and to be beautiful. The point is to recognize what kind or kinds of resonances a fictional passage highlights and invites us to pursue.) Signs of a metonymy like Scott's are everywhere apparent both in the passage and in its context—indeed, they are apparent in the way the passage itself filiates with its context. Dorothea sees the funeral, after all, because she is drawn out of the library to respond to a social call. When the narrator tells us that the "gentry of old time . . . apart on their stations up the mountain . . . looked down with imperfect discrimination on the belts of thicker life," she is obviously using a metaphor, but the metaphor refers to the life of a certain class at a certain moment.

As the scene progresses beyond the passage I've selected, our vision of the social web expands, as Mrs. Cadwallader (the wife of the clergyman officiating at the funeral) moves from visual spectacle to social and economic analysis, motivated by her own historical positions in class, gender, and politics. She is first struck by noticing among the mourners "a really good-looking woman" and a handsome young man who is evidently her son. But when the two are identified, her feelings alter: the father of the family, she announces, is "one of those who suck the life out of the wretched handloom weavers in Tipton and Freshitt. That is how his family look so fair and sleek" (327). Our sense of the power of metonymical social relations returns to the drawing room when Celia notices Will Ladislaw in the funeral crowd, and his presence is accounted for by Dorothea's uncle, Mr. Brooke, in a way that makes it seem that Dorothea had asked her uncle to invite him. But though she didn't, and though her husband falsely believes she did in defiance of his own wishes, she cannot explain this to him, now or later, because of the particular way in which the news of his arrival has come. To clear up the mistake would be to admit that her husband had reason to care about it, which is something neither he nor Dorothea wishes to do. The social conventions dictating what ought and ought not to be said or implied between members of the gentry even when they are married, and the particular inflection those conventions are given by the personalities of Dorothea and (especially) of her husband, create a chain of causality that proliferates under its own impetus, modifying the reality around it in a way we feel to be ominous. Sir James Chettam (like the reader) senses the web of meanings gathering around the mention of Will Ladislaw.[12] "His good-nature often made him quick and clear-seeing in personal matters, and he had divined from

---

[12]   Ermarth (*Realism and Consensus* 240) draws attention in a different way to the proliferation of meanings in the scene to which Chettam's tact alerts him. She uses it as an example of the way in which Eliot multiplies the number of individual viewers and viewpoints involved in any such scene: thus the mourners Dorothea observes have their own viewpoints, too. Unlike Ermarth, I do not believe that realism is definitively constituted by

Dorothea's glance at her husband [when Ladislaw is observed in the funeral crowd and mentioned] that there was some alarm in her mind" (329). It is amusing to notice how different Sir James's conception of "personal matters" is from the "deepest secrets" of Dorothea's consciousness. Yet the scene gives even those secrets a historical coloring.

We are told that "the dream-like association of something alien and ill-understood with the deepest secrets of her experience seemed to mirror that sense of loneliness which was due to the very ardour of Dorothea's nature." And the lines that follow explain how her loneliness flows from being a member of a certain class at a certain historical moment. But so does her ardor, and (remarkably) so does the very inchoateness of feeling suggested by the phrase "seemed to mirror." Our sense of the historicity of Dorothea's ardor is produced in a way that is entirely straightforward. From its opening words, the novel has connected ardor with living in particular times and particular places. St. Theresa's ardor "quickly burned up" the "light fuel" of the courtship of her day, "and, fed from within, soared after some illimitable satisfaction, some object which would never justify weariness, which would reconcile self-despair with the rapturous consciousness of life beyond self." The vagueness of "some illimitable satisfaction" received in her life the concrete embodiment of effecting "the reform of a religious order"; appropriately, she refreshed a mode of life in which one's everyday life has a connection with the Divine, and illimitable satisfaction can occur (3). For the reader, Dorothea's ardent yearnings are always shadowed by St. Theresa's; they mean in relation to the model Theresa provides.

The passage at hand enacts Dorothea's ardor, and involves both the narrator and the reader in it. "The dream-like association of something alien and ill-understood with the deepest secrets of her experience seemed to mirror [Dorothea's] sense of loneliness." On the face of it, what we hear in this sentence is the narrator giving a report about Dorothea's situation. But what is the force of "seemed" in her assertion? The word can hardly be used to suggest appearances that might be deceiving; its function is instead to suggest that the narrator is striving to deal with difficult, potent material.[13] There the narrator is, tracing the movements of Dorothea's mind and trying to make sense of it, by following out what it

---

the creation of a coalescence of disparate viewpoints; I do, however, value her work as an acute study of one quality that can help persuade us of the adequacy of a work's representation of the real.

[13] In realist novels, the verb "to seem" can have a somewhat specialized function and significance. These entered novelistic realism through Scott, who in turn appears to have found them in the Gothic. When we're told in a novel by Ann Radcliffe that "thick chestnut woods . . . seemed to form a gradation between the variegated cultivation there, and the awful wildness of the rocks above," the suggestion is not that the formation of a gradation might or might not actually be occurring. In such contexts, "seemed to form" has a

"seems" to mean. Narratorial self-dramatizations like this one always have a tendency to pull us as readers into the process: we too feel ourselves striving to make sense of the material the narrator attempts to bring into focus. The force of "seems" spreads even further than this. For, in the manner of free indirect discourse, we also hear the voice of Dorothea's consciousness as we read through the sentence. The passage thus suggests that Dorothea feels a double set of associations: the images that rise up in her mind, vaguely associated with the deepest secrets of her experience, are in turn associated with (but not identical with) her loneliness. But what *is* the connection, we feel her wanting to know. Dorothea too is involved in the difficult attempt to elicit meaning which the sentence suggests the narrator is engaged in, and which we ourselves are invited to share as we read the sentence.

Our sense of Dorothea's part in the attempt to achieve meaning fades at the end of the sentence, when the narrator tells us that her sense of loneliness "was due to the very ardour of Dorothea's nature." We don't imagine Dorothea as naming and diagnosing the force of her own ardor in the way the narrator does. Nonetheless, the impression lingers that the peculiar force of "seems" we've been tracing is something that involves Dorothea, the narrator, and us as well. But in view of the way in which Dorothea shadows St. Theresa, this means that we've been made to participate in a groping after wholeness and connection that ultimately results from history and the coming of modernity. Even the vagueness of her feelings results from history. If Dorothea were in St. Theresa's age and place, her feelings wouldn't seem, they would be: they'd find clear expression. Here again, the personal and the historical interpenetrate. We've already noted that the funeral provides an ideal metaphor for Dorothea's personal emotions. By the same token, Dorothea has local, immediate, and personal reasons for keeping the exact bearings of that metaphor from emerging, reasons that involve a kind of ardor that has more to do with what the Prelude identifies with "the common yearning of womanhood" than with Theresa's "illimitable satisfaction" or even the "vague ideal" that is its modern counterpart (3). Dorothea has a stake in feelings that remain inchoate, that fail to reach clarity of expression. She

---

meaning we could render as "*was seen* (or observed) to form"—see *The Italian*, ed. Frederick Garber (Oxford: Oxford University Press, 1981), 90. The emphasis is on visual and emotional effect. "Seemed" as "was seen" leaves room for the reader. Its purpose is to emphasize the act of seeing itself, and in the process to leave room for a certain flexibility about who is doing the seeing. Radcliffe's object is to involve the reader in the experience of viewing her verbal pictures: "seemed" is meant to fuse us with a character in experiencing the moment of initial visual impression. This holds for descriptions of persons and emotions as well: again from *The Italian*, "Vivaldi's eyes were fixed upon the building, and a violent conflict of feelings seemed to shake his soul" (73). Here the effect is differently layered: Vivaldi watches something, and we are invited to watch him.

doesn't want to admit how cold her marriage is; she doesn't want to admit the extent to which Ladislaw could warm it. Again we see how human feelings appropriate and transform the logic of the external world. On this personal level, Dorothea transmutes the reality of the funeral so that its external appearance comes to embody a realm of sadness that escapes the linguistic coding upon which all social life is based. This movement to the painful ineffable is what gives her feelings their power, for her and for the reader. Still, as we've seen, Eliot has created a context which, in our own vague but potent field of perceptions, associates the inchoateness of Dorothea's imaginings not just with her personal situation, but with her moment in time and the movement of history itself.

Dorothea's ardor comes ultimately to serve as a marker for a large faithfulness to the promise of history. On the deepest level, she needs to embrace images of frustrating opacity, with a melancholic fixation and a refusal to move on, so that she will keep alive feelings for which she has no precise names, instead of defining them into the tameness of the known. She instinctively refuses to betray the part of her inwardness that wishes to embrace history itself, in search of illimitable satisfaction, instead of looking down at it from the heights of a known categorization of experience. She thereby keeps alive a demand that history have utopian possibilities. As readers, we are invited to merge affectively with the subjectivity of Dorothea-in-history as she tries to do justice to the spectacle of a certain kind of loss. We can do so only by engaging in an active recreation of the conditions of historical possibility that inform her situation. If we do not feel our way into the historical resonances of the passage, its full meaning and affect will evade us, because Dorothea's subjective, inchoate feelings are produced under the pressure of her attempt to make a historical place for herself "here—now—in England" (29).

The Place of the Narrator

Dorothea, I've argued, never loses her place in the web of history. Even the deepest levels of her interiority are not presented as timeless; even they find a place in history. Yet isn't there a voice in Eliot's novels that escapes this placement? What of Eliot's narrative voice itself? Doesn't it gain an unearned, impossible authority, free from historical constraint? This and related claims have been a staple of Eliot criticism for some time. Steven Marcus, for instance, has written that Eliot's fiction offers a radically sociological view of human life in history, in which we are the creatures of our times and our immediate surroundings, but that Eliot then without comment or justification relieves the narrator of the epistemological limits such a view necessarily entails. According to Marcus, this is a dishonest mystification, which stems from Eliot's need to squelch the claims of desire by making the existing order of things seem inevitable and inescapable (even though the narrator seems able to escape the epistemological conditions that render it inevitable and inescapable).[14] Much that I've suggested in this book should show that objections put in these terms are beside the point, because they fail to do justice either to the historicist situation or to the resources of realism. The "sociological" viewpoint as Marcus describes it would make knowledge of other societies impossible; indeed, it would make knowledge of one's own society impossible as well. That knowing the Other while remaining a part of one's own culture is a problem for historicism, but not an impossibility, was the burden of the preceding chapter. We hear in Marcus's critique of the Eliot narrator's privilege, and others like it, the echo of an older complaint: the complaint that Eliot herself was a writer, intellectual, cosmopolitan, and someone who lived with a married man to boot, but Dorothea Brooke isn't allowed to be any of these things. This was never a contemptible objection, but it does ask for a kind of transprency of representation and application that, I've suggested, realism is quite properly not in the business of supplying.[15]

The idea that the realist narrator should be under just the same constraints as the characters in the narrated fictional world, so as to avoid philosophical and ideological contradiction, can be understood as a vari-

[14] Steven Marcus, *Representations: Essays on Literature and Society* (New York: Random House, 1975), 182–213. Marcus explicitly draws on the Barthes of *Writing Degree Zero*. As we saw in Chapter 1, critics of ideology have found in this asymmetry between narrator and characters a prime means by which realist fiction reinforces the norms of bourgeois ideology. The narrator assumes a position from which he can dictate the terms of reality, and where his exemption from the laws of the world he creates is offered not as an act of unexplained privilege, but as something that makes his creation all the more real.

[15] Significant reinforcement of the unease underlying such arguments has recently been supplied by Elizabeth Langland's suggestion that women like Dorothea Brooke were in fact never alone in the way that novels suggest, that there were always servants to marshal and household affairs to supervise. Langland's analysis is an important reminder that even Eliot's realism has its limits, and remains valuable whether or not one agrees with her assessment of the ideological implications of nineteenth-century domestic arrangements. Eliot, one feels, could have done something with such material: why didn't she? I would want to counter Langland's critique on a local level by drawing on Lukács's distinction between naturalism, which tries to include everything, and realism, which selects for emergent typicality. (Eliot herself makes scattered remarks along these lines, as Langland points out, but in my view they are susceptible to various glosses and in any case don't amount to a theory.) One then asks what simplifications and condensations need to be made to allow crucial aspects of human life (like Dorothea's inwardness) to emerge into view. Langland has an answer, which if accepted is damaging to the claims of realism as this book presents it: following Naomi Schor and others, she identifies attempts to discriminate between "typical" details and inessential ones as always a strategy of trivializing women as creatures of mere detail. See Elizabeth Langland, *Nobody's Angels* (Ithaca: Cornell University Press, 1995), 183–208.

ation on the idea that realism works by using objects in a book to represent objects in the world "directly." The fantastic requirement is now that conditions of possibility, not objects, should somehow be transported, simply and ubiquitously, into the text. Throughout this study, I have demonstrated in a variety of ways that realism has nothing to do with "transparent representation." We need instead to conceive of realist novels as creating a metonymical and rhetorical chain that runs from novel to reader to the world. If we view realism as a matter of rhetoric, not "transparency," the issue of historicizing the narrator doesn't disappear, but it becomes productive. What we would then reasonably require is that the realist narrator help to involve us in a dynamic mode of comprehension that will prove illuminating when we apply it to the realities around us. For *this* purpose, however, it might well be useful to place the narrator, like her characters, under the constraints of history. This is particularly true with Eliot, because of her wish to move the reader, through sympathetic understanding, toward action. We've seen that, in different ways, the fiction of Austen and Scott has a problematic relationship to action. One may legitimately wonder whether Austen's distinction-making might not defer action indefinitely, and whether Scott's simple delight in historical difference and his tragic and elegiac certainty that history brings loss might not also inhibit efforts to change the world. Eliot is in my view entirely aware of such problems. They become the more poignant to her because of her acute sense of human interiority and its problematic relationship with action in the external world. As a result, Eliot wishes to escape a situation in which her narrator might seem to be modeling an aloofness from history, thereby attenuating her ability to appeal to our fellow feeling. (We might think of this impulse as prompting acts of narratorial supererogation, since successful realist representation does not depend upon them.) Like Dorothea, Eliot is "not at ease in the perspective and chilliness of that height." In her fiction, historicizing the narrator means involving the narrator in the historical grain, for the purpose of enacting the possibility of responding powerfully to the situations her readers find themselves involved in as creatures of their times. Eliot seeks to give her narrator moral authority by claiming a kinship of situation with us. When Laurence Olivier was making the climactic battle scene for *Henry V*, he asked some of his extras, who were playing the parts of English soldiers, to attack a French knight by jumping down from a tree onto him and his horse. They asked him to show them how—which he did (at the expense of a twisted ankle). Then they were willing to follow his direction.

How, then, could a narrator be shown to be subject to history? What would it mean for a realist novel to have a *historicized narrator*? One tactic

would be to depict the voice and mind of the narrator in a way that implies a preoccupation with historical forces the narrator simply can't escape. Narrators who are historicized in this sense are common in nineteenth-century realism. A narrator can invite us to share his engagement
in historical or cultural nostalgia, in a way that nonetheless makes the
dangers and limitations of that nostalgia clear. Scott does this repeatedly
in *Waverley*, and it's a staple of Thackeray's novels as well. There's also
something we might call implicit thematization. Scott, as we saw in the
previous chapter, can involve us in the rhythm of passing from being in a
historical moment to being above it so often that the rhythm itself becomes palpable, and comes to seem something that has overtaken the
narrator. Yet there are moments when such resources seem not to suffice,
and novelists find themselves drawing upon the affective power they
have generated in story space to dramatize the historical nature, not only
of their characters, but of their narrators as well.

The claim that a narrator enters into the imaginative space in which the
characters live, or even seems about to enter that space, is of course para-
doxical. Mainstream narratology would suggest that it's more than para-
doxical—it's a simple category mistake.[16] Thus according to one formulation, narrators occupy one space (which is known as "discourse space");
characters another (which is known as "story space"). Discourse space
"looks out upon" the world of the story, but through a glass wall. Narrators recount what happens in that world, but by definition (and in a way
that recalls the impossibility of two objects' occupying the same space at
the same time) they cannot enter it, either to act in it or even to "see" the
events that transpire there. (Narrators don't "see," they "narrate.") In
sum, "we must recognize in discourse space a separateness analogous to
the space on this side of a pane of glass or camera lens."[17] There is intelligence, discrimination, and plain good sense in this argument, and the distinctions it offers can prove useful in many situations. From the perspective I've been developing, however, it would appear that the categorical
distinction between story space and narrative space that mainstream nar-

[16]   My construction of "mainstream narratology" here is a fiction, though I believe that
the tendencies I outline are very widely shared by narratologists. The specific formulation
I give here is based primarily on the work of Seymour Chatman, a distinguished narratol-
ogist of decided and usefully clear opinions. I offer a fuller and somewhat more technical
analysis of the issue of whether the realist narrator penetrates or seems to want to penetrate story space, and why, in "Loose Narrators: Display, Engagement, and the Search for
a Place in History in Realist Fiction," *Narrative*, 3 (1995), 95–116. In this article, as in the
discussion below, I argue that a historicist conception of history will alter the sorts of
things authors wish to do with their narrators, in ways that a purely "logical" narratology
may fail to notice—or worse, may notice only to dismiss—and I show that Gérard
Genette's narratology may not be wholly inhospitable to the claims I'm making.
[17]   Seymour Chatman, *Coming to Terms* (Ithaca: Cornell University Press, 1990), 123.

ratology insists upon is not a simple requirement of logic and good sense, but a *problem* for the realist novelist, since if strictly adhered to it would disable from the start a powerful way of making the narrator seem subject to the constraints of history. We might expect to find novelists responding as artists generally do in such situations, by taking advantage of good sense when it suits their purposes, and evading it when it does not, by drawing upon the affective powers of their art.

George Eliot grapples with the problem of historicizing the narrator as early as *Scenes of Clerical Life*, the volume that launched her career as a novelist. *Scenes* enacts and thematizes a broad range of issues involving what it means for characters to have a place in history. It also depicts, sometimes with surprising directness, the narrator's own attempt both to frame and to enter the pictures she paints. By the end of the series, a narrator richly aware of historicity finds herself turning her back on the aesthetic modes of an earlier age, as she insists upon entering the historical world of the characters and calls upon us to do the same.

Scenes of Clerical Life includes three stories, occurring in the same general locale but at different periods in the past. The most recent story, "The Sad Fortunes of the Reverend Amos Barton," opens the series. Its setting is carefully specified in time and place, and it has been praised as exemplifying a familiar notion of realism—the depiction of the ugly, mediocre, and boring.[18] (The two remaining stories in *Scenes* are a falling off from this standard.) But the story's principal contribution to Eliot's historicist realism lies elsewhere. Eliot employs a variety of modes of narrative presence and address to manipulate the distance between the reader and her fiction, ranging from the half-ironic, half-sentimental reminiscences of an explicitly male narrator, to heavy-handed attacks on the reader's supposed preference for conventional fictions over real life, to earnestly "engaging" narration ("Look at the two women on the sofa together!"[69]).[19] To some extent, this may be simple experimentation. It also arises from a well-known aim of Eliot's early realism, her wish to make us take seriously the lives of those who might otherwise seem dull and unappealing. Eliot pushes us toward her characters and pulls us back, to make us sympathetic and then to ask us whether we've been adequately so. This experimentation in the rhetorical manipulation of distance between narrators, characters, and reader has little historical valence, but it prepares for the thematization of historical positioning in the stories that follow.

"Mr. Gilfil's Love Story," the second story in the series, is an elabo-

---

[18]   See, for instance, David Lodge's introduction to his edition of *Scenes of Clerical Life* (Harmondsworth: Penguin, 1973); hereafter cited in the text.
[19]   The term "engaging narrator" is Robyn Warhol's, in *Gendered Interventions* (New Brunswick: Rutgers University Press, 1989).

rately self-conscious piece of historical re-creation, redolent of eigh-teenth-century aristocratic life. In this story, Eliot delights in a narrative method that draws on the aesthetic decorum of the period it imitates. The use of eighteenth-century architecture and painting in the following de-scription may serve as an example:

> The elder lady, who is advancing towards the cushions, is . . . tall, and looks the taller because her powdered hair is turned backward over a toupee, and surmounted by lace and ribbons. She is nearly fifty, but her complexion is still fresh and beautiful, with the beauty of an auburn blond; her proud pouting lips, and her head thrown a little backward as she walks, give an expression of hauteur which is not contradicted by the cold grey eye. The tucked-in kerchief, rising full over the low tight bodice of her blue dress, sets off the majestic form of her bust, and she treads the lawn as if she were one of Sir Joshua Reynolds's stately ladies, who had suddenly stepped from her frame to enjoy the evening cool.
>
> "Put the cushions lower, Caterina, that we may not have so much sun upon us," she called out, in a tone of authority, when still at some distance. (133)

This passage mentions a Reynolds painting as a metaphor, but it does more with the painting than that. It vivifies the process by which, we come to realize, the story itself was created. You meditate upon the arts of a period, and suddenly a period setting arises in your mind; figures begin to fill it, stepping from their canvases as Lady Cheverel seems to step from hers. Passages like this one turn the spotlight on the narrator as re-creator and magician—as someone whose voice can make the past unfold before us, with the words, "It is the evening of the 21st of June 1788" (132).

Throughout, the narrator expresses a richly historical consciousness. When the narrator defends Lady Cheverel's husband from his neighbor's criticisms—they wonder why he spends his money on architecture and not on wine and hunting dogs—she is reminding us that we, unlike his contemporaries, can read Sir Christopher in the light of the historical record:

> As for Sir Christopher, he was perfectly indifferent to criticism. "An obstinate, crotchety man," said his neighbours. But I, who have seen Cheverel Manor, as he bequeathed it to his heirs, rather at-tribute that unswerving architectural purpose of his, conceived and carried out through long years of systematic personal exertion, to

something of the fervour of genius, as well as inflexibility of will; and in walking through those rooms, with their splendid ceilings and their meagre furniture, which tell how all the spare money had been absorbed before personal comfort was thought of, I have felt that there dwelt in this old English baronet some of that sublime spirit which distinguishes art from luxury, and worships beauty apart from self-indulgence. (159)

We hear in this passage a voice capable of appreciating the extent to which a figure from another historical era might be shaped by the culture surrounding and informing him, and the extent to which he might partially transcend that culture by employing the means it itself makes available.

The heroine of "Gilfil" cannot long be contained in the spaces that frame Lady Cheverel and her husband. She is a passionate, raven-haired Italian named Tina, who brings subjective, interior passion into the story's world of polished eighteenth-century surfaces. Lest we miss the contrast, Eliot depicts a distraught Tina sitting under the gaze of a portrait that depicts a "fair blonde dame" who "seemed to look down on her with that benignant unconcern, that mild wonder, with which happy self-possessed women are apt to look down on their agitated and weaker sisters" (196). As the story develops, we find this "weaker sister," a slave to her passions of love and revenge, prowling down a country house gallery, seizing a glittering dagger, and flashing out of the house to use it on her unfaithful lover. On a less melodramatic note, the contrast between Tina's interiority and the surface world of the Cheverels is blazoned by the contrast between Sir Christopher's love of ornamental surfaces (fan vaulting, for example) and Tina's love of music. She's an accomplished singer, and when she has completely withdrawn from the outer world into the depths of a listless despair, a deep, reverberating note from a piano is required to bring her back to the surface.[20]

Where interiority prevails, the world of the nineteenth century cannot be far behind. Fittingly enough, the French Revolution enters the story, as the narrator compares Tina's emotional turmoil to the Revolutionary storms raging across the channel: "In that summer, we know, the great nation of France was agitated by conflicting thoughts and passions, which were but the beginning of sorrows. And in our Caterina's little breast, too, there were terrible struggles" (147). This comparison is re-

---

[20]   More historicizing on Eliot's part: as M. H. Abrams demonstrated some time ago in *The Mirror and the Lamp* (Oxford: Oxford University Press, 1953), the transition between eighteenth-century and nineteenth-century aesthetic theory moves from painting as the privileged metaphor to music.

peated in somewhat different terms later in the story. As in the passage relating the "deepest secrets" of Dorothea's inner experience to the world outside her, Eliot refrains from making Tina's heartaches and the upheavals of France simple metaphors for one another. Nor is the point ultimately to emphasize the power of Tina's sufferings or to put her sufferings in ironic perspective. ("They may feel severe to Tina," we'd exclaim, "but can you really compare them to the French Revolution?") Eliot is in fact balancing both views (as she will do for a different purpose when she places Gwendolyn Harleth's consciousness in the context of the American Civil War), to suggest that both kinds of suffering find a valid place as history moves in its relentless course. In doing so, she enriches the fantasia on the theme of finding a place in history for characters, narrators, and readers that informs the story as a whole.

In the end, the story returns to the contained, external, pictorial mode with which it began. The narrator creates a decorous distance between us and Tina's fate, by painting a picture. This picture, however, unlike Sir Joshua's, contains the oppositions we've noted throughout the story, between exteriors and interiors, passion and convention, the eighteenth and the nineteenth centuries. In doing so, it encapsulates and thematizes our own oscillations as readers, urged by the narrator sometimes to immerse ourselves in the story, sometimes to see it as a historical exhibit, and sometimes to do both at once. The picture that ends "Mr. Gilfil's Love Story" reveals the emotional depths hidden beneath the gnarled surface of Mr. Gilfil himself, who in his later years has come to be a gruff, aged, wholly unromantic clergyman of a predictable genre, but who in his youth had loved Tina with overwhelming passion. In the end, Tina returned his love, but she died soon after. Her memory is preserved in a chamber in Mr. Gilfil's house, which is kept locked. This room, the narrator tells us, is "a sort of visible symbol of the secret chamber in his heart, where he had long turned the key on early hopes and early sorrows, shutting up for ever all the passion and the poetry of his life" (130).

Passion and poetry of a kind flourish in the third and final story of *Scenes of Clerical Life*, "Janet's Repentance," which is set close to Eliot's present and in which the narrator seems willfully to eschew the balance so artfully created in "Mr. Gilfil's Love Story." In "Janet's Repentance," another locked chamber appears. The story's hero, Edgar Tryan, has his own secret chamber of the heart, which locks away the pathetic story of a girl he had seduced and abandoned. Unlike Tina's husband, however, he freely opens his "chamber," revealing his secret story when doing so will promote Janet's salvation. "He hesitated," the narrator tells us, "as we tremble to let in the daylight on a chamber of relics which we have never visited except in curtained silence. But . . . he went on" (358). By "going on," Mr. Tryan abandons the pictorial containment Eliot associates with eighteenth-century society, so that a new ethos—the well-known ethic of sympathy Eliot finds proper for the nineteenth century—can assert itself. This ethic, as the image of Tryan's opening up the secret chamber of his heart suggests, involves the breaking down of barriers. One of those barriers separates story space from narrative space, under pressure from the narrator's wish to enter the world of historical limitation and thereby find, for herself and for us, a real place in its moral struggles. The dramatic (sometimes melodramatic) passion that had informed Tina's inner world now touches the narrator and her relationship to us.

Signs that the narrator is taking a historically limited, even partisan position abound in "Janet's Repentance." In one remarkable sequence, the narrator compares different ways of understanding a clergyman such as Mr. Tryan. In one paragraph, she gives a gloss from above: " 'One of the Evangelical clergy, a disciple of Venn,' says the critic from his bird's-eye station. 'Not a remarkable specimen; the anatomy and habits of his species have been determined long ago.' " This cold summary is quickly corrected by a view from quite a different vantage point: "Yet surely, surely the only true knowledge of our fellow-man is that which enables us to feel with him—which gives us a fine ear for the heart-pulses that are beating under the mere clothes of circumstance and opinion. Our subtlest analysis of schools and sects must miss the essential truth, unless it be lit up by the love that sees in all forms of human thought and work, the life and death struggles of separate human beings" (322). It would be possible to interpret this fervent passage as simply one more comment made by a not-necessarily-human narrator, securely placed on one side of the glass wall that separates the space of narration from the space of story. No doubt a narrator insulated from story space *could* voice these sentiments, or any others. But reading the passage this way misses most of its affective charge, and all of its historical impetus.[21] What matters most here is not the doctrine the paragraph voices, but its mode of asserting that doctrine, a mode that is self-consciously and unapologetically emotional, willful, and partial. The passage is dramatic, and it begs to be dramatized. As a reader, I cannot react with cool aloofness to such an appeal; I must join hands with the narrator and with Tryan himself.[22]

---

[21]   The vehemence of the insistence here that we are all alike under the "mere clothes" provided by our moments in history stems precisely from the depth of Eliot's grasp of the coercive power of our historical milieu, and the need she feels to find an even more powerful force to oppose it. The issue as Eliot raises it cannot *become* an issue except in a historicist framework.

[22]   But, as a *modern* reader, I must remember to protect my cool credibility by couching this perception in the moderately derisive imitative form I've employed in the text. Few readers would mistake the writing here (and in some of the excerpts from "Gilfil" I've cited) for Eliot's best. The crudeness in some of Eliot's appeals to the reader is hard to

The reader of *Scenes of Clerical Life* knows very well that its narrator excels at the bird's-eye view. At the very moment when she castigates those who would "with the bird's-eye glance of a critic" presume to condemn Tryan's doctrinal narrowness, she specifies precisely wherein that narrowness lies, drawing her own knowledge clearly enough from a position above the historical stream. "A critic might perhaps say that he made the mistake of identifying Christianity with a too narrow doctrinal system; that he saw God's work too exclusively in antagonism to the world, the flesh, and the devil; that his intellectual culture was too limited—and so on" (322). Yet the very thoroughness of the narrator's knowledge from above calls for strong countermeasures. Mere intellectual correction will not suffice. In voicing her energetic denunciation of the bird's-eye view, the narrator seeks to bind herself to the limited view of one involved in the throes of history in the making, not one observing history already made. She seeks to immerse herself willfully in the very historical stream men like Tryan and women like Janet have helped to propel along its way—which, indeed, is the same stream in which Eliot as a writer of the present finds herself immersed. "But I am not poised at that lofty height," she declares. "I am on the level and in the press with him, as he struggles his way along the stony road, through the crowd of unloving fellow-men" (322). If this passage engages us as it means to, we will realize that in the narrator's description of Tryan's funeral at the end of the story, she not only implores us as readers to join the funeral procession that marches behind his coffin, she joins it herself. This moment, and others like it scattered throughout Eliot's works, sound a note that can infiltrate our sense of Eliot's narrative voice even when it is at its most detached and masterful, a note complexly motivated. I believe that, among other things, such moments reflect a yearning to escape the burden of a lonely authority. Eliot's stress on the need for sympathetic understanding may include a wistful wish that the reader would help her share that burden. When in *Middlemarch*, Dorothea Brooke murmurs to Rosamond Vincy "we are weak—I am weak—" (797), are we also hearing the hidden weariness of the usually masterful narrator?

To be sure, the narrator cannot remain in the thick of things with Tryan for long, because it's perfectly clear that she can't really be there at all. The rhetorical force of such moments would indeed vanish if the narrator actually made a stay in story space; then we'd be up to narratological and epistemological games, not ethical intensities. The bird's-eye view is bound to reassert itself—but it's the impulse to break down barriers that's

---

miss. This, however, helps to make crudely apparent the larger historical and narratological stakes involved, which Eliot's verbal subtlety normally obscures.

of interest here, the impulse for the narrative voice to claim a place in history. This impulse seems inevitable in a wise historicist, whether he is creating fictional or critical narratives. (In the last sentence of Erich Auerbach's "Epilegomena zu *Mimesis*," after he has outlined his methods and goals in a way that makes them seem timeless in their scope and wisdom, he adds, simply and without apology, that "*Mimesis* is a book that is quite aware that it was written by a particular man, with a particular past, living at a particular place at the beginning of the 1940's.")[23] As the narrator of *Scenes of Clerical Life* moves from "Gilfil" to "Janet's Repentance," we see her giving up a position that allows her the imaginative freedom to create a detached imitation of the past, in exchange for the moral force that stems from our amazement that such an immensely intelligent and perspicuous intellectual presence is willing to submit to the creatural limits of a given time and place. We see her entering history.[24]

In her later fiction, Eliot is less likely simply to announce that she is there in the press with her characters. Yet there are signs of a wish to join them nonetheless. We feel the narrator edging toward story space and thus toward a position in the grain of history, for instance, in moments of desire—moments some critics have deplored as embodying a simple loss of control or a failure to maintain distance. Such a dynamic informs the scenes between Dorothea and Will Ladislaw at the end of *Middlemarch*, where the narrator gives in to a weakness for merging with Dorothea, just as Dorothea gives in to her weakness for Will. These are conscious, and conscientious, surrenders.

The narrator also edges toward story space from time to time in *Daniel Deronda*. When Daniel Deronda sees the images of his, and the narrator's, and the reader's desire come to life as he rows on the Thames and looks across at the shore or up at a bridge, we discover that he, and the narrator, and we as readers, are all negotiating the same historical stream. Such uncertainty of boundaries and positions informs the very first scene in the novel, which depicts a character who feels drawn to read the riddle Gwendolyn's beautiful surface presents. "Was she beautiful or not beautiful? and what was the secret of form or expression which gave the dy-

---

[23]   Erich Auerbach, "Epilegomena zu *Mimesis*," *Romanische Forschungen*, 65 (1953), 18 (my translation). For a rich account of just how fully Auerbach was situated in the everyday not only in his thought but in his life, see Hans Ulrich Gumbrecht's remarkable " 'Pathos of the Earthly Progress': Erich Auerbach's Everydays," in *Literary History and the Challenge of Philology*, ed. Seth Lerer (Stanford: Stanford University Press, 1996), 13–35.
[24]   As we might expect from Eliot, even at this early moment in her career, there is yet another level of complication here. For though Eliot appears to be voicing a wish for immediate contact with the world of her characters, she is doing so by drawing upon a form of fiction that is itself a historical exhibit about Tryan and his coreligionists—Evangelical reform fiction.

namic quality to her glance? Was the good or the evil genius dominant in those beams?"[25] The novel opens with these words, and in its course Deronda comes to hope with some fervor that Gwendolyn will achieve deep human significance, instead of remaining part of the decorative, random meaninglessness epitomized by the roulette table over which he first observes her. These sentences enact not simply an uncertainty about Gwendolyn's character, but a confusion between speaker's and narrator's perspectives as well: for nearly a page, it's impossible to tell whether the figure who is observing Gwendolyn and asking these questions will turn out to be the narrator, or an as yet unnamed character, or some mixture of the two. No doubt this confusion is an arresting tribute to the dynamic quality of Gwendolyn's glance. The tribute gains force from its suggestion that Gwendolyn's glance is so dynamic that it suspends normal narrative boundaries and relationships, drawing reader and narrator to a position in the casino where its power may be felt.

When Gwendolyn first meets Grandcourt, there occurs another moment when the perspectives of the narrator and of one of the characters mix. The narrator comes to speak of Gwendolyn's "small inferences of the way in which she could make her life pleasant" after having presented Gwendolyn's powers of small inference busily at work as she talks with Grandcourt, in a series of literally parenthetical mental remarks made during the pauses he leaves as he responds to Gwendolyn's repartee:

> "I suppose you are a first-rate shot with a rifle."
> (Pause, during which Gwendolyn, having taken a rapid observation of Grandcourt, made a brief graphic description of him to an indefinite hearer.)
> "I have left off shooting."
> "Oh, then, you are a formidable person. People who have done things once and left them off make one feel very contemptible, as if one were using cast-off fashions. I hope you have not left off all follies, because I practice a great many."
> (Pause, during which Gwendolyn made several interpretations of her own speech.) (112)

These parenthetical thoughts continue for two more pages, and include among other things the report that in one pause, Gwendolyn "was thinking that men had been known to choose some one else than the woman they

[25] Eliot, *Daniel Deronda*, ed. Terence Cave (Harmondsworth: Penguin, 1995), 7; hereafter cited in the text.

most admired, and recalled several experiences of that kind in novels"
(114). Should we have failed to appreciate the arch peculiarity of this mode
of narration, the narrator adds, at the end of the sequence, the following observation: "How Grandcourt had filled up the pauses will be more evident
hereafter" (114).[26] Here we see a character who seems to want to act as a
narrator—indeed we find Gwendolyn narrating different versions of the
scene as she experiences it—while the narrator observes her with detachment, through the glass wall of impersonal authorial irony.

Yet at this moment where the narrator's detachment from the depicted
world appears complete, authorial intervention unexpectedly takes the
following form, attaching itself to a bit of free indirect discourse rendering Gwendolyn's reaction to the fact that Miss Juliet Fenn has beaten her
at archery:

> It was impossible to be jealous of Juliet Fenn, a girl as middling as
> mid-day market in everything but her archery and her plainness, in
> which last she was noticeably like her father: underhung and with
> receding brow resembling that of the more intelligent fishes.
> (Surely, considering the importance which is given to such an acci-
> dent in female offspring, marriageable men, or what the new En-
> glish calls "intending bridegrooms," should look at themselves dis-
> passionately in the glass, since their natural selection of a mate
> prettier than themselves is not certain to bar the effect of their own
> ugliness.) (114)

Here the disengaged narrator suddenly imitates Gwendolyn's own way of
"filling in the gaps"—the more unmistakably, in that we might for a line or
so identify the parenthetical commentary as Gwendolyn's! Is the narrator
at such a remove from the scene that she can play tricks with the forms she
has created, or has she suddenly (and inexplicably) entered the fictional
world? Why should the narrator mimic Gwendolyn here, to be sure in a
different key? If the purpose is to raise the possibility of movements between narrative world and story world, whether this moment itself embodies such a shift hardly matters. What does matter is that we may subsequently be more inclined to recognize in fictional passages and sequences
an expression of the narrator's desire to intervene, the kind of desire all of
us, whether in fictional histories or in the world of history, must share, as
events unfold, promising and threatening. Eliot's historicized narrator

---

[26]   In a letter to Eliot written while he was reading the proofs of *Deronda*, William Blackwood noted that Gwendolyn's "running mental reflections after each few words she has
said to Grandcourt" were "as far as I know a new device in reporting a conversation." See
Gordon Haight, *George Eliot: A Biography* (1968; Harmondsworth: Penguin, 1985), 481.

would seem to merge here with a "desiring narrator." How better to dramatize desire than by drawing on the resources of story space?

One of the more surprising passages in *Daniel Deronda* places Gwendolyn in the context of the American Civil War:

> Could there be a slenderer, more insignificant thread in human history than this consciousness of a girl, busy with her small inferences of the way in which she could make her life pleasant?—in a time, too, when ideas were with fresh vigour making armies of themselves, and the universal kinship was declaring itself fiercely: when women on the other side of the world would not mourn for the husbands and sons who died bravely in a common cause, and men stinted of bread on our side of the world heard of that willing loss and were patient: a time when the soul of man was waking to pulses which had for centuries been beating in him unfelt, until their full sum made a new life of terror or of joy.
>
> What in the midst of that mighty drama are girls and their blind visions? They are the Yea or Nay of that good for which men are enduring and fighting. In these delicate vessels is borne onward through the ages the treasure of human affections. (124)

Though this passage shares the fervor of the narrative interventions we've noted in *Scenes*, its blurring of narrative boundaries is more complex than theirs. We don't find the narrator here announcing that she is there with Gwendolyn, that she has herself become a delicate vessel. What the passage does contain is a notable mixing of voices and viewpoints.[27] On the one hand, the narrator speaks with Olympian detachment about the importance of "girls and their blind visions." On the other hand, if we try to apply these pronouncements to Gwendolyn, we hear the narrative voice shift from a mode of detachment to one of hope and desire, a mode that seems more appropriate for a character than an extradiegetic narrator. As we'll see more fully in a moment, the narrator insists on her status as narrator, judging and disposing of characters and events, at the very time when she seems full of the sort of earnest, open-

---

[27] In "George Eliot's Pulse," *differences*, 6 (1994), 28–45, Neil Hertz discusses what I take to be a similar oscillation in a network of passages, including this one and the passages from "Gilfil" comparing Tina's sufferings with world-historical problems; he persuasively relates these passages to problems of female authorship and of writing itself. David Carroll (*George Eliot and the Conflict of Interpretations*, 50) also finds a connection between Tina and Gwendolyn in this context. Nancy L. Paxton, in *George Eliot and Herbert Spencer* (Princeton: Princeton University Press, 1991), 257 n. 20, takes the passage to be a "heavily ironic" critique of Spencer's views of manhood: war would simply bring out the qualities in men most likely to jar with the feminine.

ended desire to make sense of the historical stream we might expect a character to feel. There may be worse ways of attempting to describe this remarkable bifurcation and coalescence than to suggest that the narrator seems, at crucial moments in *Daniel Deronda*, not quite to enter story space, but to evince a strong impulse to attempt such an entry.

On the face of it, one could hardly imagine a narrator more securely removed from the world of the characters than this one is, with her talk about Gwendolyn's "small inferences," her comprehensive view of the larger historical context, and her secure analysis of the way in which a small character and a large historical moment are intertwined. Her confident ease extends astonishingly far. "Ideas" are magisterially depicted as "with fresh vigour making armies of themselves"—as if the only question that might arise concerning the relationship between an idea and an army involved the degree of "vigour" with which the one could transform itself into the other! There is, however, a remarkable gap between the certainty with which the narrator defends the importance of the inner dramas of "girls" and the bemusement we feel as we try to view Gwendolyn in the narrator's light. The point of the passage would seem to be that, appearances to the contrary notwithstanding, Gwendolyn's inner life is significant. Visions of Civil War heroism may seem to make her concerns unspeakably trivial; in fact, though, she and other girls like her embody the point of that heroism, the reason why strife and suffering are justified. Yet when we think of Gwendolyn concretely, this noble justification seems to evaporate. "Girls" may be the "delicate vessels" in which "human affections" are borne; but Gwendolyn's "human affections" seem at best embryonic at this point in the novel. (Selfishness and a primitive fear she possesses in abundance.) And though we may find Gwendolyn at certain moments brittle, does she really seem "delicate"? Thus we find ourselves back where we were when the passage began, wondering why Gwendolyn, of all girls, is worthy of so much scrutiny. To be sure, Gwendolyn as an *empty* vessel might be intended to demonstrate the bankruptcy of the upper-class English society that she takes to be her natural setting: if ideas made armies arise around the likes of her and them, they would be making a mistake. But such a reading fails to account for the positive aura that hovers around the "girls" in the passage.[28]

---

[28] Alison Booth, in *Greatness Engendered: George Eliot and Virginia Woolf* (Ithaca: Cornell University Press, 1992), finds a different kind of "flaw in the image of the passive vessels of affection" (247). For her, the passage momentarily occludes Gwendolyn's connection with age-old female oppression, and also with forms of communal consciousness and action that stand as alternatives to the official version of history and social relations enshrined in the "realism" of English society (and of the realist novel). "Gwendolyn, crea-

We can account for that aura if we speak in terms, not of what Gwendolyn's "blind visions" represent at the moment, but of what they *might* and *should* represent—if we think of potentiality, not actuality; of the future, not the present; of the optative, not the indicative. Then we begin to hear in the narrator's voice not only Olympian certainty with respect to the worth of "girls" in general, but hope and wishfulness with respect to Gwendolyn. The narrator blends two voices—one that generalizes from a vantage point securely removed from story space, and another that desires and hopes, in the teeth of present evidence, as a character *in* story space, and in the space of history, might do. Such a narrator has gained an aura of historicity, by engaging in a complicated interplay with the problems and energies of the historicized fictional world she has created.

In the frail vessels passage, then, Eliot gives a visionary extension to Scott's movement between narrative foci in and above the world he depicts. One might deal with Scott's oscillation and remain within the terms of mainstream narratology: employed in a somewhat Pickwickian sense (which would include a liberal sprinkling of Seymour Chatman's useful notion of an "interest" focus), the concept of narrative "focus" could account for Scott's narrative practice in this regard.[29] I've been arguing that for Eliot, such terms don't quite suffice. Because of the depth of her recognition of the problems involved in historicist realism, she finds herself putting pressure on the normal narrative distinctions, and we need a way of formulating this pressure as more than just a violation of logic or convention. In "Janet's Repentance," this is relatively easy to see: after all, the narrator *tells* us that she's down there with Janet. In the later novels, the impulse to descend isn't expressed in bodily terms, but it remains, making itself felt in Eliot's rhetorical stance and practice. The stakes here are high. If we fail to register this aspect of Eliot's representation, we are in danger of neglecting something central to the view of our predicament in history as defined by the works of this clairvoyantly intelligent author.

Eliot's optative appeals to her characters' potentialities are part of an attempt to forge a historicist ethics. They insist on our need to imagine possibilities not already realized by the web of historical causality surrounding her characters, and surrounding us as well. They are based

---

ture of the marriage market, is fighting the world's battles in her own spirit, and the conflict reveals a gothic version of the unconscious" (247). I would modify this reading by suggesting that though the rhetoric of realism regularly draws on other genres, such as the Gothic, the generic "dominant" (to recall the parlance of the Russian Formalists) in *Deronda* remains a metonymical realism. This realism mirrors the conditions of our own reality; it is our court of appeals, against whose judgments the claims of other modes of imagining life in history gain their meaning, and their power.

[29] Chatman, *Coming to Terms*, 148.

upon a sense, like Austen's, that the grain of society can be negotiated by following a number of paths, which produces the effect of a certain amount of play in the system. But the optative in Eliot is a form of narration in the historical grain pointed toward the future. This differentiates her from both Austen and Scott. Viewed in this light, there may be more to Gwendolyn Harleth's taut, anguished attempt, at the end of *Deronda*, to attain a state of expectancy than at first meets the eye. The Messiah cannot in fact be expected to enter the strait gate from outside; we must, however, keep ourselves in active readiness for moments when the grain of a historical moment works itself into a form that will simulate such an entry from within, so that we can help to narrate it into being.

Eliot's projections of a redemptive history for individuals may seem to be special cases of a general "providential" narrative. But there's a difference between potentially redemptive narratives and providential narratives. Eliot's future-directed narratives of personal redemption and of national redemption (like the one Daniel Deronda imagines) come from a position within the historical grain, and they depend on individual action. Providential narratives, by contrast, proceed from above, and they minimize the importance of the individual will.

Is Eliot's Narrator Gendered?

The nature of the claim I've been making for Eliot's narrator, and its limits, may be clarified by raising a parallel issue. We can ask, not whether Eliot's narrator is shown to be historical, but whether her narrator is shown to be gendered. If we take the default gender to be masculine, then this becomes the question of whether the narrator can be shown to be feminine.[30]

No recent critic has spoken of the narratological issues that matter in this regard with more authority than has Susan Lanser. Lanser's *Fictions of Authority* gives a powerful account of the pressures women novelists have felt in attaining an authoritative narrative voice. She sees Austen, for instance, as having been badly burned by the experience of finding

---

[30] In approaching issues of gender and realism in Eliot, I have found judicious and stimulating Penny Boumelha, "Realism and the Ends of Feminism," in *Grafts: Feminist Cultural Criticism*, ed. Susan Sheridan (London: Verso, 1988), 77–91. For women's narration, my touchstones have been Robyn R. Warhol, *Gendered Interventions*, Alison Case, *Plotting Women* (Charlottesville: University Press of Virginia, 1999), and Susan Sniader Lanser, *Fictions of Authority* (Ithaca: Cornell University Press, 1992). Lanser works from a view of realism informed by most of the tenets I contest here. I believe that her valuable insights about female narration can be disentangled from what I can only consider a mistaken view of realism.

Northanger Abbey's publication indefinitely postponed. It seems to Lanser no coincidence that the overt dicta voiced by the narrator in *Northanger Abbey* (for instance, her ringing praise of other women novelists) are toned down in subsequent works. Austen learned the dangers of producing novels likely to raise male resistance by unseemly displays of female authority, and she adjusted her narrative apparatus accordingly. In the same way and for generally similar (though more complicated) reasons, as Eliot progresses in her career from being an author who can pass herself off as a male to one who is known to be a woman living in sin, she alters her narrative techniques. In the later novels, the narrator dissolves into a dispersed, if always masterful, presence. In the process, Eliot's narrator merges with a "naturalized" male discourse itself, according to Lanser.

Lanser's exploration of changes in narrative style during the careers of Austen and Eliot adds an element my own book omits. Though I don't entirely agree with her descriptions of their careers, I find them useful and stimulating. My reticence in this matter stems primarily from my wish to emphasize the opportunities of readers, not the predicaments of authors. Accompanying and in important ways organizing Lanser's account, however, is a view of realism that I find unacceptable, for it draws heavily on assumptions about realism I wish to move beyond. According to Lanser, realism works to totalize the orthodox ideology supporting male hegemony. She treats the appearance of dialogic possibilities in the realist novel with great suspicion. Lennard Davis may go a bit too far in denying the possibility of the dialogic altogether, but what dialogue exists is likely to involve "playing the game" as D. A. Miller describes it, as at best a Saturnalian exercise that in the end only strengthens the grasp of the dominant ideology. In Lanser's account, narrators reinforce orthodoxy in one of two ways: they assert a strong, authoritative presence, or they seem to disappear. What unites these antithetical possibilities is the logic of naturalization, for both stances affirm a "totalizing 'we' " which allows "the language of any ideologically dominant group" to lend its own ideology a spurious universality.[31] The realist narrator presents himself as omniscient, and omniscience is male. I trust that by now, readers of this book will find inadequate such a conception of the way in which the realist narrators engage with their readers, and I do not intend to contest it further here. I will ask instead whether we can discover signs within Eliot's novels that invite the reader (and especially, though not exclusively, the modern reader) to consider the narrator's voice to be more than simply male. Lanser's work helps to make this an urgent question,

---

[31]   Susan Sniader Lanser, *Fictions of Authority*, 96.

for her account of the pressures mounted against female authority in novels remains formidable, reminding us that gendering the narrator female would be more than a technical or intellectual achievement.

It would of course become an impossible achievement if the novelistic discourse available to an author were seamlessly masculinist. My account of the language of reference denies that our perceptions and our linguistic tools are totally colonized in advance by any one ideology: if they were, the possibility on which I've insisted of referential productivity would evaporate. Yet the strength of patriarchal institutions governing the production of novels and (I believe to a lesser extent) their consumption seems undeniable. Then too, historicist thought itself has tended not to make sufficient room for gender as a category, and probably it cannot make room for gender as the fundamental category. Historicism, as we've seen, is happiest in the area of human experience existing from the skin out and inflected toward the institutional and the economic and public spheres. We have yet to work out entirely satisfactory ways of finding a place for gender here, and the historicist thinking that informs the nineteenth-century novel had hardly begun to consider them. (Yet isn't one of Eliot's achievements, in *Romola*, say, precisely to add considerations of gender where the men in her novels think they don't belong?)

Can the realist narrator I've described present herself as gendered? What would it mean for her to do so? Well, if what would be required would be a narratorial enactment of *écriture féminine*, the answer seems a clear negative: at best, historicist realism could serve as a grain for such a voice to violate. If the stakes are less total, the question is more open. The question might then conveniently reduce itself to whether the narrator can act as a feminine "role model." Despite the unfashionableness of this term these days, I don't find its use trivializing: with about the same degree of reductiveness, my main concern in the previous section could be described as an attempt to gauge the extent to which realist narrators can serve as historicist role models. I have suggested that by hovering at the edge of a historicized story space, the narrator can dramatize the pressure of the historical and a mode of responding to it. This is what it would mean to create a historicized narrator. The problem of creating a narrator gendered feminine cannot be solved in quite this way, because (from a historicist point of view), it exists on a more concrete level: femininity would need itself to be historicized, would need to be femininity at a certain historical moment. We would then expect a feminine narrator to enact the pressures of being a woman in history, as well as a characteristically feminine response to those pressures.

A classic criticism of *Middlemarch* is that its narrator allows herself to be taken over by Dorothea, losing critical distance. In my view, one grain of truth in this criticism is that, during the course of the novel, Dorothea comes to function as a role model for the narrator. What the narrator calls "the great powers of her womanhood" (772) are powers the narrator also draws on—among other things, in the warmth of tone with which she bathes Dorothea's attempt to save Rosamond in the extended sequence in which that phrase occurs.[32] The narrator thereby recommends Dorothea's powerful generosity and selflessness to us. This has occurred before. In her interchange with the cautious, reasonable, unmistakably male Farebrother (who, in the course of the novel, becomes ever more "manly" in the typical nineteenth-century sense of "possessing the power to restrain one's own desires"), Dorothea's feminine ardor has for both narrator and reader the last, best word:

> "But, my dear Mrs. Casaubon," said Mr. Farebrother, smiling gently at her ardour, "character is not cut in marble—it is not something solid and unalterable. It is something living and changing, and may become diseased as our bodies do."
> "Then it may be rescued and healed," said Dorothea. (734–35)

If, following the lead of some of the dominant voices in feminist narratology, we must code the brainy, ironic, distanced aspect of Eliot's narration as male, then I'd argue that the narrator draws on Dorothea's example to supplement these qualities with what the novel's ideology (not without problems in this regard) considers an essentially feminine strength. As with historicized narrators, what gets dramatized here is more than anything a stance, a mode of understanding and possible action. The exploration of such problems in their concrete, metonymical specificity remains a task to be accomplished by the characters in story space.

Eliot, Realism, and Modernity

When Eliot's narrator shifts into an optative mode in positing the potential significance of Gwendolyn Harleth's consciousness, we observe historicist realism responding to the force of modernity. Modernity, Habermas reminds us, begins as society finds itself compelled to create

---

[32] "Dorothea's nature was of that kind: her own passionate faults lay along the easily-counted open channels of her ardent character; and while she was full of pity for the visible mistakes of others, she had not yet any material within her experience for subtle constructions and suspicions of hidden wrong. But that simplicity of hers, holding up an ideal for others in her believing conception of them, was one of the great powers of her womanhood" (772). I am indebted to Alison Case for pointing out the relevance of this passage to me, and for suggesting that Dorothea comes to serve as a role model for the narrator.

its values from its own resources, instead of drawing them from tradition. A characteristic response is to imagine values along the axis of the future, as that which we are on the path toward attaining. There are, however, very significant variations on this theme. Providential history is only one of many paths one can follow. Habermas wishes us to maintain a connection with tradition in the process of value formation, but to shift a regulative and evaluative role to such agencies as the "ideal speech situation." Eliot, though in quite different ways, also works at making a place for tradition (for instance, in her translation of the *Ecclesiasticus* passage to fit *Adam Bede*) while at the same time honoring the insight that in a secular world our values must emerge from the grain we confront and inhabit. Her use of what I've called the optative is one of several techniques that work from this premise of modernity. All of them may be seen as aspects of a larger process of "perfecting."

By "perfecting," I mean to describe a process in which the full significance of an entity is developed, so far as is possible, by drawing upon the entity itself. At the very least, one tries to adjust the terms one brings to the object so that they are in the same key as those of the object. I'm drawing here on the relationship between the words "perfect" and "unfold," and this gives the process of perfecting an inherent narrative dimension. "Perfecting" as I'm using the word involves an unfolding that aims to achieve ever greater completeness of historicized specification; perfecting is an unfolding given a direction or vector. In law, a decision is perfected as it is practically and concretely applied. A lien can be judged to hold in some circumstances only if it's been "perfected"—that is, if its inherent requirements and procedures have all been drawn out of it and put into concrete action in a given place and at a given time. In printing, perfecting means printing the reverse side of a leaf on which one page has already been printed. In the process of perfecting, a book becomes itself, is realized. Realist perfecting follows a mundane, immanent logic. It tries to stay in the grain of historical reality, while employing the productive powers of language to move toward a comprehensive view. It thus embodies one mode of negotiating between positions "in" and "above" a mundane world, imagined or real.

Realist novelists are necessarily involved in one form or another of this process of fictional perfecting. Indeed, one could say that realist novelists create characters and situations so that they can be perfected. Their characteristic density of metonymic specification both enables and calls for perfecting. This might be seen as organicism run wild—novels are constructed so that they will grow their own interpretations—except that the connections we are called upon to make are themselves by no means "organic." The connection between Lydgate's soul and his furniture is not organic in any sense of the word. Nor is the connection between Sir Everard and his newsletter, though that connection can be called upon to support an ideology favorable to "organic society." Then too, perfecting calls for the collaboration of the reader, a collaboration in which one feels a pressure to make meaning in the mode of asymptotic approximation. Austen leads us to participate in the perfection of a class-based language so that it can embody with perfect adequacy a set of values that seems latent within it—values that, as Raymond Williams suggests, arise from, but are in the end irreducible to class ideology. But our feeling of linguistic exhilaration at her virtuosity is always shadowed by a recognition of effort and difficulty, so that the statement that "seldom, very seldom, does complete truth belong to any human disclosure" is an earned and integral part of the climax of *Emma*. Scott, through a variety of means, strives to perfect a different set of potentialities—the "ideal type" potentialities of past societies—by setting them in motion before us. With Jeanie Deans, for instance, he creates situations in which the historical Other speaks itself, acting out permutations and combinations of its potentialities that may never have had a chance to unfold in history itself. This speaking is perfected only when we help construct a voice that cannot be heard directly. Perfecting depends upon involving the reader in a hermeneutical enterprise.

Eliot's fiction follows the logic of perfecting, nowhere more forcefully than with its free indirect discourse, in which the narrative voice mingles with and perfects the voice of a character, and each phrase and sentence comes to seem saturated with a definitive meaning, perfectly realizing the character and situation at hand. Sometimes, this process produces what seem final, even totalized results. Thus Mr. Brooke is definitively captured in *Middlemarch* by the following perfecting of his motivations for retaining Will Ladislaw as his secretary, despite the urgings of his friends:

> It would have been highly inconvenient to him to part with Ladislaw at that time, when a dissolution might happen any day, and electors were to be convinced of the course by which the interests of the country would be best served. Mr. Brooke sincerely believed that this end could be secured by his own return to Parliament: he offered the forces of his mind honestly to the nation. (486)

The last sentence here has the effect of fixing Mr. Brooke's ingratiating muddle-headedness for time and eternity. It does so in a way characteristic of realism, by placing Brooke in the metonymical context of a cultural discourse—here, the discourse of political speeches, which have set words ringing in his head he is foolish enough to wish to realize in action. (The less specialized meanings of "honestly" suffice to reveal his fatuity.) The economy of method here can lead critics to find Eliot's narrator quietly and smotheringly domineering: there are few things more exasperating than being condemned by the words of your own mouth.[33] We can reply by noting the sentimentality inherent in supposing that what serves as a mind for characters (and people) like Mr. Brooke can't be summed up with precise, exhaustive rapidity. Perfecting the thoughts of such characters functions as a five-finger exercise; we're shown how the thing is done in simple terms, so that we can learn to appreciate and perhaps even to apply similar techniques to more complex cases. The narrator's easy mastery here need not imply that all aspects of reality can be rendered so transparently available to us, or betray a wish to install one or another ideology as "natural." The truth about a phenomenon like Mr. Brooke is a truth realism can claim to tell, simply.

When Eliot's free indirect discourse encounters subjects and situations of greater complexity, it invites us to participate in a more open process of understanding. After her traumatic break with Will Ladislaw and Dorothea's healing visit, Rosamond Vincy turns to her husband, whose reaction is described in the following terms:

> Poor Rosamond's vagrant fancy had come back terribly scourged— meek enough to nestle under the old despised shelter. And the shelter was still there: Lydgate had accepted his narrowed lot with sad resignation. He had chosen this fragile creature, and had taken the burthen of her life upon his arms. He must walk as he could, carrying that burthen pitifully. (800)

The passage concludes with what, in the first instance, we take to be Lydgate's own thoughts.[34] Yet it's also clear that the narrator is perfecting, not simply reproducing, the thoughts here. The word "burthen," for instance, is the narrator's, not Lydgate's, and its religious pathos and Wordsworthian echo give it the ring of external moral authority. To be sure, such

---

[33] Eliot's narrator provides the following commentary on Peter Featherstone: "If any one will here contend that there must have been traits of goodness in old Featherstone, I will not presume to deny this; but I must observe that goodness is of a modest nature, easily discouraged, and when much elbowed in early life by unabashed vices, is apt to retire into extreme privacy, so that it is more easily believed in by those who construct a selfish old gentleman theoretically, than by those who form the narrower judgments based on his personal acquaintance" (323–24). Mutatis mutandis, this will serve as a response to the objection that Eliot is violating Mr. Brooke's inner complexity.

[34] Suzanne Graver (*George Eliot and Community*, 142) seems right in suggesting that this passage acts as a record of what Lydgate understands to be his own situation.

language may suggest that Lydgate, like Mr. Brooke, is using a general cultural discourse to clothe his thoughts and feelings: the poetic, biblical ring of the phrases evokes a supportive aura of quasi-religious, dutiful compassion. But the force of the language here transcends the purpose of depicting ideology at work: though Lydgate may or may not have read Wordsworth and gives no indications of devoutness, the passage invokes positive, indeed peremptory ethical standards.

It's at just this point that one can accuse Eliot's narration of a coercive totalization that seeks to make contingent political and ideological forces seem natural and inevitable. Her free indirect discourse, one might argue, smuggle such values—and worse, a sense that these values are inevitable—into the novel in the guise of what a character learns about "life," blending her voice with the character's the better to conceal its ideological designs. Raymond Williams finds in the phrase "sad resignation" a way to characterize the affective mode he believes Eliot creates to control her later fiction, as social concerns are recoded into personal concerns, and a probing awareness of human (and class) separation gives way to a mellow acceptance of what is made to seem the human condition.[35] "Sad resignation," according to Williams, hides a quietist turn toward individual inwardness that can support the status quo only by rendering invisible the real forces that might disrupt it.

In my view, the passage opens up in other directions. In Eliot, when we're dealing with characters more complex than Mr. Brooke, perfecting brings to light situations that are themselves likely to contain the seeds of self-contestation. I would claim there is an inherent tendency in historicist realism to contest the ideological homogenization and stultification Williams imputes to "sad resignation," and others have imputed to Eliot's narrative arrangements in general. In my first chapter, I suggested that critics have taken antithetical views concerning whether historicist realism is dispersed or totalizing because they have paid attention to only one pole of its constitutive tension between seeing history whole and honoring its concrete complexity. Here I want to suggest that novelists who maintain

---

[35] "From the social history, which had been seen as determining but as narrowly determining, there is a contraction [at the end of *The Mill on the Floss*] of sympathy to the exposed and separated individual, in whom the only action of value, of any full human feeling, is located. And then what in *The Mill on the Floss* is an active, desperate isolation becomes, in a new way of seeing, a sad resignation." In Eliot's subsequent works, we find "evidence of growing maturity and control," but this is "a control, precisely, based on sad resignation" (173–74). Williams uses the phrase "sad resignation" repeatedly in his chapter on Eliot after it appears in this passage, but he never refers overtly to its occurrence in *Middlemarch,* and he exempts that novel from what he takes to be the general tendency in Eliot's career to turn away from depicting how conditions of economic scarcity structure the power relations between upper and lower classes.

this tension transcend the "bad" totalization that's often ascribed to realism. Realism's search for metonymical connections in the world, and its attempt to forge a rhetorical relationship with the reader, mean that, when it has gathered steam, it is unlikely to settle into a seamless, transparent ideological totality. This is not to endorse the liberal view of realism I've associated with J. P. Stern, which celebrates realism for affirming human freedom by refusing to see larger patterns in history and society. The grain of the realist world can be crossed by many paths, but there is a grain. The imaginative oscillation between positions in and above fictional worlds suggests limberness and the existence of a multiplicity of viewpoints, but it is an oscillation in search of the truth. Much of the affective pleasure of historicist realism comes from its attempts to present us with materials that interest us just because they don't fit our normal notions—with glimpses of the Other—but it presents those glimpses as knowable and authentic. Realism is a restless mode whose energy is neither exhausted nor contained by endings, but it believes that the modes of processing historical experience it invites us to learn point to an end.

Let's return to Lydgate and his "burthen." The narrator's free indirect discourse, as we've seen, reveals Lydgate at work, drawing upon the ethical discourses available to him to clothe the nakedness of his unenviable lot with Rosamond. Given the particularities of his situation, this seems understandable. As he admits to Dorothea, he has lost trust in himself: his admirable capacity for care and compassion, however, is something he can keep. Even on this level, however, misgiving and resistance arise. "Sad resignation" may be the best Lydgate can do, but how good is it? Are ugly realities being clothed with fine-sounding terms that preclude clarity and the possibility of a real solution? Is this the underside of the studied hopefulness we've seen the narrator in *Daniel Deronda* voice concerning the potentialities of Gwendolyn Harleth? And can we—and should we—bear with the picture of Rosamond painted here? She may be "frail" at the moment, because her egotism has been badly shaken, but over the course of the novel, she has proved anything but a fragile creature requiring pitiful carriage. Is Lydgate simply digging himself more deeply into an ideology of gender she has shown herself wonderfully adroit at manipulating to her advantage? In his sad acceptance, is he perhaps exhibiting the same "pitiable infirmity of will" he earlier deplored in Farebrother (187)? And so on. I do not offer these objections as striking discoveries that others have missed. In the wake of feminism, I find it hard to imagine readers to whom all of this and more hasn't occurred. My purpose is to suggest that the manner in which the text helps to produce such doubts has implications for our understanding of how realism itself operates.

"He must walk as he could, carrying that burthen pitifully." The narrator's stake in the "must" here deepens our resistance. Why must Lydgate bear his burthen? Well, one reason involves something like authorial revenge. Lydgate is being punished for his trivializing view of women. The irony of the notion that Rosamond is essentially fragile would make the punishment seem positively gleeful in a less serious context. But the sources of the narrator's leap to the imperative go deeper. Who that cares much about George Eliot's novels can fail to hear, at least briefly, echoes in the announcement that Lydgate "must" bear the burden of Rosamond, must stick to his lot and his place beside her? Maggie Tulliver, too, must stay near the mill on the Floss; Gwendolyn Harleth must have a home endeared to her by childhood memories, even though she doesn't. Eliot's insistence on staying in your place is never entirely explained. It has connections with other motifs in the thought informing the novels, but it remains enigmatic and excessive, with an energy that is simply there, perturbing the rest of the system. The insistence on staying in a known place has, for example, a relationship with the doctrine of sympathy, but you can't deduce its peculiar force from that doctrine, nor can you deduce that doctrine from it. A nostalgia this strong for a world in which you are forced to stay in your place betrays an intense uneasiness that we are approaching a point in history where one place is as good as another, and no ties bind. This fear marks the historicity of Eliot and of her narrator; for the world seen through historicist eyes, as we've repeatedly seen, gains its form, inevitability, and pathos from lacking any recourse to the dignity and finality of philosophical or theological necessity—a pathos that puts notions of what any of us "must" do in a peculiar and difficult light. A profound (and I believe entirely intended) effect of Eliot's insistence on staying in one's place is, then, to mark the historicity of the world of her novels, and of the one she shares with us, a weight that transforms its seemingly definitive pronouncements into attempts to cope. If we listen carefully enough, we hear the weight of history in her narrative voice.

Staying in your place is an impossible injunction to honor wholly if you take it personally, for you can't really know that you're in your place if you are only and therefore fully there. I suggested in the previous chapter that in *The Talisman*, Scott takes great imaginative pleasure in creating a fantasy world, both for a privileged character or two and for his narrator, in which moving between positions in and above a situation is simply exhilarating. Eliot finds it hard to allow her characters or her narrator this sort of freedom with a clear conscience. No doubt Eliot's fierce insistence on attaching so many of her characters to their places stems both from considered intellectual roots and from the guilt of an Evangelical country

girl who grew up to be an agnostic cosmopolitan; it may also reflect uneasiness at her narrator's own masterful ubiquity. The oddness, in a sense
the quaintness, of Eliot's insistence that it is good for her characters to
stay in place is that this insistence offers, by way of producing a series of
utopian vignettes (such as those Maggie Tulliver imaginatively produces
or tries to produce for herself in the closing pages of *The Mill on the Floss*),
static answers to a problem that Eliot knows can be met only on the run,
by the use of narrative expedients. We are shown Mary Garth's face as
the epitome of generations of women who have remained in their places,
and we momentarily forget we are walking past and beyond her, part of
a moving crowd—and so is Mary Garth herself, in the action of the novel.

Eliot's voicing of Lydgate's thoughts, then, bears the weight of historical circumstance. Her use of free indirect discourse reveals much about
the nature of reality and our situation in history as construed by historicist realism. It arises in response to a modernity in which meanings and
values must be unfolded from our place in history. If it appears to achieve
a crystalline perfection requiring no effort on our part, this is deceptive,
for we are called to participate in its realization and to respond to its implications all along. In all, it represents a remarkable expression of the realist habit of mind, a limit case of the historicist balancing of local and
global consciousness. Realism doesn't always work in this register. It
does, however, work cumulatively, if we allow it to. The acts of attention
evoked by Austen and Scott and Eliot can create, if we enter into them, a
readiness to encounter subsequent unpredictable but cognizable movements of reality.

Historicist realism reaches a culmination in such passages as the one
we've been considering. Given enough time, visions of the world exhaust
themselves, as do aesthetic forms and accomplishments. Major realisms,
however, do not lose their grip until the world changes radically for
human beings, and such changes occur infrequently. If we are attentive to
its grain, nineteenth-century historicist realism has a staying power that
exceeds what we would expect from the standard literary critical discourse about it. If our own world had really altered enough to make historicist realism irrelevant, could we recognize it? Which is not to say that
things haven't changed or that bridges don't need to be built. In my own
view, the realism I have been exploring is still powerful enough to make
worthwhile the effort of hermeneutical recovery involving not only individual works but the general habit of mind they invite us to share. The
discovery of such continuities makes historicist realism *our* realism,
which is why perfecting a connection with a great, seemingly superseded
realist literary critic of the past is of exemplary importance for my project
in this book. My return to Auerbach attempts to model the relationship

we can maintain with historicist realism, by developing from his work implications and conclusions to answer concerns and questions that were not altogether his, to meet the needs of a moment, our moment, which he did not quite imagine in his talk of the "approaching unification and simplification," but which nonetheless has a living connection with his own time.

Powerful arguments have been offered to suggest that we have indeed turned a corner, entering a reality for which historicist realism can have at best a symptomatic interest. For those who are persuaded that historicist realism is no longer our realism, I hope this study may still have some value. If the corner has been well and truly turned, it should no longer be necessary for new intellectual and aesthetic forms to assert themselves by obscuring their distinguished predecessors. For such readers, this book is offered as a way of freeing realism from serving simply as a defining Other of new, more vital things.

Afterword

As the twentieth century draws to a close, our intellectual and cultural lives have become permeated with suspicion. A hermeneutics of suspicion underlies much of the most vital literary criticism of recent years, and the practice of political criticism has come to be largely identified with it. Sixty years ago, Yeats announced that things thought too long can be no longer thought, but this ringing statement seems questionable. The real problem is that things thought too long are thought too easily. (Which of course may be what he meant—that they are not really thought at all.) Suspicion, too, can be thought too long.

For anyone who believes we are radically historical in our being, however, the notion that a strong current of human thought, even if it becomes automatic, is simply a mistake must itself be suspect. We find ourselves in a place that has been partly made by the hermeneutics of suspicion, and it is ours. I would be distressed though not entirely surprised if the reader were to take anything I've said as simply dismissive of the suspicious positions I contest. Not surprised, because one of the things too often thought these days is that if one engages with the dominant forms of political criticism with anything but acceptance, one must be motivated by a wish to turn back the clock and wash those forms away. Political criticism is by now well enough entrenched that we do not owe it an unthinking solidarity. I have learned from the positions I contest, but one of the things I've learned is that they haven't done justice to realist fiction.

I believe that we have come to a point where, in literary criticism and also in politics, the hermeneutics of suspicion has become a stumbling block. We need to find paths around or through it. How you go about dissenting from a tradition without dismissing it remains a thorny problem, and I'm not entirely satisfied in my own attempts to solve it. I've described a certain style of criticism as "sublime." I suppose that some note of derision must attach itself to any such label; I hope that respect for the power of the sublime lingers in mine. Who would wish away the insights into Austen peculiar to our times? Who, indeed, would wish away the writing of Walter Benjamin? It's obvious enough that my own commentary on Austen is informed by the views of those whose procedures I contest.

A promising route through and beyond the hermeneutics of suspicion is offered by the work of Jürgen Habermas. Habermas himself mounts a sufficiently suspicious objection to Gadamer's hermeneutics of merging and acceptance, but in the end what matters most may be that he sees the issues between them as a problem, instead of viewing a mode of objecting as a method that solves the problem. Habermas takes with utmost seriousness the fact that being situated in modernity means generating our values from the place in which we find ourselves. I believe that meditating on the workings of the nineteenth-century realist novel can help us in this endeavor. We must at any rate stop ignoring the origins, indeed the existence, of the values we use to mount political critiques of literature and of society. Amanda Anderson's commentary on the "cryptonormativism" of the suspicious, referred to earlier in this book, seems very much to the point. One reason why realism matters is that it provides a model of how we might go about construing the world in a way that gives us a reliable enough sense of our place within it to facilitate discovering and discussing values and norms.

It is easier to know what to avoid than what to embrace. I nonetheless venture to believe that Habermas's stress on the norm of the "ideal speech situation" offers a powerful way for us to make sense of our situation within the confines of history. This book is largely concerned with imagining what it would be like to encounter realist fiction in an atmosphere of uncoerced speech. In the first part of the work I argue that nothing prevents us from achieving such a relationship with realism, or prevents realism from creating such a relationship with the world in which an evolving sense of what is real and valuable can emerge. In the ideal speech situation, the constraints of power are wholly (and counterfactually) absent. Comparing this ideal situation with our own can help us to recognize the ways in which power inflects our discussions and actions—and the ways in which it does not. We can take the power of ideology seriously without swallowing it whole. By denying that realism must be malignly totalistic in my first chapter, I seek to leave room for some maneuvering that isn't choreographed by power. In a similar way, my second chapter makes room for significant encounters between novels, readers, and an objective world, and my third chapter precipitates a theory of the workings of realism through a hermeneutic encounter with Auerbach. In all of this, I try to escape the picture of a world of passive things onto which we simply project meanings, and a collectivity of passive readers onto whom ideology simply projects itself. The regulative goal of discovery through discussion has been very much in my mind as I have attempted to conceive of better alternatives.

My conception of realism is fundamentally involved with what I have defined as historicist metonymy. This involvement generates what I hope is a productive suspicion of the timeless proclivities of metaphor, which translates into a questioning of what I have called the critical sublime (a mode of criticism that discovers, in a flash, unexpected identities between disparate objects). In discussing Austen, Scott, and Eliot, I have been much concerned with formulating and testing the strengths and limitations of realist metonymy. Can following up on the metonymical links Austen creates lead us to discover areas of play in the highly organized linguistic and social situations of her novels? If she isn't dealing in the imaginative sublime, what sources of imaginative energy does she tap, and to what ends? To what extent does Scott's voice dominate his metonymical representation of history? Does it leave a place for other voices from other times? Does the complex texture of his historical awareness include a recognition of the tenuousness of his attempts to make peace with what history brings? These questions all resonate with the notion that realism opens up the possibility of multi-voiced discussions and opposing perspectives. In my final chapter, the relationship Eliot's narrative voice creates with us as readers is shown to rest upon her vision of what it means to live in history. For Eliot, the germinal issue for this study is a central and explicit concern: how can we develop norms and values from within our own historical situations? Aspects of this problem live in the realist imaginings of Austen and Scott as well. These are works that repay our efforts to engage them in an ongoing conversation. My aim has been to indicate that such a conversation is both conceivable and desirable, and to suggest some of the conclusions we might draw from it.

Appendix: On Tropes and Master Tropes

The trope of metonymy, I have contended, provides a convenient way of describing the habit of mind central to realist fiction. It also raises epistemological dilemmas. When it is suggested that the "master tropes" of metaphor, metonymy, synecdoche, and irony provide us with "possible alternative paradigms of explanation" and that they do so as a matter of "linguistic usage itself," the specter of a linguistic determinism of thought lurks in the background, in which these tropes would provide alternative grids that allow us to identify objects and imagine them in a rigidly preordained set of ways.[1] I believe that the tropes have considerable cognitive power, but not of this kind. In this Appendix, I shall give a number of reasons for denying tropes a determining power over our cognition of the world, and I'll explore ways in which they do help us make sense of the world.

The master tropes are procedural, not substantive: they give us directions for how to make connections, but they don't of themselves predict results. Their operation parallels the operation of reference, which we saw in Chapter 2 is potentially productive of new meanings. They can in this regard be seen as particular inflections of our general referential powers. We can add that the master tropes produce results only when embedded in a given set of beliefs about reality. They are not indepen-

---

[1] Hayden White, *Metahistory* (Baltimore: Johns Hopkins University Press, 1973), 36; hereafter cited in the text.

dent enough to make our worlds for us. Different tropes point us toward different kinds of relationships between entities, but what counts as an example of a given kind of relationship depends upon our prior commitments with regard to reality—upon our beliefs about what is real, whether knowledge about the real is possible, and if so, how it can be best obtained. I've given a striking example of this dependence in my third chapter, where I show that both figural realism and historicist realism, despite their very different metaphysical and ontological assumptions, can lay claim to the trope of metonymy. Our assumptions about reality result from a variety of disparate, contingent forces that cannot be credibly imagined as direct effects of the built-in powers of any single aspect of linguistic usage. They arise from traditions of thought and practice; they involve interactions with the powers, latent and apparent, operative in nature and society. The master tropes may play their part in these interactions, but they do not control them. This isn't of course to say that a given metaphysic will find each of the master tropes equally congenial. Hayden White's talk of "elective affinities" in such matters is very much to the point (29). The master tropes do not dominate our ways of making sense of reality; they do provide useful ways of conceiving of different possible relationships *within* a given view of reality.

In Chapter 3, I briefly suggested that metonymy from its own point of view is a very different entity from metonymy viewed from the point of view of metaphor. I now want to generalize this insight, by suggesting that in any system of master tropes, there always exists a master of masters (whose status is usually hidden away from sight) that determines the ways the other tropes are characterized, and in doing so reveals the orientation characteristic of that particular system as a whole.[2] Our prior metaphysical commitments, I'm suggesting, will lead us to favor one of the four master tropes: this super-trope will then redefine the other master tropes in its own image—or, more precisely, in the image imprinted upon it by our metaphysical and ontological commitments. And so we find ourselves in the familiar situation in which a hidden binary opposition emerges to organize a set of distinctions, and then promotes one term at the expense of the others.

Two of the most interesting writers on tropes, Kenneth Burke and Hayden White (who draws on Burke), seem to escape the problems that so easily arise in such bipolar thinking, by producing systems incorporating not just metaphor and metonymy, but the four master tropes we have already identified. Yet in both cases, the four-part system is in fact gener-

[2] Compare Hans Kellner's remarks on the "Over-Trope" in his valuable article "A Bedrock of Order: Hayden White's Linguistic Humanism," *History and Theory*, Beiheft 19 (1980), pp. 15–29.

ated by precisely the sort of dichotomy it seeks to evade. For both Burke and White, there is a hidden master of masters among the tropes and a scapegoated antitype of that trope, and the system as a whole arises from their opposition. We might suspect that for Burke (who uses the four tropes to supplement his more fundamental apparatus of the "five key terms of dramatism"), irony would turn out to be the master of masters, for it comes last on his list and draws up all the others into itself.[3] In fact, however, the ultimate though hidden master trope for Burke is his version of synecdoche, which is based on the relationship between microcosm and macrocosm. Burke imagines (and defines) all the other tropes under the aegis of this vision of synecdoche, and this is why each trope can, in his account, slide into the next one in a smooth ascending spiral. In its fully developed form, Burke's system might seem to avoid the use of a binary opposition, since Burke's version of synecdoche appears neither to require nor to allow negatives to its positive: it asks only for partners to join in the dance it founds. But in fact, there is a "negative" trope in hiding even here, which turns out to be the trope of metonymy. Burke has recourse to the tropes in the first place in order to reveal the inadequacy of what he terms metonymical "reduction," which in his view implies a one-way explanation of the nonphysical by the physical. Metonymy here serves as a stand-in for those intellectual operations Burke most disliked—behaviorist psychology, crude materialist metaphysics, and in general the "scientism" that attempts to reduce human thought and behavior to numbers. Behind Burke's four-part system, then, there's a struggle between a trope that, in its unredeemed form, is radically reductionist and scientistic, and the more complex, two-way, microcosmic-macrocosmic relationships incarnate in Burke's notion of synecdoche. In the final system, most of the signs of this struggle are effaced, as even metonymy is reclothed in a more synecdochic garb.

A similar dynamic underlies the work of Hayden White. For White, our hypotheses (themselves based on tropes) efficiently determine how we slice up experience into coherent units of perception, and there can be no real translation between different modes of slicing. One tropically based mode of viewing the world can never be disproved by another, because each mode constructs its own confirming evidence. Some have seen White's vision as nihilistic in its relativism; in fact, in his own hands it becomes sternly ethical. If we accept White's vision, we can no longer suppose that the tropes will reveal an external logic in history that will make our political and moral decisions for us. The logic of history will not tell

---

[3] Kenneth Burke, "Introduction: The Five Key Terms of Dramatism" and "Appendix D: The Four Master Tropes," in *A Grammar of Motives* (1945; Berkeley, University of California Press, 1969).

us what cause to espouse, because our view of history itself flows from the trope we favor; as a result, "the best reasons for being a Marxist are moral ones, just as the best reasons for being a Liberal, Conservative, or Anarchist are moral ones" (284). Such a principled relativism is, however, itself informed by the master trope of irony, which White revealingly suggests is "transideological" (38) in a way the other tropes are not. This is not to say that, were White to make an ethical choice among systems, it would have to be a choice of irony; it does, however, suggest that the way in which White conceives of *all* the tropes in his system reflects a basic allegiance to irony as his founding intellectual operation.[4] It is precisely the element of voluntarism injected into White's system by making irony "transideological" that allows him *not* to choose irony as the basis for ethical and political judgments.

In White as in Burke, the promotion of one trope as master comes at the expense of another, and a hidden binary opposition between the master trope and the scapegoated one informs his system as a whole. The trope White's system strives to disarm is, again, metonymy.[5] For if metonymical connections, and especially connections of cause and effect, could make good their claims to explain the world and to influence actors in it, then the power of the tropes to organize all aspects of reality for us in advance would be threatened. Reality might, through its chains of causality, impinge on us and alter our views. The best reason to be a Marxist or anarchist might turn out to involve not simply a Pascalian wager, but a genuine and objective knowledge arising from interaction with the workings of society. We might then be able to refer to a real world, and to produce

[4]   Irony would appear to be the trope White would most like to transcend: see, for instance, *Metahistory*, 433–34, and more recently, his assertion in *The Content of the Form* (Baltimore: Johns Hopkins University Press, 1987), 184, that for Hegel, Nietzsche, and Ricoeur "the overcoming of irony was the central problem of a distinctively human thought." But this does not make irony any less the central, mastering category for him: one sign of its power is that it defines the problems that really matter. As we saw in Chapter 4, White is "inclined to think" that a "visionary politics," the only kind of politics he considers capable of effecting true liberation, can proceed only from the assumption that history "makes no sense whatsoever" (*The Content of the Form*, 73). Is this his ultimate reason for rejecting the sense metonymy would make of history?
[5]   A telltale sign of White's attempt to foreclose metonymical possibilities involves his use of the philosopher Stephen C. Pepper's *World Hypotheses* (Berkeley: University of California Press, 1942). White brilliantly draws on everything Pepper has to offer that would support an ironic relativism arising from the point of view of single-observer epistemology. He ignores, however, a crucial part of Pepper's conceptual system—the part that describes how knowledge can be produced by groups of people who pool their observations to create a kind of knowledge supported by what he calls multiplicative corroboration (47–48). Pepper's concept of multiplicative corroboration is, to be sure, heavily informed by a positivistic notion of scientific inquiry: his favored example involves a series of observers pointing to the position of needles on dials. Yet, as the example of Habermas reminds us, a social model of knowledge needn't be so restricted in scope.

knowledge about it by our acts of reference. To be sure, this would not involve a situation in which knowledge about the world was so "transparent" and conclusive that it made our choices for us. Ambiguities and opacities would doubtless persist; our choice of a political position would continue to rest, in part, on ethical grounds.

In my own use of the master tropes, I do not follow Burke and White in specifying four, but return instead to the familiar dichotomy between metaphor and metonymy. My justification may already be apparent from my demonstration of how, in both Burke and White, the definition of a hidden "master" master trope controls the characterization of the other three tropes as well: instead of a four-part system, we have a set of terms that derive from the workings of a binary opposition plus a value judgment. I choose to fall back to the metaphor-metonymy dyad, then, because I believe that it is merely obscured, not superseded, by four-trope systems.

That I should discover the "bad" trope for both Burke and White to be metonymy, the trope I myself associate with realism, might seem to reflect a certain paranoia, induced perhaps by the persistence and variety of the attacks on realism I've documented in the first part of this book. I prefer to consider the recurrent resistance against metonymy as a sign that my association of realism with metonymy is correct. White and Burke are reacting to something real about metonymy and the claims of realism it underwrites. For the opposition between metaphor and metonymy involves a distinction between mental operations that work with (or, as I've argued in my chapter on Austen, *through*) the grain of our social and historical reality, and those that work against it or transcend it. Metaphor promises artistic creativity and autonomy. With metaphor, we need not replicate the lines of causality informing the world history has made; instead, we make our own connections (which, to be sure, can then be further valorized by the claim that they penetrate to the essence of reality).[6] The political and ethical senses of the word "realism" soon come into play here, with those who prefer metaphorical modes of thought playing the role of "visionaries" to the metonymical "realists."

To be sure, there are ways of defining metaphor and metonymy that reverse the association of metaphor with the creation of areas of freedom from real-world constraints. Jean Laplanche, for example, has shown that in the work of Lacan, there is a bias in favor of metonymy. Lacan, Laplanche points out, demotes metaphor because (given the way the rest of his system operates), it's *metaphor* that threatens to link the linguistic sig-

---

[6] On different reasons for valuing metaphor, see Jonathan Culler, "The Turns of Metaphor," in *The Pursuit of Signs* (Ithaca: Cornell University Press, 1981), 188–209.

nifier to the real world (in the way that, for most other systems, metonymy does).[7] Similarly, de Man describes and values metonymy as autonomous from real-world determinations, through an implicit "inclination to identify metonymy with the code, with language itself as a system of arbitrary signs."[8] Yet even in the speculations of such theorists, I would argue, both metaphor and metonymy are, as in Burke and White, defined from the point of view of metaphor, in a way that tends to empty metonymy of substantial cognitive force. Where these theorists differ from Burke is in valuing a "merely" contiguous, materialist (Burke would say the mechanistic) version of metonymy, instead of deploring it. We're left, then, with a situation in which even those who value metonymy do so under a definition that robs it of what I'm claiming realist fiction depends upon it to provide—a way of bringing into focus and following real-world connections.

What would happen if we turned the tables? What if we attempted to imagine the master tropes from the point of view of a robust, realist and historicist metonymy? How would our characterization of the other tropes shift? The vision of metonymy that informs this book would produce the following results. Irony, from the point of view of metonymy, would become the ultimate expression of the workings of metonymy, involving a developing dialectic based upon metonymical, "real-world" relations: it would serve as a way of figuring the workings of historical process itself. Metaphor and synecdoche, by contrast, would assume the roles of the disreputable, mystified opposites of metonymy and irony. Synecdoche, given its associations with macrocosms and microcosms, would be particularly suspect, because of the way its underlying metaphysic recalls an earlier and now intellectually discredited world. (Alternatively, one could redefine synecdoche as involving the creation of a metonymic model through the summation of a series of acts of metonymical representation, not a summarizing model based on the relationship between macrocosms and microcosms, in which case it would become respectable again.) And the consequences of promoting metonymy would extend even further than this, with metonymy becoming a "master" trope in more senses than one. If you say that metonymical or "real-world" relations are fundamental, you're implying that there is a real world, with a determinate, metonymical structure, which is knowable or at least representable. To make a version of metonymy (or

---

[7]   Jean Laplanche, in *Life and Death in Psychoanalysis* (1970), trans. Jeffrey Mehlman (Baltimore: Johns Hopkins University Press, 1976), 127–39, provides perhaps the most balanced view of the claims of metonymy and metaphor currently available.

[8]   Culler, "The Turns of Metaphor," 199–200.

any other trope) one's dominant trope is thus, to borrow a phrase from the Old New Critics, to make a choice of worlds.

Is it also to make a choice of political ideologies? That both Marx and the Tory Scott may be plausibly ranged under the sign of metonymy should cast doubt on any direct derivation of ideology from tropical deep structures, even if viewed in terms of the metaphysical and ontological presuppositions with which they are intertwined.[9] We may imagine society as constituted by an intricate web of causal links, but the way in which we conceive of those links—their number, their robustness or fragility, above all their likely effect on individual subjects—will make a difference, will determine among other things whether we think of the links as heavy fetters to be broken or as fragile bonds to be strengthened. Yet the choice of master trope nevertheless matters, because certain kinds of questions are much more likely to arise, and to be thinkable, in one tropical system than in another. In particular, the level or levels of generality on which we can easily focus will shift. A metonymical vision will tend to focus on relations between subjects: it will find the ultimate human reality in the realm of the social, which provides the only field in which metonymical relations can fully extend themselves. Systems based on the other tropes are likely to resist the primacy of this field, less propitious to their own claims. We may have here an explanation of what Engels identified as "the triumph of realism" in the novels of Balzac, as Lukács after him did in the novels of Scott. An interested reader can evoke from the works of both Scott and Balzac objects of attention which allow metonymical analysis full play.

[9] White (*Metahistory*, 281–330) finds in Marx a fertile attempt to bridge metonymical and synecdochic modes. I've already argued at length in these pages that metonymy is fundamental to Scott's mind and art.

Index

Althusser, Louis, 22, 35
American Graffiti (film), 18–20
Anderson, Amanda, 174, 189, 266
Auerbach, Erich
  on Dante, 93, 95–98, 112, 115, 118–20, 122
  on figural realism, 92–99, 103, 107
  on Flaubert's "mystical-realistic in-
    sight," 41, 112
  as a hermeneutical object, 262–63
  on his own historicity, 246
  on historicism, 96, 113–14
  as narrator, 5, 91–92, 109–23, 115,
    130–31
  "randomness" in, 120n32
  on realism after Dante, 96–99
  on Scott's historicism, 169
  mentioned, 4, 200
Austen, Jane
  Emma, 144, 146, 257
  Mansfield Park, 157–58
  Northanger Abbey, 135, 147–61, 163, 165,
    178, 253
  Persuasion, 108, 126–27, 160–66, 230
  Pride and Prejudice, 118
  areas of freedom in, 148, 152, 157,
    161–62, 165, 209, 252, 267
  and distinctions, 147–65, 227, 267
  mentioned, 6, 63, 171, 218, 231, 238, 252,
    266

Austin, J. L., 74, 82–90
  as narrator, 86, 122
Avni, Ora, 64–65

Bakhtin, Mikhail, 29–30
Balzac, Honoré de, 5, 7, 12, 23, 75, 96, 123,
  169, 275
  Sarrasine, 100–101
Barthes, Roland, 8, 32, 53, 76
  S/Z, 22, 72, 91, 100–101
  on "naturalization," 9, 21
  on Verne, 21–22
Beer, Gillian, 142
Belsey, Catherine, 54, 58
Benjamin, Walter, 135, 266
  Theses on the Philosophy of History,
    135–37, 139–43
  on historicism, 136
Benveniste, Emile, 71
Booth, Wayne, 50, 187n28
Boswell, James, 201
Bourdieu, Pierre, 138
Brecht, Bertold, 7, 17, 22–23, 28
Burke, Kenneth, 101, 270–74
Butler, Marilyn, 135–36, 143

Caruth, Cathy, 67
Cleishbotham, Jedediah (schoolmaster),
  59–61, 67–69

Complicity, 133, 141, 146–47, 181, 202–3
Comte, Auguste, 225

Dante. *See* Auerbach, Erich: on Dante
Davidson, Donald, 106–7
Davis, Lennard, 27, 253
Defoe, Daniel, 49
de Man, Paul, 66, 74, 274
Descombes, Vincent, 53, 58, 65–66
Detachment, problem of, 20, 115, 242. *See also* Austen, Jane: areas of freedom in; Eliot, George: and staying in your place; Eliot, George: and transcendence; Historicism: and knowledge of another age or culture; Historicism: and the loss of organic ties to one's culture; Narrative Voice: "in" or "above" the world; Reading and "the grain"; Realist Fiction: and action; Realist Fiction: and the will; Scott, Sir Walter: narrative/cultural embeddedness and transcendence in
Dickens, Charles, 34
    Bleak House, 23, 26, 51, 79–80
Distinction-making and power, 25–27. *See also* Austen, Jane: and distinctions
Dostoevsky, Fyodor, 29
Dummett, Michael, 69
DuPlessis, Rachel Blau, 128

Eagleton, Terry, 16–17, 23, 135–36, 142
Ecclesiasticus, 220–21, 256
Eliot, George
    Adam Bede, 49, 219–22, 225–29, 256
    Daniel Deronda, 246–52, 255, 260–61
    Felix Holt, 222–25, 231
    Middlemarch, 59n25, 129, 226–27, 229, 231–36, 245–46, 254–62
    The Mill on the Floss, 261–62
    Romola, 222, 254
    Scenes of Clerical Life, 240–46, 251
    Silas Marner, 227
    and the everyday, 51–52
    external representation in, 219–25
    historicist ethics in, 251
    and historicity, 162, 167, 178
    human interiority in, 225–36, 242–44
    narrator in, 17, 220, 236–62, 267
    and staying in your place, 261–62
    and transcendence, 242, 262
    mentioned, 28, 168, 170–71, 217
Emergence, doctrine of, 189
Engels, Friedrich, 12n15, 27, 123, 275

Epistemology
    experience as flux, 24n27, 102–3, 138
    fixed-frame, 121
    single-observer, 36, 57, 71, 79–80, 87–88, 120n32, 272n5

Foucauldian criticism, 23–24, 27, 32–34
Fielding, Henry, 43, 63, 188
Flaubert, Gustave, 41, 97–98, 112
    Madam Bovary, 61–63, 96
Flew, Antony, 87–88
Frazer, J. G., 111–12
Free Indirect Discourse (FID), 117–21, 215, 235, 248, 257–60, 262
Frege, Gottlob, 60, 69, 76n47

Gadamer, Hans-Georg, 190n32, 266
Gallie, W. B., 86–87
Gaskell, Elizabeth, 49
Genette, Gérard, 223
Goethe, Johann Wolfgang von, 185

Habermas, Jürgen, xi, 4, 88, 174, 272n5
    on Benjamin, 140–41, 143, 148
    versus Gadamer, 190n32, 266
    on modernity, 35–36, 97, 180, 255–56
Hall, Stuart, on "articulation," 178
Harding, D. W., 144
Hardy, Thomas, 130
Heath, Stephen, 16
Hegel, G. W. F., 4, 35–36, 40n1, 97, 140, 145, 168
Historicism
    and contingency, 102–3, 261
    enters the novel, 5–7, 107–8, 165–66, 168
    and gender, 254
    and human interiority, 108, 165
    and knowledge of another age or culture, 91, 121, 125, 130–31, 188, 214, 226–27, 237, 260
    and the loss of organic ties to one's culture, 162, 165, 181
    and memory, 165
    and metonymy, 103–4, 113, 229
    and "providential history," 131
    and subject-formation, 162
    tendency toward exoticism, 225
    texture (particularity) versus structure in, 16, 32, 44, 189
    See also Auerbach, Erich; Benjamin, Walter
Historicism, the New, 5n2
Hume, David, 139

Jakobson, Roman, 8–9, 102–3
James, Henry, 169
Jameson, Fredric, 27–29, 179
Johnson, Claudia, 135–38

Kant, Immanuel, 29, 58
Kripke, Saul, 69

Lacan, Jacques, 16, 19, 273
Lanser, Susan Sniader, 252–54
Laplanche, Jean, 273–74
Leavis, F. R., 228–29
Levine, George, 24, 71
Lodge, David, 8–9
Lubbock, Percy, 50
Lukács, Georg
    versus Brecht, 7, 28
    on the development of realism, 5–6,
        107–8, 169
    on modernism, 6–7
    on "necessary anachronism," 185
    and the reader, 34–35
    on realism and totality, 11–16, 24
    on realist representation and history,
        22–23, 44–45, 99, 106
    on Zola, 75
    mentioned, 27, 30–32, 49, 275

Macaulay, Thomas Babbington, 110–12,
        115, 130
    on Scott, 111
MacCabe, Colin, 17–20, 23n26, 76n47
MacDiarmid, Hugh, 183
Macherey, Pierre, 21–23, 32–34
Mandelbaum, Maurice, 131
Mann, Thomas, 75
Marx, Karl, 27, 178, 275
Metonymy, 101–9, 137, 166, 188, 229, 260,
        267, 269–75
    "dead metonymy," 200
    versus metaphor, 232–33
Mill, John Stuart, 232
Miller, D. A., 23–27, 253
Miller, Nancy K., 128
Ms. (magazine), 138

Narrative Voice
    as gendered, 252–55
    as historicized, 238–52, 261
    "in" or "above" the world, 115–22,
        185–90, 251, 260–61
    "narrator's privilege," the, 52, 174n8,
        188, 237

as productive over time, 189
as suspect, 8, 176

"Optative," the, 193, 251–52, 256

Pavel, Thomas, 54–55
"Perfecting," 256–59, 262
Petrey, Sandy, 71, 73–79, 84–85, 88
Pinch, Adela, 126–27
Plots and plotting in realism
    endings do not fix a narrative's mean-
        ing, 122, 130, 134, 160
    as energizing, rhetorical, and instru-
        mental, 109, 114, 126–31, 134, 142,
        155–56, 160
    marriage plot, 132–38, 164–66
    "story-telling" by characters, 128–29,
        133, 160–63
    as templates, 128–29, 131, 133, 164, 176
    See also Providential history/narrative
Popper, Karl, 131
Procedural versus substantive thinking,
        xi–xii, 211
Providential history/narrative, 56, 99,
        109–15, 122–23, 130, 209, 252, 256
Putnam, Hilary, 69–70, 77, 177

Radcliffe, Ann: *The Italian,* 234n13
Rader, Ralph W., 129
Readers
    active readers are central to realism, 30,
        109, 134, 212, 216, 235, 253, 257
    and the marriage plot, 132
    neglected or denigrated in accounts of
        realism, 19–20, 26, 30–35, 109, 267
Reading and "the grain"
    reading against the grain, 135–44
    reading through the grain, 125, 143,
        147–48, 157, 163, 226, 273
    reading with the grain, 20, 142
Realist fiction
    and action, 69, 77–79, 191, 238
    definition of, 5–7
    development of, 5–6, 31, 36, 165–69,
        217–18, 262–63
    involves a habit of mind, 16, 48, 92, 109,
        117, 131, 166, 188–89, 225, 262
    and the "Other," 19–20, 121–22,
        168–217
    as philosophically naive, 14–15
    and the representation of lower-
        class/vernacular mentalities,
        59–61, 212–17, 219–29

Realist fiction (*cont.*)
  as rhetorical, 238
  as transparent, 8–10, 38–63, 85, 131, 137,
      176, 238, 260
  as totalistic, 9–37, 94, 98, 109, 137, 144,
      174, 253, 259–60
  and the will, 39, 44, 78, 212
Reference, 53–89
  as productive, 59, 123, 131, 180, 254, 269
Regulative ideals, xi, 52, 174
Reynolds, Sir Joshua, 241, 243
Richardson, Samuel
  Clarissa, 43–44, 163n37
  Sir Charles Grandison, 185
Ricoeur, Paul, 71, 75
Rigor, philosophical, 68, 91
Robbins, Bruce, 30n41, 110, 113, 115,
      164n39, 209, 227
  on "transient utopias," 110, 209n41
Russell, Bertrand, 59

Said, Edward
  Musical Elaborations, 210n42
  Orientalism, 170–76, 190–91, 196–97,
      210n42, 213
Sacks, Mark, 29, 58
Saussure, Ferdinand de, 53–56, 65, 71
Schiller, Johann Christoph Friedrich von,
      21, 145
Scott, Sir Walter
  The Betrothed, 191
  Journal, 183–85, 189–91, 204
  The Heart of Midlothian, 130, 193–94,
      213–17, 257
  The Minstrelsy of the Scottish Border, 199,
      211
  Old Mortality, 230–31
  Redgauntlet, 1–3, 151–52
  "Tales of My Landlord," introductory
      material to, 59–61, 182
  The Talisman, 175–76, 188, 190–98, 203,
      209, 213, 261
  "The Two Drovers," 197–212
  Waverley, 45–48, 104–7, 123–25, 186–88,
      201, 213, 239
  on Austen, 166
  cultural/narrative embeddedness and
      transcendence in ("in or above?"),
      167, 183–212, 239, 251, 261
  characters imagined "from the skin
      out" in, 36, 162, 169, 214, 219, 230

  Waverley hero in, 185–86, 197
  mentioned, 5–6, 31, 143, 165, 218, 227,
      233, 238, 252, 267, 275
Screen (journal), 16–17
Searle, John, 86–87
Seltzer, Mark, 25
Semiological (semiotic) hypothesis, 53–63,
      72
Shakespeare, William, 188
Silence, 127, 149–50, 158–59, 163, 212, 236
Speech-Act Theory, 73–79; 82–89
Stendhal (Henri Beyle), 96
Stern, J. P., 6n5, 14–17, 21, 23, 32, 34, 260
Sterne, Laurence, 187
"Sublime Criticism," 137–39, 142, 159,
      203, 266–67
Suspicion, hermeneutics of, 265–66

Teleology, 52, 99, 109. *See also* Providen-
      tial history/narrative
Thackeray, William Makepeace, 171, 239
  Vanity Fair, 50–51
Thompson, E. P., 132
Tolstoy, Leo, 29–30, 130
Trilling, Lionel, 3, 144–47
Trollope, Anthony
  An Autobiography, 41n3
  Barchester Towers, 25–26
Twain, Mark, 144

Universalism versus cultural particular-
      ism, 176–83
Utopias, transient, 110, 124, 209–12

Verne, Jules, 21–22, 34
Villañueva, Darío, 40–41

Warnock, G. J., 87
Watt, Ian, 40–53, 63–64, 72, 80–82
Welsh, Alexander, 143
White, Hayden, 101–2, 135, 137–39,
      270–75
White, Laura Mooneyham, 132–34
Williams, Raymond
  on Austen, 152, 228, 230, 257
  on Eliot, 222–29, 259
Woolf, Virginia, 116–18, 120, 169

Žižek, Slavoj, 179–81
Zola, Emile, 4, 40–41, 96, 112
  Germinal, 75–76